T0386173

Dick Schoech, PhD

Human Services Technology
Understanding, Designing, and Implementing Computer and Internet Applications in the Social Services

Pre-publication
REVIEWS,
COMMENTARIES,
EVALUATIONS . . .

"Information technology is oozing into human services. It is no longer a question of whether to engage in using information and communication technology in human services, but how to get the most out of it. And here is a unique source of information and ideas to efficiently deal with the challenges.

From the very first pages, the reader's attention is captured. Sections include introduction of technology, the variety of available applications, designing and implementing applications, and maintaining and supporting technology. What can sensibly be added to these 400-plus pages and supporting Web site that tell it all? No human service practitioner, manager, policy maker, scholar, or student will have an excuse not to engage in sound usage of information technology. Not with such a comprehensive and authoritative source of information close at hand."

Jan Steyaert, PhD
Senior Consultant,
Fontys University
of Higher Professional Education,
The Netherlands

More pre-publication
REVIEWS, COMMENTARIES, EVALUATIONS . . .

"*Human Services Technology* provides a comprehensive, clearly written text for students and human service professionals who need to understand the impact and use of information technology in human service practice. This text is not merely an introduction to computer literacy or a compendium of human service Web sites, although it contains these elements. It explains the social forces, ethical dilemmas, applications, impact on staff and clients, and future potential of information technology using vocabulary, concepts, and examples familiar to human service workers.

Human Services Technology focuses on human service organizations as engaging in information-based decision-making activities that increasingly require a variety of information technologies. As such, the text describes issues and applications related to management, practitioners, clients, and the larger community that will be changed by new developments in information technology. Understanding and critical thinking related to human service information technology is enhanced in the text through the author's extensive use of analogy, charts, and diagrams as well as through the inclusion of discussion and review questions at the end of each chapter. Another outstanding feature of the text is the companion Web site that provides links to further information and real-world examples to supplement material in the text, thus promoting greater student involvement and interaction with the material.

The study of information technology in human services was once considered supplemental to human service education. It is increasingly seen as an essential component. *Human Services Technology* will be an indispensable reference for senior-level elective and master's social work courses on information technology. It will also provide an important means of integrating information technology throughout the curriculum, especially in practice and management courses. Dr. Schoech has made a major contribution to social work and human services education by providing a text that is strong on theory, critical thinking, and pragmatic information."

Jerry Finn, PhD
Associate Professor,
Department of Social Work,
University of New Hampshire

"In this revised text, Dr. Schoech acts as a skillful interpreter, guiding the human service professional gently into the unknown territory of information technology. Offering an extensive array of content from computer fundamentals to ethics in information technology, this text manages to present it all in a clear and understandable fashion and balanced with a sense of humor.

Infused with practical insights and enriched with extensive tables and illustrations, *Human Services Technology* offers the reader content ranging from fundamental to sophisticated, and across all levels of practice, from clinical, through management, to policy.

Internet-ready, *Human Services Technology* explores IT from the unique perspectives of a wide range of users, providing historical contexts, basic concepts, and rich, detailed applications. Supplemented by its own Web site, *Human Services Technology* is an excellent reference text for the human service professional's desktop.

A primary focus and strength of this text is the application of information technology to human service organizations in particular, including database management, the development of information systems, decision making, telecommunications, and the World Wide Web. Decision makers at all levels of practice will appreciate the detailed information and extensive insights offered."

Robert J. MacFadden, PhD
Associate Professor,
Associate Dean,
Faculty of Social Work,
University of Toronto,
Canada

Human Services Technology
Understanding, Designing, and Implementing Computer and Internet Applications in the Social Services

CRC Press
Taylor & Francis Group
Boca Raton   London   New York

CRC Press is an imprint of the
Taylor & Francis Group, an **informa** business

Human Services Technology

Understanding, Designing, and Implementing Computer and Internet Applications in the Social Services

Second Edition of
Human Services Computing:
Concepts and Applications

Dick Schoech, PhD

The Haworth Press, Inc., 10 Alice Street, Binghamton, NY 13904-1580

Cover design by Monica L. Seifert.

The Library of Congress has cataloged the hardcover edition of this book as:

Schoech, Dick.
    Human services technology : understanding, designing, and implementing computer and Internet applications / Dick Schoech.
       p.   cm.
    Includes bibliographical references and index.
    ISBN 0-7890-0108-X (alk. paper).
    1. Human services—Data processing. 2. Social service—Data processing. 3. Human services—Administration—Data processing. I. Title.
HV29.2.S364 1999
361'.00285—dc21   98-48698
                                                       CIP

ISBN 0-7890-0943-9 (pbk.)

CONTENTS

PART II: APPLICATIONS OF INFORMATION TECHNOLOGY IN THE HUMAN SERVICES

ABOUT THE AUTHOR

Dick Schoech, PhD, is Professor of Administrative and Community Practice at the University of Texas at Arlington School of Social Work. Previously, he worked as the Executive Director of a comprehensive health planning council in Columbus, Indiana, as a regional health planner. Dr. Schoech is the Founder and Coordinator of the Computer Use in Social Services Network (CUSSN), as well as Founder and Editor of the *Journal of Technology in Human Services,* a Haworth Press journal. He has written two books and numerous articles on human service computing and has been principal investigator on grants to human service computing applications in the areas of child protective services, aging, HIV/AIDS, and developmental disabilities. With the help of his graduate students, Dr. Schoech has developed several software packages, including Keisha, Kids HIV and AIDS Training, and the Worker Safety Advisor (http://www. uta.edu/cussn/). His research interests include distance education, performance support systems, knowledge engineering, and high technology culture. Currently, Dr. Schoech is developing multimedia and World Wide Web-based training and decision-making materials.

Introduction

Delivering human services to clients involves large amounts of information. Information is exchanged during practitioner-client interactions, during agency management, and in documenting accountability, efficiency, and effectiveness to stakeholders. Since information is a pervasive and essential ingredient of service delivery, technologies that collect, store, manipulate, and communicate information have a dramatic impact on human services.

Although delivering services generates much information, agencies currently capture and use only a small portion. For small, locally supported agencies, this lack of formal information is not a problem because community members have personal knowledge of the agency's performance. However, as human services become professionalized and agencies connect to form large systems, formal information becomes a key for survival. Consumers and funders demand more formal information to make up for their lack of personal knowledge about agency performance. Technology helps meet this demand by allowing agencies to capture and use much more of the information generated during service delivery.

Simply capturing and disseminating information is not enough. As more information is made available, we often use less of it. The common complaint that "we are drowning in information but starved for knowledge" illustrates this problem. Human service practitioners often complain that they rarely have the right information at the right time and in the right format. Experience and expertise is required to provide the analysis and synthesis that turns data into knowledge that is used in decision making.

Since the 1940s, the world has been developing and assimilating a new group of information technologies that are based on microelectronics, telecommunications, and the computer. The computer and the Internet are the most important information technologies for the human services. The impact of these new technologies on information and its use is proving to be as dramatic as the impact of previous information technologies. For example, the Renaissance is often attributed to the invention of the printing press. Electronic technologies can inexpensively collect and store large libraries of information in media the size of a coin. Once stored in electronic form, information can be rapidly searched, manipulated, transmitted, and displayed to humans or to other devices around the world. This power to easily manage, manipulate, interconnect, and disseminate large volumes of information is radically changing information-based segments of society, such as the human services.

Societies adopt new technologies in three phases that can be illustrated by the adoption of the internal combustion engine:

1. A new technology is applied to things that exist. For example, the internal combustion engine was seen as a better horse and used to produce the horseless carriage.
2. Existing things are rethought with the new technologies in mind. For example, the Model T Ford was produced based on the internal combustion engine and mass production.
3. Things are invented using the new technology that were not considered or not possible before the technology existed. For example, the internal combustion engine resulted in the invention of the airplane.

Adoption of information technologies into the human services is probably between phases one and two. To continue the automobile analogy, some professionals are still in the pretechnology horse-and-buggy stage. They are constantly angered at the many horseless carriages creating unnecessary noise and stirring up dust. Others are entering phase two, applying technology to carriages and developing automobiles that are noisy and unreliable. However, some of these inventions are fast, powerful, and have great potential. Some agencies are in the middle of phase two: they have very usable, efficient, and effective computer applications performing major accounting, testing, data management, and networking chores. A few professionals are thinking about phase three: they are imagining new ways to use technology in the human services; they are experimenting with simulated human expertise, creating self-help virtual worlds on the Internet, and designing robot caretakers.

Our current adoption of information technologies is analogous to the early days of the automobile when motoring was popular. Then, motoring clubs of automobile enthusiasts existed for exploring country roads. However, the real societal change came when roads were connected into highway systems. Currently, computer clubs that once catered to the personal computer enthusiast have been replaced by Internet conferences for sharing experiences and exploring the information highways of the world. Not all is positive, however. Experience reveals that the pleasures of motoring can quickly vanish in smog-choked cities and traffic jams. Similarly, unwise use of information technologies can create unforeseen problems.

Although development of automobile technology is analogous to computer technology in many ways, the analogy fails to demonstrate the speed at which computer technology is advancing. If the automobile and airplane business had developed at the rate of the computer business, a Rolls Royce would cost $2.75 and would run for 1 million miles on a gallon of gas; a Boeing 767 costing $500 could circle the globe in twenty minutes on five gallons of gas (Forester, 1985). With information technologies developing so rapidly, their assimilation is likely to produce equally rapid change and disruption.

Information technologies are being developed that are small, easy to work with, and require little technical knowledge from the user. In human-technology interaction, humans no longer need to think and perform like machines because technology is enabling machines to perform more like humans. Two capabilities that illustrate this phenomenon are natural language processing and speech recognition. In adapting to humans, information technologies have also undergone a revolution in the complexity of the tasks they perform, for example, reasoning and learning. However, even when new technological applications have proven valuable and easy to use, their widespread use takes years because assimilation requires individual and organizational change.

As information technologies mature from performing routine, repetitive work to mimicking sophisticated human activities, we are beginning to question the direction in which these new technologies are leading us. Jobs are threatened as "steel-collar" robots replace people in the industrial blue-collar workplace and as "smart machines" move into the white-collar workplace. Technology-savvy companies use temporary employees who have few benefits and move work around the globe to find the lowest-cost employees, with little regard for worker and community well-being. Privacy is threatened as databases store and exchange information about most members of society. A more basic challenge may be our beliefs about human nature. Humans have always seen their ability to reason and communicate as unique. As smart machines become more sophisticated and supplement human intelligence, we are forced to reexamine our beliefs about what makes us human.

The human services are at the center of this reexamination, since highly educated and trained professionals interact with people about basic human needs. Also, since human services involve people-intensive work, policy planners and agency directors are constantly under pressure to replace expensive human expertise with inexpensive information technology. Although we readily accept the idea of humans and machines working side by side in the industrial workplace, the idea of human service practitioners and smart machines working together to serve clients has not been fully accepted.

Learning about a subject involves understanding the vocabulary in that field. This is difficult with human service technology because both the human services and technology contain many new and evolving concepts. In this book, electronic technologies that process information are referred to as information technology, or IT. Sometimes in this book, the term technology alone is used when it is obvious that IT is meant. Other electronic-based technologies besides IT exist in the human services. For example, robotics can physically assist people with a disability. Phrases that describe the changes caused by electronic technologies are also evolving. Some examples are "the age of information," "the information revolution," "the cyber society," and "the wired society." Underlying these phrases is a perception that computers and telecommunications are combining with other technologies to alter the way we work and live. Human services' use of technology must be understood as part of this larger change occurring throughout the world.

This book provides human service professionals with a basic framework for moving into the information age. It synthesizes information in the fields of computer science, systems analysis, information management, and telecommunications, within the context of the human service environment. This book not only presents types of applications and examples of applications but also focuses on how an agency or individual designs, develops, implements, and manages those applications. Throughout this book, descriptions of technology and its application are tailored for human service professionals with little or no systems, business, or IT background.

ASSUMPTIONS

Several underlying assumptions in this book should be explicitly stated.

The first assumption is that the primary activity in the human services is decision making. All human service professionals continually go through the decision-making process. This process involves investigating situations, gathering information, negotiating alternatives, helping implement the preferred solution, and using the results to guide future actions. Technology is becoming the basis of most decision-making tools. Although technology applications can store and manipulate information, today they can make only routine decisions without human assistance. For the foreseeable future, both humans and technology capabilities are needed in the complex decision making required to help clients.

A second and similar assumption is that human service decision making is information intensive. Serving clients, managing agencies, and reporting to funding sources involves collecting, storing, manipulating, reproducing, and communicating large volumes of information. Some is collected and stored just in case it is needed, for example, for liability protection or to seek funding.

A third assumption is that information technologies are combining to form a low-cost universal IT appliance. This appliance will combine the telephone, television, and computer and connect to other devices via the Internet. The IT appliance will collect, store, manipulate, and disseminate information in the form of data, text, audio, graphics, animation, video, and virtual reality environments.

A fourth assumption is that many clients in the information age will often have better technology and better information than their practitioners. Two factors account for this assumption. The first is that with hardware and telecommunications costs declining, individuals can purchase and implement personal IT faster than agencies. Large organizations and multiorganizational systems will have the most difficult time keeping abreast of the latest technology. Consumers also have the time to gather the information specific to their problems. Their information will be more current and problem specific than the information the practitioner has time to collect and assimilate. Although clients will have more current and detailed information, they will not have the expertise to synthesize, interpret, integrate, and apply the information to their problem. The client and practitioner must work together to understand and use all the information available.

A fifth assumption is that human service IT is not always a simple matter of transferring technologies previously developed in the business or governmental sectors. Adapting IT applications to the human services requires not only a basic understanding of technology but also an understanding of human problems, agencies, human service professionals, and human service decision making. Human service agencies and professionals should not be changed for the sake of using technology. Rather, technology should be adapted to practitioner work patterns, agency operations, and human service procedures wherever possible.

A sixth assumption is that successful IT applications require much more than just knowing about technology. Understanding and managing the people and organizational components of change are more difficult than the technology components. Therefore, understanding what practitioners do when helping clients is the most important task for successful IT. This assumption implies that IT cannot be left to developers or outside consultants, but must be the responsibility of all potential users. Technology professionals have the same difficulty in understanding human services as human service professionals have in understanding technology. Both fields are highly specialized, complex, laden with jargon, and require experience to understand the subtleties of practice. Both fields have credibility problems, in that they frequently overpromise what their services can accomplish. In addition, good intentions often fail to produce results, even with long, hard, and frustrating work. The necessity of putting technologists under agency and user control has been a very difficult lesson to learn, as many without a basic understanding of technology delegate the design and adoption effort to technologists.

A similar seventh assumption is that assessment is one of the most important aspects of change. Human service (HS) professionals know from working with clients that the key to successful intervention is the assessment. The same exists for IT.

An eighth assumption is that human service practice can be improved by changing:

1. people, for example, through education or motivational training;
2. the goals people strive to achieve, for example, through strategic planning;
3. the tasks people perform, for example, through task analysis and job restructuring;
4. the process by which people perform tasks, for example, through policies and procedures;
5. the environment in which people work, for example, through office design; and
6. the information with which people work.

Changing item 6, the information base of practice, is one of the easiest and least disruptive ways of improving performance, given recent advances in technology.

A final assumption is that IT will continue to have a pervasive influence on society. Human service professionals must view IT as a force to harness, control, and use. They must explore new technologies and be in the forefront of their adoption. Only when they are in control can they ensure that these technologies will be used in accordance with professional ethics and in the best interest of clients. If human service professionals are not in control, others will readily take their place. However, other professionals may have different values and different commitments to clients.

ORGANIZATION OF CHAPTERS

This book is divided into four parts: Part I consists of two chapters that introduce technology use, basic terms, and history. Chapter 1 introduces the reader to human service IT using scenarios that present typical uses. The reader is given an idea of what IT means to the client, practitioner, manager, and policy planner. Chapter 2 introduces human services and IT concepts and presents their historical context.

Part II consists of three chapters that present the variety of technology available in the human services. Chapter 3 presents generic IT applications that one would find in the human services. Chapter 4 discusses several types of management applications. Chapter 5 presents human service applications at various levels of the human service delivery system.

Part III consists of six chapters that discuss designing and implementing IT applications and the influences on IT design and implementation. Chapter 6 presents the process of developing any IT application. Chapter 7 describes the systems and decision-making theories underlying IT applications. Chapter 8 shows how the information needs of human service professionals and organizations influences IT development. Chapter 9 discusses hardware and software influences, and Chapter 10 examines database management influences on IT development. Chapter 11 completes Part III by discussing the networking and telecommunications influence on IT development.

Part IV consists of two chapters concerned with maintaining and supporting IT. Chapter 12 discusses managing, supporting, and evaluating IT. Chapter 13 presents future trends and issues.

An analogy used throughout this book compares a computing system to a transportation system. This analogy can illustrate the goal of this book. To use a transportation system successfully, one does not need to be an auto mechanic or design engineer. What is required is a thorough understanding of one's transportation needs and how to use the available transportation system to meet those needs. A driver's education course is preferable to a course on auto mechanics. Similarly, using IT requires an understanding of one's information needs and how to use IT to support one's decisions. Information about the technical details can be obtained from specialists.

In essence, the focus of this book is to assist human service professionals to become intelligent designers and users of IT to support practice. We become intelligent users by understanding IT, both as a societal phenomenon and as a tool for improving the decisions made when helping clients.

Finally, this book is caught in the information revolution it describes. Printed books, such as the one you are reading now, are antiquated technology for informing about human services IT. The applications described in this book change too rapidly for books to keep up to date. Also, books lack the connectivity and interactivity that supports information gathering and learning. Readers should be able to quickly explore a resource or application mentioned in this book by touching or clicking. Book references should be linked to the original source. Examples should link to demonstration software and Web sites. To try to accommodate these needs, the Web site http://www.uta.edu/cussn/ contains supplemental materials, class exercises, and resources associated with this book. Content with supporting information from the Web is designated by the symbol ✿.

PART I:
BASIC CONCEPTS AND HISTORY

Chapter 1

Personal Views
of Human Service Technology

INTRODUCTION

This chapter introduces information technology (IT) by presenting nontechnical scenarios from different levels of the human service delivery system. It will describe IT from the perspective of a client, paraprofessional, professional practitioner, midlevel information manager, executive director, and community volunteer. The scenarios are written from a personal perspective to allow for easy expression of feelings and attitudes. Although the experiences presented are hypothetical, they are typical of actual situations. IT jargon has been largely eliminated, but the glossary may be needed for unfamiliar terms. Following each scenario is a list of questions that highlights the themes and issues addressed in future chapters. In essence, this chapter previews the book through hypothetical scenarios presented as personal case histories.

INFORMATION TECHNOLOGY
AS SEEN BY A PERSON WITH A DISABILITY

Linda's cerebral palsy keeps her confined to a wheelchair. She is unable to communicate with anyone except those willing to listen carefully to what she is saying. Linda's control over her limbs is minimal. She is only able to press a button or move a lever with her foot. Linda is above average in intelligence, but has few avenues available for using her abilities.

Her first exposure to IT occurred in the early 1980s when she received an experimental computerized wheelchair developed by a local university. The wheelchair was coupled with a voice recognition device that translated thirty sounds into commands which drove the wheelchair. The basic set of commands consisted of Linda's pronunciation of start, stop, right, left, slower, faster, etc. Fascinated with the capacity of this equipment, Linda soon persuaded the researchers to add a keyboard to the wheelchair's computer. By using her television as a computer screen, Linda began programming the computer. Through practice, she was able to write simple entertainment programs that increased her knowledge of the computer and its operation. Although she could press only one key at a time with her toe, Linda had plenty of time to teach herself about the computer.

A big step forward came in the mid-1980s, when the local computer club set up an electronic bulletin board system (BBS) that provided local e-mail, file transfer, and conferencing. Linda could access the BBS using her computer and telephone. The BBS allowed her to send a message to anyone in the computer club and receive files on many topics. She joined many BBS conferences where people with disabilities "hung out." The BBS allowed Linda to communicate without others recognizing that she had a disability. Linda began trading computer programs with other computer hobbyists and picking up additional programming skills. She discovered that employers often posted programming jobs on the BBS. If she got a job, Linda wrote the computer programs on her home computer and uploaded it to her employer. She used e-mail to report progress and ask for additional instructions. She used BBS conferences to seek technical support.

In the early 1990s, the BBS was connected to the Internet. Whereas the BBS connected Linda with a local social group and information, the Internet connected Linda globally. Besides connections to global social support groups, the Internet provided Linda information on almost any topic. She often completed courses via distance education and was a sophomore majoring in computer science at an Internet-based virtual university.

Linda now found that she had little free time. Because of the time she dedicated to her work, Linda developed a reputation for dependability and error-free computer programs. She spent the money she earned from programming on new computer equipment (hardware) and programs (software). A new device on which Linda was spending most of her time and money was a programmable mechanical arm on wheels. A computer program along with a joystick device and a speech recognition application controlled the hydraulic pinchers of the arm. Talking the arm through a detailed series of movements would program it. This robotic arm allowed Linda to move prepared food from the refrigerator to the microwave oven, to get food from a specially designed plate to her mouth, and to do physical exercises. The mechanical arm was like the canister-shaped *Star Wars* character R2D2, but Linda fantasized about the day when it would be more like the humanoid C3PO.

Today, Linda's continuous speech recognition application operates all the electronics in her house. Although many people had difficulty understanding Linda's speech, her computer did not. She continues to work with researchers on additional applications for people with disabilities. Linda tested a product for researchers in England that linked speech recognition to speech synthesis in order to translate unintelligible utterances to understandable human speech. However, the current version produces a voice that is unfeminine, has a funny accent, lacks expression, and often mispronounces complex words.

Linda's computer has broadened her life by providing a way to communicate with the outside world. Linda no longer feels frustrated, useless, and isolated. She now has friends and colleagues around the world, many of whom she has met in person. She earns money and is becoming more independent. Her understanding of technology, her distance education coursework, and her on-line activities got her involved with research that has had important implications for persons with disabilities. Her long-range goal is to teach a course on technology for a virtual university. Linda does not fear IT or the so-called information society. Talk of a computerized society and technology as "Big Brother" is not negative; technology and all it represents are indeed like a helpful "big brother" to her.

Themes and Issues in the Scenario

1. What groups, other than those with disabilities, can IT empower?
2. What types of professionals are needed to help clients use new technologies? Where should they be trained?
3. How can service providers keep up to date on what technologies are available to empower their clients?
4. How can society pay for the research, development, training, and follow-up required by people with disabilities?
5. What roles can clients play in IT? Is the role for those with physical disabilities and mental disabilities the same?
6. What future technologies will allow people with mobility and communication disabilities to use their abilities?

INFORMATION TECHNOLOGY
AS SEEN BY AN EXECUTIVE SECRETARY
IN A MENTAL HEALTH ASSOCIATION

For the last four years, Mary worked as the executive secretary of an urban Mental Health Association (MHA), an organization of citizens interested in promoting mental health. The MHA lagged behind most agencies in using IT, although in the 1980s, an accounting firm computerized the MHA's bookkeeping. The MHA had initially hoped the accounting firm would help agency staff learn more about computers and their potential for the agency. However, the bookkeeping service was so distant, and their programs so self-contained, that this learning did not occur.

In the late 1980s, an MHA board member who worked for a computer manufacturer donated several computers to the MHA. Several of the less experienced secretaries had expressed fears that the computer would replace them. Fortunately, the agency director kept these fears to a minimum by stating that IT did not reduce work, but changed the nature of work, so she did not intend to reduce staff. Since funding sources were demanding better records, the director wanted the computers to do a better job with the ever-increasing paperwork burden.

The executive director was right about computers changing the quality of work and the way it was done. Since word processing was introduced, Mary found that typed information became more standardized, yet more personalized. Standardization occurred because the same basic reports and letters were used repeatedly by all staff, with only minor changes. Personalization occurred because personal information could easily be added to the standardized text. Mary became more conscious of the need to manage paperwork and its flow through the office in order to use secretarial time more efficiently. The computer created new tasks, such as ensuring that all computerized information was periodically copied and that these "back-up" files were stored in several safe places. Mary became the person responsible for keeping the executive director informed of new secretarial computer programs that appeared on the market. She frequently stopped at computer stores during lunch hour to check for new training and office management applications. Mary also attended a class on Web site development. Her exposure to the Internet through her son revealed its potential for informing the public about the MHA, developing e-mail-based advocacy campaigns, and fund-raising.

Besides changing the way work was performed, the IT created new dependencies, as did other technologies, such as electrical power and telephones. This dependency became apparent when lightning damaged the computers and they were not repaired for two days. Changing back to the old way of working was impossible. Staff could do very little since most of their work involved computer files. Another problem was that the technology was not designed for comfort. Since distributing memos and filing documents no longer required getting up from one's chair, secretaries spent hours in front of the computer display. Backaches and eyestrain were common complaints. Another problem was that the donated computers were not well matched to the MHA's needs. The agency should have completed a detailed study of IT needs before accepting the equipment. The agency had spent a lot of time and effort setting up and learning an application that was not designed for its needs and was relatively obsolete. Overall, Mary felt that agency IT had been a success. No one wanted to go back to doing things as they had been before the computers were introduced. However, they had learned by making mistakes rather than from the mistakes of others.

Themes and Issues in the Scenario

1. What steps can/must an executive director take to ensure that an IT application will be introduced with minimal resistance?
2. How does IT change work, that is, what type of tasks are eliminated, changed, or created?
3. What questions should an agency ask before accepting donated computer equipment?
4. How can an agency minimize dependence on an IT application?
5. Can technology be purchased and quickly introduced in an agency, or must an agency "reinvent the wheel" to ensure that the necessary learning occurs?
6. How can the Internet help an agency such as the MHA?

INFORMATION TECHNOLOGY AS SEEN BY A CLINICIAN IN A MENTAL HEALTH CENTER

Countywide Mental Health Center (CMHC) was organizationally part of the county hospital district and physically located next to the county hospital. As CMHC's Director of Clinical Services, Bill became involved in CMHC's IT efforts when they purchased an accounting application in the mid-1980s. Bill had used a computer in graduate school for statistical analysis and realized that computers potentially could help clinicians. Bill's experience with computers, his present interest, and his position resulted in his membership on the CMHC Information Systems Committee. CMHC managers appreciated Bill's interest in computers, but saw the computer primarily as a management tool. Management saw Bill's role as helping "sell" technology to the clinicians so they would complete the computer forms that management needed.

One of Bill's biggest problems was convincing managers that clinicians also needed support. Bill saw case management and therapy as the primary function of CMHC and therefore felt that IT should primarily help clinicians serve clients. Management was sympathetic to Bill's position, but argued that agency survival depended on computerized management information systems, not clinical-oriented applications.

After implementing the accounting application, CMHC purchased applications for fee determination, client scheduling, and client billing. These applications calculated the sliding scale fee, sent bills and reminders to clients, maintained appointment calendars, and produced periodic progress reports. Next, CMHC purchased a client-record-keeping application that automated all client records except nonstandard information such as progress notes. The standardized information in the application included client characteristics, client problems, level of functioning, and treatment plans. An automated intake application and a computerized testing application, on which the client or guardian typed in responses to questions presented on a computer display, later complimented this application. The application stored the information in the client's file and printed standardized physical, social, and psychological reports. Bill and his colleagues appreciated these computer reports, such as the list of daily appointments generated from the automated calendar application and the histories generated from the automated interview. However, these applications helped administrators manage clinicians more than they helped clinicians serve clients. Clinicians could keep schedules by hand as easily as they could by computer. Although the computer-generated histories were acceptable for agency records, they were too limited to replace the detailed case histories that clinicians needed.

One application that helped clinicians perform their work was a goal attainment scaling (GAS) application that allowed clinicians to pick from a list of previously developed attainment measures associated with standardized treatment goals. If no existing measures fit their need, clinicians could develop new measures to add to the list. Before each session, clients would enter their current attainment on the scales, and the computer would print a graph of the past and current attainment. During therapy, the clinician would check the client's input for accuracy, make necessary changes, and discuss the progress with the client. Clinicians found this an easy way to collect detailed information on client progress and to focus each session on client achievements. Clients appreciated receiving the detailed graphs of their progress.

In response to Bill's concern about the lack of clinical IT support, management purchased palm-sized computers and Internet access. Clinical staff used the Internet to keep current with research and practice. This became increasingly necessary, as clients often educated themselves using the Internet before coming to treatment. Clinicians also became involved in Internet-based discussion groups on their area of specialty and emotional support groups to prevent stress and burnout. One popular Internet site helped identify contraindications and negative reactions to drugs. Another provided self-help exercises for clients who had Internet access. Clinicians also liked a site that provided specialized training along with the Continuing Education Units (CEUs) needed for accreditation. Training with the site involved several steps. The clinician chose a client problem on which to receive training. After administering a pretest, the site presented videos of three clients with the specified problem. It then questioned the user about possible intervention strategies. Next, it compared the user's response to the responses of experts. Finally, the training application presented video of experts from different therapeutic perspectives working with the clients. The training session concluded with a site-administered posttest and suggested additional training, if indicated. A detailed analysis of the user's performance throughout the session and the user's training history was available anytime.

Considering the popularity of the training site, CMHC planned to develop an education Web site usable by clients at any time in the privacy of their home. This site would provide information on mental health problems, their prevention, and treatment along with an agency orientation. The orientation would allow potential clients to see pictures and video of the facility, staff, intake procedures, and CMHC's accomplishments. CMHC hoped this orientation would encourage earlier and more appropriate requests for services. Early intervention would increase CMHC's chances of intervening with low-cost preventive approaches that had a higher success rate.

One of Bill's colleagues in another CMHC was helping to develop an application that would mimic the decision processes of an expert diagnostician. After a clinician provided the "expert system" with details about a client, the system would display the most appropriate diagnosis and the reasoning behind the diagnosis. Currently, the expert system agreed with the human expert on whom it was based 70 percent of the time. Unfortunately, the system only agreed with an independent group of diagnosticians 50 percent of the time. Until the experts could agree among themselves, the expert system was seen as a training tool for illustrating diagnostic reasoning. Although Bill realized that accurate and reliable expert systems took years to develop and refine, he hoped they would be developed for more phases of the therapeutic process.

Overall, Bill and the other clinicians were satisfied with CMHC's involvement with IT. The clinical applications were providing support and helping staff refine their skills. The management applications kept clinicians informed of who provided what services to whom, when, and with what results. Statistical analysis of management-oriented information was influencing therapy decisions. For example, profiles were being developed to see why clients progressed differently than expected in various treatment programs. If predicting client outcomes from historic data was possible, then the computer could estimate a new client's chance of succeeding in each agency program.

Several clinicians in CMHC had no interest in using the support provided by IT. These individuals fell into two categories. Some were experts in a specialty field for which no IT applications were available. Others used very prescribed approaches with clients and had no interest in changing their techniques. Skepticism of IT did not bother Bill. He believed that change takes time and that a critical perspective was healthy. The skeptics brought IT problems to Bill before large mistakes were made.

Bill believed major benefits of IT would occur in the rural suboffices opening next year. IT would help connect the suboffices to CMHC and would be valuable to rural clinicians who did not have on-site collegial support or in-depth experience.

Because of IT, CMHC experienced a series of small changes that combined to produce a major change in the way services were delivered. Old issues and practices had to be continually reinterpreted in the light of new technology. For example, CMHC was examining its malpractice liabilities as more clinicians provided follow-up using the Internet. Bill believed that staff were recognizing which aspects of therapy were a science based on information and which were an art based on experience and intuition. In essence, Bill's agency had finally progressed beyond management IT. Clinicians now viewed IT as a tool that could quickly and cheaply perform mundane tasks and provide valuable expertise and assistance in the difficult process of helping clients.

Themes and Issues in the Scenario

1. What conflicts exist between therapeutic and management needs for IT?
2. What types of assurances must a practitioner have before using new, "unproven" technologies in client care?
3. Where should clients get consumer information on the appropriateness of self-help software and Internet support groups?
4. What should be the role of national professional associations in new IT applications such as self-help software and Internet-based therapy?

5. What is the difference between resistance to IT and healthy opposition to IT, and what can be done to alleviate resistance and encourage healthy opposition?
6. What clinical tasks can IT applications do well, and what tasks do they perform poorly?

INFORMATION TECHNOLOGY AS SEEN BY THE DIRECTOR OF INFORMATION MANAGEMENT AT A LOCAL STATE DEPARTMENT OFFICE

Tina had a busy job as the Director of Information Management for a local office of the State Department of Children's Services. In 1980, the department promoted Tina from a child welfare worker to her present position because she had undergraduate coursework in computer science. Initially, Tina's title was Management Information System (MIS) Liaison. Her job was to implement a centralized statewide information system. This statewide MIS computerized national and state reports. Although the system's function was relatively simple, it required new forms and statewide standardization of data.

The saying "You can tell the pioneers by the arrows in their backs" certainly applied to this initial centralized MIS. The state had been a pioneer in MIS. However, many good initial decisions resulted in long-term problems that were difficult to correct. Other state MIS personnel visited their system and analyzed their mistakes. By 1985, their initial effort was viewed as overly complex compared to newly designed systems. Their MIS was seen by staff as a data "monster," requiring increasing paperwork and constant changes.

Tina realized that one of the biggest initial mistakes had been the way the state "sold" the system. To gain acceptance and accurate reporting on the new forms, the state stressed the usefulness of system reports for local managers, supervisors, and workers. However, the system was designed for national and state reporting and provided little usable local information. This overselling resulted in a skeptical view toward all new applications.

Constant revisions were another problem. The system initially was state of the art, but it became outdated within four years. The initial MIS was revised and expanded before many local offices were familiar with it. The revised MIS was more responsive, flexible, and changeable, but it did not mesh well with local needs. It still took over a month to get reports back to local workers. Special requests for information took from two weeks to two months. One problem was that centralized hardware resulted in a centralized MIS being implemented in a decentralized organization.

A third revision moved IT to the local level. The important terms used to describe the third change were "distributed," "networked," and "database." Distributed meant putting computers in local offices under local control so local data needs could be better met. Networked meant linking central and local computers together to function as one statewide system. Database meant organizing all state and local data into an easily accessible pool of information for use at any office. With these changes, Tina's local department was renamed from the MIS Liaison Department to the Information Resources Management (IRM) Department. Tina now represented the state to local IT efforts rather than being a local liaison to central IT. Tina's office provided:

- national and state reports from the distributed system,
- technical assistance on the MIS to local offices,
- training for all MIS users,
- hardware and software to ensure compatibility and reduce costs with bulk purchases, and
- standardized statewide taxonomies and data definitions to ensure local and state systems could exchange information.

The department delegated all other MIS activities to local offices.

The distributed network was used for non-MIS purposes. An example was the new employee training application. The state developed computer-based training packages that were delivered over the computer network. Workers were required to complete one training session before the state issued their monthly paycheck. The training sessions took ten to thirty minutes, depending on a worker's knowledge of the topic. However, if an employee did not retain what they had learned, the application required them to repeat sections of previous training. Employees readily accepted training using the computer and preferred its flexibility to hour-long, scheduled training sessions. Local offices were allowed to develop additional training packages. The state offered technical assistance and required that locally developed training be usable at other local offices.

Tina believed the distributed and networked approach was a step in the right direction. However, as the number of computers proliferated throughout the state, the pace of development became too fast and complex for state control. Local offices were developing many applications, often with different hardware, software, networks, and terminology. Tina saw the difficulties of ensuring standardization and coordination as the weak link in the distributed approach.

On the positive side, a few statewide applications had originated from experimentation at the local level. For example, several local offices automated a child risk assessment process, each learning from the other's mistakes. After three years of local development, the state agreed to refine and maintain a standardized, statewide risk assessment application. Several other local applications were expanding statewide. One application matched children in state conservatorship to foster and adoptive homes using past data to predict future outcomes. Another automatically forwarded names of reported child abusers requiring a home investigation to law enforcement computers for matching. A match could indicate a simple parking violation or a history of violent behavior. If a match occurred, the system would suggest the worker contact law enforcement before going to the home. To protect client confidentiality, names were coded during transmission and no permanent record of the names was kept. This automated record check worked so well that some local agencies were experimenting with using the Internet to support workers. One project encrypted and e-mailed records of difficult or unique cases to national experts for consultation within twenty-four hours.

Looking back, Tina realized that IT in her department had come a long way. However, the unsettled nature of the present distributed application suggested that the department was far from meeting both state and local information needs. IT development had not been easy for state and local staff. Most applications were especially difficult for workers who continually had to learn new procedures and use new forms. Although no one calculated the cost of computerization, Tina thought it would be more expensive than anyone realized if staff time and effort were considered. Nevertheless, computerization enabled the department to handle the increasing workload and paperwork demands with the same number of staff. It also provided the detailed reports the legislature wanted before deciding on agency funding.

Tina considered herself an information broker who negotiated, coordinated, and provided technical assistance about the agency's information. Her job was similar to the Director of Financial Management, who negotiated, coordinated, and provided technical assistance about the agency's money. Tina wondered if one coordinated system of local and state IT could ever be completely developed. She also wondered what new changes would result from the rapid growth in technology and what "good" present decisions would create problems several years in the future.

Themes and Issues in the Scenario

1. Is it more difficult for large multisite organizations to computerize than small ones?
2. Does the development of an IT application follow a definable pattern?

3. Is work on an IT application ever complete?
4. What qualifications should human service personnel have who are in charge of agency information management?
5. If pioneering in IT is risky, should an agency attempt it? If not, who should?
6. What are the characteristics of a centralized and decentralized information system?
7. What could Tina do to help workers cope with the rapid changes associated with IT?
8. What are three IT challenges Tina will face in the next five years?

INFORMATION TECHNOLOGY
AS SEEN BY THE EXECUTIVE DIRECTOR
OF A MULTIPROGRAM HOME HEALTH AGENCY

Community Home Health (CHH) provides a diverse mix of low-income human service programs in many locations throughout a low-income neighborhood of a large city. CHH operates programs for the homebound such as Meals-on-Wheels, Homemaker Services, and Home Health Care. It also operates well-baby clinics and health-screening clinics. All programs are small and program staff range from two to fifteen paid employees. Maria, the agency's executive director, installed a computerized accounting application in the early 1980s to track agency funds. A computerized accounting application was necessary because each agency program could be funded by national, state, county, city, client, United Way, church, foundation, and other sources. Each funding source could have a different fiscal year, spending restrictions, and reporting requirements. Although the overall budget of the agency was relatively small, the computerized accounting application was very helpful in handling the massive paperwork involved in keeping the agency's books.

After several years of developing and debugging the accounting application, Maria decided to allow each agency program to purchase computers. The only condition was that the programs develop a plan for their use. Maria knew little about computers and considered her expertise to be in leadership, management, and coordination rather than in technical areas such as financial or information management. Her philosophy of IT stressed local initiation and operation, combined with centralized development and coordination. Maria felt that if staff were trained to understand what IT could do, they could determine if IT would be useful in their work. If an agency program wanted a computer, Maria believed central management should determine the feasibility and cost benefit of the applications through traditional decision-making channels. If management decided the applications were worth developing, they would convene a team to develop, manage, and monitor the development and implementation processes. This centralized development ensured agencywide service definitions and compatible system designs. Frequently, an agency program had to make changes in an application for the good of the total agency, for example, to add data to implement an agencywide total quality management initiative.

When Maria purchased the computer for the accounting application, she hired someone to be Director of Financial Management. However, she also gave him the title of Director of Information Management. As the Director of Information Management, he coordinated the agency IT effort and helped staff choose, implement, and maintain IT applications. He was supported by, and responsible to, an advisory committee. The advisory committee included Maria, a representative from each agency program, a CHH board member, and a client.

Each of CHH's programs used its IT differently. The Home Health Care program used client scheduling and case management applications. Each morning, nurses and health aides connected to the CHH computer to receive a list of patients to visit, the dates of previous visits, services rendered, a health summary, and present medications. The nurses added new information on their palm-sized computers. At the end of the day, they connected their palm-sized computer to the agency computer and uploaded new data.

The Meals-on-Wheels program used a diet management application that planned meals for diabetics and others with special dietary needs. When planning a client's menu, the application considered client characteristics such as age, weight, height, and physical activity. Meals-on-Wheels also automated its roster of volunteer drivers and the hours they were available to deliver meals. If a volunteer was unavailable, the application would search the volunteer file and list all available volunteers and the dates they previously volunteered. Volunteers could complete all forms on their activities over the Internet. Volunteers could also use the Internet to designate the hours they were available and view their records.

The agency's most ambitious computer application was in scheduling and assisting Meals-on-Wheels volunteers in locating meal recipients. The list of volunteers and meal recipients changed frequently, resulting in many last-minute changes in routes and schedules. The person who currently routed and scheduled the volunteers was a former taxi driver who knew the city well. However, this expertise was rare, and this person was nearing retirement. Since it would take years for someone to learn the job, the time was ideal for implementing a computer-based application.

This new application used a street database developed and maintained by the city police, fire, and transportation departments. This database contained all the streets in the city, their features, the distance and travel time between streets, and the traffic characteristics of each intersection. For example, it contained whether each intersection contained a stoplight or was a through street. Using the database, Meals-on-Wheels could find a route between two points, using criteria such as shortest distance, best roads, least travel time, greatest access to main roads, or fewest stops. Meals-on-Wheels provided each volunteer driver with his or her meal recipient's name, address, and a map of the best route based on the criteria selected. Meals-on-Wheels was developing an application that would match drivers with meal recipients based on the number of hours the driver could volunteer and the shortest travel time for all drivers. In essence, the application would contain much of the knowledge of the retiring scheduler. The homemaker and home health programs were also interested in this routing application.

Maria felt many of these applications saved money, although application development had often been costly. As a member of the CHH Information Management Advisory Committee, Maria insisted that the agency develop applications only after searching for existing software. CHH had worked with a university to design one application that turned out to be more complex, costly, and time-consuming than anticipated. Although the application was working, the operating manuals were not well prepared or easy to use. Currently, the application had several minor flaws or bugs, but debugging was too expensive because the professor and students who designed the application using foundation grant money were no longer at the university. Debugging would require paying an expert to comprehend the overall design and detailed programming before changes could be made or flying in the professor to make the changes. Maria's agency also had commercial software with problems, but software companies offered revised and enhanced versions at a reasonable cost. Maria thought that software development was risky and better left to the private marketplace. Her agency was currently trying to sell the university-developed package to a private vendor for a small royalty on future sales.

IT had changed Maria's management style. Since IT regularly monitored program progress, supervisory meetings focused on how well things were done rather than whether things were done. At times, a quick computer analysis would provide help with a management decision. For example, the health-screening clinic wanted to buy a van to transport clients to neighborhood sites. Maria had both the Home Health Program Director and the Health Screening Clinic Program director establish the "cost per client served" for each program over the last year. They then determined if the van transportation and "clinic costs per client" were greater than the cost of serving a client at home through the Home Health Program.

This interprogram analysis pointed out a weakness in the agency's present IT applications. Although it was easy to get staff together, getting all the computer applications to share data was not possible. An overall information system that could easily access data from the many separate IT applications was needed. Maria's agency was a combination of many programs, or a system made up of many subsystems. Yet the agency did not have an overall information system, only a collection of specialized IT applications. Maria needed to network the information systems of all agency programs together, but could not afford the dedicated, high-speed communication lines required at all locations. Maria was hoping to develop an "intranet," that is, to use Internet tools for this connectivity. Many staff currently used the Internet to send e-mail, transfer documents, and access resources. Developing the input forms and reports that connected program information systems through the Internet, while maintaining security and privacy, would be a big task. To handle this new effort, Maria was planning to separate the information management function from the financial management function. She would then hire a full-time information manager with Internet expertise to link the present applications into one integrated system.

Maria saw future IT allowing her agency to not only link programs together but to link programs more closely with the community. With most residents having Internet access from their homes, many programs could use Internet video to make frequent "house calls." The agency could also electronically connect neighbors with Web sites, so neighbors could help neighbors and reduce the waiting list for many of the services Maria's agency offered.

Agency complexities had forced Maria to use IT, yet she continually found IT applications inflexible and incapable of adjusting to quick changes. So although IT applications provided the data and analysis that indicated changes were necessary, they also prevented those changes from rapidly occurring. Developing, updating, and managing the technology the agency needed seemed an endless process.

Themes and Issues in the Scenario

1. How would the job of a fiscal manager and an information manager be similar?
2. During the many years that the Community Home Health Agency was developing IT applications, what type of tasks were created, discontinued, or changed?

3. Explain what central coordination and development and local initiation and operation of an agency information system mean.
4. What could Maria have done to ensure the agency would have an overall integrated information system rather than many separate systems?
5. Can IT be used to reconnect neighborhoods and make them more cohesive?
6. What other IT applications could Maria's agency use?

INFORMATION TECHNOLOGY AS SEEN
BY A UNITED WAY COMMITTEE MEMBER

United Way (UW) agencies play a vital role in the human services through fund-raising and service planning. Esther began her volunteer involvement with the United Way in the early 1980s as a member of the Information and Referral (I&R) Advisory Committee. Her interest in serving as a volunteer was to establish an I&R application whereby clients needed to call only one telephone number to receive help. When Esther's volunteer committee work began, several I&R services operated eight hours a day, five days a week. The only source of I&R information was a UW book that was updated, reprinted, and distributed yearly to the 250 agencies in the community. The person who operated the I&R service had been working in the human service field for many years. She knew most agencies and their staff and rarely had to refer to the I&R book. When this staff person retired, the I&R service went through a minor crisis. Referrals had to be made by inexperienced staff from an incomplete and outdated resource book. The I&R Advisory Committee decided to prevent this problem from occurring in the future by computerizing the I&R service. They believed computerization would allow them to store much of the information on computer that experienced I&R staff kept in memory. Also, the I&R service wanted to expand its hours of operation by using volunteers. This expansion was only possible if I&R information was readily available on computer.

The initial task of developing the I&R application took over a year, but the payoffs were immediate. Anyone with training could respond to a caller by working through computer screens. These screens displayed lists of problems and became more and more specific until the particular problem was identified. Once the problem was identified, the application asked for demographic information about the client. Then, information on possible resources appeared on the screen. If additional problem solving was necessary, the I&R database could be searched by categories. Typical categories were zip code, telephone exchange number, census tract, and service needed.

The I&R application was easy to update and change. An I&R resource book was still printed, but only on request. Several books could be printed overnight or sent in electronic form to the requesting agency. The I&R application could produce reports on the application's use, for example, reports on the number of times a problem was identified, the number of agencies addressing a problem, the characteristics of clients seeking help for a problem, and frequently reported problems for which no resources existed. Other UW staff found the I&R database helpful. The I&R database became the UW's source of agency mailing labels, and I&R reports were used for the planning and resource allocation process. For example, during a UW planning meeting, the I&R database was queried for a list of I&R calls during the previous eight months by type of problem and for a list of community resources by type of problem. The I&R application provided printouts of this information in fifteen minutes. Since the I&R application was serving more users, a redesign was needed. One redesign added more detailed information on each agency. In addition, statistical software was added to allow better analysis and modeling of information. Finally, graphics software, along with a color printer, was added to produce charts, graphs, and city maps that volunteer committee members could better understand.

The biggest change occurring in the I&R service began several years ago when Esther and other I&R advisory board members formed a county-wide consortium of human service agencies. These agencies had previously agreed to share their information for planning, fund allocation, and service delivery purposes. Most agencies kept computerized client data, such as age, sex, address, presenting problem, services provided, and outcome. Present database technology allowed this data to become one easy-to-use pool of information. The Human Service Consortium was the organizational umbrella that would develop the technology to collect, manage, and generate reports from this pool of information.

The board of the Human Service Consortium included the executive director and a board member from each participating agency. A consortium of agencies was a better structure than a single new agency because the major tasks of the consortium were not technical, but concerned the policies on data sharing. The consortium finally agreed on the essential pieces of information that all agencies would encrypt and electronically send to the consortium's database. The most difficult technical problem among the agencies had been to protect client privacy between agencies while sharing client-identifying information. A task force on security and privacy decided to code client names into a list of unduplicated identification (ID) numbers and client addresses into street coordinates. The consortium developed and maintained the software that encrypted names and addresses into codes and maintained strict control over this software and the database. Using the database, agencies could only discover which agencies of the consortium served their clients. Detailed information about the services provided to clients was handled among agencies in the traditional manner.

The UW and other agencies were just beginning to realize the power of the consortium's community-wide data and to use it in their service decisions. For example, a consortium study could quickly identify gaps in community services by problem, service, and geographic area. A model could be constructed to simulate the impact of a new service and to find locations that would place the service close to potential users. In addition, by matching census data to consortium data, the size and mix of future suburban services could be estimated.

The I&R Advisory Committee had two future projects. One was to make the I&R application available over the Internet. The committee hoped that Internet access would let volunteers work from their homes and free staff to spend more time collecting information. A second five-year project involved having the consortium maintain indicators of community strengths and problems, for example, church attendance and child abuse rates. Indicators would be available over the Internet by clicking on maps. Users would identify the indicator desired and click on a map to select the geographic area. The application would then produce tables and shaded maps containing the indicators requested.

Using IT, Esther began to realize her goal of a community-wide human service delivery application that helped clients find appropriate services from the many uncoordinated agencies. The effects of linking agency and community data and of having a more coordinated community-wide service delivery application were just beginning to be realized.

Themes and Issues in the Scenario

1. What are the benefits and drawbacks of a computerized I&R service? Do most of these benefits and drawbacks apply to other IT applications?
2. Describe the ideal I&R worker in an agency without a computerized application and in an agency with a computerized I&R application.
3. Considering the problems and liabilities associated with protecting client data, is multiagency sharing of client data desirable?

4. Assuming that client confidentiality can be protected, list some of the potentials and liabilities associated with a community-wide information system composed of agency client data.
5. Should client and client advocate groups be given access by agencies to nonidentifiable client data?
6. What are some of the uses of a geographic Web site of community strengths and problem indicators?

CONCLUSION

This chapter presented personalized scenarios of human service IT from the client to the policy level. The scenarios illustrated the processes, attitudes, and feelings that often underlie the more technical discussion in the remaining chapters. They also pointed to the larger political, economic, and cultural issues that society must face as we move into the information age.

REVIEW AND DISCUSSION QUESTIONS

1. What common themes and principles occur throughout all scenarios?
2. Which of the scenarios gave you the most positive opinions of IT? Which gave you the most negative? Why?
3. Several scenarios described the development of an IT application. By examining all the applications in the scenarios, list at least four steps that seem to be common in developing any IT application.
4. List some early decisions in the scenarios that caused future problems.
5. Identify two different approaches agencies used in developing IT applications. List the advantages and disadvantages of each developmental approach.
6. Considering the many IT applications in the scenarios, list three sources of user satisfaction and three sources of user dissatisfaction with IT applications.
7. Which setting in the scenarios had the most success with IT? Which had the least? Why?
8. List three approaches taken in the scenarios that seemed to increase the chances that the IT applications developed would be successful. List three factors that decreased the chances for the application's success.
9. From the scenarios, list three ways in which IT changed the nature of the work of those involved.

Chapter 2

Basic Concepts and Historical Context

INTRODUCTION

As we enter the twenty-first century, information technology (including both computer and telecommunications) has become the United States' largest industry, ahead of construction, food products, and automobile manufacturing. This fact illustrates the rapid growth in IT over the past fifty years. Society is in the process of assimilating electronic IT. How a society assimilates technology is related to the characteristics of the technology and to the receptivity of society. The mechanical clock is a good example of a technological invention with characteristics that resulted in dramatic changes in a receptive society. Monks used water-driven clocks to remind them of the correct time to pray. When Christianity spread into the colder climates of Northern Europe, they found that their water-powered clocks froze. To solve this problem, monks invented a mechanical clock that used levers and weights instead of water. The mechanical clock had increased accuracy, along with decreased size and cost. These characteristics and society's receptivity enabled the mechanical clock to have dramatic impacts on business and science. For example, the scientific community achieved major advances due to the increased precision of the mechanical clock.

Compatible technologies can combine to increase their impact on society. An example is the automobile. It combined the technologies involved with steel, the pneumatic tire, the internal combustion motor, and petroleum fuels. Technologies can also affect various segments of society differently. The clock and the automobile had little effect on human service delivery, because human services involve the transfer of information and emotions rather than the measurement of time or the transportation of individuals. Although mechanical technologies had little impact on human services, IT technologies dramatically affect human services because agencies store, manipulate, and communicate large amounts of information while serving clients.

This chapter introduces IT and provides the historical context in which human services IT is developing. It first defines basic concepts. Then it compares the components and functions of a computing system to those of a stereo system. Next, it traces the history of information storage, information processing, programming, languages, and telecommunications technologies. Finally, it explores IT as the latest in a series of information technologies that have revolutionized society. The chapter concludes with a historical analysis of information's use in the human services.

BASIC CONCEPTS OF HUMAN SERVICES IT

Human Services

Human services facilitate daily living by enabling individuals, families, and other primary groups to function, cope, and contribute. Human services address the problems that people, individually or collectively, have with:

- themselves, for example, emotional and mental difficulties;
- primary groups, for example, family conflict, divorce, child abuse;
- other nonrelated individuals, for example, crime;
- organizations, for example, unemployment, poverty; and
- communities and the larger society, for example, deviance.

Human services are provided by a delivery system consisting of consumers, laws, regulations, resources, organizational structures, and professionals. A typical way to classify human service professionals is by their function or position in the multitiered service delivery system. These positions are policy planner, community practitioner, top-level managers, midlevel managers, administrative support staff, and direct service practitioners. The direct practice level can be divided into professional practice and paraprofessional practice. Professional direct practitioners usually have an advanced degree or certification in a human service field, for example, psychologists, psychiatrists, or social workers. Paraprofessionals are those who receive their expertise through on-the-job training, such as psychiatric attendants and welfare eligibility determination workers. Professional practitioners are more skilled and more highly paid than are nonprofessionals. In this book, the term *practitioner* refers to professional practitioners unless otherwise indicated.

Technology

Technology is a combination of tools and actions that are grounded in scientific knowledge, practice, or ideology and which direct one's activities and decisions. Technology encompasses the tools, techniques, and procedures of a profession or trade. A professional is a person who has the knowledge and skills to competently use a set of professional technologies.

Technology that involves machines or tangible items can be thought of as "hard." Technology can be thought of as "soft" when it involves intangible guidelines, techniques, or a structured series of procedures. Accounting involves both hard technology, such as the calculator, and soft technology, such as budget techniques and auditing procedures. The technology of a visiting nurse consists of medical instruments (hard), along with diagnostic techniques and rehabilitation procedures (soft). The technology of a counselor may consist of biofeedback devices (hard) and counseling techniques such as hypnosis (soft). IT involves both hard and soft technologies.

The distinction between hard and soft technologies is especially helpful in the human services because most human services include both soft and hard technologies. It is easy to see how IT can support most hard technologies because they are based on the cause-and-effect principles of physics, mathematics, and engineering. In contrast, it is often difficult to see how IT can support the soft technologies of the human services that are based on less quantifiable scientific knowledge, such as theories of behavior. When human service activities are not derived from scientific knowledge or codified expertise, professional decisions are often guided by ideologies, for example, psychotherapy. Consequently, human service delivery is often seen as more of an art than a science. Education often involves improving the artfulness of the practitioner rather than acquiring professional technologies. This book assumes that human services are heavily based in hard and soft technologies that are open to definition, measurement, and IT support.

Information Technology

The term *information technology* (IT) is commonly used as the overarching term to describe technologies that process information in electronic form. In the past, some information technologies have been nonelectronic, for example, a book or typewriter. Sometimes the term information is dropped and the term technology is used alone. Although the computer is the basic IT, IT also includes telecommunications, networking, and any other electronic technology used to collect, store, process, and disseminate information. Not all electronic technologies are for processing information; for example, a robotic arm is designed to produce movement.

The introduction pointed out that we first apply new technology to the present ways of doing things, for example, the horseless carriage. As we become more familiar with technology, we use it to invent totally new ways of doing things, for example, airplanes. IT can be divided into similar types. Horseless carriage IT would include word processing, data processing, statistical analysis, spreadsheet analysis, presentation software, groupware, robotics, and computer-based training. Airplane IT would include multimedia, neural networks, virtual reality, and the Internet.

Computers, Computing, and Applications

The term computer is derived from the Latin *computare*, meaning to reckon together. A *computer* is an electromechanical device that accepts data and instructions, manipulates the data according to the instructions, and outputs the results. Computers are often linked to other technologies such as printers and telephones. These related technologies increase the power and accessibility of the computer. Computers process data in electronic form, that is, as a series of electronic pulses. Data in nonelectronic form can be processed by hand or with the help of mechanical devices, for example, by abacus, typewriter, or mechanical calculator.

Throughout this book, analogies are made between a transportation and an information system. In these analogies, the computer is analogous to the motor. Both are devices that carry out a process. Gasoline motors convert the energy stored in petroleum into the rotational energy of a spinning shaft. Computers transform electrical energy into arithmetic and logic operations. The computer is the basic device underlying information technology, just as the internal combustion engine is the basic device underlying automobile technology.

Computing refers to the total process of collecting, storing, manipulating, communicating, and disseminating information in electronic form. Computing can support secretaries, as in word processing, or provide pleasure, as in computer games. Figure 2.1 illustrates that a computer performs the core functions of computing, just as a motor performs the core functions of traveling.

Applications are systems of IT, people, and procedures that solve a problem. Cars and trucks are transportation applications, just as word processors and treatment planners are IT applications.

Confusion sometimes occurs because computers can be smaller than one's fingernail or large enough to occupy an entire room. Computers come in many sizes, just as motors come in many sizes. With hardware undergoing rapid miniaturization, size distinctions such as supercomputer, mainframe, minicomputer, microcomputer, and personal computer are becoming less meaningful. These distinctions also ignore that most computers are networked together. The basic components of a computer system are a processing unit, memory, and input/output components. All these compo-

FIGURE 2.1. Motoring and Computing Operations

Motoring/Traveling Operations

Input of gasoline into automobile gas tank
Long-term storage of gasoline in automobile tank
Operating automobile (turn steering wheel, push gas pedal, etc.)
Retrieval of gasoline from automobile tank
Internal combustion

> Input of gasoline into motor
> Input of user instructions (gas pedal, etc.)
> Firing of spark plugs
> Movement of piston
> Turning of crankshaft

Operations of the Motor

Turning of wheels
Movement of automobile according to user instructions, for example, steering wheel
Travel by passenger

Computing Operations

Collection of data
Input of data to computer or storage device
Programming of instructions for processing data
Long-term storage of data and instructions
Retrieval of data and instructions from storage device
Processing of data

> Input/output of data
> Input of user instructions (programs, keyboard, etc.)
> Manipulation of data according to instructions
> Temporarily stores results in short-term memory

Operations of the Computer

Storage of processed data
Formatting of processed data according to user instructions
Communication of processed data according to user instructions
Reproduction of processed data according to user instructions
Use of processed data in other operations

nents may be integrated on one tiny chip called a microprocessor. Such a chip can be used as a complete computer by other electronic devices.

Computing often involves other technologies such as the telephone, television, copiers and printers, satellites, lasers, and robots. The transportation analogy helps illustrate this combination of technologies. Although the motor is the basic technology in today's transportation system, transportation involves much more than just motor technology; it involves technologies such as steel manufacturing, petroleum refining, asphalt preparation, and road and bridge building. The importance of the motor in early transportation can be seen in the common use of the term "motoring" to describe going from one place to another. Today, other terms have evolved to replace the overall concept of motoring. Similarly, new terms may evolve to replace the term "computing" as the information revolution matures.

Hardware, Programs, and Software

The term hardware in traditional usage denotes metal goods such as the tools and equipment that can be purchased in a hardware store. Hardware has a similar meaning in computing terminology. *Hardware* refers to the physical, tangible components of computing systems, for example, a printer. One can touch and see computing hardware.

Hardware must have instructions to operate. *Computer programs* are stored instructions that guide the computer's operations. Computer programs are written in *computer languages* that have characteristics similar to human languages and must be learned, just as one learns a foreign language. A *programmer* is a person who writes computer programs using a computer language.

Software consists of computer programs and the accompanying documentation (see Figure 2.2). Software guides the computer, aids the computer programmer, and interacts with the user. Software is the nontangible part of a computing system, just as music is the nontangible part of a stereo system. One cannot touch the sound of music or the logic of software. One touches only the hardware components that contain music or software, such as tapes and disks, or the symbols that represent music or software, such as notes and characters. Hardware with limited software is like a stereo system with a limited record collection.

Two types of software exist. *System software* manages the computer and its use, for example, the Windows operating system, server software that handles a network, or virus detection software. *Applications software* solves a user problem, for example, word processing. Software that requires little user customization before use is often referred to as a *software package,* for example, a statistical software package. Chapters 3, 4, and 5

FIGURE 2.2. Classification of Software

System Software

Definition:

Helps the system run correctly and helps programmers develop programs for users

Examples:

Operating system

Utilities that perform system tasks, such as checking for viruses

Languages, such as HTML and BASIC

Local area networks

Application Software

Definition:

Helps solve a user problem

Examples:

Packaged software that solves a well-defined and common problem, such as word processing

Custom-developed software that solves a unique problem, such as an agency information system

Documentation

Definition:

Describes software and its use

Examples:

Instructions internal to a computer program

Manuals for the computer operator

Manuals for the users of an accounting software package

Interactive user help

present many IT applications relevant to the human services. Chapter 9 discusses hardware, programming, and software in more detail.

Data, Information, and Knowledge

Communication involves sending and receiving verbal and nonverbal signals. What we communicate takes many forms. In IT, the three common terms to designate what is communicated are data, information, and knowledge.

Data are numbers that have no inherent meaning. For example, the numbers 76019 are data; they have no meaning other than their arithmetic value. *Information* is data organized to communicate a meaning. If 76019 is a zip code, then one could discover that this arrangement of numbers denotes the University of Texas at Arlington. *Knowledge* is information in the form of descriptions and relationships. For example, that the University of Texas at Arlington is part of the Texas State University system is a piece of knowledge. In certain sections of this book, the distinction between data, information, and knowledge is unimportant. To enhance readability, any one of the terms may be used to denote all three. Typically, information is the most commonly used term.

Media other than text and numbers can be used by IT, for example, graphics, pictures, animation, sound, and video. When several media are combined, the term *multimedia* is used.

Data Processing

Many different terms define what occurs with IT and data. A human analogy of data processing is when humans act on visual input (see Figure 2.3). Humans perceive reality through a series of sensory inputs. They process the inputs by use of cognitive models that are either inherent in their genetic predispositions or acquired through learning. Two humans may process the same facts differently. A cow may be seen as something to eat by a farmer in midwestern United States. However, in certain parts of India, a cow is seen as a sacred animal that should not be eaten.

Figure 2.4 illustrates that IT applications are often seen as processing data into information in ways similar to the human brain (see Figure 2.3). The processes in Figure 2.4 are involved with all IT applications whether they are adding two numbers, processing monthly paychecks, or operating a robot helping a bed-confined patient. However, as the complexity of the data processing task increases, the number and the repetitions of the operations increase. Table 2.1 presents technical terms and examples for these operations. This book often lists these operations as capturing, storing, manipulating, and communicating data. Thus, *data processing* is the capturing, storing, manipulating, and communication of data. When data processing is performed by many computers linked to operate as one computer, the term *parallel processing* is used.

Connectivity, Communications, Networks, and the Internet

Connectivity refers to the extent of the linkages and the sharing of IT resources between two or more systems. Connectivity involves *data communications,* or the sending and receiving of data using IT. Data commu-

FIGURE 2.3. Human Processing

**Sensing and
Recognition**

Cognitive Processing

Action

Source: Compliments of Mike Petree.

nications over telephone lines is called *telecommunications*. Some of the hardware involved in telecommunications includes the telephone, modems, telephone lines, optical fiber, satellites, microwave stations, and sophisticated switching and signaling networks. *Bandwidth* is the term that describes the speed at which data travels over data communication networks.

Computer *networks* are linked software and hardware systems that share resources. Computers on a network are called *nodes*. A *local area network* (LAN) connects computers to share IT resources within one organization. A *wide area network* (WAN) connects computers to share IT resources in many agencies. The Internet is a network independent of any

FIGURE 2.4. Computer Processing

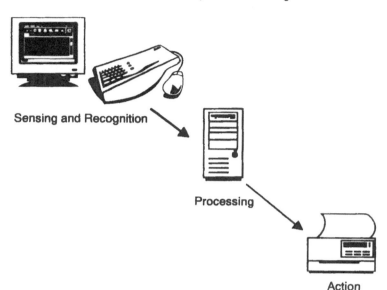

Sensing and Recognition

Processing

Action

application or organization. The *Internet* is a network of networks that has many features to meet users' needs, for example:

- *E-mail* for sending and receiving messages composed of text, graphics, pictures, voice, video, Internet links, etc.
- *Lists* to distribute all e-mail they received to all subscribers to the list
- *FTP (file transfer protocol)* to provide a standard for uploading and downloading files
- *Chat* to allow real-time communications between multiple people connected simultaneously to the Internet
- *Discussion groups (conferences, bulletin boards, newsgroups, and threaded forums)* that make it easy to follow and reply to messages on a topic
- *Search engines* that use keywords to locate information
- *Internet telephone* that allows a person to make local or long-distance calls over the Internet
- *Telenet* to help access a remote Internet computer as if one were directly connected to that computer

New features are constantly being developed.

TABLE 2.1. Data Processing Operations: Human and Computer Examples

Operation	Definition	Human Services Example	Computing Example
Recognizing	Sensing what exists in reality and sorting what was sensed into accepted symbols, numbers, and words	A counselor recognizes the client's symptoms during the intake interview.	A computer recognizes a command typed on the computer keyboard.
Storing	Depositing data on media such as paper, film, magnetic tape, or electronic circuitry	A counselor-client session is stored on videotape.	A word processing file is stored on computer disk.
Retrieving	Locating, gaining access to, and restoring stored data	A clerk pulls a client's record from a file cabinet.	Client data is located on computer disk and loaded into computer memory.
Verifying	Checking to ensure that what is recognized accurately reflects what actually exists	A counselor interviews a client to ensure agency records reflect client-provided information.	A software program checks to ensure data received over telephone lines are exactly what was sent.
Classifying	Placing data into types based on a predetermined scheme	A counselor uses client symptoms to classify problems according to the *Diagnostic and Statistical Manual*.	A computer uses a coding scheme to classify a stream of electronic signals into known commands.
Comparing	Examining data for a predefined relationship	Client symptoms are compared to the adverse reactions of a drug.	Two databases are examined for matching names.
Arranging	Placing data in an order or sequence	A human sorts a mailing list in zip code order.	A computer program sorts a mailing list in zip code order.
Aggregating	Assembling smaller units into a larger unit	Symptoms are combined into a diagnosis.	Weekly totals are assembled into a monthly report.
Calculating	Adding, subtracting, multiplying, and dividing	A client's bill is determined based on a sliding fee scale chart.	A client's bill is determined based on rates and sessions.
Reproducing	Copying data from one media to another or to another location on the same media	Notes from a counselor's intake interview are reproduced on an intake form.	Notes from a counselor's intake interview are moved from the database to a report.
Disseminating	Transferring data from one location to another or from one person to another	A client's record is forwarded to an internal review committee.	An e-mail message is sent to all employees on a list.

The *World Wide Web* (WWW or Web) is a network of Internet nodes that adhere to standards which allow user access via a graphical software package called a *browser*. Most people experience the Internet using a browser on the Web. Browsers display node information that is stored in a standard format called hypertext transmission protocol (HTTP). HTTP allows information to be presented as scrollable pages of information organized into a Web site. Web pages may contain text, graphics, and pictures, as well as links to downloadable text, programs, audio, and video files. Links may also connect users to a different section of the same page, other pages, or other Web sites. The first page of a site is called the *home page*. Home pages are similar to an agency brochure because they present the initial image of the site. Since Web site addresses change frequently, those relevant to each chapter of this book will be made available on the Web site associated with this book.

Human-machine communication. Several terms are concerned with the way people interact with IT applications. On-line means the user has a direct communication link to the computer. In contrast, off-line refers to a mode of operation in which the individual and the computer are not connected. An example of off-line interaction occurs where Internet access is costly. Often e-mail messages are downloaded to a local computer in on-line mode. Then each message is viewed and answered in off-line mode. Once completed, the local computer is again connected on-line with the Internet so that the new e-mail messages can be sent.

The term *interactive* is used to describe a processing mode in which each user command elicits a response from the computer. For example, an Internet site that presents text is not very interactive, while a chat room is very interactive.

A computer interaction is in *real time* if the time between the user entering a command and the computer responding is fast enough to affect subsequent use. Real time for an airline reservation system may be twenty seconds, while real time for an air traffic controller at a busy airport may be three seconds.

INTRODUCTION TO IT

Since the computer is the most pervasive IT, examining a computing system will help illustrate basic IT concepts. An easy way to examine the components and functions of a computing system is to compare them to the more familiar components and functions of a stereo sound system, often called a stereo. In this section, stereo and computing systems will be compared using system purpose, functions, and components. Table 2.2 summarizes the comparison. For simplicity, the comparison will use terms related to music in describing the stereo system, although a stereo system can produce other sounds as well. Similarly, the generic term data will be used to discuss the computing system in this comparison, although information and knowledge can be processed as well. This comparison is simplistic, as digital multimedia have blurred the lines between sound and computer systems.

Stereo System

A *system* is a group of components in interaction. A *subsystem* is a smaller group of system components that functions as a unit. Computing systems and stereo systems have a purpose and storage, input, processing, and output subsystems.

Purpose

The purpose of a stereo system is to serve the user by converting stored signals into sound, according to user specifications. Two major subsystems comprise a stereo system, the music subsystem and the control subsystem. The music subsystem retrieves sound stored on disc or tape. It then trans-

TABLE 2.2. Hardware Components of a Stereo System and a Computer System

	Components	
Function	**Stereo System**	**Computer System**
Storage	Cassette tape	Reel-to-reel tape
	Reel-to-reel tape	Cassette tape
	Phonograph record	Hard disk
	Compact/DVD disc	Floppy disk, CD-ROM, DVD disc
Input	Turntable	Video display terminal
	Tape player	Tape drive
	Disc player	Disk drive
	Buttons	Voice recognition device
	Levers and switches	Scanner or optical character reader
	Microphone	Joy sticks or mouse
Processing	Amplifier	Central processing unit
Output	Speakers	Video display terminal, lights
	Meters	Printers
	Lights	Speech synthesizer
	Cassette tape	Hard disk, floppy disk
	Reel-to-reel tape	Cassette tape, reel-to-reel tape
	Compact disc	CD-ROM

forms the stored information into music for listening or into signals for recording. The control subsystem allows the user to set performance specifications such as volume and tone. Lights and meters of the control subsystem allow the user to observe whether the system is performing according to specifications.

Mass Storage Media

Data and music reside in one of several types of media. A medium for holding large amounts of information is commonly called mass storage. Large amounts of sound are stored on media such as phonograph records, tapes, and discs. One important difference between tape and disc storage is the way sound can be accessed. Playing a song from an audiotape requires searching each song successively until arriving at the desired song. This access method is called sequential access. The term sequential indicates that one must proceed sequentially, or song by song, to access the desired track. With a record or disc, a song can be rapidly located because the turntable needle or disc laser beam can quickly be moved to any track. This nonsequenced access method is called random access because sound can be stored in random locations on the storage media and yet be quickly accessed (see Figure 2.5).

Input

Inputs into a stereo system serve two functions: the first is to control performance such as volume and tone (control subsystem); the second is to perform a task for the user, for example, play prerecorded music (music subsystem). Input devices for the control subsystem consist of levers, buttons, and switches for relaying user specifications. Input devices for the music subsystem consist of turntables, compact disc players, or tape decks. These input devices detect and transmit stored signals to the processing subsystem.

Processing

To produce music on a stereo, the amplifier processes control information and music signals into signals the output devices can use. During processing, signals are enlarged and adjusted according to the volume, tone, filtering, balance, and other characteristics specified by the user.

Output

A stereo system outputs music signals and control information. Output devices, such as speakers, convert output signals into sound for listening.

FIGURE 2.5. Cartoon About Random Access

"Cleo, some idiot outside claims he has a random access device which is going to revolutionize the way we do our work!"

Source: Compliments of Mike Petree.

Other output devices, such as a cassette tape, store signals for future input. Control outputs indicating system performance are presented to the user on displays such as meters and lights.

Computing System

The familiar functions and components of a stereo system are analogous to the less familiar functions and components of a computing system (see Table 2.2).

Purpose

The purpose of a computing system is to serve the user by rapidly and reliably processing data to solve user problems. This same purpose exists whether the computing system is responding to the voice commands of someone in a wheelchair or calculating payroll checks. Similar to a stereo system, the computing system has a control subsystem and a data subsystem. The data subsystem manipulates data according to user instructions processed by the control subsystem.

Mass Storage

Data and processing instructions are stored as electrical pulses on the surfaces of magnetic tape or disks. Computer storage media function similarly to the storage media of a stereo system. Disk storage allows for random access, while tapes allow sequential access. Computer disks and tapes are coated with iron oxide, the material on the surface of a cassette tape. Various other media can be considered computer storage, although a computer cannot write information directly on them. For example, a scanner with optical character recognition (OCR) software can transform handwriting on specially designed forms into computer-usable data. Or, a speech recognition device can transform speech into computer-usable text.

Input

As in a stereo system, inputs into a computer system serve two functions: one is to control the computer's performance (control subsystem); the other is to perform a task for the user (data subsystem). Two types of devices input data into a computing system. One type allows direct user input and the other type retrieves stored data. The keys of a computer keyboard are analogous to the levers and buttons on a stereo system. Each allows the user to input nonstored data. Devices that read tapes and disks allow the input of stored signals.

Processing

The processing unit of a computer receives the instructions and data from the input devices. It then transforms the data according to the instructions and stores the results for immediate use by the system or by an output component. This processing involves three basic tasks (the data processing operations in Table 2.1 are listed in parentheses after each task):

Task 1. Data and instructions are accessed, and depending on the instructions, either 2a, 2b, or both are performed (recognizing, retrieving, verifying, classifying, reproducing, storing).

Task 2a. Arithmetic operations of add, multiply, subtract, and divide are performed (retrieving, calculating, storing).

Task 2b. Logical operations such as equal to, greater than, and less than are performed (comparing, arranging).

Task 3. The results are written to memory or transferred to an output device (storing, reproducing).

Output

Typical output devices are a television-like screen called a display, a printer, and mass storage devices such as a disk drive. A computing system, similar to a stereo system, produces two types of output: one output is the result of user-specified tasks (data subsystem); the second is information on how the system performed the task (control subsystem). Data subsystem and control subsystem outputs are often displayed on the same output device, the computer display. In addition, a few lights and meters also display control information.

One major difference between a stereo system and a computing system is that the computing system is capable of handling very complex control instructions. In a stereo system, control inputs are limited to lever and switch settings. Control output information is limited to displays by lights and meters. In a computing system, massive amounts of control information can be entered. Sophisticated control output messages can be displayed, printed, or stored for future input. This very complex control subsystem gives the user tremendous power over the data processing capability of a computer.

HISTORICAL PERSPECTIVE

IT involves technological developments in areas such as information storage, processing, programming, languages, and telecommunications. This section presents a brief history of these areas. The viewpoint reflects the IT history of the United States. Other countries, such as the United Kingdom and Hungary, would have a similar history of IT. Pictures of some of the IT devices mentioned in this section are available from links provided on the Web site associated with this book.

Storage

Technology for storing and retrieving information by machine has been available for hundreds of years. Weaving looms, which typify this technology, used punched paper cards banded together. This series of cards directed the loom in making complex woven patterns.

The technology of storing data on cards advanced in 1900 when Herman Hollerith used punched-card technology to store U.S. census information. The new storage mechanism and automatic tabulator completed the 1900 census in half the previous time and at a considerable cost savings.

The punch card developed by the Census Bureau was the forerunner of the computer card. Computer cards and punched-paper tape provided the mechanical storage technology of early computers. Later electronic technologies, such as magnetic tapes, disks, and memory chips, resulted in the mass storage devices so essential to today's computers.

Processing

In 1823, Charles Babbage became frustrated with the time-consuming process of checking calculations. This frustration led to his building a mechanical calculating device called a "difference machine" for the British government. In the process of building the difference machine, Babbage proposed that the government finance a steam-powered "analytical machine." The proposed machine would be capable of automatically calculating any mathematical function without human intervention. Babbage's machine was to have a punch-card input system, a memory unit capable of storing 1,050-digit numbers, an arithmetic unit, a "sequence mechanism" to supervise the order of operations, and a typesetter output system. Babbage's mechanical computer was never finished, however, because his design did not become feasible until major developments in electronics a century later.

The late 1930s saw the first efforts in electromechanical computing. In 1937, researchers John V. Atanasoff and Clifford Berry at Iowa State College in Ames, Iowa, began building the first electronic digital computer. The ABC (Atanasoff-Berry Computer) was completed in 1942. Also, in 1937, Howard G. Aiken, a Harvard graduate student on an International Business Machines (IBM) grant, began researching the idea of an electromechanical calculating device. In 1944, Aiken and IBM completed the electromechanical calculator called Mark 1. The Mark 1 was capable of performing three additions every second.

During World War II, computer-like devices were developed for quickly calculating artillery trajectories and breaking enemy codes. In 1943, the U.S. Army commissioned John W. Mauchly and J. Presper Eckert Jr. to build ENIAC (Electronic Numerical Integrator and Computer). ENIAC, the first large-scale digital computer, was completed in 1946. It was developed to reduce artillery trajectory calculations from fifteen minutes to thirty seconds. ENIAC cost $400,000, weighed thirty tons, was the size of a three-bedroom house, consumed 150,000 watt-hours of electricity each day, and failed every seven seconds. ENIAC was less powerful than today's pocket-size computers.

The Army commissioned John von Neumann, during 1945 to 1951, to develop EDVAC (Electronic Discrete Variable Automatic Computer), a more powerful computer than ENIAC. EDVAC's most significant improvement was a stored computer program. Stored programs alleviated the problem of rewiring thousands of switches to reprogram the computer to perform a new task.

Shortly after ENIAC was developed, Eckert and Mauchly formed the Eckert-Mauchly Computer Corporation. They built UNIVAC 1 (UNIVersal Automatic Computer). Their first commercially available computer was delivered to the Census Bureau in 1951. UNIVAC 1 performed about 3,000 additions every second and could hold approximately 1,000 words of internal memory. In comparison, the internal memory of most personal computers sold today holds approximately one-half million words.

Other important developments in hardware soon followed. The transistor, developed in 1947, replaced the troublesome vacuum tubes. In 1958, the development of electrical circuits on silicon chips, called integrated circuits, decreased computer size and enhanced capabilities. Computer-controlled mass production of computer chips and other developments allowed decreases in cost and size and increases in capacity. The result was large, powerful, expensive computers capable of simultaneously serving many users.

In the mid-1970s, these same trends led to the development of single-user computers that were affordable by home computer enthusiasts. The development of this personal computer was analogous to the mass production of the Model T Ford. The Model T Ford increased the availability and use of automobiles and had a major impact on today's transportation system. Similarly, inexpensive, powerful, personal computers are driving our transition into the information society.

Table 2.3 presents the generations of computer hardware development. Computer generations change when a major technological development occurs. Table 2.3 documents the phenomenal speed at which computer size and costs have declined as computer power has increased. Considering the relatively short history of electronic processing by computer, it is remarkable how pervasive computing has become. The unconnected computer is not having a dramatic impact, but the networked computer, combined with other technologies such as lasers and satellite communications, is. The ability to quickly collect, manipulate, and communicate large volumes of information worldwide has radical implications for society and for human services.

TABLE 2.3. Computer Hardw;

Characteristic	1950-1958 1st Generation	1958-1964 2nd Generation	1964- 3rd G	-1980+ ;enera
Size of the smallest computer	Room size	Closet size	Desk	writer s
Basic circuitry	Vacuum tube	Transistor	Integi	large-s egratio
Predominant data entry device	Paper tape	Cards	Cards ten	oard, t iuse
Speed in instructions per second	1950=244	1958=2550	1964:	, Intel !00,00C
Cost of 100,000 manipulations	1952=$1.26	1958=$.26	1964: 197	=$.01
Computers in an organization	One	One/several	Seve un(	i, conn
Typical information processed	Large calculations	Accounting, inventory	Mana info	le- and el info
Key personnel	Computer scientist	Systems analyst	Syste	sion sc
Primary computer user	Technician	Technical manager, researcher	Midle	anage
Predominant business use	Data processing	Management information system	Inforr	sion su stem
Responsibility for	In the department	Accounting	A ton	v denar

Programming

The previous discussion indicated that for hundreds of years, instructions inscribed on storage disks and cards have controlled devices such as antique music boxes and weaving looms. Technicians who calculated the locations of the holes in these disks and cards could be considered the forerunners of computer software developers. One of Babbage's colleagues, Ada Augusta, is often credited as being the first computer programmer. The Department of Defense recognized her achievements by naming a computer language ADA.

The process of writing separately stored instructions for computers preceded the term software, which was not coined until the 1950s. John von Neumann's use of computer instructions stored in computer memory began the development of modern programming. One major drawback of early computer instructions is that they had to be written in code that was different for each computer. In the early 1940s and 1950s, programmers saved time and energy by collecting, reusing, and exchanging portions of code that they called subroutines. To ensure the accuracy of copying these subroutines, they were stored in machine-readable form. The computer was programmed to pull the necessary subroutines out of memory and to combine them into a machine language program. The result was the beginning of machine-readable code that could run on a variety of computers.

Languages

A computer language is a generic set of symbols, conventions, and rules that allows humans to write instructions for a computer. The language software takes written instructions and translates them into computer-specific code. Primitive forms of computer languages existed for early computers. The development of standardized computer languages for generating machine code marked a breakthrough in software development. In the late 1950s, an IBM team designed FORTRAN (FORmula TRANslator). The two and one-half years it took to develop the translation program from the FORTRAN design specification illustrates the complexity of a computer language. FORTRAN proved that programs could be written in a language which bore no resemblance to machine code and which could run on many computers. With the success of FORTRAN and the availability of fundamental language concepts, the 1960s saw the development of over 200 new languages. Even today, new languages, such as Java, are being developed to extend the capabilities of the Internet.

Another milestone language was COBOL (COmmon Business Oriented Language). COBOL was commissioned by the Defense Department to replace the many different languages used by each military branch. COBOL became the standard language for business applications. Another important language, BASIC (Beginner's All-purpose Symbolic Instruction Code), was designed for multitasking and education. Another primary language, called C, was designed for transferability of programs from one computer to another. Program transferability is important because it allows existing software to be easily adapted to the latest hardware. Overall, languages are becoming much more powerful in controlling the computer and much easier to use.

Telecommunications

Telecommunications began in 1844 with the first public demonstration of Morse's electric telegraph. Another milestone occurred in 1876, when Alexander Graham Bell spoke the first complete sentence over a telephone, "Mr. Watson, come here. I want you." Other milestones involved the digital transmission of information, satellite communications, optical fiber data transmission, computer networks, and microwave relay of data. The integration of these technologies is resulting in a telecommunications network capable of linking most electronic devices and transmitting large volumes of data, such as in video broadcasts. Telecommunications allows IT to be linked together in networks.

SOCIETAL IMPACT

Information exists in many forms, including sound, gestures/symbols, dance, painting, writing, pictures, and film/video. Several basic media exist for working with information, for example, psychic, print, and electronic. Digital electronic-based media, on which signals are transmitted as a series of ones and zeros, are the latest for storing, manipulating, and communicating information.

The introduction of a new information medium into society can cause significant societal changes. Analyzing the impact of writing and mechanical printing can provide insights into the impact digital electronic media will have on society. This section presents the information revolutions that followed the introduction of writing and printing. It will also examine the possible revolution that will result from the introduction of electronic media.

Writing to Capture the Spoken Word

One of the first revolutions in information media began with the introduction of pictographic writing about 3,000 B.C. Later, phonetic writing was developed, in which a symbolic representation of speech was used rather than a picture of the idea to be communicated. The ability to capture speech on wood, stone, or other objects was significant. It made the communication of information independent of the human voice, the storage of information independent of the human mind, and the manipulation of stored information possible.

The impact of writing on society was dramatic. Before writing, memory was considered a skill and virtue that ruled daily life, as the following quote illustrates:

> The elder Seneca (ca 55 BC-AD 37), a famous teacher of rhetoric, was said to be able to repeat long passages of speeches he had heard only once many years before. He would impress his students by asking each member of a class of 200 to recite a line of poetry, and then he would recite all the lines they had quoted—in reverse order, from last to first. (Boorstin, 1984, p. 107)

The value of such feats of memory began to decline with the introduction of writing. Today, such feats are practiced only as entertainment.

Writing helped bring about the demise of the oral tradition and the displacement of the storyteller. It led to the replacement of "one's word" by a more precise, written contract that could be stored for future reference. Public ceremonies such as marriage, which allowed the tribe or clan to witness an oral agreement, began losing their importance. With thoughts written, orders and procedures were more accurately transmitted. This enabled church, state, and military bureaucracies to grow in size and control. Crafts and industries grew around the establishment of a writing system. For example, scribes became important professionals and monks labored in medieval monasteries to write, translate, and copy books.

Writing also caused fear and resistance. Some Greeks considered writing a passive impersonal medium and feared its ill effects. They believed writing discouraged dialogue, prevented ideas from being tailored to the listener, and destroyed memorization skills and memory.

Printing

Another information revolution began in Western society in 1440 with the invention of printing from movable type by Johannes Gutenberg. The Gutenberg press advanced the media for storing, manipulating, and transmitting information from written to printed form. Mechanical printing resulted in accurate and rapid reproduction, inexpensive mass storage, and the widespread, inexpensive dissemination of information.

The impact of mechanical printing on society paralleled that of handwriting. For example, job displacement occurred as monks were no longer needed to hand copy books. Bureaucracies grew as orders and procedures were capable of being quickly printed and widely distributed. Education was decentralized as inexpensively stored information could be communicated to a much wider audience. Cultural ideas and scientific knowledge spread as books became available to the common person. Printed books played an important role in the European Renaissance of the fourteenth through sixteenth centuries.

Nevertheless, not all impacts were beneficial. Because the spread of ideas was feared, printing was opposed, controlled, and licensed. Readers, accustomed to handwritten books, proclaimed that the new printed books were impersonal. Leibniz in the late 1600s was said to have proclaimed, "the mass of books will surely exhaust people's curiosity." Printed information was also misused. The church, state, and other powerful institutions that feared change used printed works to identify and punish those considered heretics or traitors.

A third information revolution occurred with the invention of film for pictures and movies. Although this revolution has greatly influenced the arts, a fourth "digital" revolution is producing results that are even more pervasive, since most forms of information are stored, manipulated, and communicated in digital form.

Electronic Media

Digital electronic media for storing, manipulating, and communicating information is causing the current information revolution. This fourth information revolution began around the middle of the nineteenth century with the invention of the telegraph and the telephone. It leaped forward with the invention of the digital computer in the 1940s and is now flourishing, as computers are combined with other technologies. These technologies are telephones, televisions, lasers, holograms, fiber optics, satellites, robotics, and microwave transmission.

The current information revolution is impacting society similarly to previous revolutions. Jobs such as typesetting are being eliminated. Bureaucracies are able to grow into large multinational conglomerates because they can quickly disseminate information to remote locations. Education is becoming more self-guided and home centered, for example, through distance learning. Language barriers and geographic distances are becoming less important. The popular terms "global village" and "wired society" imply these changes. Negative effects also exist, such as the increased ability to make large mistakes and to identify deviates and enemies of powerful institutions (see "Clients," "Issues," in Chapter 13).

To understand the impact of digital media on the human services, it is helpful to examine the role information plays in the human services as a culture moves from a tribal to an information society.

INFORMATION USE IN HUMAN SERVICE DELIVERY

Since human service delivery is information based, the history of service delivery and information technology will help understand human services IT. In this section, preindustrial, industrial, and postindustrial societies are described, along with the accompanying service delivery system and information technology. Table 2.4 is a summary of the following discussion.

Human Services in Tribal/Agricultural Societies

Preindustrial or tribal/agricultural societies are dominated by hunting, farming, and animal-rearing technology. Real and perceived threats from the world outside the tribe form powerful socialization mechanisms. Human services in preindustrial societies are delivered within the clan. Family, clan, village, or tribal members care for the ill, injured, insane, aged, retarded, handicapped, deviant, and needy. Delivery systems that transcend ancestral or tribal groupings rarely exist. Human service problems often concern physical illness and the problems of people living in an isolated cohesive community.

Human service delivery technology in tribal/agricultural societies is based on remedies derived from plants and animals, as well as, on a rigid set of beliefs, customs, rituals, and relationships. Most tribal societies entrust human service expertise to a professional healer such as a shaman. The policies and guidelines governing service delivery are handed down by tradition and reinforced through symbols and rituals. Nonconformists are considered outcasts. A shaman may recommend reconciling with one's self and others as a preliminary step for dealing with the petitioner's problems.

All members of a clan financially support the service delivery system. For example, members may provide the shaman with living necessities. Individual offerings may be expected when healing is requested. A sliding scale fee often exists. A person's wealth, as well as the type of problem presented, may determine the size of the individual offerings.

TABLE 2.4. Evolution into an Int

Characteristic	Agricultural, Tribal Society	Industrial Soci	Posti
Basic resource	Land, animals	Raw materials	Infor
Source of identity	Clan, family	Company of wo	Indivi
Most common work	Hunting, gathering, farming, physical labor	Manufacturing, clerical labor	Servi
Basic form of power	Physical, animal	Physical, hydro	Elect
Location of workers	Home in rural areas	Factories in citi	Office
Form of information	Oral, painted, written	Printed	Digit
Basic information tools	Voice, paper, pen and ink, ballad, ritual, ceremony	Printing press, mechanical dup	Comp satell
Jobs diminished	Storyteller, heralds	Scribes (monks	Type
Jobs created	Sage	Publishers, cler	Prog know

Although service guidelines and procedures are often rigid, little formal information is recorded. The delivery systems are small and personal, and the necessary information can be learned and passed on to apprentices. Drawings are sometimes used to record details about rituals and ceremonies to ensure their correct performance. However, drawings are seldom used to record data about service recipients' problems and individual treatments.

Human Service Delivery in Industrial Societies

Industrial society is dominated by factories that process natural resources, such as oil, timber, and steel, into commodities, such as cars and appliances. The change from agricultural villages to industrial cities precipitates the breakdown of the shaman/clan human service delivery system. During industrialization, able-bodied workers typically leave their villages to earn money in distant factories. Cities develop to provide housing and other necessities for the workers. Since personal worth and socialization in cities is determined more by the workplace than by kinship, clan-based service delivery systems break down and eventually cease to exist. The consequences can be seen in the human suffering described in such industrial society novels as *Oliver Twist* by Charles Dickens.

Human service problems during industrialization concern illness, lack of resources, and lack of socialization, for example, addictions and violence. Western society has had a difficult time adjusting to these problems. Particularly difficult is obtaining consensus on the responsibility for solving problems now that a clan no longer exists. We have yet to agree on which responsibilities should be borne by the individual, family, business sector, voluntary sector, and various levels of government.

Industrial society's human services are frequently delivered through a variety of unconnected and uncoordinated government and independent agencies. Delivery technologies are often seen as based on common sense, good moral principles, or the art of practice gained from experience. Information is gathered to support management and rarely the client/practitioner interaction. Agencies seek multiple funding sources to ensure fiscal viability, but these funding sources differ in the data needed to document accountability. Human service agencies typically collect more information than internal operations require simply to satisfy the external accountability demands. Thus, agencies are tremendous information generators, but inadequate information users. Delivery systems designed in the industrial age are the basis of our present service delivery system. Industrial society's human services are ripe for applying the information technologies.

Human Service Delivery in Information Societies

Some interesting differences exist between the essential resources of an industrial society and information, the essential resource of a postindustrial society. In contrast to timber, metals, and oil, information is not consumed as it is used. In fact, its potential as a resource grows the more it is used. Even obsolete and erroneous data are useful once automated. Obsolete data are useful in trend analysis, and erroneous data can be manipulated to determine the source of the error. Another difference is that electronic technologies have few, or no, moving parts and rarely wear out.

The information society is predicted to be as different from industrial society as industrial society is from agricultural society. If this prediction is true, our human service delivery systems can be expected to experience changes as dramatic as those which occurred when large industrial cities replaced clans. However, the change may be even more dramatic. Although human service delivery had little use for industrial technology, it is potentially a large user of information technology. Information technology can impact the way information is communicated between service recipient and practitioner, between practitioner and management, between agency and funding source, and between a funding source and its constituents. Chapter 13 will further discuss the changes that occur as a society moves from a tribal to an information society and speculate on their impact.

CONCLUSION

IT involves the linking of many old and new technologies. This linking exposes human service professionals to many new terms and concepts. The most fundamental IT is the computer. Similar to all systems, a computer has a variety of input, processing, and output operations and components. IT, in its short history, has advanced rapidly and is having dramatic effects on all aspects of society. The information society will be as different from industrial society as industrial society is from tribal/agricultural society.

Although people's basic human service needs have remained relatively constant over time, the structures society uses to address these needs continue to change. The human service delivery system of a postindustrial/information society will use IT to support all levels of the organization. In addition, services will have to continually change to handle the new human service problems an information society creates.

REVIEW AND DISCUSSION QUESTIONS

1. Name the major information technologies in society today.
2. What is the history of the major technologies listed for question 1?
3. State how the technologies listed for question 1 have been, and will continue to be, impacted by digital communications.
4. Name the major components of a computer system and what each component does.
5. Discuss how human services in a country village differ from human services in a high-tech city.
6. What human service problems are associated with high-tech culture and the information age?

PART II: APPLICATIONS OF INFORMATION TECHNOLOGY IN THE HUMAN SERVICES

Chapter 3

Professional Generic Applications and Assistive Technology

INTRODUCTION

Information technology is best seen in its applications. An application is IT that helps end users to accomplish a task or solve a problem. Most users do not care about the underlying technology as long as an application solves their problem. Similarly, most people do not care about the underlying technology in their automobile as long as it gets them where they want to go. This chapter presents the common computer and Internet applications that human service professionals use at work or home. Chapter 4 presents management applications, and Chapter 5 presents human services specialty applications. The technology underlying the applications is presented in Chapters 9 through 11.

The categorization and classification of applications is problematic. With rapid advances in technology, applications evolve and new applications are invented. For example, although speech recognition was a specialized application in the past, today it is becoming part of other applications, for example, word processing. Also in the past, users bought an application on disk or CD-ROM and installed it on one computer or a computer network. Today, applications may be downloaded and continuously updated from the Internet with no user involvement. Applications are also becoming more connected; they can be integrally linked to a component on the Internet anywhere in the world. This categorization problem exists with other technologies. To use the transportation analogy, cars are classified as subcompact, compact, and sedan, but users experience difficulty placing automobiles into these categories.

GENERIC APPLICATIONS

Word Processing Publishing

Writing text is a common task for most human service professionals. Human service agencies frequently need letters, reports, forms, brochures, and other specialty documents. Today, almost all professionals use a word processing program to collect, store, manage, edit, proofread, format, and print text and images. Since most agencies generate a large amount of repetitive paperwork, word processing is often the most cost-beneficial generic application available.

Publishing

Sometimes agencies need more flexibility and greater capacities than are available with word processing applications. Print shop capabilities on a small computer were first made available in 1985 with the introduction of the Apple Macintosh and the laser printer. Today, with a low-cost computer, printer, and desktop publishing software, professionals and agencies can typeset text, draw illustrations, design page layout, and print high-quality "camera-ready" output. Applications that allow a desktop computer to perform print shop design and layout tasks are known as *desktop publishing*.

Other publishing media are becoming popular, for example, CD-ROMs (compact discs) and DVD-ROMs (digital versatile discs). *Multimedia publishing* applications support the user in writing scripts, storyboarding, and integrating text, data, images, sound, video, and special effects into a packaged product. These applications use hyperlinks and multimedia. Hyperlinks allow users to jump from one topic to other related topics rapidly and nonsequentially. These applications are also called *authoring systems* (Bolen, 1997) (Schoech, 1994). Authoring systems are often used in developing training applications.

A more recent medium for publishing is the World Wide Web. *Web publishing* allows users to design and construct Web pages, post files to a Web server, and manage the files as part of an integrated Web site. Web publishing applications may include features that search sites for key words, present audio and video, track site use, post forms to capture information in a database, and publish database results.

Speech Processing

Speech processing applications perform *speech recognition* to execute user commands to the computer, convert dictation into text for word processing, or place user responses into forms. They also perform *speech synthesis,* whereby the computer speaks text to the user. Although speech processing has been available in specialized applications for a long time, it is just beginning to be integrated into other applications, for example, data entry for mental health professionals (Butterfield, 1998). Speech recognition and speech synthesis are important to the human services because they open the computer interface to clients and others who have limited keyboarding skills.

Spreadsheet Analysis

A *spreadsheet* is an electronic version of an accountant's columnar tablet, and each square created by the intersection of a horizontal row and a vertical column is called a cell. When using a paper columnar tablet, a cell may contain only a label or a number. However, when using an electronic spreadsheet, cells can contain other entities, such as a complex equation. The spreadsheet's advantage over the columnar pad is the rapid recalculation of each cell when the contents of any cell are changed. Spreadsheets can also be linked, causing any cell changes to result in rapid recalculation of all linked spreadsheets.

Since the first spreadsheet, VisiCalc, was introduced in 1979, spreadsheets have been widely employed by many professions for "what if" analysis. For example, if an agency's budget was in spreadsheet format and the agency board wanted a budget representing a 4 percent salary increase, inputting a few numbers and commands would generate the new budget. Spreadsheets can perform "what if" analysis in nonbudget areas. For example, Janzen and Lewis (1990) present the use of a spreadsheet to develop foster care performance indicators.

Databases and Information Systems

Data storage and retrieval is performed by file management or *database management system* (DBMS) applications. DBMSs allow users to design data entry forms, data storage structures, and output reports. Some DBMSs allow users to store hyperlinks, images, sounds, and video as well as data.

DBMSs typically form the basis of other applications, for example, agency information systems. However, *information systems* are more than databases for they include the people, procedures, and documentation for collecting, processing, and disseminating the information. Specialized information systems exist; for example, *geographic information systems* (GIS) work with geographic and spatial information using database tools, geographic analysis, and maps for visualization and presentation. With GIS, data are referenced by spatial or geographic designations such as street address or global positioning coordinates. Thus, spatial data analysis is possible, with the results presented to users on a variety of maps. A typical use of GIS involves an Internet user continually narrowing a search for information about a community by clicking on maps of the county, city, neighborhood, block, and plot. The information sought could be real estate values, crime statistics, churches, or social service agencies. For a more in-depth discussion of GIS applications, see Hoefer, Hoefer, and Tobias (1994) and Thompkins and Southward (1998). Chapter 10 covers data management in more detail.

Presentation Managers

Presentation management applications allow the user to sequence text, graphics, sound, and pictures into a presentation using the computer display. Presentation software replaces slides and overhead transparencies and adds new features such as animation and interesting transitions between slides. Some presentation software allows the user to imbed Web links into the presentation and to publish the presentation for Internet use. Presentation management applications are used primarily in meetings, conferences, and the classroom.

Project Managers

Project management applications allow users to input project activity information such as tasks, prerequisite tasks, responsible persons, due dates, costs, resources, and milestones. Once entered, project activities can be arranged in a variety of lists and charts with key dates and activities highlighted. The shortest possible series of tasks to perform a job can be quickly calculated. If one of the entered variables on a project is changed, the charts and lists are rapidly reconfigured. E-mail can be incorporated into project management software, allowing upcoming events and updates to be automatically distributed to project team members. Grant applications often make use of project management software to develop work plans and to list the tasks of grant personnel.

Browsers and Mailers

Browsers are software programs that make the many features of the Internet available to users. Browsers perform functions such as customizing the look and feel of the user interface, maintaining a list of favorite sites, handling Internet security and cash transactions, downloading files, and printing, sending, or saving information from a site. Most browsers allow users to add applications, called *"plug-ins,"* as integrated components of the browser. Common plug-ins allow users to participate in voice meetings or three-dimensional games. Popular plug-ins are often incorporated into the next version of a browser.

Browsers also include a *mailer*, which once was a separate application. Mail applications allow the user to retrieve and read e-mail messages, compose and send text and graphic documents and files, maintain an e-mail address book, sort and store messages, and search messages for phrases or names. Most browsers also allow users to read and send messages to Usenet newsgroups (see Chapter 11).

Communications

Communication links are to the information society what railroads, canals, and highways are to an industrial society. Communications applications allow a computer to interact with peripherals or other computers over standard telephone lines or special data lines. Using communications software, one computer can connect to another computer and operate as a remote terminal. The two computers can also perform more sophisticated operations, such as sending and receiving files or becoming one node of a wider area network. For two computers to interact over telephone or dedicated lines, software must provide communication standards called *protocols*. One common Internet protocol is TCP/IP (Transmission Control Protocol/Internet Protocol). FTP (File Transfer Protocol) is a communication standard for sending and receiving files. Communications is discussed further in Chapter 11.

Other Applications

Thousands of generic software applications exist, as illustrated by advertisements in popular computer magazines. Human service agencies often use these generic applications to perform, for example, inventory management, and appointment scheduling. Generic applications could be considered information tools. Having the right tools is very important for getting a job done; using the wrong tools can frustrate work efforts as one tries to adapt and modify the tool to fit the use. Inventive users who are knowledgeable about a variety of applications can often find one or more that will solve a problem, thus preventing costly software development.

Internet conferences are a valuable source of expertise on the best applications to accomplish a human service task. The Internet often allows users to download a trial or demonstration version of an application to determine if it is appropriate for the user.

RESEARCH APPLICATIONS

Research refers to the structured analysis of data, information, and knowledge in an attempt to scientifically predict or learn new relationships among variables. Classic research seeks to develop and test theories using various designs, methodologies, and statistical tests. A more applied form of research is program evaluation that attempts to determine program outcomes, results, and impacts. Several applications help researchers complete their tasks.

Research Tutors and Advisors

Since research is an extremely specialized area, tutorial and advisory applications exist to help users understand and perform key tasks, such as determining sample size, designing appropriate methodologies, and selecting relevant statistics (Bordnick, 1997).* Although tutors and advisors are often independent teaching tools, similar content is being integrated into applications that perform statistical analysis.

Statistical Analysis

Statistical analysis applications help users to perform descriptive and inferential statistical tests on data and to report the results. Statistical analysis applications vary widely in features. Some products provide a variety of statistical techniques and output charts and graphs. Others emphasize user-friendly features or integration with a DBMS. Often, the discipline that a statistical application targets (e.g., business or psychology) will determine the features included.

Qualitative Analysis Software

Qualitative research encompasses a variety of techniques that allow researchers to think and hypothesize about nonnumeric and unstructured data and text (Drisko, 1998). Qualitative analysis applications help researchers by managing text, segmenting text, coding, annotating, and developing theories. Qualitative analysis applications perform such operations as indexing all terms and categories of interest, accumulating text of similar content, and counting instances of the use of terms and concepts (Quinn, 1996).

Neural Network Analysis

Neural network applications have their roots in brain and artificial intelligence research. They use data analysis models based on nodes and synapses for classification, modeling, optimization, estimation, and pre-diction. A typical problem addressed by neural networks is mortgage loan risk assessment, for which data on as many variables as possible about previous loans are entered into a neural network. Also inputted is whether the loan in each case was repaid. The neural network uses previous cases to construct formulas and weights that guide the firing of synapses that change the formulas and weights and then fire additional synapses. In essence, the neural network application develops models that fit all past cases to predict future cases (Steyaert, 1994).

Although the human services have not made great use of neural net-works, their applications have proven very promising. One study to differ-entiate between juvenile recidivists and nonrecidivists found that discrimi-nate analysis differentiated 63 percent of the cases, while neural network analysis differentiated 99 percent of the cases. (Brodzinski, Crable, and Scherer, 1994). Another study found a neural network to predict medical diagnoses 9 percent better than linear regression because it could better adjust to patterns in the data (Armoni, 1998).

Conducting and Analyzing Surveys

Some research applications perform specialized functions, such as managing telephone surveys. These applications help construct computer screens that guide surveyors through the questions, record the respon-dent's answers, analyze the data, and graphically display the results. Some survey tools are designed to administer Internet surveys that allow re-sponse through e-mail and Web site survey forms.

EDUCATION APPLICATIONS

Another group of IT applications help educate or train. The distinction between training and education is not always clear, although education is typically long term, such as that found in a university, and training is typically short term and job related, such as that found in on-the-job training. In this section, the term education will cover both professional education and training.

In the United States, no national effort has existed to develop and use technology for education in the human services. In some countries, such as the United Kingdom (Rafferty, 1998) and the Netherlands (Grebel and Steyaert, 1993), a central accrediting body determines how technology will be integrated into the curriculum and allocates funds for application development. One problem with national efforts is that rarely does agreement exist on what IT should be taught and how IT should be taught. Consequently, these efforts take a long time to reach consensus and develop applications. With technology changing so rapidly, applications just a few years old can seem outdated. For example, early text-based applications seem awkward and unfriendly compared to those involving multimedia. Also, upgrading applications can be as costly as their original development.

In the United States, the marketplace, along with uncoordinated government grants, has influenced education applications. Government efforts often produced education applications that were not commercialized and did not survive. Even commercial applications have not been used enough to keep the vendor in business. Examples of applications that are no longer actively marketed are IV-Skills for teaching interviewing skills, OUTPST simulation to teach management (Luse, 1980), AGENCY simulation developed to emulate service delivery in an agency (Cox et al., 1989), and CCAATS (Computerized Child Abuse Assessment Training System) to teach child abuse investigation (MacFadden, 1991).

Education applications are in their infancy and little agreement on terms exists. This section will discuss six common types of education and training applications: computer-aided instruction, simulations, games, wizards and coaches, education management, and distance learning.

Computer-Aided Instruction

Before the 1950s, few instructional technologies existed other than the book and chalkboard. The expense and complexity of early computers hindered their use for instructional purposes. Early applications proved computers to be endlessly patient, thorough, and persistent teaching machines capable of providing individualized instruction along with immediate feedback and reinforcement. The introduction of low-cost Apple computers and their popularity for K-12 education resulted in a large base of instructional applications.

Computer-aided instruction (CAI) is a popular term for describing education and training applications. Many other terms exist, for example, computer-based training (CBT), computer-assisted learning (CAL), technology-based training, and Web-based instruction. One distinguishing feature of CAI is that a coherent body of information is typically delivered at one time. Users spend from fifteen minutes to several hours interacting with a CAI application. Often the training is broken into small modules that are delivered in a step-by-step fashion, with each module becoming progressively more challenging. CAI can also involve tracking and testing, with scores presented to the user and used to determine which module the application should deliver next.

Considerable research has been conducted on the effectiveness and efficiency of CAI. These evaluations are mostly positive, showing CAI to be as effective as other forms of training and to reduce training time (Lambert and Vieweg, 1990). Reasons often cited for the reduction in training time include tighter instructional design; users' capacity to learn and test out of sections; and the use of text,' animation, simulation, and other modes that reinforce rapid and sustained learning. Other CAI advantages include continuous availability for training, when and where it is convenient, and the use of standardized curricula and tests so that more uniform outcomes are achieved. One problem with many CAI studies is that by the time the study is finished, the technology used for the training is obsolete.

Given all its advantages, the use of CAI has not seen the growth in the human services that many anticipated. One problem is that, currently, few rewards exist for producing CAI. Another problem is that most human service curricula are difficult to specify in small step-by-step segments. A third problem is that substantial resources are needed to keep CAI products current with new research, hardware, software, and networking.

Table 3.1 contains some examples of CAI in the human services. Unfortunately, many of the applications mentioned in the table are not commercially available.

Simulations

Another type of education and training application involves interactive simulations that allow learners to make decisions in a simulated reality. A *simulation* is an experimental method that attempts to replicate a system or activity without building or operating the actual system or performing the activity.

Developing simulations to support complex phenomena requires that we:

- identify the elements of the phenomenon,
- measure the attributes of the elements,
- measure and map the flow of the interactions between the elements,
- represent the measures and mappings in a form that a computer can manipulate,
- build a model that satisfactorily relates measures and interactions to the phenomenon, and
- validate that the model represents the phenomenon. (McLaughlin and Pickhardt, 1979)

TABLE 3.1. Examples of Human Services Computer-Assisted Instruction Applications

CAI	Problem/Situation Addressed	Source
Paraphrase	Train students on listening skills such as paraphrasing	Resnick, 1998
Health Guide Depression, Stress, etc.	Provide information on the causes, symptoms, and treatment of depression	www.healthguide.com
Cognitive Therapy	Teach the basic concepts and techniques of cognitive therapy	http://mindstreet.com/
Understanding Schizophrenia	Explain schizophrenia as a disability within its context	Celia@scs.cmm.unt.edu
Mental Health Studios	Educate the public on mental health and mental illness	Renz-Beaulaurier, 1997
HyperCDTX	Train on skills in assessment, diagnosis, and treatment of substance abuse	Patterson et al., 1997
Training Kids About HIV/AIDS	Present multimedia HIV training for youth ages 6 through 9 and 9 through 12	www.uta.edu/cussn/ kidsaids.html
Methodologist's Toolchest	Assist in developing research projects and grant proposals	Bordnick, 1997
Basic behavioral principles	Teach behavioral principles and procedures to staff	Desrochers, 1996
CCAATS	Teach child abuse investigation	MacFadden, 1991
Videodisc Series	Discuss cultural diversity related to Southeast Asian refugees and Native Americans	Falk et al., 1992
IV-Skills	Teach interviewing skills	Poulin and Walter, 1990
Mr. Howard	Present behavior therapy training	Lambert, 1989

The complexity of many human service processes means that few usable training simulations have been developed. However, simulations do exist to educate students and the public about policy issues (Flynn, 1985; Flynn, 1987). Another simulation, Keisha, allows a child maltreatment professional to work a failure-to-thrive case.* The Keisha simulation allows the user to review the intake for risk, view and assess pictures of the home and the baby, work the case with supervisor consultation, complete the risk assessment form, and receive feedback on how well the case was worked (Satterwhite and Schoech, 1995; MacFadden, 1997). The Interactive Patient is an Internet-delivered simulation that allows users to assess a patient and receive feedback on their diagnosis.* Table 3.2 lists several training simulations.

TABLE 3.2. Examples of Human Service Simulations

Simulation	Problem/Situation Addressed	Source
Interactive Patient	Allows users to assess a patient and receive feedback on their diagnosis	http://medicus.marshall.edu/medicus.htm
World Game	A simulation to distribute energy, technology, food, etc., worldwide	www.worldgame.org/workshops/
Evergeen	Strategic planning of health and welfare services for the elderly	Vaarama, 1995
SimHealth	Discusses making health policy	Hoefer, 1996
MERGE	Computer simulations of social policy process	Flynn, 1985
Keisha	How to work a child neglect case from intake to placement	Satterwhite and Schoech, 1995
PIC	Teaches students case managment skills	J. I. Gray, 1994
No name	Provides realistic situations for practicing microcounseling skills	Engen et al., 1994
Life Choices	Helps adults think through decisions of daily living	Thomas, 1994
How to Get Out and Stay Out: The Story of Cathy	Stress management and medication compliance for the chronically mentally ill	Olevitch and Hagan, 1994
No name	Teaches crisis counseling and organizational assessment	Seabury, 1993
AGENCY	Emulates service delivery in an agency	Cox et al., 1989
OUTP ST	Teaches management	Luse, 1980

Lambert, Hedlund, and Vieweg (1990) reviewed educational simulations in mental health and broadly categorized them into five groups: (1) interviewing simulations, (2) clinical diagnosis/treatment decision-making simulations, (3) case management simulations, (4) organizational management simulations, and (5) psychopathology models. They conclude that:

> Unfortunately, few of the currently reported simulations have advanced beyond initial development and limited testing. Despite the potential advantages of computer simulations, and the considerable face validity of many applications, there has been relatively little systematic research that would provide objective information about the "validity" of computer simulations in mental health training. (p. 223)

Games

A *game* is a simulation that uses techniques such as challenge and competition to amuse or entertain. IT-based games are an extension of the older style board games, although technology allows more complexity.

Table 3.3 lists examples of human services, IT-based games. Commercial games can be used to achieve human service educational objectives. One popular game format concerns the allocation of scarce resources to address social problems and the trade-offs associated with various policy alternatives (Hoefer, 1996). One popular adolescent game, Ages of Empires, allows players to allocate resources to build communities and advance civilizations (Thomas, 1998). Players learn policy and management skills because each decision involves balancing the advancement of society against meeting people's needs. Thomas contends that Age of Empires teaches the critical thinking skills necessary for IT policy analysis and information systems development. He suggests that adults should play games because the young game players of today will design the future digital human services systems of tomorrow using gaming principles.

The Internet makes it easier to deliver games, to keep them continually updated, and to add nongame features. One example is the Web site that allows players to balance the federal budget of the United States.[*] Game results are summarized and forwarded to policymakers in an attempt to influence public policy. The Internet also allows multiplayer games in which one user's actions impact all other players. With multiplayer games, players from around the world can interact, compete, and learn in a controlled environment. This interaction of people from various cultures on a common project has the potential to achieve human service goals. As new tools are developed, Web games will become a popular medium that human service professionals can exploit.

After reviewing the literature on human service computer games, Resnick and Sherer (1994) concluded:

> Computerized games are only a tool, one of the many that may be useful in enhancing the therapeutic process. Choosing which suits a certain objective best depends upon an assessment of the situation itself. Thus computerized therapeutic games, like any other professional tool, must be properly designed. The games must grow out of a solid theoretical base which will address the objectives of therapy and find ways to achieve them. Proper study and research will secure development in this subfield and, at the same time, shed light on its contribution. (p. 27)

TABLE 3.3. Examples of Human Service Games

Game	Problem/Situation Addressed	Source
Reinventing America	A game to balance the U.S. budget	www.crossover.com/reus/
World Game Workshops	Puts participants in charge of the world for four hours to become global problem solvers	www.worldgame.org/workshops/
Memory for Goblins	Assessing and training memory skills in senior citizens	Ryan, 1994
Convict	Meeting financial responsibilities as one interacts with the criminal justice system	Stull, 1994
The Poverty Game	Social problems of poverty and problems of poverty policy	S. H. Gray, 1994
Health Works	Teaches youth ages 6 through 8 about AIDS	Cahill, 1994
SMACK	Illustrates the negative consequences of drug use	Oakley, 1994
OPTEXT	Helping clients explore life choices	Cowan, 1994
Busted	Links choices with consequences and reduces antisocial behavior in youth offenders with addictions	Resnick, 1988
The Computer Marriage Contract Game	Help parents and children resolve family conflicts	Bleckman, Rabin, and McEnroe, 1986
Commerical games such as fishing and casino	Helps with the loss of intellectual activity and memory for stroke victims and the aged in nursing homes	Schueren, 1986
No name	Teaching kids impulse control	Clarke and Schoech, 1984

Help Systems, Coaches, and Wizards

A more recent form of training involves providing extensive systems of help inside applications. Traditionally, small text-based help files were available inside applications. Newer help systems contain substantial amounts of well-indexed text, animation, audio, and video. This information is often accompanied by wizards that lead the user through a process while monitoring and providing guidance along the way and coaches that take control from the user and demonstrate correct performance. Help systems can monitor user activity and tailor help accordingly. Some help systems interact with other systems over the Internet. Internet-based help is easier to upgrade and maintain so users always have the latest help information available.

Human service agencies have not made extensive use of help systems to deliver training and education. One reason is that the tools for developing help systems have not been readily available. Another is that workers have not had adequate access to networked computers in most agencies. However, help systems can be an important part of an overall environment that educates workers and supports practice. One obvious first choice for an agency use of a help system would be putting the agency's manuals and operating procedures on-line. Vendors see the help system as one of the most cost-effective components of their technical support program.

Education Management

CAI uses technology to deliver education. *Computer-managed education* (CME) or *technology-delivered instruction* (TDI) applications help the user manage the education environment and curriculum delivery. CME/TDI applications help users plan curricula, register learners for a course, protect materials with passwords and other security mechanisms, customize a curriculum for the learner, develop and administer tests, track learner progress, evaluate overall learning, and produce reports.

Technology-Based Distance Learning

Education began by using a learning model in which the student studied at home during convenient times. As the body of knowledge to be learned became greater, education moved from the home to the school or monastery. This first "distance learning" involved transporting students large distances from their homes to learn at prescribed times from specialists. Curriculum was structured so that students had summers off to work in the fields. Educational technology consisted of the lecture, the chalkboard, and books. The teacher was often the "sage on the stage," dispensing knowledge to a room full of learners. These trends continue today, with most education being offered by specialists at remote sites. Graduation regalia from the Middle Ages symbolize our educational system's close ties to the past.

Although correspondence courses and open universities have been with us for some time, their growth has been hampered by the difficulty of putting educational content into pencil-and-paper format. However, technology now allows a second distance-learning shift from educational institutions to the home or workplace. CAI, video conferencing, and e-mail allow an education specialist to train students at their homes, anywhere in the world. Since the term distance refers only to the geographical barriers overcome, the term virtual learning is often used to imply the ability to time shift as well. For many learners, eliminating the time barrier seems to be more important than eliminating the geographic barrier. The combination of the Internet and multimedia technology has resulted in other terms, for example, multimedia training, Web-based training, on-line training, or interactive training. In another distinction, *asynchronous training* refers to training in which all participate on their own time, compared to *synchronous training* in which all participants interact simultaneously.

Distance education (DE) is the common name given to the process of using technology to overcome the physical and time distance barriers between the learner and the instructor. DE concepts are rooted in the old philosophy of education, that of the active teacher-educator and the passive student-learner. *Distance learning* (DL) is a term some prefer, as it moves the focus on learning by the student rather than information dispensing by the instructor. In distance learning, the instructor acts as a guide, expert, and resource person. Distance learning can supplement the classroom, or it can replace the classroom. Four levels define how dependent DL is on technology:

1. Informational: IT applications support other modes of course delivery. A course Web site may contain the syllabus, announcements, articles, PowerPoint presentations, resource links, and an FAQ (frequently asked questions) section.
2. Augmented: Required IT applications support other modes of delivery. Students must use the IT applications to complete the course.
3. Dependent: The course is delivered primarily via IT. Classroom meetings and other materials may still be used, but the majority of the course resources and activities are delivered using IT.
4. Delivered: All instruction is delivered using IT. The course may be delivered via two-way video or over the Web.

Some argue that technology allows a fundamental shift in the way we perceive and structure education. Technology, more than ever before, allows learners to:

- receive training anywhere in the world that has access to electricity and a telephone;
- progress at their own speed, that is, interactive self-paced;

- chart their own path through the material, that is, interactive self-directed;
- receive continuous and detailed feedback throughout the learning process; and
- track and monitor their learning.

The term *electronic-mediated learning environment* describes this fundamental shift. Creating electronic-mediated learning environments represents a different way of approaching education, that is, the teacher creates the environment in which the learner participates. The teacher becomes a creator, guide, and learner-helper rather than an expert dispenser of information. The teacher sets up learning opportunities and makes them available for students to access and interact with at their own pace.

Summary of Education Applications

Human service trainers and educators can learn much from software vendors who understand IT and have an education and training task similar to that in the human services. For example, compare vendors' education and support for operating systems over the years. Early support for the DOS system consisted primarily of a manual that was organized alphabetically by software command. Today, vendors create a support environment by cost-effectively combining manuals, tutorials, interactive help within the software, faxed answers to frequently asked questions, Internet sites, and telephone technical support. Manuals are highly indexed and organized by user task, for example, "getting started." Often, software contains help systems that are fun to use and demonstrate how to perform a task. Human service educators and employers are beginning to use a variety of technologies to develop learning environments.

Instructors are fearful of the amount of learning and feedback that can be provided through IT, even if two-way video is used. The question is always asked: "Would you go to a counselor or medical doctor who received a degree via distance learning?" It will take time to determine what content can be effectively taught using distance learning techniques and what content is best taught in the classroom. Another issue is that distance learning requires different skills on the part of the instructor. A good classroom instructor may not make a good distance learning designer or instructor.

ASSISTIVE TECHNOLOGY

People have always used devices to compensate for human deficits. For example, a pencil is a memory device because it helps us write down things that we cannot remember. A car is a mobility aid because it allows us to travel farther than we can walk. IT provides the basis of many new devices that are allowing people to overcome deficits and lead more normal and productive lives. Technology that helps people overcome their disabilities is referred to as assistive technology and the devices are called assistive devices. According to the Rehabilitation Act of 1973 (as amended), "*assistive technology* means any item, piece of equipment, or product system, whether acquired commercially off the shelf, modified, or customized, that is used to increase, maintain, or improve functional capabilities of individuals with disabilities" (emphasis added).

The 1990 Americans for Disabilities Act (ADA) requires accommodations to be made by employers and the service sector for persons with disabilities. The ADA stimulated the movement of technology from the research labs to work and leisure settings. The number and types of assistive devices are as large and complex as the disabilities and the services they support. Currently, over 20,000 assistive technology products exist in the Disability and Adaptive Equipment Resource Library CD-ROM.✺

Assistive devices are unlike other human service applications in several ways. They are typically applications of both hardware and software and they serve a narrow market. Consequently, research, development, and manufacturing costs can rarely be recuperated from future sales. In addition, expensive professional services, such as the following, are associated with their use:

- Assessing a client's need and potential to use an assistive device in his or her customary environment
- Locating, funding, and acquiring the most appropriate assistive device
- Matching the assistive device to the client
- Fitting or customizing the assistive device and training the client to use the device and, where appropriate, training others in the client's environment
- Repairing, maintaining, or replacing the assistive device as technology and client needs change

Although commercial hardware and application costs are decreasing, the costs associated with the development and use of an assistive device are increasing. Some simple devices may cost substantially more than the sophisticated generic computing technology to which they are attached.

One of the leading research institutions in the United States is Trace R&D Center, University of Wisconsin at Madison.✺ Trace is working with major technology corporations to make hardware and software accessible to people with disabilities. The belief behind this initiative is that, very often, small and inexpensive design modifications can make technology much more accessible. Corporations have also found that modifications which make technology accessible for people with disabilities can make it more usable for everyone and increase sales. The wheelchair icon in the control panel of Windows 95 is the result of teamwork between Trace and Microsoft.

Sixteen specialty Rehabilitation Engineering Research Centers are funded by the National Institute on Disability and Rehabilitation Research (NIDRR), U.S. Department of Education. The centers investigate the following areas:

- Accessible and universal design in housing
- Adaptive computers and information systems
- Applications of technology to the rehabilitation of children with orthopedic disabilities
- Assistive technology and environmental intervention for older persons with disabilities
- Augmented and alternative communication
- Hearing enhancement and assistive devices
- Lower back pain
- Modifications to work sites and educational settings
- Personal licensed transportation for disabled persons
- Prosthetics and orthotics
- Quantification of physical performance
- Rehabilitation robotics
- Rehabilitation technology services in vocational rehabilitation
- Technology for blindness and visual impairments
- Technology evaluation and transfer
- Technology to improve wheelchair mobility

This section will cover assistive technology for physical access and mobility, environmental controls, communication and sensory aids, and mental augmentation and learning. This brief coverage provides only an idea of the types of applications available.

Mobility and Access

In an industrial age, physical movement and strength are of primary importance. A physical disability results in less work and less participation in society. In an information age, mental capacity is of utmost importance. If access to information is provided, persons with physical disabilities are as capable of mental work as are the able-bodied.

Physical access devices may be as simple as a mouth stick that allows a person to lock down special function keys on a computer keyboard or as sophisticated as a robotic hand. Some devices are highly experimental, such as a mobility device that stimulates nerves to help a quadriplegic walk. Some researchers are experimenting with virtual environments in which people with physical disabilities can be just as capable as everyone else.

Environmental Controls

Client groups such as the aged and disabled need to control their environments to maximize their self-sufficiency and independent living. Computing applications that turn on/off appliances and lights, lock and release doors and windows, answer the telephone, and call for help in emergencies are becoming popular. Since environmental controls are often associated with security and safety, a large general market exists that is being filled by the private marketplace. Many general purpose devices are appropriate for persons with disabilities, and others require only minimal modification.

Communication and Sensory Aids

Speech, vision, hearing, and the other senses provide vital links to active participation in society. Communication and sensory aids can be simple. For example, communication boards can speak messages by pressing a button, or sonar canes can send messages to those with visual impairments. Some applications are very complex, such as direct stimulation of the vision area of the brain using electronic signals from a camera.

Attitude changes must accompany technological changes, as the following story about one of the first augmented communication experiments indicates. The experiment provided a computer-generated voice to someone who had difficulty speaking due to cerebral palsy. The researchers had concluded that one success milestone would be reached when the person could use the device to order a meal over the telephone. After device design, user training, and practice, the user called a pizza parlor. Responding to user commands, the device stated, in a somewhat mechanical voice, "I would like to order a pizza." The person at the pizza parlor, suspecting a practical joke, replied, "We don't sell pizzas to computers," then hung up the telephone.

Mental Augmentation and Learning

Technologies can provide rehabilitation and compensation for defects in memory, perception, concept formation, and problem solving (Burda et al., 1994). For example, persons with brain damage and memory problems can be taught to dress themselves by going through several detailed series of procedures. Although these individuals may have mastered each separate series, they often have trouble getting dressed because it requires placing all the series together. A pocket-sized computer with a speech synthesizer can be programmed to talk the person through the detailed dressing instructions. Such a device could be customized to the limitations of each user, with only the problematic instructions spoken at the user's requested pace.

More complex devices could be used to augment the information processing of the aged, persons with brain damage, and persons with learning disabilities. Memory augmentation could occur with the use of frequent reminders presented throughout the day and special reminders on certain occasions such as appointments and birthdays. The reminder could be as unobtrusive as a vibration from a wristwatch or belt, as with an electronic bladder sensor for those who are incontinent.

CONCLUSION

Software applications operationalize the capacity of IT hardware. With hardware becoming a commodity item, software applications are becoming the key to successful IT use. Knowledge of a variety of IT applications is important. Developers may use an application that is not well suited to solving a particular problem because they know the application and do not have the time to locate or learn a more appropriate application. In carpenter's terminology, "when all you have is a hammer, everything looks like a nail." Many agencies and systems suffer due to not devoting enough time and resources to finding the most appropriate IT applications.

REVIEW AND DISCUSSION QUESTIONS

1. Which generic application is the most cost-effective for a typical human service organization?
2. Should we expect new research and analysis IT applications in the future? Can you speculate what they might look like?
3. Would you go to a counselor who received his or her bachelor's and master's counseling degrees via distance learning? Explain the rationale behind your answer.
4. List all the assistive devices you encountered this week and the disability they helped overcome. Which device is the most common? Which is the most sophisticated? Which is the most important for the user's quality of life?

Chapter 4

Management Applications

INTRODUCTION

Human service professionals need to be aware of the variety of management IT applications to communicate with IT professionals and to select applications that support their work and solve their problems. This chapter attempts to organize, clarify, and simplify terms and concepts related to management applications relevant to the human services. Table 4.1 presents and compares the five categories of management applications discussed in this chapter. Although this categorization is imprecise, and the popular literature not always consistent, it is useful for discussion purposes. Since new terms are often coined without regard for overlap with existing terms, new applications will appear in the future that will expand this classification.

HISTORICAL PERSPECTIVE

The IT applications in Table 4.1 have their roots in efforts to improve organizational decision making, to create artificial intelligence, and to train workers. Examining their historical roots will help understand these applications better.

Organizational Decision Making

Before the 1950s, organizations processed data by hand or with the support of mechanical or electronic calculators. The first IT applications were computerized versions of these manual systems. In the 1950s, large, expensive, and slow mainframe computers processed routine data in specialized areas such as inventory. Electronic data processing (EDP) or

TABLE 4.1. Categories of Management Applications Relevant to the Human Services

Term	Focus	Problem Addressed	Predominant Process	Example
Data processing (DP)	Efficiency	Processing routine transactions	Calculations	Payroll system
Management or agency information system (MIS)	Reporting	Collecting and using basic agency information	Aggregating and formatting of data	Client information system
Knowledge-based system, expert systems, etc. (KBS)	Extracting knowledge for decision making	Advising, predicting, decision making, explaining rationales	Finding patterns, reasoning from cases, presenting codified advice	Child abuse risk advisor
Decision support system (DSS)	Effectiveness	Answering "what if this were the case"	Modeling, statistical analysis	Optimum allocation of agency resources
Performance support system (PSS)	Performance	Instructing and providing advice on a subject or how to complete the task at hand	Guided instruction, interactive dialogue, monitoring user performance	Providing safety advice on the case being worked

automated data processing (ADP) were the terms used for routine clerical computing applications, such as accounting and inventory control. As EDP applications were developed for many routine problems, and computers became synonymous with data processing, the term electronic or automated was often dropped. Today, the term data processing usually implies computer-based automation of routine clerical tasks.

In the 1960s, data processing (DP) applications to support middle management proliferated. These DP applications were often linked to form a management information system (MIS). MIS denoted the connection of separate DP applications into an integrated reporting system of hardware, software, computing technicians, computing managers, and users. As MISs expanded beyond the management level of the organization, the word management was often dropped and the term information system (IS) used.

The database management technology of the 1970s enabled information systems to be more flexible and accessible. Flexible, user-friendly information systems, which contained modeling techniques for answering "what-if" types of user queries, were labeled decision support systems (DSS). DSS focuses on complex decision making, such as that at the policy/top management and professional direct service level of human service organizations.

Artificial Intelligence

Whereas EDP, DP, MIS, IS, and DSS applications are rooted in organizational decision making, another group of IT applications is based in the artificial intelligence (AI) field. Artificial intelligence applications model human intelligence and acquire knowledge to solve intellectually challenging problems. Since AI applications work with knowledge, the term knowledge-based systems (KBS) is often used as an overall term. The study of knowledge and its use became known as the field of knowledge engineering, which involves knowledge acquisition, representation, manipulation, and use. Knowledge acquisition focuses on how knowledge is extracted from experts, literature, and research. Knowledge representation involves how knowledge and expertise (knowledge derived from experts) can be stored in computer-usable form. Knowledge use concerns how human decision makers assimilate computer-generated knowledge. Knowledge-based systems include areas such as natural language processing, speech synthesis, robotics, pattern recognition, case-based reasoning, and expert systems.

In the 1960s, AI research focused on using powerful computers to imitate human intelligence in cognitive processes such as reasoning, thinking, learning, and creating. The goal was to develop general-purpose problem-solving machines. Computers that play chess resulted from this line of AI research. During the 1970s, AI researchers grasped the overwhelming complexity of their task. Consequently, they gradually changed their goals from creating general-purpose thinking machines to developing applications with a more limited focus. Their research indicated that the key to expert decision making in a specific area was the knowledge base. Other elements of the decision-making process, such as representing knowledge to computers or developing inference schemes, could be considered tools for using a knowledge base. Following this line of reasoning, AI researchers began developing knowledge bases in specialized domains. They also began developing the mechanisms for extracting decisions from these knowledge bases. Expert systems, or computer programs that mimic human expert decision making, are the most predominant AI technology in the human services literature.

Training

Early computer-assisted instruction (CAI) programs were primarily linear or step-by-step text-based presentations of information. The development of the graphical user interface (GUI) allowed graphics, icons, text, pictures, sound, video, and other media to be incorporated into CAI. The development of hypertext allowed CAI content to be delivered more flexibly and nonlinearly. *Hypertext* involves document linking so that information in one document connects to information in another. By creating user-controlled links, training content could be tailored based on the interactions of the user. The term *multimedia* was coined to describe applications that relied primarily on linked graphics and text.

In the 1990s, corporate experience with CAI suggested that training IT could be more effective if it were focused on improving the performance of specific tasks. IT applications that improve performance by providing content-specific training when it is needed and in the format it is needed are called *performance support systems* (PSS).

Having provided a general overview of how management IT applications have historically evolved, the following material presents more detailed examinations of each type of application.

DATA PROCESSING APPLICATIONS

In popular literature, the terms data processing and computing often denote the basic process of manipulating data with computers. However, a narrower view of data processing denotes the automating of routine clerical tasks by a computer, which is often called automated data processing (ADP) or electronic data processing (EDP). This section discusses the narrower ADP-EDP view.

Definition

A *data processing* application consists of machines, people, procedures, and equipment for working with routine clerical data. Data processing tasks include collecting, storing, retrieving, manipulating, transferring, and outputting data.

Examples of Data Processing Applications

Figure 4.1 presents a noncomputerized DP application. As the number of transactions and the complexity of the information increase, many of the components of a noncomputerized DP application exhibit problems. A

FIGURE 4.1. A Noncomputerized Data Processing System

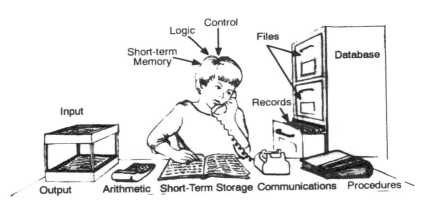

calculating machine is too limiting. The file cabinets become overloaded. The human feels like a machine from doing routine data entry and calculations and may suffer burnout.

Automated data processing applications are designed to reduce clerical costs by processing the routine transactions of secretaries and clerks. DP applications are usually controlled by accounting departments or by specialized data processing departments. An example of a data processing application is a system that processes payroll checks. The inputs to the DP application are data and information, for example, time worked, base salary, and deductions. The outputs are data (paycheck totals) and information (payroll reports). The data processing tasks are narrow and routine. An example of a key question answered by the payroll application is "What are the check totals?" Some routine decisions may be made during payroll data processing. For example, if the cumulative salary is more than $40,000, the application may automatically decide to use the next higher tax rate.

INFORMATION SYSTEMS

The words in the term *management information system,* or simply information system, illustrate the type of IT applications implied. *Management* implies that the application primarily serves the middle-level needs of the organization. *Information* implies that processing data into information is the underlying task. *System* implies that all forms, processing, and reports create an integrated whole. Information systems are often developed using database technologies that provide efficient data storage and easy access.

Definition

An *information system* is a collection of people, procedures, and technology that gathers data and information, enhances it through processing, and disseminates the results (O'Brien, 1995). An information system may be informal, such as when people get their office information in the coffee room, or it may be formal, as with an agency newsletter. An information system need not be computerized. Conversely, just because an agency has a computer does not mean that it has an information system. One agency may have a highly developed manual information system, while another may have a computer-based, haphazard, and uncoordinated system of information gathering and retrieval. In this section, the term information system refers to a formal, computerized, application that processes basic organizational information.

Information systems have many of the characteristics of DP applications. Moreover, they usually integrate many separate DP applications, process nonroutine information, serve many levels of the organization, and produce information in the form of reports. The focus of most information systems is to collect, manage, and manipulate information to answer queries and generate reports. Most information system outputs are designed to help managers or practitioners handle their work. Infrequently, outputs are designed to enhance the client-practitioner relationship. One example is a tickler report that reminded practitioners of the birthdays of foster children in their caseloads. However, rarely do information systems provide substantive support for practitioners' work with clients. Supporting practitioner-client interactions requires more complex applications, such as those described in the following sections.

Since information systems are integral to the basic functioning of an organization, they are heavily influenced by the environment in which they operate. For example, fear and lack of trust in an organization might result in an information system being neglected or sabotaged. In one large state agency, when managers needed to be sure of data accuracy, they would request that regional managers bypass the information system and do a hand count from records. In this case, technology may be working well, but the people or the procedures part of the information system did not perform as expected. Thus, information systems have differing levels of effectiveness, depending on how well the information generated matches the needs of its environment.

Examples of Information Systems

Figure 4.2 presents a simple, noncomputerized information system previously used by many human service agencies. This simple manual system has some of the basic elements of an automated system. Client data are written on a record (5″ × 8″ card) that is sequentially stored in a file. The most frequently manipulated fields are indexed on the outside of the card by notching a hole in the outer edge. For example, all cards of Anglo clients would be notched in the "a" position above ethnicity, all African Americans in the "b" position, and so on. Thus, each hole forms a key by which the file can be manipulated using a metal rod. Inserting the metal rod through the Anglo key of the file and lifting would extract all races

FIGURE 4.2. A Noncomputerized Information System

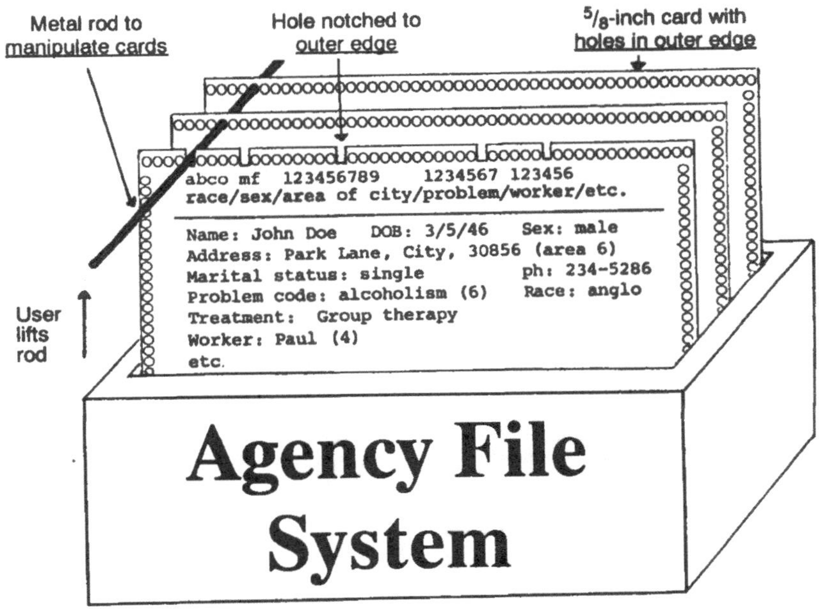

Source: From "Strategies for Information System Development" by D. Schoech, L. L. Schkade, and R. S. Mayers, 1982, *Administration in Social Work*, 5(3/4), p. 13. Copyright 1982 by The Haworth Press, Inc. Reprinted by permission.

except Anglos. Additional extraction of cards using the rod could result in the file containing Anglo males in a given age group who live in one geographic area, who have a specific problem, and who visit the same practitioner. Table 4.2 presents the subsystems, files, and information of a typical agency information system. Most information systems are modular, in that independent subsystems are designed and implemented in stages.

TABLE 4.2. A Typical Human Service Information System

Agency Information System	
File Type	Types of Data/Information Included
Resources Subsystem	
Agency resources	Programs, geographic areas served, admission criteria, etc.
Community resources	Agencies' services and admissions criteria, agencies referring clients, agencies receiving discharges, etc.
Client Subsystem	
Client data	Age, gender, address, previous treatment, medications, etc.
Client problem	Presenting problems, problem type and severity
Service Subsystem	
Treatment information	Psychological/social history, treatment activities, events, and progress, discharge summaries
Case management	Type and date of treatment, appointments kept, follow-up information, other agency involvement
Management Subsystem	
Office management	Supplies, mailing lists, inventories
Personnel	Hours worked, caseload, performance reviews
Fiscal management	Revues, expenditures, billing, grants, payroll
Analysis and Evaluation Subsystem	
Planning	Population at risk, target population, census data
Evaluation	Efficiency, effectiveness, and productivity measures and peer review data
Monitoring and control	Data on fulfillment of agreements, contracts, and certifications and licensure requirements

Note: Activities common to all subsystems include data input and modification, report generation and distribution, and data manipulation.

Source: Adapted from "A Microcomputer-Based Human Service Information System" by D. Schoech, 1979, *Administration in Social Work*, 3(4), p. 427.

KNOWLEDGE-BASED APPLICATIONS

Knowledge-based applications, or knowledge systems, rely on large stores of task-specific knowledge as a base for high performance in complex tasks. Since knowledge contains more meaning than data or information and the structure of knowledge is more complex, different processing techniques are required. Human service knowledge-based applications are still experimental, but important, because they handle the complexity to support practitioners' interactions with clients. Three types of knowledge-based applications with particular relevance to the human services are expert systems, case-based reasoning, and natural language processing.

Expert Systems

Expert systems are useful in supporting human service practitioners because many human service tasks involve expertise that is "a mile wide and a 100 feet deep"; that is, many independent groups of knowledge must be linked to perform a job. A child protective services worker, for example, can encounter a wide variety of abuse and neglect situations, each requiring different identification and intervention techniques. An expert worker requires a modest amount of knowledge about each type of maltreatment.

Definition

Expert systems are software applications that mimic processes to perform tasks at skill levels comparable to human experts. Expert systems make decisions about a case by applying knowledge stored in the computer to user-supplied facts (Schoech et al., 1985) (Schuerman and Vogel, 1986). They work well in the following situations:

- Recognized experts exist who make decisions better than novices and whose expertise can be routinely taught to novices.
- The task takes an expert a few minutes to a few hours to complete.
- The task is primarily cognitive, requires expertise rather than common sense, and is characterized by the extensive use of judgment, probabilistic knowledge, experience, and less than certain solutions to problems.

Expert systems are typically more narrowly focused than information systems and make decisions rather than generate reports. A noncomputerized equivalent of an expert system is a case conference during which a practitioner provides case facts to the questions of experts. The experts apply their knowledge to the facts and provide their decisions and the supporting reasons.

Developers of expert systems use the computer in two ways: (1) to rapidly process masses of nonnumeric symbols and (2) as a large powerful number-crunching machine. Table 4.3 offers some differences between expert systems and a mathematical or statistical approach to problem solving.

The four major components of an expert system are the knowledge base, the inference system, the facts of the case under consideration, and the user interface (see Figure 4.3).

The *knowledge base* stores the expertise or knowledge in the form of descriptions and relationships. Descriptions are statements that identify and differentiate objects and classes. For example, the statement "a divorced person is one whose marriage has been legally terminated" is a description. Relationships are particular kinds of descriptions that express associations. For example, the relationship between parents who have abused and the risk of reabuse may be expressed as follows: "25 percent of

TABLE 4.3. Statistical versus Expert System Approach

Comparison	Statistical Approach	Expert System Approach
Purpose	Find new knowledge	Store expertise for future decision making
Unit of analysis	Numeric data	Variable descriptions and relationships
Number of variables	Small number of predictors	Large number of variables
Sample size	Large number	One or several experts
Analysis	Statistical and mathematical	Logic and inference
Validation	Validity/reliability tests	Agreement with experts
Output format	Graphs, charts	Decisions, certainties, logic trails
Uncertainty	Unable to address	Handled with statistics or logic

Source: Adapted from "Computerizing Protective Services Intake Expertise" by J. Wick and D. Schoech, 1988, *Children and Youth Services Review,* 10(3), p. 238.

FIGURE 4.3. Basic Components of an Expert System

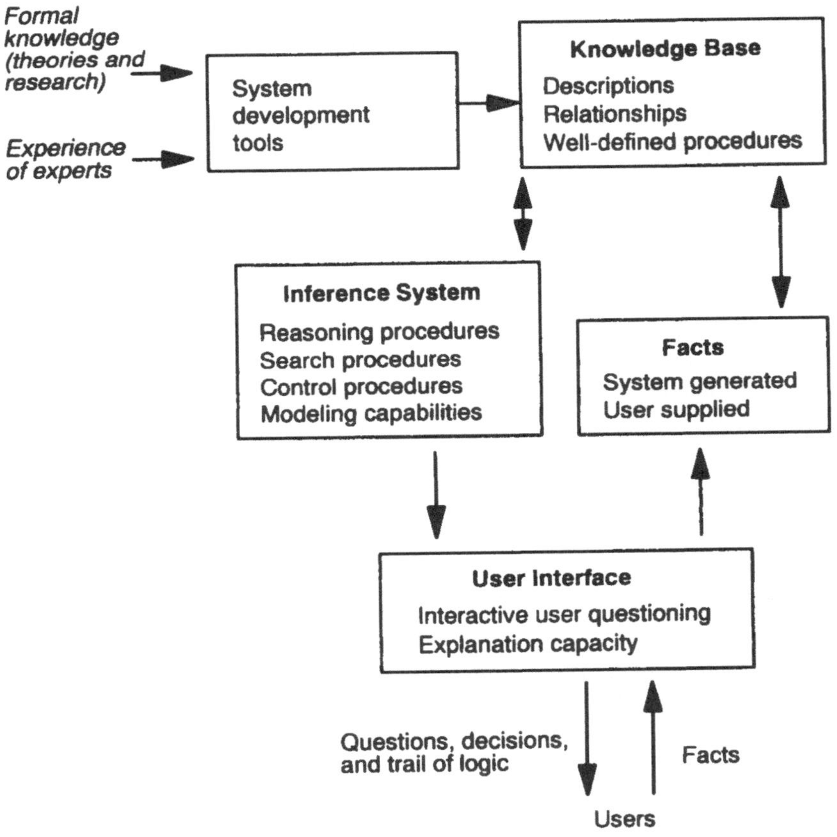

Formal knowledge (theories and research)

Experience of experts

System development tools

Knowledge Base

Descriptions
Relationships
Well-defined procedures

Inference System

Reasoning procedures
Search procedures
Control procedures
Modeling capabilities

Facts

System generated
User supplied

User Interface

Interactive user questioning
Explanation capacity

Questions, decisions, and trail of logic

Facts

Users

Source: Adapted from "Expert Systems: Artificial Intelligence for Professional Decisions" by D. Schoech, H. Jennings, L. L. Schkade, and C. Hooper-Russell, 1985, *Computers in Human Services, 1*(1), p. 89. Copyright 1985 by The Haworth Press, Inc. Reprinted by permission.

the substantiated abuse cases not placed in foster care were re-reported and substantiated over seven years of follow-up period." Knowledge statements are often called heuristics, which are statements containing rules of thumb, aids in guessing, plausible reasonings, or judgments that increase the likelihood of reaching a successful decision.

In "rule-based" expert systems, knowledge is stored in the knowledge base in the form of "if-then" rules. The premise of a rule is the "if" statement and the consequence of the rule is the "then" statement. A child welfare "if-then" rule might be the following:

> IF a child less than one year old has been severely spanked, THEN the child should be physically examined by a physician.

Knowledge can also be stored in formats other than rules. Two common formats are semantic nets and frames. Each storage technique has advantages and disadvantages and is a feature of the expert system development software chosen.

Expert systems often allow measures of information completeness and user confidence. For example, the previous rule might be modified as follows to handle measures of information completeness and user confidence:

> IF one unreliable source states that a child less than one year old may have been severely spanked, THEN a physician's exam is recommended 50 percent of the time.

Information completeness and confidence levels are important because human service information is rarely complete or certain. Uncertainty can be handled by fuzzy logic, a superset of conventional (Boolean) logic that concerns values between "completely true" and "completely false."

Facts are the second component of an expert system. *Facts* are case-specific information that is supplied in response to user questions or automatically generated from reasoning. An expert system may request only those facts which are needed as it searches along different logical paths, following some paths and discarding others. Thus, different cases will require different facts before an expert system reaches a conclusion. An expert system also uses system-generated facts, such as successful lines of reasoning and accepted subhypotheses.

The third component of an expert system, the *inference engine,* provides the reasoning or the "thinking it through" capacity. The inference engine supplies the general procedures and operations the expert system uses as it searches through the knowledge base. In this search, some knowledge is used, or processed, and the results are stored for future use. Other knowledge is examined and discarded as irrelevant to the present situation. The inference engine is typically purchased as part of expert system development software.

The *user interface* is the final component of an expert system. The user interface contains mechanisms to request information and display conclusions, certainties, and the logic behind conclusions to users.

Examples of Expert Systems

A simple expert system is illustrated by the session presented in Figure 4.4. This session depicts the use of a simple expert system by a child maltreatment worker. The goal of the expert system is to arrive at the service priority level of a case. In this session, priority 1 indicates very serious abuse and a high need for protection. The Web site associated with this book contains the inference engine written in BASIC. Figure 4.5 presents the knowledge base in a BASIC program written in the form of if-then rules. The inference engine uses the knowledge base to examine facts supplied by the user to arrive at a conclusion. At any time, the expert system can explain the rationale it is using to reach its conclusion. This system begins by gathering facts to prove or disprove specific rules, presented in Figure 4.5, lines 4100-4300. As rules are found true or false, the system works toward one of the hypotheses listed in line 6000 of Figure 4.5. Through proving and disproving rules and subhypotheses, the hypotheses are selected or discarded. The search process is represented graphically in Figure 4.6.

Figure 4.6 illustrates several expert system characteristics. One is selective search in which the system automatically examines key factors, such as the child's age, to eliminate unnecessary rule processing. Figure 4.6 also illustrates the complexity of expert system construction. For example, if one goal was that users spend a minimum of time interacting with the system, which fact should be requested first? Since the system handles only yes/no responses, the importance of a rule and user confidence in a fact are not considered. Therefore, no confidence level is provided with the conclusion.

Few functional human service expert systems exist. One is ECS (Expert Counseling System), which helps clients identify employment problems, sets goals to resolve these problems, provides tips on how to do this, and makes referrals to appropriate resources that can help clients achieve their goals.[*] Another is ICS, which checks medication orders against patient records in a hospital to reduce the number of drug interactions. ICS prevented 1.2 drug-related mistakes each day at one hospital (Paul, 1996). For an updated list of human services expert systems, check the book's Web site.

FIGURE 4.4. Interaction with a Simple Expect System to Prioritize Intakes

> The user's case involves a child with limited physical abuse in need of a high degree of protection. The primitive dialogue of this illustration results from a poor user interface. In the following dialogue, capitalized text is from the inference engine program, italicized text is from the child welfare knowledge base. The Y (yes), N (no), or W (why) are input by the user.

HELLO. THIS PROGRAM DEMONSTRATES HOW AN EXPERT SYSTEM WORKS. I (THE EXPERT SYSTEM) WILL USE MY 13 RULES TO TRY TO ESTABLISH ONE OF THE FOLLOWING 4 HYPOTHESES

> *is priority 1*
>
> *is priority 2*
>
> *is priority 3*
>
> *is no priority*

PLEASE ANSWER MY QUESTIONS WITH Y (YES), N (NO), OR W (WHY).

IS IT TRUE: *history of abuse exists?* N

IS IT TRUE: *child left alone?* Y

IS IT TRUE: *child under age 6?* W

I AM TRYING TO USE RULE 8. I ALREADY KNOW THAT: CHILD LEFT ALONE. IF CHILD UNDER AGE 6, THEN HIGH PROTECTION NEEDED.

IS IT TRUE: *child under age 6?* Y

RULE R8 DEDUCES *high protection needed*

IS IT TRUE: *burns exist on child?* N

IS IT TRUE: *child has broken bones?* N

IS IT TRUE: *discipline is excessive?* W

I AM TRYING TO USE RULE 1. IF DISCIPLINE IS EXCESSIVE AND NO PHYSICAL INJURY EXISTS FROM DISCIPLINE, THEN ABUSE NOT SERIOUS.

IS IT TRUE: *discipline is excessive?* Y

IS IT TRUE: *no physical injury exists from discipline?* Y

RULE 1 DEDUCES *abuse not serious*

RULE 10 DEDUCES *is priority 2*

I CONCLUDE THAT: *is priority 2*

Source: From "Expert Systems: Artificial Intelligence for Professional Decisions" by D. Schoech, H. Jennings, L. L. Schkade, and C. Hooper-Russell, 1985, *Computers in Human Services, 1*(1), pp. 92-93. Copyright 1985 by The Haworth Press, Inc. Reprinted by permission.

FIGURE 4.5. The Knowledge Base of the Rule-Based Expert System in Figure 4.4

```
10 REM Developed 5/16/84 By Dick Schoech
20 REM Rules For Child Abuse Domain
30 REM note: use the merge command to insert this program
40 REM into the inference engine provided with this program
4030 '
4040 ' Data Evidence Suggests—
4060 Data
4070 '
4080 ' Data For Rules
4090 '
4100 DATA R1, If discipline is excessive
4105 DATA No physical injury exists from discipline
4106 DATA Then, abuse not serious
4110 DATA R2, If bruises exist in nonvital areas
4115 DATA No other signs of injury exist, then abuse not serious
4120 DATA R3, If poor care provided child
4125 DATA Child not functionally impaired, then low protection needed
4130 DATA R4, If child left alone
4135 DATA Child over age 6, then low protection needed
4140 DATA R5, If burns exist on child, then abuse serious
4150 DATA R6, If child has bruises in vital areas
4155 DATA Inadequate explanation given for bruises, then abuse serious
4160 DATA R7, If history of abuse exists, then high protection needed
4170 DATA R8, If child left alone
4175 DATA Child under age 6, then high protection needed
4180 DATA R9, If abuse not serious, then low protection needed,
4190 DATA chronic poor care provided, then is priority 3
4200 DATA R10, If abuse not serious,
4210 DATA high protection needed, then is priority 2
4220 DATA R11, If high protection needed,
4230 DATA abuse serious, then is priority 1
4250 DATA R12, If low protection needed,
4255 DATA abuse serious, then is priority 2
4260 DATA R13, If abuse not serious, low protection needed,
4270 DATA caretaker capable of caring for child,
4280 DATA caretakers express concern, then is low priority
4300 DATA Stop
5970 '
5980 ' Data for hypotheses
5990 '
6000 Data is priority 1, is priority 2, is priority 3, is low priority
6020 DATA Stop
6030 '
6040 End
```

Source: From "Expert Systems: Artificial Intelligence for Professional Decisions" by D. Schoech, H. Jennings, L. L. Schkade, and C. Hooper-Russell, 1985, *Computers in Human Services, 1*(1), p. 115. Copyright 1985 by The Haworth Press, Inc. Reprinted by permission. You can download this demo expert system from http://www.uta.edu/cussn.

FIGURE 4.6. The Graphical Design of the Rule-Based Expert System in Figure 4.4

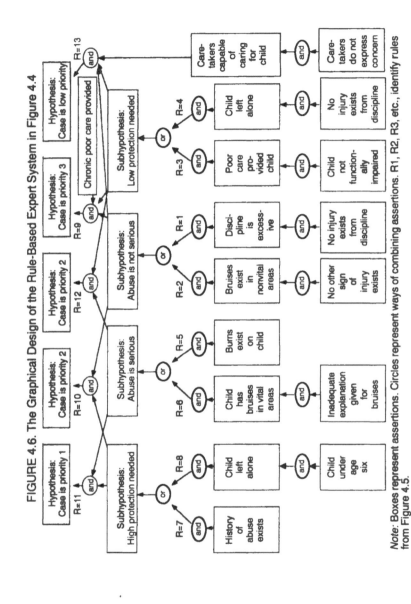

Note: Boxes represent assertions. Circles represent ways of combining assertions. R1, R2, R3, etc., identify rules from Figure 4.5.

Source: From "Expert Systems: Artificial Intelligence for Professional Decisions" by D. Schoech, H. Jennings, L. L. Schkade, and C. Hooper-Russell, 1985, *Computers in Human Services, 1*(1), p. 94. Copyright 1985 by The Haworth Press, Inc. Reprinted by permission.

Developing usable expert systems in complex human service domains is currently an experimental process. In some cases, the expertise that is most difficult to represent in a knowledge base may be the most crucial to making a decision. In addition, as the number of complex relationships in an expert system increases, so too does the potential for problematic interactions between the relationships. A related issue is the difficulty of combining the uncertainties associated with each fact and combining many uncertainties into an overall decision certainty. Another problem in the human services is that experts may not always agree among themselves. When future events will not verify the correctness of a decision, the accuracy of an expert system must be determined by its agreement with experts. If experts cannot agree, then developing generalized knowledge bases is impossible, and an expert system can mimic the decision making of only one expert.

Time also presents limitations. Three to five person years of effort are typically required to develop, field test, and refine an expert system. Another limitation is that expert systems are typically expert in only one specialty. Since they cannot transfer expertise from one area to another, they are blind or ignorant of all other knowledge. For example, although the expert system PUFF can diagnose lung disease, it does not know that lungs are in the chest (*MacNeil-Lehrer Report,* 1983). Expert systems can be compared with the psychological phenomenon of an idiot savant: they are experts in a specialty area, yet have no common sense. Therefore, expert systems may be used primarily for training or for second opinions when practitioners are interested in the logic behind a recommended solution.

We may find that the human parallel to an expert system, a consultation session with an expert, involves much more than expert decision making and explanation. Consultation with an expert may involve sympathetic listening, emotional support, the exchange of sentiments, and an affirmation of self. These aspects may be more important than the solutions and rationales that expert systems can provide.

Case-Based Reasoning

Another way to obtain knowledge is by mining thousands of client cases, especially if the cases contain information on client demographics, services, and outcomes. The name given to this technique is case-based reasoning.

Definition

Case-based reasoning (CBR) is an AI technique that has potential in extracting knowledge from data stored in client cases. *Case-based reasoning* is the process of developing solutions to unsolved problems based on preexisting solutions of a similar nature. CBR is the problem-solving paradigm that uses exact and "good enough" past experiences stored in cases to develop "plans" that solve a current problem. CBR requires a "memory" subsystem in which past cases are organized. A plan subsystem stores and indexes successful plans by the goals they satisfy and the problems they avoid so they can be used to solve similar future problems. By storing failures as well as successes, the plan subsystem is able to anticipate and avoid future failures. At the end of problem solving, the memory subsystem is updated with the new problem-solving experience. Thus, learning is integrated with problem solving (Leake, 1996).

Example

CAMP (CAse-based Menu Planner) plans daily menus to meet individual nutritional and personal preference requirements. It employs case-based reasoning to plan new menus by retrieving and adapting menus previously designed to meet dietary and aesthetic guidelines (http://toros.ces.cwru. edu/~marling/camp.html).*

Natural Language Processing

A final knowledge application is called natural language processing (NLP). NLP goes beyond converting speech to text by trying to understand and speak human languages such as English and Japanese. The complexity of understanding language is often demonstrated by the spoken sentence "They're going to park their car over there." They're, their, and there all sound alike yet have different meanings. Hal, in the film *2001: A Space Odyssey,* is an example of a robot with NLP capabilities.

One typical NLP application is translating text from one language to another. Computer translation of agency forms, documents, and reports would be beneficial for many clients who experience language as a barrier to services. The problems of language translation are often illustrated by one English-to-Russian NLP program that translated "out of sight, out of mind" to "invisible maniac" and "the spirit is willing, but the flesh is weak" to "the vodka is good, but the meat is rotten."

Future natural language applications will include the ability to request clarification and to learn the user's unique meaning, language structures, and jargon. Users will then be able to talk to their IT applications to obtain the information needed for work and play. Natural language processing will make available the human-computer interface to many in the human services who do not have keyboarding or computer literacy skills. It will also allow clients to interact directly with computer applications.

DECISION SUPPORT APPLICATIONS

Another type of application provides information and models that allow users to explore the decision at hand. Many authors define these applications as decision support systems, or DSSs (Keen and Morton, 1978). Whereas DP and IS applications focus on efficiency, DSSs focus on effectiveness. The effective decision-making process is not always efficient or cost beneficial. Obtaining the best decision may require adaptation, new learning, redundancy, false starts, and failure. The focus of an information system is on providing reports, while a decision support system (DSS) focuses on the decision-making process. Expert systems focus on making decisions, while a DSS focuses on exploring the nature of the decision. As with most concepts in the computing field, these distinctions are evolving as the applications mature and merge.

Definition

A *decision support system* (DSS) is a computer-based application designed to assist professionals in making complex decisions (Keen and Morton, 1978). A DSS helps the user retrieve, manage, and display information about a decision. A DSS works with data to answer "what if" types of questions about the decisions at hand. With a DSS, users can search for trends or evaluate alternatives in highly flexible ways. Users can generate graphs, run data through models, and view various information simultaneously using familiar language and logic.

A DSS consists of three components. The first is a database and computer modeling capabilities, such as that provided by a statistical model, a spreadsheet, or an expert system. The second element, tied to the modeling capacity, can be computer storage to retain the processes, interaction, and results the decision maker uses in examining a problem. This is similar to saving the scratch paper of a mathematician or the rough drafts of a writer. A final component of a DSS is a user-friendly interface, for example, software that allows dialogue with the database in familiar logic and language.

A DSS is not a substitute for the user's experience and judgment. A DSS contains only data and models, not the experience and the politics surrounding a decision. For example, the most appropriate option indicated by a session with a DSS might be to abolish the department directed by the boss's son. However, experience and politics are needed to evaluate such an option.

Examples of Decision Support Systems

Figure 4.7 presents what could be considered a noncomputerized equivalent of a DSS. The forty-four-item checklist illustrated in Figure 4.7 is a tool to help the practitioner gather and relate the appropriate knowledge regarding a case. The checklist structures the practitioner's decision making and helps obtain the most appropriate facts using a paper-and-pencil interface. The checklist is based on underlying decision models. These models are implicit in how facts are requested, how the questions are asked, and the branching from one section to another based on the user's response. It is a decision support tool because it does not derive an overall conclusion but aids in the decision-making process.

An example of a DSS is an IT application that predicted and improved service equity in an aging agency (Miller, 1993). The DSS helped workers determine what services clients needed to allow them to stay in their homes. The DSS resulted in an increase in client home stay of 15.4 percent. It also resulted in a decrease in accountant-like job content and paperwork. Other findings were that practitioner's jobs were not lost, practitioner discretion increased, and deviance from DSS predictions was not punished but instead used to improve the prediction.

Figure 4.8 presents a hypothetical child welfare DSS containing the interactions of a practitioner returning from a child abuse investigation (Schoech and Schkade, 1980). The hypothetical DSS illustrates several modeling capabilities. The first three options present some of the most frequent models requested, while option number 5 offers the capacity to build new models. As practitioners learn to use the DSS and realize its capabilities, the use of option number 5 to answer "what if"-type questions should increase. Thus, actual development and use of a DSS alters the decision-making process. The DSS must be flexible enough to change as user sophistication increases and user needs change during the interaction.

Several problems exist in developing human service DSSs. The decision-making process must be modeled and "outcome," "success," or "effectiveness" of decisions must be established. This is a long and difficult task (Texas Department of Protective and Regulatory Services, 1997).✳ Professionals must trust the validity and reliability of the information and

FIGURE 4.7. A Noncomputerized Equivalent of a DSS

Checklist: Observations from First Home Visit

Part I: Supervision

	Yes	No
1. Supervision was an issue?	—	—
(a) If NO, go to Part II: Child's Condition		
2. If YES: Was there a caretaker in the home?	—	—
(a) What is the caretaker's relationship to the child?	_____	
(b) If not a parent, was the caretaker there by arrangement with a parent?	—	—
(c) Regardless of relationship, was the caretaker able to supervise the child?	—	—
(d) Regardless of relationship, was the caretaker willing to supervise the child?	—	—
(e) etc.		

Part II: Child's Condition

1. Was the child's condition an issue?	—	—
2. If NO, go to Part III: Condition of the home		
3. If YES, did you observe an injured child (burns, lacerations, bruises, etc.)?	—	—
(a) If YES, use the narrative section to report the caretaker's and child's explanation of how injuries were sustained.	—	—
(b) etc.		

Source: From *Decision Making at Child Welfare* (pp. 42-43) by T. Stein and T. Rzepnicki, 1983, Washington, DC: Child Welfare League of America. Copyright 1983 by Child Welfare League of America. Reprinted by permission.

the models before they will use it. Although developing a DSS is expensive and complex, it could be cost beneficial when viewed over time. DSSs have potential benefits beyond decision support. A DSS could help prevent burnout by supporting practitioner judgments with logical explanations or statistically validated models. In addition, workers and clients will be confident that all appropriate data and expertise were considered.

FIGURE 4.8. A Hypothetical Child Welfare DSS

CWDSS: You are using the Child Welfare Decision Support System called CWDSS. Please enter your name and unique password.

Worker: Joe Smith, AZURE

CWDSS: Since this is your first use of CWDSS, please select the interaction type you desire.
1. No explanation (expert user)
2. Brief explanation (experienced user)
3. All explanations (novice user)
4. All explanations and personalized dialogue (new user)

Worker: 4

CWDSS: Thank you, Joe. The CWDSS has now been set to provide you all explanations using personalized dialogue. CWDSS can do the following five tasks to assist with your case decisions:
1. Provide a summary narrative on similar cases that were resolved successfully according to a panel of experts.
2. Identify key activities of cases similar to yours that were judged to have been handled successfully.
3. Compare the series of activities you are planning with your case and see what outcomes these activities achieved in previous cases.
4. Provide abstracts on subjects related to your case. (The CWDSS will search for the topic you specify.)
5. Present the procedure for asking additional questions. Type the number you want performed.

Worker: W

CWDSS: The W entered does not correspond to one of the five items. Joe, please read the information above and enter either 1, 2, 3, 4, or 5. If you still do not understand, and if you have a question, just type a ? and our dialogue will be stored and instructions for using the system will be presented. Please type one of the five numbers or a ?.

Worker: 2

CWDSS: Have you filled out form 1045 on this case? Yes or No? {If yes, the computer automatically gets the information from form 1045 and requests only the data missing or needed in addition to form 1045.}

Worker: No

CWDSS: Joe, in order to perform the activity specified, background information is needed about your case. If you do not know the answer to the questions asked, press the "enter" key. Is there a father in this case? Press Y for Yes or N for No. {If No, the CWDSS automatically branches to the next series of questions.}

Worker: Y
CWDSS: Is the father in the home? (Y or N)
Worker: Y
CWDSS: How old is the father?
Worker: 37
CWDSS: What kind of work does he do? (Press appropriate letter)
    A. Unskilled Laborer
    B. Semiskilled
    C. Professional
    D. Other {For brevity, additional categories are not shown.}
Worker: C
CWDSS: Has he been convicted of any crime? {If Yes, the computer branches to the questions that search for more detail, e.g., a crime involving aggression on another person or a crime involving alcohol or drug abuse.}
Worker: N {Similar information would be gathered for the mother, household, and family, based on the variables found applicable in abuse situations.}
CWDSS: All the information needed has been collected. Before reviewing similar cases, would you like Form 1045 to be typed from the information you provided and put in the appropriate files?
Worker: Y
CWDSS: Form 1045 is in your files. A search of the database has found the following information:
    1. Three similar cases with up to five exceptions.
    2. Five cases similar to yours with five to ten exceptions.
    3. Seven cases similar to yours with ten to fifteen exceptions.
The most similar case is identical to yours with the following exceptions:
    1. There is no grandmother in the home.
    2. The mother has divorced and remarried twice.
    3. The abused child's older brother was age 4.
Do you want to continue with the most similar case summary?
Worker: Y
CWDSS: MOST SIMILAR CASE SUMMARY: The worker removed the children from the home immediately and placed them in foster care for one week. The father and mother were referred to financial counseling to obtain guidance and consolidate their bills. The parents were required to go to Family Services for marital counseling for three sessions the first week and one session a week for the following three months. The children were reinstated in the family after the third week, and the older children were involved in the marital counseling every third week. The case was resolved successfully based on the following facts.

FIGURE 4.8 (*continued*)

1. The family unit was quickly restored.
2. Six monthly follow-up visits by the worker gave the impression that the major problems were being solved.
3. No future complaints were received by the unit since reinstatement of the children.
4. Records reveal no case activity, since it was closed 30 months ago. Do you want more details on this case? (Y or N)

Worker: N

CWDSS: Do you wish to have a summary of the second most similar case displayed? (Y or N)

Worker: Y

CWDSS: The second most similar case was identical to yours with the following exceptions, etc.

Source: Adapted from "Computers Helping Caseworkers: Decision Support Systems" by D. Schoech and L. L. Schkade, 1980, *Child Welfare 59*(9), pp. 568-570.

PERFORMANCE SUPPORT APPLICATIONS

Another type of application focuses on "just in time" training to improve worker performance. Some authors use the term performance support tools (PSTs) or electronic performance support system (EPSS) when discussing these applications. Others simply use the term performance support system (PSS).

Definition

A *performance support system* is a computer-based application that improves workplace performance by providing on-demand access to the integrated information needed to complete a task or solve the problem at hand, with minimal support from other people (Grey, 1991; Reynolds and Araya, 1995; Brown, 1996; Schoech, 1996). A PSS provides information support when it is needed, where it is needed, and in the format it is needed. Information may be imbedded in text, sound, graphics, animation, pictures, and video. Support may be in the following forms:

- Interactive access to agency databases
- Interaction with experience and expertise stored in knowledge-based systems

- Guided interaction through sequences
- Agency documents in hypermedia or multimedia form
- Specialized software tools or "agents" that perform routine tasks such as managing a consultation (Carr, 1992)

PSSs consist of a database with a sophisticated user interface that builds on the natural way users perform their jobs. They also allow users to control the interaction. Important design considerations of a PSS are flexibility, ease of maintenance, and the ability to accommodate changes.

One way to understand a PSS is to compare it with a DSS. A DSS contains advice or algorithms that help explore a decision. A PSS focuses on increasing practitioner performance; no decision making need be involved. For example, if high stress impinges on practitioner performance, then a PSS could be designed to lower practitioner stress by talking practitioners through a stress-reduction process. Since decision making is not the focus, a PSS may be less complex than a DSS. A PSS may simply lead one through a complex process without helping answer the "what if" questions that DSSs typically address.

Another way to understand the PSS concept is to compare it to CAI. With CAI, the user stops work and devotes a set amount of time to training. Curriculum specialists design CAI into a structured series of training modules. Although CAI is interactive, users have minimal control over the curriculum content and structure. Typically, users are required to complete module 1 before module 2 and to complete each module in a structured fashion. The goal of CAI concerns learning for future practice, whereas the goal of a PSS concerns improving immediate performance. Thus, a PSS presents information drawn out of its larger context. This larger context is usually obtained during training. This point can be illustrated using an analogy. If training is analogous to watching a movie, then a PSS is analogous to users selecting and viewing short clips of the same movie. What is gained by training is the same as what is gained by viewing a movie as a whole. The gain is the bigger picture, suspense, entertainment, the context of action, and the process of discovery once a conceptual framework is established.

In contrast, a PSS may apply the task the user is performing to help determine what information is needed. For example, if the user is assessing a six-month-old child, a PSS may exclude information not relevant to a six-month-old child. The PSS could also allow the user to specify exactly what information was needed, for example, specialized information related to the child's ethnicity and gender. The user may also specify the output format desired, for example, text with citations, video clips, pictures for printing, and so forth. Whereas a CAI session may occur infrequently and take from fifteen minutes to an hour to complete, a PSS may be used frequently throughout the day in two- to five-minute episodes.

A PSS works well in the following situations:

- Voluminous instructions and procedures exist about how to perform the work.
- Staff turnover and on-the-job training are common.
- Agencies have basic computer systems in place.
- Pressures exist to reduce budgets and improve quality.
- Staff reside in many geographic locations, making the informal sharing of information difficult. (Ladd, 1993)

Choosing an appropriate area to support is important given the long-term commitment required for PSS maintenance. Good areas for PSS development are those containing large amounts of agreed-upon expertise or infrequently used or complex procedural steps that are difficult for practitioners to remember. Bad areas are those which do not immediately impact practitioner performance or in which controversy and change exist that are beyond the agency's control.

A PSS is not altogether a new tool, but rather the combination of existing tools to place the agency technology and its information under user control. PSSs focus IT tools on practitioner performance instead of on making reports, predictions, and decisions or on practitioner training. In fact, some authors suggest that the first and most difficult task in PSS development is distinguishing performance that is critical to an agency's mission from noncritical performance (Carr, 1992). The PSS concept is a good conceptual base for agencies desiring to move beyond their information systems or traditional training.

Examples of Performance Support Applications

A human service application with PSS features is CASP, Computer-Assisted Services Planning (www.psp.info.com).✿ CASP helps users define and structure problems, measures, and interventions and to use the setup to support practitioners. One use of a CASP setup is to help practitioners develop treatment plans.

Another human service PSS is the Worker Safety Advisor, which a worker can consult for several minutes prior to going out on a case for which safety is a concern. Worker Safety Advisor presents workers with several computer screens on which they specify the situation they face. Worker Safety Advisor then searches a database of worker safety information and presents relevant information in an easy-to-select format (Schoech and Bolen, 1998) (see Figure 4.9).✿

FIGURE 4.9. Illustrations from the Worker Safety Advisor

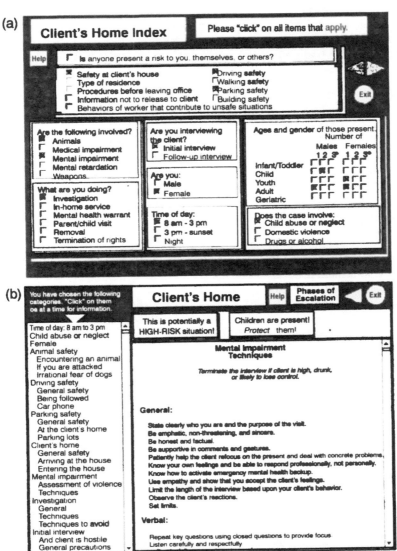

Source: From "The Worker Safety Advisor: A Performance Support System" by D. Schoech and B. Bolen, 1998, *Computers in Human Services 15*(2/3), pp. 143-158. Copyright 1998 by The Haworth Press, Inc. Reprinted by permission.

Some may see a PSS as replacing traditional practitioner training. One temptation may be to cut the training budget after several PSS modules are developed. However, a PSS is better viewed as a productivity aide that builds on traditional training. One solution to this dilemma of training versus PSS is to use training content to develop a PSS and then to integrate PSS use into traditional worker training.

CONCLUSION

Those involved with IT have noticed a gradual progression in applications from supporting routine management decisions to supporting complex practitioner-client interactions. Our understanding of applications has evolved also. From developing data processing applications, we found that practitioners wanted more timely, organized, and complex information, such as that available in integrated or agencywide information systems. However, even with integrated information systems, practitioners have problems getting the information they need, when it is needed, and in the format it is needed. They also have problems when applications contain only information because knowledge is needed to support many worker decisions. While developing expert systems, we discovered that many practitioners do not need sophisticated applications that make a decision. Instead, they need basic information and knowledge to help with the variety of complex tasks they perform (Schoech, Cavalier, and Hoover, 1993). In developing training applications, we discovered that CAI is effective (Kulik, 1994), yet practitioners often forget much of the detailed information and do not have time to use the training software to refresh their memories. Practitioners only have time to examine information that is necessary to get on with their work. Performance support systems offer one way to customize information to specific situations and work habits. However, they require a substantial amount of information and, therefore, need to be integrated into the agency IS. Knowledge systems and decision support systems offer potential to support more complex decision making, but their development has been hindered by cost and complexity.

Eventually, the applications discussed in this chapter will merge into an intelligent supportive environment that improves the efficiency, accountability, and effectiveness of human services. This environment will combine interactive manuals, tutorials, interactive help, answers to frequently asked questions, Internet sites, and telephone technical support. The goal is to support the user on the concept or task at hand and to direct the user through a process while monitoring and providing guidance along the way.

Although supportive environments for complex human service problems may be years away, adding intelligence to traditional applications is currently possible. For example, a psychological test may have an intelligent "front end" that initializes the test to the characteristics of the client. Or, training software may have a diagnostic module that analyzes user mistakes and successes and adjusts the learning style, timing, and phrasing to ensure that an optimal learning strategy is employed. Another way for applications to become more intelligent is by allowing users to add their personal expertise. IT applications that learn are important due to the difficulty of human services knowledge engineering. Codification of professional knowledge and concepts into software will be a primary human service task.

Although applications that provide support to managers and practitioners are important, we should also think about providing more direct support to clients to allow the service delivery process to become more efficient and effective. Similar to practitioners, clients also need a supportive information environment to help them meet their needs. If delivered over the Internet, such applications could educate, prepare, advise, and empower clients. These applications may also help clients collect their own data for intake and service monitoring or coach clients through self-help processes for solving basic human service problems. By applying IT applications to client needs, we can help them become intelligent consumers of human services and empowered partners in service delivery. Realizing the potential of IT applications will be an important task for human services in the future.

REVIEW AND DISCUSSION QUESTIONS

1. Pick a critical human service decision made in an agency. What support tools now exist for making that decision?
2. What distinguishes a data processing application from an information system? An information system from a knowledge-based system? An expert system from a decision support system? A DSS from a PSS?
3. Would a new employee who is a novice react differently to a DP application than an expert who is a longtime employee? To an MIS? To an expert system? To a DSS? To a PSS?
4. What are two noncomputerized decision-making models in your specialty area?
5. List several human service IT management applications we can expect to see in the future.

.

Chapter 5

Human Services IT Applications

INTRODUCTION

This chapter presents an overview of computer and Internet applications from the policy to self-help levels of the human service delivery system. A historic and summary overview is provided for several major categories of applications at each level. Accompanying figures present typical applications for each level. Since lists of applications quickly become outdated, a current list is provided on the book Web site.

POLICYMAKING LEVEL

This section describes two major categories of IT applications that support policy—information analysis and dissemination and social action. A list of typical applications is presented in Table 5.1.

Information Analysis and Dissemination

Traditionally, social policy IT applications concerned storing and analyzing information for policy staff. Political leaders and elected officials infrequently used IT applications to enhance their policy decision making. Occasionally, computer models were developed for interpreting policy data or predicting social problems. One experimental effort used an expert system to model the U.S. foreign policy belief system to simulate foreign policy arguments (Taber and Timpone, 1994). The Policy Arguer was most useful in mapping the logic behind policy alternatives. Another effort created the equivalent of a flight simulator for "taking off," "flying," and "landing" welfare reform without risking the lives of children and families (Rohr-

TABLE 5.1. Policy Applications

Problem/Situation	Technology Used	Example	Source
How to make wise decisions in designing welfare reform	Computer models, DBMSs	System Dynamics model of welfare reform	Rohrbaugh and Johnson, 1998
Monitoring the status of social problems	Web site with social indicators and geographic information system (GIS)	The Social Well-Being of Vermonters	www.dsw.state.vt.us/ahs/swb97/swbcover.htm
How to find and interact with public officials on issues	Web site, database of officials, on-line petitions	E-The People	www.e-thepeople.com/
Educating on the impact of policy legislation	Web site presenting studies, data, news, meetings, conferences, links	Colorado Welfare Reform Web site	http://carbon.cudenver.edu/public/cwr/
Mobilizing people on the ill effects of social policy	Web site providing information, links, sign-up campaigns, and resources	Fight managed care "horror stories" Web site	www.his.com/~pico/usa.htm
Teaching youth IT skills and social values such as equal rights	Communication IT, group process, mentoring	Camp to educate youth on IT and social responsibility	Harkonen, 1995

baugh and Johnson, 1998). This model of the welfare system allowed users to ask "what if" questions about alternative strategies and policies while maintaining a safety net for the needy. For example, the model identified the important effect that self-sufficiency promotion could play in welfare reform and spurred appropriate policies. It caused one government official to appoint task forces on the special needs of teenagers, child care availability, and cross-agency employment services. Users found that the model challenged some deeply held beliefs and ideas.

The Internet has greatly expanded the capacity of IT to support policymakers, and the Web is quickly becoming a major policy tool. The Internet allows for easy and quick collection and dissemination of information at very little cost. By the late 1990s, most government agencies and research centers used Web publishing to release studies for maximum circulation and impact. Also, most political and policy leaders used e-mail, and most government and corporate databanks became available through the Web.

One increasingly popular way to provide policy information is to track indicators on an area's social problems and strengths, for example, poverty rate or volunteerism rate. Since social policy often concerns a geographic area, Web sites that allow users to retrieve indicators as maps can be very powerful. Some policy Web sites allow users to map the indicators of interest onto any geographic area. As more agencies become connected to the Internet, the linking of indicators from many local Web sites will become common (Schoech et al., 1998).

Social Action

Computers have traditionally played an important role in speeding up the creation, management, tracking, and mass mailing of literature on policy issues. However, paper-and-mail campaigns are costly and lack the quick action required to retain momentum or achieve an impact. Another problem with computer-assisted advocacy has been that many human service advocacy agencies have not had the resources and skills to purchase, implement, and support a technological approach to advocacy.

The Internet provides important technology for advocacy due to its interactivity, speed, universality, low cost, and massive number of available resources. Currently, e-mail is the Internet tool most frequently used for advocacy. Some Web sites specialize in helping citizens design and manage petition campaigns and contact their representatives.

The Internet makes powerful advocacy tools and resources so readily available that even nonprofessionals can develop advocacy campaigns. An example is a schizophrenia self-help discussion forum that used the Internet to spontaneously mount an effective media campaign against discriminatory policies toward one of its members. Currently, the key problem is that Internet access is not universal; some of the most disenfranchised populations are not connected to the Internet, e.g., the homeless.

COMMUNITY LEVEL

Applications to support community practice are not well developed. A 1990 conference on computers for social change and community organizing suggested that computers are primarily used to manage data and to create, manage, and disseminate documents (Downing et. al, 1991).

Internet applications are now being used for information collection and dissemination, multiagency coordination, planning and committee work, building a new community, and strengthening neighborhoods (Nartz and Schoech, 1998). Table 5.2 lists several community applications.

TABLE 5.2. Community Applications

Problem/Situation	Technology Used	Example	Source
Helping communities solve their problems	Citywide discussion forums, links to resources	Seattle Community Network	www.scn.org/
Connecting people to community resources	Information and referral database with case management features	IRIS	www.irissoft. com/
Giving communities access to demographic and geographic information	CD-ROM with U.S. Department of Housing and Urban Development information	Community 2020	www.hud.gov/ cpd/c2020ad. html
Bringing people and professionals together to form interest-based communities	Web publishing, discussion forums, membership database	Child Abuse Prevention Network	http://child. cornell.edu/
Linking community agencies into a network	Internet, I&R database, e-mail	National Telecommunications and Information Administration	www.ntia.doc. gov/otiahome/ tiiap/(Alabama United Way)
Getting neighbors to care about their neighborhoods	Web publishing of news, discussion forums, links, etc.	Neighborhood Knowledge Los Angeles	http://nkla. sppsr.ucla. edu/

Information Collection and Dissemination

Word processing, desktop publishing, and Web publishing have been the primary applications for collecting and disseminating community information. Most agencies that develop Web sites and track use are surprised at the number and variety of visitors and the relevance of site contents to visitors' needs.

Specialty information and referral (I&R) applications have been used for many years by community agencies, especially United Way agencies. I&R applications support a trained practitioner or volunteer in providing information to callers seeking help and referring them to the appropriate services. One benefit of community I&R applications is that they formalize and standardize the I&R process and knowledge. Once computerized, an I&R application can be easily updated and distributed to all agencies performing I&R. Although an I&R application allows the I&R novice to perform better, it may be a burden to the sophisticated I&R specialist. IT often provides the sophisticated user little new information and may overstructure the interaction with the user in order to collect information systematically. Another problem with I&R applications is that they centralize data collection and dissemination for a network of agencies. However, once community agencies have Internet access and agency Web sites, the I&R function in a community can become more distributed and can even be available directly to citizens.

Multiagency Coordination

The concept of linking multiple agencies into a coordinated system of services for clients has been a dream of community practitioners for years. Traditionally, wide area networks (WANs) linked offices or similar agencies using dedicated telecommunication lines. Linking of agencies via telephone and modem has also been tried, with some success. Problems include agency politics, the lack of a central agency to set up and manage the community network, the lack of top management involvement, the change in work patterns required, and the lack of service standardization (Schoech, Cavalier, and Hoover, 1993). Most successful multiagency networks involve agencies in which clients may frequently move from one agency to another to obtain services, such as with food pantries and homeless shelters. Many of these networks exist to exchange client information to coordinate services and prevent their abuse.

The Internet makes multiagency networking easier and less expensive by providing agencies with a well-supported and inexpensive networking infrastructure. It also takes many networking tasks away from each agency and centralizes them through the use of networking specialists. The Internet offers the capacity for intra-agency e-mail, discussion forums, common databases, and linkages to resources. It also offers ways for the clients and the public to network with agencies. Client and citizen networking with agencies can have a substantial impact on agency operations and services.

One problem with multiagency networks sharing client information is protecting data security and confidentiality. The United States has few restrictions regarding corporate database security and confidentiality. Consequently, some Internet service providers may not have the security and confidentiality tools and procedures that human service agencies need. Also, no guidelines exist for agencies regarding the sharing of client information. For example, the courts have not decided what constitutes informed client consent in relation to the sharing of agency records in a multiagency network.

Planning and Committee Work

Computer applications that help committees perform their work have not been used by many agencies. Applications have been developed to generate ideas, work on common projects, automatically record group interaction, and structure committee voting and decision making on controversial issues (Simmons, 1979). Studies suggest that group decision support systems increase participation, help members generate a higher number of original ideas, and reduce intergroup conflict (Daily and Steiner, 1998). Generic, Internet-based groupware applications that support information sharing, issue tracking, calendar coordination, task assignment, document management, and deadline setting are becoming popular in business and will be used more in the human services.

The Internet is proving useful not only in making documents readily available but also in communicating with committee members. E-mail and discussion forums are the most common Internet applications used for committee work. The Internet also allows committees to meet interactively in text-based chat rooms or for audio and video conferencing. Internet tools have successfully supported national and international advisory committees through good Internet access for all members. As agencies' experience with virtual meetings and other Internet tools improves, Internet use will increase substantially.*

Building and Strengthening Community

Applications to build new communities and strengthen existing ones have been limited due to the availability of computers and the technical difficulties involved with networking individuals. Rheingold (1993) documented early Internet-based community-building efforts around the world. Most early efforts involved like-minded IT professionals coming together on-line to share information, research, resources, and ideas. However, Rheingold reported that interest groups' members quickly became involved in social support and interpersonal activities that are common to communities. Some groups held small, intimate chat or voice interactions during which members were linked physically and electronically, such as multiple, video-linked, local dinner parties.*

Many initiatives involving agency and community networking have been funded by approximately 100 million dollars awarded annually by the Telecommunications and Information Infrastructure Assistance Program (TIIAP) of the Department of Commerce. Many community networking projects are described on the TIIAP Web site.✿

In addition to being useful for building virtual communities of interest, the Internet also helps strengthen geographic communities. Most cities have a home page on the Internet that performs some community strengthening functions. One promising use of the Internet is at the local neighborhood level (Doheny-Farina, 1996). The Internet can be used to re-create connections between neighbors that have been lost due to our modern lifestyle. E-mail newsletters are easy and inexpensive to produce and distribute. Social indicators available at the neighborhood level allow citizens to document their concerns. Neighborhood discussion forums allow people to post and read neighborhood news on a schedule more suitable to today's lifestyle.

An ambitious IT community-building project is the new town of Celebration, Florida, which includes a joint venture between the Disney Development Corporation and a Florida Hospital to create a twenty-first-century health care system that makes the town a healthier place to live, partly by taking full advantage of the Internet (Bezold, 1994). Another noteworthy project, Access Colorado, provided Internet access and resource links to citizens of Colorado through a networked state libraries system.✿

AGENCY MANAGEMENT LEVEL

Agency management's first priority is to develop an information system that integrates independent applications and links to outside resources. Such a system primarily serves management needs but can be useful throughout the agency. For example, the capacity to project the impacts of budget increases and decreases is useful for strategic planning. Many vendors offer "generic" information systems for agencies. However, these vendors usually struggle to make the application generic enough to serve the needs of many agencies, to keep the application as up to date as users expect, and to increase sales so that costs associated with application updates are spread out over a large user base.

Since some management functions are similar throughout all organizations, many generic management applications can be used in human service organizations, for example, spreadsheet and project management applications. However, many human service management applications are unique to the human services, for example, nonprofit accounting. In addition, many agencies have a nonstandard way of implementing generic management concepts, for example, services planning and case management. Thus, most human service applications tend to be custom-built. This nonstandard mode of operation has limited the number of human service management applications because of the expense of application development and maintenance.

Internet technology has not yet had a substantial impact on agency management applications in the human services. However, intranets are popular in business and will be popular in the human services. Intranets, or internal agency Internets, allow agencies to standardize networking and take advantage of the large number of Internet tools to design applications, such as information systems, scheduling applications, e-mail, and so on.

The categories of management IT applications covered in this section are collecting and reporting management information, accounting and fiscal management, personnel and volunteer management, public relations, marketing, and fund-raising (see Table 5.3).

TABLE 5.3. Agency Management Applications

Problem/Situation	Technology Used	Example	Source
Providing information for agency decision making	Customized DBMS and MIS	Community Services Network of Central Florida or CMHC systems	www.sundial. net/~csn/ software.htm or www.cmhcmis. com/
Billing and bookkeeping	Bookkeeping systems	Therapist Helper	Lambert, 1994
Matching clients to services	Matching programs, DBMSs	Target Cities Projects	Hile, 1998
Optimal and equitable allocation of personnel	Computer models, caseload reports, group decision-making reports	Model for computerized allocation of personnel resources	Margaliot, 1997
Fund-raising	Customized DBMS	RccDonor or RMsoftware	Fortuna, 1996; www. rmsoftware. com/
Tracking progress on grants	Customized DBMS and MIS	Grant tracker	www. granttracker. com/
Technical support on how to manage an agency or program	Database of innovative programs, CAI on evaluation and planning	Innonet	www. inetwork.org/

Collecting and Reporting Management Information

Support of management decision making via agency information systems represents the majority of human service applications to date. One reason is that managers make decisions on what applications are developed. They understand their needs best and tend to meet them first. Another reason is that management information needs are more routine and easier to support than practitioners' needs. Finally, management information needs are critical to agency survival, as agencies must have basic data to demonstrate progress to their funding sources. The data provided by the information system are often the basis of quality assurance programs, program evaluation efforts, and reports to funding sources. Mature information systems can integrate data for all users in the organization (Oyserman and Benbenishty, 1997).

After basic agency information systems are developed, management typically focuses on improving connectivity, for example, better internal networking and networking with other agencies. A common application is the construction of computer models to help make difficult and complex decisions, such as the allocation of personnel (Margaliot, 1997) or services (Miller, 1993). Another frequent application that uses agency and community databases is the matching of clients to services (Hile, 1998; Schwab, Bruce, and McRoy, 1985).

Accounting and Financial Management

Perhaps the oldest human service applications concern financial management. These packages are very popular because many small nonprofit agencies do not have the resources to hire a professional bookkeeper and their financial management needs are complex. Nonprofit financial management is complex because oftentimes agencies receive money from a variety of funding sources, each on a different fiscal year, and each with its own reporting requirements. Services for the same client may be charged to many different funding sources. Also, funding sources prefer grant applications that link services from a variety of agencies. These coordination projects are politically attractive, but they require complicated bookkeeping.

Personnel and Volunteer Management

Many specific personnel applications exist in business, some of which are appropriate for human service agencies, for example, managing employee training. In addition, applications that help recruit, schedule, and manage volunteers have been developed. Managing volunteers is different from managing personnel, as the rewards for volunteers and staff are different. Thus, volunteer applications allow more individualization and flexibility in scheduling and detailed tracking of efforts for funding sources. Volunteer applications are important because oftentimes the task of managing volunteers is not adequately resourced or is left to a newly hired employee with little management or personnel experience.

Public Relations, Marketing, and Fund-Raising

Traditionally, most human service agencies have not been involved in service marketing, public relations, and fund-raising. However, with privatization initiatives, these tasks take on increasing significance. Fund-raising is a generic function common to many nonprofit organizations, such as foundations and museums. Therefore, applications to support fund-raising are well developed. IT to support public relations and marketing has traditionally consisted of word processing and desktop publishing for producing brochures and reports, along with a DBMS for mailing list management.

Agencies are discovering that the Internet is an ideal public relations, marketing, and grant-seeking tool. Using the Web, agencies can inexpensively publish text, images, and video about themselves worldwide. The first Internet application for most agencies is a home page for public information, public relations, and marketing. Other applications follow, depending on the specific needs of the agency. One application that has quickly proven the power of the Internet is adoption Web sites for hard-to-place children. Adoptive families find the Internet an easy and private way to find pictures, videos, and background information on available children. Another use of the Internet is to connect foundations and government funding agencies with those seeking financial support. Some Web businesses specialize in e-mailing information about funding that is customized to a user's interests. Another Web application provides technical support to agencies in areas such as program evaluation and fund-raising. On such sites, agencies can work through structured processes and receive feedback and advice from experts.

DIRECT SERVICE LEVEL: HELPING PRACTITIONERS MANAGE AND REPORT WORK

Practitioner applications can be divided into two categories. The first category, discussed in this section, helps practitioners manage and report on their work. The second category, which supports practitioner interactions with clients, is discussed in the next section.

Applications that help practitioners manage their work perform functions such as record keeping, scheduling, service monitoring, and following processes and procedures. Table 5.4 presents typical practitioner applications.

Record Keeping, Scheduling, and Monitoring Services

Although agency information systems are available to support practitioners in managing and reporting their work relatively few generic applications support practitioner management activities. Human service practice varies by agency and client to the extent that one-of-a-kind applications must be built, and these may only work in a few locations. An example of a common task that varies by agency is case management. Agencies face the difficulty of determining whether any vendor produces applications that reflects how their practitioners operate. The Internet can be helpful in this search.

TABLE 5.4. Applications That Help Practitioners Manage Their Work

Problem/Situation	Technology Used	Example	Source
Obtaining information and consultation on specialized topics	Web site with chat rooms and discussion forums	Mental Health Conference Room	http:// mentalhealth. miningco.com/ mpchat.htm
Evaluating severity of client problems, tracking progress, and managing case notes	DBMS integrated with assessment scales and reports	CASS	www.syspac. com/~walmyr/
Developing treatment plans quickly and uniformly	Database with interactive front end to structure process	CASP or Clinical Planner	www.pspinfo. com/ or www.cedrus. com/cplanner/
Keeping personnel up to date and certified	Streaming audio, text instruction, and testing	AudioPsych	www. audioPsych. com/
Delivering services to remote areas	Electronic network, two-way video in homes	TeleHealth Project, Georgia	http:// catelehealth. org/sect1.html
Finding an appropriate assistive device	Database of assistive devices	Hyper-ABLEDATA	www.trace. wisc.edu/tcel/

IT applications exist that record baseline data, schedule clients, monitor client progress, and track client movement through the agency (Nurius and Hudson, 1993). Scheduling applications can manage staff calendars, schedule appointments and meetings, produce daily client appointment listings, and provide reminders of important dates, such as client birthdays or anniversaries of significant events that increase clients' risk. Multiagency networks may allow practitioners to determine if other agencies have provided services to a client and to schedule case conferences with these other involved agencies.

Another type of application involves service monitoring by placing IT on or near the client to record and send information to the agency. A well-developed area of monitoring is biofeedback (Hartje, 1993). Other monitoring applications involve clients maintaining detailed information on their progress, using forms available from the agency's Web site. Progress charts can then be available to the client and the practitioner at any time. Another example uses global positioning coordinates and telecommunications to relay whether a client is staying in a confined area. This technology is used with criminal justice clients and with elderly persons who tend to wander away from their homes.

Given the acceptance of IT by clients, it is surprising that more agencies have not involved the client more in their basic record keeping. For example, clients could enter detailed tracking information on their treatment at an office computer or by using the Internet. The Internet allows tests to be administered in a client's home and the interpretation is automatically scored and stored in the agency's information system. Internet data input by clients would help relieve the paperwork burden and get clients more actively involved in monitoring their own progress. Voice recognition systems and the Internet might spur more clients to input data on their situation.

Research on telephone interactive voice response systems has proven that data collection IT applications are effective. One monitoring application involves using a telephone interactive voice response system to track and monitor client progress. The system periodically contacts clients, administers interviews and tests, stores the results in the agency database, flags problematic results, and graphs the results for the practitioner to review (Mundt et al., 1998). Another automated telephone system delivers a stress management program. Schneider, Schwartz, and Fast (1995) reported a high demand for the telephone stress management program and found that offering personalized messages and homework motivated users to continue the program, comply with program suggestions, and report whether the program was helpful. Similar interactive telephone systems have been used to keep track of available treatment slots so that assessment applications could recommend the most appropriate, available agency programs.

Teleconferencing software is becoming increasingly popular for quick and cost-effective interaction with clients. These telehealth applications are especially popular in areas where client access is difficult, for example, in prisons or in rural areas. Even with expensive satellite communications, two-way video with clients has proven to be cost-effective, especially when the time and travel costs of the client are included in the calculation. As two-way video becomes available over the Internet, telehealth applications will grow as an alternative way to deliver and monitor services to clients.

Following Procedures and Processes

Several applications help practitioners structure a process, provide advice about completing a process, or make completing a process easier. These applications are important, given the high workloads and turnover in some human service jobs. Some of these advisory applications are little more than elaborate decision trees or expert coaches that ensure that workers perform a process correctly, for example, monitoring of data input. Others make the most common activities that practitioners perform easier by organizing information and putting it in the format required by the agency, for example, treatment planning. Treatment planning applications lead practitioners through the treatment planning process and allow them to select components of typical treatment plans for standard DSM (*Diagnostic and Statistical Manual of Mental Disorders*) categories. These applications allow practitioners to generate standardized and professional-looking treatment plans in less time. Similar applications exist for constructing problem-oriented records and goal-attainment scaling. The difficulty that all specialty applications have is exchanging data with the agency information system. This is especially problematic in complex organizations such as hospitals.

DIRECT SERVICE LEVEL: SUPPORTING PRACTITIONER-CLIENT INTERACTIONS

Using an agency's information system to support practitioners' interaction with clients seems practical, but few applications have been developed. For example, few agencies have information systems that answer questions such as "What is our agency's most effective intervention strategy for this client diagnosis?" One problem is that such predictions require accurate data and service outcome measures. Given that most information systems are designed for accounting, accountability, and efficiency purposes, data on client problems, services, and outcomes may not be clinically accurate. One insurance company found many counterintuitive and inexplicable findings when they used their large mental health data sets for such analysis.

One solution involves companies that use the Internet to receive, analyze, and return data from agencies. These companies distribute the cost of developing sophisticated analysis applications among many agencies. Other promising technology for using data in information systems involves neural networks and case-based reasoning, but little use has been made of these tools in the human services (Modai et al., 1995).

Applications that support the **practitioner-client** interaction perform functions such as assessment, testing, consultation, analysis, structuring, and treatment. These categories are not mutually exclusive. Applications may perform several, or all, of these functions. Table 5.5 presents some common applications designed to support the practitioner-client interaction.

Assessment and Testing

IT applications have proven to be very accurate and reliable in gathering information from clients. This is especially true when the client interview is primarily for gathering information and not considered part of the therapeutic process. An application can patiently and consistently present questions, check for errors, store the information in the agency database, and print a report for client verification and immediate use. If client satisfaction is one essential element of success, then IT has consistently proven as, or more, successful than some human-client interactions (Erdman et al., 1981). The following quotes emphasize this point:

> A study of 398 people who tried the DHSS experiment [a computer asking all eligibility questions] suggested that a substantial majority (85 percent) preferred a computer to a DHSS *officer* while fewer (58 percent) would rather have benefits assessed by the machine than by a *social worker*. The main reason for the preference was that the computer did not keep people waiting for attention. (emphasis added) (Glastonbury, 1985, p. 61)

> Fifty-seven percent of the 135 patients stated that they liked using the computer "quite a bit" or "extremely" while only two percent (three patients) did not like the interview at all. Most patients felt that they were able to communicate their ideas and feelings to the computer and agreed that the questions were appropriate. Several spontaneously mentioned that they wished that their psychiatrist had been as

detailed as the computer in examining them. No patients reported serious difficulties with using the computer terminal and most seemed to learn how to interact with it quickly. In general, the patients' evaluations of the computer interview were positive indicating that acute psychiatric inpatients can complete the computer interview successfully. (Mathison et al., 1984, p. 4)

TABLE 5.5. Applications That Help Practitioners Interact with Clients

Problem/Situation	Technology Used	Example	Source
Matching kids to out-of-home placements	Web data collection, databases, algorithms	Youth for Tomorrow	www.yft.org/
Helping practitioners structure and analyze client information	Software that generates genograms	Relativity	www.clark.net/pub/wware/dldemos.html
Assessment and testing of clients	DBMS with assessment and testing front end	Department of Veterans Affairs	www.va.gov/
Screening for assistive device readiness	Decision tree and advice-giving software	Augment, an augmentative communicative readiness screener	www.uta.edu/cussn/diskcopy.htm or ftp://ftp.uta.edu/cussn/augment.zip
Delivering counseling independent of time and place	Professionally monitored support groups	CYBERPsych	www.win.net/cyberpsych/
Reducing the 10 to 14 hours required to diagnose dyslexia	Knowledge-based system based on heuristic rules	DYSLEXPERT	Blonk, Van Den Bercken, and De Bruyn, 1996
Identifying child development benchmarks	Internet-based presentation of theories and norms	The child development Web site	http://idealist.com/children/
Protecting oneself from dangerous situations	Multimedia, performance support system, knowledge base	Worker Safety Advisor	www.uta.edu/cussn/cussn/wsa/

Hile and Adkins (1997) found the reasons that clients sometimes prefer IT assessments to their human counterpart as being due to their completeness, enjoyability, and ease of use.

The administration, scoring, and interpretation of psychological tests is a time-consuming activity, and many testing applications exist. Assessment applications go beyond data collection and testing by applying norms or expertise to interpret the information collected. Results of IT assessments are comparable to practitioner assessments in mental health and substance abuse (Hile and Adkins, 1997). Hile's and Adken's research produced the Initial Standardized Assessment Protocol, which has three IT administered measures, a symptoms checklist, a readiness to change questionnaire, and a quality of life survey.

Studies have consistently found that people will reveal more sensitive information on subjects considered embarrassing, wrong, illegal, or deviant to a computer or Internet application than to another person. The reason for this phenomenon is not clearly understood, although the opportunity to interact in private with no fear of immediate consequences seems to be a factor. For this reason, and others presented in Table 5.6, an IT-mediated client interview is often considered superior to a human interview (Malcolm et al., 1989).

Consultation and Analysis

Consultation and analysis applications examine information for trends or patterns or consult codified expertise for advice. For example, some applications use statistical analysis and formulas to recommend the most appropriate services for clients (Hile, 1998). One consultation application checks client background and prescription guidelines to identify potential prescription contraindications. Another application matches child behaviors to acceptable age norms and displays potential problems and recommended solutions. Still another screens a client's potential to benefit from an assistive device. Experimental applications have mapped behavioral patterns and made predictions in specialized areas.

One interesting application helps family physicians diagnose and track mental health problems. SDDS (Symptom Driven Diagnostic System) administers a fifty-two-item symptom checklist to patients while they are in the physician's waiting room. This screening application detects from 62 to 90 percent of all patients having histories of (1) suicidal ideation, threats, or attempts; (2) major depression; (3) generalized anxiety disorder; (4) panic disorder; (5) obsessive-compulsive disorder; and (6) substance abuse. SDDS prints a preliminary diagnosis and list of questions the physician may ask the patient to probe further and refine the diagnosis. It also gives tips on

TABLE 5.6. The Advantages and Disadvantages of Technology-Mediated Interaction with Clients

Practitioners

Advantages	Disadvantages
Increases gathering of sensitive information in areas such as suicidal ideation, sexual dysfunction, and substance abuse	May interfere with the therapeutic benefits of information gathering
Eases the collecting and graphical representation of repeated measures over time	May hinder relationship building
Can check every item for accuracy and ask for clarification on "out of range" responses	Verbal and body language cues are missing
Can apply expertise to the information provided (for example, comparing data to norms or actuarial predictions)	Lack of a variety of "good" interviewing applications
Can use formats such as text, graphics, touch, voice, and video	Inability to explore beyond the information sought
Can collect information about the data collection process, for example, delays in responding, patterns of hyperlink use, etc.	Validity and reliability of application difficult to establish
Can automatically repeat or rephrase questions in a consistent way	

Clients

Advantages	Disadvantages
More convenient and flexible, e.g., can accommodate people with busy schedules, disabilities, or homes in rural areas	Few ethical standards and regulations exist for new techniques
Can be self-paced and "patient"	Some clients may not feel comfortable using IT
Can be personalized by consistently using the client's name, offering encouragement, and presenting positive reinforcement and immediate feedback	Digitized information is easier to transmit, thus increasing the potential for privacy violations
Can automatically skip irrelevant questions based on previous answers	Mechanical interaction because IT structures processes too tightly
Can provide clients with an educational experience while they wait for services	Difficult to bypass "the system" for nonroutine situations
Offers more privacy and decreased embarrassment about sensitive issues	Lack of research on its effectiveness

TABLE 5.6 (*continued*)

Agency

Advantages	Disadvantages
More thorough and consistent administration	Increases IT dependency
Structures the data-gathering process to en-sure that information is collected consistently	Applications take time to develop and integrate with agency procedures
Less overhead so more efficient operations	Requires hardware, soft-ware, and networking
Widespread acceptance by clients	Less flexible and more diffi-cult to change
Transcription and coding errors are reduced	Increased complexity and development time

what diagnoses to consider and which to rule out. SDDS also prints a list of questions the physician can use to track patient progress through nine future visits.

Clinical decision support systems that use complex statistical models or expert systems are rare (Gingerich, 1995). The few agencies that have developed practitioner-oriented DSSs have had difficulty using them (Miller, 1993) (Schwab and Wilson, 1989). As mentioned previously, Miller developed a DSS that determines the best configuration of in-home support services, given the agency's resources and the goal of maximizing client stay in the home. Schwab and Wilson developed a DSS that recommended the best out-of-home residential placement for children.

Several advisory or performance support systems have been developed, for example, systems that advise on worker safety (Schoech and Bolen, 1998) or on the treatment of aggressive, self-injurious, and destructive behaviors displayed by individuals with developmental disabilities (Hile and Desrochers, 1994). To date, the use of these advisory applications has not justified their development costs. Researchers have found many seemingly simple human service processes to be extremely costly to document, program into software, and evaluate. Often what seems like a simple advisory application becomes a major undertaking in terms of complexity, cost, training, implementation, and maintenance. In addition, a rigorous evaluation of advisory applications is often demanded, although few agencies have applied these high evaluative standards to the traditional practices that the IT application replaces.

The advantages of using consultation and analysis applications include the following:

- Scarce expertise can be codified, improved upon, and provided inexpensively to numerous users.
- A practitioner or group of practitioners can consistently implement an intervention approach.
- The practitioner and clients can immediately receive analytical feedback.
- Client progress can be easily tracked and monitored.
- Work can be undertaken by clients alone, thus saving the practitioner's time.
- Clients have more involvement with, and control over, the treatment process.

These advantages are leading to new methodologies in which IT applications take over routine information collection, monitoring, analysis, and feedback tasks. The practitioner is then free to engage in more complex work with the client.

Treatment

Treatment applications can deliver services to clients with minimal practitioner supervision. Several research efforts in this area deserve mention due to their seminal work and findings. One impressive effort is CATCEC (Computer-supported Assessment and Treatment Consultation for Emotional Crisis), an expert consultation application to aid navy corpsmen in evaluating and treating emotional or behavioral emergencies onboard submarines (Lambert, Hedlund, and Vieweg, 1990). The corpsman conducts a clinical interview and physical examination and then enters observations and ratings in response to CATCEC questions. CATCEC generates likely diagnosis, prognosis, treatment suggestions, and treatment side effects concerning the emotional and behavioral problems. An accompanying CAI application with case simulations (CATSIM) was developed to educate corpsmen about basic principles for approaching emotional/behavioral emergencies.

Another experimental effort, called MORTON, was designed around Beck's cognitive treatment model for depression. MORTON includes six educational sessions reinforced by homework assignments that emphasize learning the cognitive theory of emotions. Research demonstrated that mildly to moderately depressed patients improved as much with computer treatment using MORTON as did patients in treatment with a human therapist, and more than did patients in a control group (Selmi et al., 1982; Selmi et al., 1990).

Sexpert, an application program for providing sex therapy, combined traditional sex therapy techniques with a dialogue module, an advice module, and a text-generation module. In the initial session, Sexpert uses a natural language interface to collect information. It then presents clients with the dysfunction suspected, the context of the dysfunction, and a tailored treatment program. Later sessions consist of sexual exercises and a review of how previous exercises were carried out. Troubleshooting takes place throughout the treatment, and the couple is referred for professional help if necessary. An evaluation of Sexpert found that couples perceive interaction with Sexpert positively and that such interaction may change sexual behavior (Binik, Meana, and Sand, 1994).

Although IT-based treatment applications are rare; applications that assist in the treatment process are more common. One example is MAGIE, an interactive video application that can be incorporated into a traditional intervention strategy. The first step is to videotape a couple's discussion on a predetermined topic. Then the videotape is played to each member of the couple separately, with the tape stopping at key discussion points. At these points, each member answers questions presented on the computer screen. For example, the system might ask how relaxed or anxious each person was at a key discussion point. The couple's numerical responses to important questions are then computer analyzed and charted. The results form the basis of discussion with a therapist (Wakefield, 1985). Other practitioners have experimented with computer-mediated group therapy (Sander, 1996).

Some applications focus on making treatment more efficient by allowing technology to perform routine therapeutic tasks. These applications are often accompanied by protocols for integrating them with traditional practice. For example, Fear Fighter, an application for phobias, requires the practitioner to conduct a traditional evaluation of the client for the nature of the phobia and the appropriateness of computerized treatment. Appropriate clients then interact with Fear Fighter to identify fear triggers, set detailed goals, closely monitor their progress, and receive routine advice on their treatment. During the technology-mediated part of treatment, the practitioner is available to answer questions and monitor overall progress. Fear Fighter can reduce the total cost of treating a phobia by as much as 50 percent (Shaw and Marks, 1996; Marks, Shaw, and Parkin, 1998).[*]

Other research has shown that using IT applications, such as self-help on-line conferences, in conjunction with face-to-face treatment reduces the number of treatment sessions. One application helped clients clarify their concerns and identify goals for behavioral change prior to their first session with a counselor. Research that compared three computer sessions followed by two counselor sessions to five sessions with a counselor found no difference in behavioral change outcomes. However, clients were more satisfied with the face-to-face counseling (Arbona and Perrone, 1989).

Research is needed to answer many of the questions concerning treatment IT. One example is research by Weinberg (1996) who found no significant differences on several supportiveness scales between face-to-face and technology-mediated counseling. Consistent with previous research, Weinberg showed that members of the computer-mediated counseling group were less guarded in their self-revelations.

CLIENT LEVEL

Applications at the client level provide education and information, virtual support groups, self-help, insight, and treatment (see Table 5.7). The client level could be the "sleeping giant" in the human service application market, since the number of potential users is large and the Internet allows developers to directly deliver applications to consumers.

Education and Information

The largest number of client IT applications involves education and information. Some of these were discussed in Chapter 3. A typical CD-ROM example is the Mental Health Studio designed for schools and museums to educate kids about the nature and symptoms of mental illness (Renz-Beaulaurier, 1997). Other examples are the multimedia-based Risk Advisor and RiskTeacher that provide a personalized assessment of risk of HIV exposure and education to reduce risk.

Since most agencies, educational institutions, and research centers have a Web site, consumers can quickly find the latest information about treatments and medications. Some agencies and research centers loosely link together to form a virtual network for providing quality information about particular topics, for example, Mental Health Net and CancerNet.[*] CancerNet has patient, health professional, and researcher interfaces with access to expert-reviewed information in the form of publications, databases, research and treatment summaries, and frequently asked questions.

Expert review allows consumers to trust the information provided by a Web site. Knowing what Web information to trust is a difficult issue for consumers. For example, one Web site operated by a physician who owns FEN/PHEN drug patents, included the following statement: "I have found that FEN/PHEN consistently and rapidly remits alcohol, heroin, and cocaine craving. . . . Furthermore, FEN/PHEN has been highly effective in the

TABLE 5.7. Applications That Support Client Self-Help

Problem/Situation	Technology Used	Example	Source
Reducing exposure to HIV/AIDS/STDs	CAI and multimedia	RiskAdvisor and RiskTeacher	www.path.org/ html/ riskadvisor. htm
Building a support group of people to help cope with HIV/ AIDS	Networked computers, discussion forums, resource database	CHESS	Boberg et al., 1995
Helping persons with depression	CAI and interactive dialogue	Overcoming Depression	www.MAIW. COM/
Treating agoraphobia and panic	Multimedia guides, DBMS, behavioral therapy	Fear Fighter	www. qualcare. demon.co.uk/
Reducing stress and improving self-esteem	CAI, cognitive intervention techniques	HELP-Esteem and HELP-Stress	www.catsco. com/
Providing enjoyable education for youth about difficult life decisions	Educational and entertaining stories, role-playing	Drunken with Love, a Path Interactive Story	www.path.org/ html/path_ interactive_ stories.htm
Help families and individuals cope with disabilities by planning	Information, resources listing, databases, listservs	National Institute on Life Planning for persons with disabilities	www.sonic. net/nilp/
Self-monitoring to find patterns and solutions for mood disorders	Database and custom-designed forms and reports	Mood Monitor	www. ourcorner. com/wt/
Preventing suicide	Informational text and links to resources	Suicide . . . read this first	www. metanoia.org/ suicide/

management of affective and obsessive-compulsive disorders previously refractory to conventional therapy." As major problems were reported with FEN/PHEN, this wording was removed and the site renamed to the FEN/PHEN Crisis Center. The site still claimed FEN/PHEN was safe, but only if following the physician's treatment protocol. The site also solicited patients by offering a toll-free telephone number and e-mail address. As of this writing, the site had only one link to another drug site.

This example illustrates that self-promotion and conflict of interest are not policed on the Internet. A similar problem exists regarding psychological tests that are published on the Internet without proper validation and consumer education. Consumers also have difficulty placing Internet information in its larger context and integrating it with previous research. The saying that "a little information is dangerous" applies, as consumers can quickly develop only a superficial understanding of many complex problems. Every practitioner remembers their first abnormal psychology course in which students applied abnormal labels to the behavior of friends, family, and themselves. Practitioners and agencies must help consumers become "educated" about problems by guiding their Internet use with links to reputable and responsible sites and incorporating the discussion of Internet information as part of their intervention.

Virtual Support Groups

On-line support groups have been very popular since bulletin boards were developed in the 1980s (Schneider and Tooley, 1995). Self-help discussion forums exist on almost any topic; typical support groups focus on alcoholism, cancer, and various other health and mental health disorders. Large network providers, such as CompuServe and America Online, offer many self-help forums. Groups communicate via e-mail in a discussion forum or in on-line chat rooms. Often a volunteer or professional moderator exists. Groups have primarily been text based, although voice and video options are becoming available. Internet discussion forums provide a support community and often result in more extensive one-on-one support. Various lists of Web support groups are available over the Internet.* Finn (1996) and others (Ferguson, 1996; Lambert, 1998; Schneider and Tooley, 1995) describe support group advantages and disadvantages, some of which are summarized in Table 5.8.

Professionals' roles in on-line groups are still evolving. Some professionals do not identify themselves for fear of liability and violating ethical codes that do not sanction on-line therapy. Others identify themselves and try to assume a professional role. The recent case in which one longtime member of an on-line support group confessed to murder suggests that professionals may have certain legal responsibilities even if they do not reveal their professional status.

One well-researched self-help project is the Comprehensive Health Enhancement Support System (CHESS) (Gustafson et. al., 1993; Boberg et al., 1995). CHESS is an integrated set of computer services that allows

TABLE 5.8. Advantages and Disadvantages of On-Line Support Groups

Advantages	Disadvantages
Greater access to support	Destructive interactions
Use from the privacy of one's home at any time	Lack of clear and accountable leadership
Large variety of groups to meet the needs of those with esoteric concerns	Promotes social isolation
Reduction of barriers related to social status	Limited access to non-computer-using populations
Encouragement of reluctant participants	Lack of research about benefits
Enhances communication of those with interpersonal difficulties	Difficulty in providing emotional cues
High level of concern for other participants	Easy domination by one or a few people
Users think before they type and submit	Dependent on good keyboarding skills
Availability of a searchable, historical written record	Difficulty in following streams of conversation

people with serious health issues, such as breast cancer or AIDS/HIV, to form a support community. CHESS uses personal computers that are placed in users' homes and linked together via modem through a central computer. CHESS services include information, referrals, decision support, and social support. CHESS goals are to improve the emotional health of users, increase the cost-effectiveness of health and human services, and reduce the incidence of risk-taking behaviors that can lead to injury or illness. CHESS users reported improved cognitive functioning, increased social support, greater participation in their health care, a more active lifestyle, and fewer negative emotions, as compared to control subjects who reported that they remained the same or became worse regarding these variables (Boberg et al., 1995).

Another type of mutual support application uses the Internet and video cameras to help people stay connected to family and friends receiving care. With this technology, child care centers and nursing homes can place cameras in service areas and broadcast a continuous video feed over the Internet to friends and loved ones at work or home.

Self-Help, Insight, and Treatment

Applications that are mass-marketed to help clients obtain information and advice independent of practitioner supervision are often referred to as self-help applications, which parallel the self-help book market. They are seen by many as "pop" psychology rather than "true" therapy. However, self-help applications have greater potential than books. They can contain sophisticated presentations along with monitoring techniques that continuously analyze progress and prescribe personalized remedial work.

Sophisticated self-help applications can provide self-insight and treatment. One of the first self-help application programs was Eliza. Joseph Weizenbaum developed Eliza in 1964 to illustrate the conversational limitations of a computer. It was named Eliza after Eliza Doolittle in the play *My Fair Lady*. In the play, Eliza Doolittle was taught to speak "proper English," but in reality, she was only a commoner pretending to be upper class. Eliza is a computer application that pretends to be a therapist by speaking the "proper" jargon of a nondirective therapist. During the interaction, Eliza rephrases client questions and presents emotional and psychological statements. Although Eliza is simple and often meaningless, it fascinated users and sparked interest in the use of computers to provide therapy.

A subsequent program, Racter, combines user narrative with stored phrases to converse with the user. Racter can also be absurd and meaningless; nevertheless, people enjoy the conversation and some even claim they benefit from its use. One user confessed to me that, one time, when she could not get to sleep after an argument with her spouse, and it was 2:30 A.M. and she could not telephone anyone, she had a long conversation with Racter to relieve her loneliness and depression. Other self-help packages focus on areas such as dream analysis, personal intimacy, marital relations, sexual dysfunction, stress management, assertiveness training, and diet management.* One self-help program, Mind Prober, constructs narrative psychological profiles of the user based on responses to an adjective checklist. Mind Prober was marketed as entertainment, although it's assessment is based on psychological research. The popularized "parlor game" version of Mind Prober sold hundreds of thousands more copies than the version for human service professionals.

Colby (1979) summarized the advantages of a self-help treatment application over seeing a human therapist:

> It does not get tired, angry, or bored. It is always willing to listen and to give evidence of having heard. It can work at any time of the day or night, every day and every month. It does not have family prob-

lems. It does not try to perform when sick or hungover. It has no facial expressions of contempt, shock, surprise, etc. It is polite, friendly, and always has good manners. It is comprehensible and has a perfect memory. It does not seek money. It will cost only a few dollars a session. It does not engage in sex with its patients. It does what it is supposed to do and not more. (p. 151)

Colby's application, Overcoming Depression, provides cognitive therapy for mild to moderate depression (Lambert, 1998).* The program consists of a text mode interwoven with a dialogue mode. The text mode provides facts, concepts, and explanations about depression, along with cognitive strategies for alleviating the disorder and preventing its recurrence. The dialogue mode involves the user in therapeutically directed conversations by interpreting and responding appropriately to the user's everyday language. The purposes of the dialogue mode are to encourage free expression, provide support, arouse hope, individualize therapeutic learning, and promote cognitive action, thereby helping users put their innermost thoughts and feelings into words that can be looked at and thought about. In follow-up studies, Overcoming Depression achieved a satisfaction rating of 96 percent, taken from a sample of 142 users. However, its validity and reliability have not been established.

Apprehension about self-help consumer applications is not coming from consumers but from professionals. Although professionals should be concerned about unethical and problematic IT applications, some of their apprehension is due to a lack of understanding of technology and of the time needed to relearn and change traditional approaches. Valid professional critique of self-help applications is necessary to give consumers the information they need to evaluate the appropriateness and effectiveness of self-help applications.

CONCLUSION

Although human service IT applications are currently not numerous, their rate of development has been increasing. This increase will continue as human service professionals become more IT literate and user-friendly development tools become available. The Internet will lead to many IT applications and allow direct distribution between developer and consumer. Overall, we are in the beginning phase of using the potentials of IT to support practice and create new practice methods.

REVIEW AND DISCUSSION QUESTIONS

1. Which IT applications in this chapter have the most profound effect on IT professionals, clients, agencies, and citizens?
2. Can you think of additional human service IT applications that could be helpful?
3. Do human service problems exist for which IT applications would never be appropriate?
4. What problems do you foresee with self-help applications?
5. What role do professionals have in helping clients use self-help applications?

PART III:
DESIGNING, DEVELOPING, AND IMPLEMENTING INFORMATION TECHNOLOGY SYSTEMS

Chapter 6

The Process of Developing IT Applications

INTRODUCTION

Developing and implementing IT applications is a major, often irreversible, change. With any change, something new is gained as something old is lost. Therefore, we can expect resistance to leaving the old behind and discomfort about the new situation and the unknowns. The adage "garbage in, garbage out" (GIGO) suggests that organizations have had problems developing and implementing IT applications. GIGO may be caused by users purposely inputting incorrect information, by accidental errors made during data entry, or by an application that does not contain the appropriate information. The first two causes of GIGO reflect implementation failures and suggest better user involvement and training. The third cause reflects application design failure and suggests a better understanding of what information is needed, how to process it, and how to present it to users. Both application design and implementation will be covered in this chapter. Excluded from this discussion is the development of software applications that address nonorganizational needs (for example, a computerized wheelchair or a home computer game).

Minimizing the human impact of IT applications has been a challenging management task. Because of the money, time, effort, commitment, trust, and habit changes required, agencies should address some difficult questions before developing IT applications:

- How is IT similar to other organizational changes the agency has successfully implemented?
- What change stages and activities are involved?
- What approaches or strategies are recommended?
- What expertise is needed, how can it be obtained, and where should it be placed in the agency?
- What tools, techniques, and skills are needed?

This chapter addresses the answers to these questions. IT applications have a greater chance of success if they follow the well-proven development process presented in this chapter.

BASIC CONCEPTS

IT Applications As Change

Whether an IT application is a generic package or custom developed, changes in processes and people are involved. The extent of change depends on factors such as the number of processes affected by the application, the differences between the old and new systems, and the number of people affected. Because people are involved, developing IT applications is a "people change" process as well as a technical process.

According to the National Science Foundation (NSF), people and organizational change is as important as technical developments. NSF's research indicates that a "rule of thumb" when developing IT applications is that hardware absorbs 10 percent of the overall cost, software and software development absorb 40 percent, and implementation and training absorb 50 percent (Neilson, 1985). When developing IT applications, agencies often devote resources in the reverse proportion. That is, they spend 50 percent on hardware, 40 percent on software and software development, and 10 percent on implementation and training. Sometimes agencies consider implementation and training as additional tasks for a staff already overburdened with a new application.

The processes that IT supports are rarely new in an organization. Similar noncomputerized processes usually already existed, although these may be simple and disorganized. Developing IT, then, is system improvement. The system currently in operation becomes the starting point for the development of any new system.

Information technology rarely operates in isolation. Even a small application, such as a computerized mailing list, will influence other agency processes. Eventually IT spreads beyond one application to all information-based agency processes. Since IT rarely occurs in isolation, planning for overall agency IT is necessary before any development is attempted because detailed plans for specific applications need to be developed within the framework of an overall IT plan. IT that follows a planned change process has a better chance of success.

The Change Process and Change Management

Much of the information on change and change management is very familiar to human service professionals. We are experts in changing clients and their environments. However, human service professionals tend to become fascinated with technology and have difficulty applying their expertise to IT. The situation is similar to the old adage about "the cobbler's son not having shoes." Figure 6.1 presents the basic change process for individuals. It is important to understand that this process occurs with any change and often involves resistance and fear on the part of those involved. The impact of change can be minimized if users are well informed, if they are involved in the process, and if the change is gradual and aligned with user values. Being able to visualize the end result also helps reduce resistance.

The changes involved in IT follow a process very similar to other changes, and the process of planned change is well researched. At its simplest, the stages of any planned change effort involve feasibility, assessment, implementation, and evaluation. The following quotation compares the changes associated with developing IT to the stages of psychotherapy:

> Just as psychotherapy begins with an analysis and assessment of the client's psychological needs, the system development process begins with an analysis of information needs. The psychotherapy process proceeds to helping the client discover and design new ways to meet his or her psychological needs; the information system development process proceeds to the design of a system of gathering, processing, and producing information. Psychotherapy concludes with the successful integration of new attitudes and patterns of behavior; information system development concludes with the installation of a new, successful information system. (Zefran, 1984, p. 21)

Although the change process can be stated simply and logically, implementing change often becomes a process of "muddling through." In muddling through, the overall plan is kept in mind as one struggles to find the most appropriate solutions to day-to-day problems. Stated more bluntly, "When you're up to your elbows in alligators, it's hard to remember that the initial objective was to drain the swamp."

Often, IT is only one component of a larger change process. Figure 6.2 illustrates the stages in developing a multiagency information system simultaneously with a multiagency collaborative effort. Since the information system is often the driving force behind establishing a multiagency collaborative effort, its planning is often confused with the planning for the overall effort. Developing a multiagency collaborative effort is a more complex change than developing a multiagency information system.

Having presented some basic concepts, the following material discusses several information management tasks in more detail.

FIGURE 6.1. Individual Change Process

> When involved with change that is beyond one's control, an individual may go through the following intellectual and emotional phases.

Phase 1: Discomfort and resistance
Definition: The individual fears the unknown, laments the loss and comfort of the old, and may not believe that change needs to occur.
Example: Why change at this time? Things were not great, but they were going OK.

Phase 2: Search for information
Definition: The individual tries to find out as much as possible about the change and its source. If little accurate information is available, rumors are accepted as valid information.
Example: What have you heard? Mike heard from a friend that the IT Department ordered the change.

Phase 3: Anger and blame
Definition: The individual reviews the past, seeking a cause or blame for the discomfort.
Example: I'll bet this is part of a larger scheme to remedy the problem of continually late reports.

Phase 4: Despair
Definition: The individual feels hopeless, helpless, and has a sense of loss and emptiness. The past keeps going through the individual's thoughts.
Example: We might as well go along. We certainly have no influence here. Why does this always happen where I work?

Phase 5: Humor
Definition: The individual uses humor to relive the past and heal the pain and frustration.
Example: Do you remember the look on Mike's face when we told him about the change?

Phase 6: Reaching out
Definition: The individual talks to others to share the frustration and to see how they are handling the change.
Example: You sure look sad. Can you believe it has come to this?

Phase 7: Rationalization and accommodation
Definition: The individual begins looking for reasons to accept the change.
Example: The only good thing about the change is that we won't have to do hand counts anymore. I say, if you can't fight it, join it.

Phase 8: Emotional reorientation
Definition: The individual emotionally accepts the change.
Example: Maybe it won't be so bad after all. It will be nice to be working with new computers for a change.

Phase 9: Acceptance
Definition: The individual comes to terms with the change intellectually and emotionally.
Example: If we have to do it, let's get it done and do it right.

Phase 10: Involvement and stability
Definition: The individual accepts the change and uses it in a positive manner.
Example: I don't know what we did without this new system.

FIGURE 6.2. Community Change and Information System Activities

Stage 1: Engagement and Sensing

Community activities: Determining who supports multiagency collaboration and why.

IT activities: Determining which stakeholders have similar views toward IT.

Stage 2: Clarifying Overall Direction

Community activities: Identifying the conditions of concern, assumptions, vision, and guiding principles for multiagency collaboration.

IT activities: Clarifying the role IT might play in the overall effort.

Stage 3: Assessing the Situation

Community activities: Collecting data/facts and prioritizing needs/strengths for multiagency collaboration.

IT activities: Completing an IT needs and strengths analysis (see Figure 6.3).

Stage 4: Intervention Planning

Community activities: Developing goals, objectives, and work plans for multiagency collaboration.

IT activities: Developing the IT plan, including implementation and system design options.

Stage 5: Implementing

Community activities: Deciding the course of action and doing what is planned.

IT activities: System development and deployment.

Stage 6: Monitoring and Evaluating

Community activities: Monitoring the overall change and determining if it accomplishes the collaboration goals.

IT activities: Monitoring IT application performance and maintenance and determining if the IT goals were met.

THE APPLICATION DESIGN
AND DEVELOPMENT PROCESS

Agencies progress through major stages, engage in complex activities, and face important decisions when developing IT. Figure 6.3 summarizes the activities involved at each stage of the application development process. The process is both sequential and repetitive. As decisions are made throughout the process, some stages are repeated, while other new stages are entered. Each stage builds on and amplifies the activities of the previous stage and addresses some of the tasks in future stages. For example, the first stage, feasibility and preparedness, must be given repeated consideration throughout the process. In addition, success criteria developed in the feasibility stage are used during the evaluation stage.

The stages in Figure 6.3 can be applied to any IT application development. Slight modifications of the process often occur for different types of applications, but the basic stages remain the same. Figure 6.4 illustrates the stages in the development process for designing an agency Web site. Figure 6.5 presents the stages in the development process for a distance education workshop.

The amount of time devoted to each stage can vary substantially, depending on the size and complexity of the application. The 80/20 rule suggests that you can complete 80 percent of an application using only 20 percent of total resources. However, completing the remaining 20 percent of the application requires 80 percent of total resources. This final 20 percent can cause frustration, especially to users who see little progress as they eagerly wait for the final application.

The progression of the stages in the development process may appear scientific and precise, but the process is more of an art than a science. The time and effort devoted to each activity varies for different applications. For example, if an agency purchases an information system from a vendor, it may skip some design phase activities because the vendor completed them. However, the agency should compile documentation on all stages, no matter when they were completed, where they were completed, or who completed them.

Exploration of Feasibility and Preparedness

The first stage is to assess preparedness and feasibility. The activities in this stage establish communication channels that help identify the resources, support, and concerns. Communication at this stage helps staff develop realistic expectations of the changes that may occur and the anticipated results. The decision to proceed with the application should be well-

FIGURE 6.3. Stages in the Process of Developing an IT Application

Stage 1: Exploration of Feasibility and Preparedness

Communicate about the IT effort to all staff.

Establish an agency steering committee and application-specific subcommittees.

Define the application's purpose, development timetables, and responsibilities.

Estimate resources for change, i.e., money, time, expertise, and commitment of key individuals.

Estimate improved application impacts (positive and negative).

Assess the expectations and reactions of those who will be affected by the application.

Draft continuous improvement mechanisms and success measures.

Prepare and circulate preparedness and feasibility report.

Decide to proceed or terminate effort.

Stage 2: Assessment (Systems Analysis)

Identify the major needs and decisions the application will address.

Define the characteristics of the information needed, its source, and collection methods.

Analyze current and future data input, processing, and output operations and requirements, e.g., forms, data manipulations, files, reports, and flow of information from collection to dissemination.

Evaluate problems with how things are currently done.

Identify resources on which to build the new application.

Collect baseline data on success measures.

Review similar efforts in other agencies and request help from national or state associations.

Prepare and circulate assessment.

Decide to proceed or terminate effort.

Stage 3: Conceptual Design

Finalize application scope, goals, objectives, continuous improvement measures, and success measures.

FIGURE 6.3 *(continued)*

Develop alternative conceptual designs (i.e., fields, records, files, data manipulation, forms, reports, and graphics).

Apply design specifications such as flexibility, reliability, processing and statistical requirements, growth potential, life expectancy, and tie in with other applications.

Apply restrictions to designs (i.e., required and desired data frequency, volume, security, confidentiality, turn-around time, money, time, and expertise.

Design mechanisms to collect and report continuous improvement information.

Translate designs into software, hardware, and networking configurations.

Detail the advantages, disadvantages, and assumptions of alternate designs.

Prepare and circulate conceptual design and decide to proceed or terminate effort.

Stage 4: Detailed Design and Development

Set up controls and technical performance standards for chosen design.

Select the software for the chosen design.

Select the hardware to match the software.

Select the necessary networking and communications.

Design and develop data collection forms, data manipulation, operations, file specifications, database structures, error checks, storage mechanisms, backup procedures, and output reports.

Prepare documentation and instruction manuals.

Stage 5: Testing and Preparation

Prepare system operators, users, and others to receive the application.

Develop agency policy and procedural changes necessary for the new application.

Develop performance specifications and testing plan.

Test programming, forms, operational procedures, instructions, reports, and the use of outputs.

Educate and train system operators, data users, and others affected.

Stage 6: Implementation

Develop and approve conversion plan (e.g., stop old system when new system starts or run old and new systems simultaneously for comparison).

Incorporate application into standard operating procedures (e.g., performance appraisals, new employee orientation, and training).

Reorganize staff and space if necessary.

Convert from old to new equipment, new processing methods, and new procedures.

Ensure all systems and controls are working.

Stage 7: Monitoring and Evaluation

Compare application performance with initial application objectives (e.g., outputs used in decision making, users satisfied, client services improved).

Relate benefits and costs to initial estimates.

Ensure continuous improvement mechanisms are working and remedial action is taken.

Stage 8: Operation, Maintenance, and Modification

Prepare backup and emergency plans and procedures.

Complete documentation (e.g., instructions for adding to, deleting from, or modifying application).

Assign persons responsible for data integrity, system maintenance, backup, new software appropriateness, virus protection, etc.

Provide continuous training of users.

Continue to add desired enhancements and to maintain and debug the application.

Begin Stage 1 if additional subsystems are to be developed.

Source: Adapted from "Strategies for Information System Development" by D. Schoech, L. L. Schkade, and R. S. Mayers (1982), *Administration in Social Work,* 5(3/4), pp. 25-26.

FIGURE 6.4. Stages in the Application Development Process Applied to Designing an Agency Web Site

Stage 1: Feasibility and Preparedness

- Develop an overall concept, create a development team, and locate political and financial sponsors.

Stage 2: Assessment

- Determine potential users and the activities, type of access, etc., needed for each user.
- Determine your organization's needs, e.g., tracking use, public relations, confidentiality, indexing on national lists, etc.
- Determine the hardware, software, and resources available.

Stage 3: Conceptual Design

- Develop a prototype.
- Load prototype onto server.

Stages 4 and 5: Detailed Design and Development and Testing and Preparation

- Test the prototype with a wide variety of potential users and refine.

Stage 6: Implementation

- Notify Internet search engines of your site.

Stage 7: Monitoring and Evaluation

- Compare use statistics to those planned.
- Report use statistics to key decision makers.
- Continually seek feedback.

Stage 8: Operation and Maintenance

- Upgrade the hardware, Web applications, and connectivity.
- Upgrade the information, links, and functions on the Web pages.
- Add new functions and enhancements.

FIGURE 6.5. Stages in the Application Development Process Applied to Web-Delivered Distance Learning

Stage 1: Feasibility and Preparedness

This stage involves the trainer, curriculum specialist, technology specialist, and sponsor/funder determining whether the content and situation being considered is appropriate for distance learning. Some content, such as teaching of certain interviewing or reflective skills, may require face-to-face interaction. Some working environments may not be capable of accepting distance learning due to technological or political realities. In determining feasibility, the group must think through all the remaining stages.

Stage 2: Assessment

Identify the needs of all parties involved that might impact distance learning. These include the learning style of trainees and the needs of trainees, trainers, trainees' organizations, and the sponsoring organization. Also, assess the content to be delivered and the technologies currently available.

Stage 3: Conceptual Design

This stage involves dividing the training into small independent modules. Next, for each module, the best distance learning techniques should be selected. Before new materials are developed, a thorough search should be conducted to ensure that existing materials or workshop modules are not currently available, for example, via a WWW link.

Stage 4: Detailed Application Design and Development

Develop and test the materials and get the teacher, trainees, and trainee organization prepared for the training. The following items need to be prepared:

- A syllabus including textbook(s), assignments, and evaluation and grading policies
- Lecture notes
- A glossary of terms
- A set of frequently asked questions
- Handouts and discussion questions
- Examinations
- WWW links
- Practice quizzes and tests

FIGURE 6.5 *(continued)*

Stage 5: Testing and Preparation

If this is the instructors' first distance learning experience, they may need assessment and training in two areas. The first area is giving up control by backing off so learners can think on their own and by focusing on the process of learning rather than the product of the learning. The second area is creating a pleasant learning environment from the moment the learner registers and keeping students prepared and motivated despite the distance.

If this is the students' first distance learning experience, they might need training on the technology used and ways to acquire the motivation and discipline that distance learning requires.

Stage 6: Implementation

This stage involves delivering the course.

Stage 7: Monitoring and Evaluation

This stage involves administering and evaluating the assignments and using the evaluation instruments that were derived from the course objectives and needs identified in the assessment.

Stage 8: Operation, Maintenance, and Modification

This stage involves making any needed changes if the course is offered again.

founded and well-supported. However, tangible benefits do not always exist to justify this decision. Sometimes the desire to proceed must be based on only a belief that the application will allow the agency to function better, serve its clients, and survive.

Implementing a sophisticated application may be too much change for an agency with a haphazard manual information system, little computer or telecommunications expertise, and little experience in using data for decision making. Careful planning, preparation, and staff training can ease this transition. Alternatively, agencies could develop small applications of limited scope, with the intention of making a step-by-step transition from a manual to an electronic environment. Assessing preparedness for change is of crucial importance because the changes involving IT cannot be mandated. Staff can easily sabotage an application through activities such as withholding data or entering incorrect data.

Assessment of the Situation (Systems Analysis)

The second stage is to undertake an analysis of the existing system. The existing system, no matter how underdeveloped, evolved to meet agency needs. Consequently, it should be a source of ideas for designing any new application. Studying the existing situation involves analyzing data collection processes and forms, the flow of information from one person or operation to another, information manipulation, and information use in agency operations. Examining how staff make day-to-day decisions can uncover and document that agency practices deviate from agency image or stated policies and procedures. Those providing information during the analysis stage must trust that it will not be used punitively or for non-application development purposes.

Another activity at this stage is to examine similar applications locally and nationally. A representative group from the agency can visit its counterparts in similar agencies or agencies that have similar applications. Internet discussion groups can be used to connect to similar agencies nationally. Personal visits and conversations with key personnel are often worth the time and cost. Most agencies are very willing to share their successes and mistakes, as long as their mistakes are held in confidence. Part of the search for outside expertise should involve an examination of the literature.

A final activity at this stage involves checking with national associations and experts for advice. Often national associations have someone specializing in IT who has familiarity with similar applications. They can also refer agencies to consultants who can provide expertise on structuring the change process and designing and developing the application. Expenditures at this stage often save time, money, and frustration in later stages.

The result of the assessment stage is documentation on how the present system functions, why it functions the way it does, and the needed and desired improvements.

Conceptual Design

The third stage involves conceptual design. Expectations and resources identified in the feasibility stage and the problems, information needs, and desires uncovered in the assessment of the existing situation guide the activities in this stage. The conceptual design stage investigates several options for the application. Hardware, software, and networking options are examined with regard to agency and design requirements. The advantages and disadvantages of each design are explored. A major decision is whether to use packaged software or to custom develop software. Another decision concerns how to connect computers together into a network. The result of this stage is a chosen design to be modified through more detailed developmental work.

Detailed Design and Development

The detailed design and development stage produces a working application of software, hardware, communications, and procedures. Often, this stage requires professional IT expertise.

A discussion of the hardware and software options illustrates the decisions and problems of this stage. Choosing hardware and software can be a difficult task because many other decisions are dependent on what is chosen. In addition, few agency staff have the expertise to make or monitor these purchases. A transportation analogy is helpful in understanding the problem inherent in hardware and software purchase decisions. Most people recommend buying the car that they know and use rather than thoroughly analyzing the transportation needs of the buyer. Similarly, IT specialists like to develop applications based on IT they already understand. That is, hardware, software, and networking recommendations often reflect product familiarity rather than a rational selection based on user needs. Another problem is that computer vendors, similar to automobile dealers, have a financial incentive to recommend high-profit or overstocked products. Complicating the decision is that no "best" application exists just as no "best" car exists. Many hardware and software combinations will meet present and future agency needs. The success of the choice is heavily dependent on how well the assessment specifies these needs and if the needs are considered in the selection process.

Because of the technical complexity of this stage, human service personnel often become overinvolved in the technical aspects. This overinvolvement satisfies the challenge to control the technical process, but should not be used to escape from more people-oriented activities, such as user involvement and documentation.

Testing and Preparation for Change

Once the application is developed, staff must determine if it and users are ready for implementation. Testing is extremely important. Introducing a faulty application frustrates staff, wastes time, and threatens credibility. The application should be tested with standard and nonstandard conditions, i.e., infrequently used data as well as routine, high-volume data. Testing is especially important for complex applications that integrate many systems and perform core operations for the agency.

Although open communication prepares staff to receive an application, certain groups, such as operators and users, require special preparation for accepting and using the application. As with application testing, spending the time and money to educate, involve, and train staff pays off through more trouble-free conversion and less resistance to change.

Implementation

Implementation is the process of installing a new application or converting from an old to a new application. It involves integrating the application and the changes it brings into the total agency structure, procedures, and work habits.

Four basic approaches exist to convert from an old to a new application. A combination of these approaches may also be used. The first approach is total or *direct conversion,* whereby the agency discontinues the old application when it implements the new application. Since direct conversion is abrupt, it is most suitable when the old application is significantly different from the new application and involves little comparable data. The second approach, *parallel conversion,* involves operating the old and new applications simultaneously until the new application meets predetermined performance standards. Parallel conversion allows a continuous comparison of the outputs of the old and new applications. However, running parallel applications is costly, and maintaining two applications can overwhelm users. The third approach is *phase-in, modular,* or *gradual conversion.* This approach divides the application into independent modules and implements one module at a time. The fourth approach, *pilot conversion,* implements a section of the application in one part of the organization at a time, thereby producing minimum disruption. Whatever approach is taken, conversion can still become a costly, frustrating, and never-ending process.

Monitoring and Evaluation

To monitor and evaluate results requires feedback loops throughout the application development process. Feedback compares actual performance to design criteria and expectations. Studies have found that continuous improvement mechanisms are essential for identifying potential problems and fine-tuning the application (Hile, 1998). Although evaluation is one of the final stages, success criteria must be a consideration from the very beginning of the application development process. Feedback is especially important during continued operation to ensure that the application continues to be cost-effective in meeting the needs of the agency.

Operation, Maintenance, and Modification

Since no agency is static, application development is a continuous process. The activities during the operation, maintenance, and modification stage ensure that the evolving application will continually meet the agency's needs. The life of an application depends on the changes occurring in an agency. Applications in highly volatile agencies may require major changes after one to two years. Those in very stable agencies may function well for three to seven years with minimal changes. Agencies often rapidly outgrow the first application as they discover the potential of IT. However, the learning that occurs with the initial application will help the agency make longer-lasting choices in the future.

Each stage in Figure 6.3 begins with the determination of goals, objectives, tasks, schedules, checkpoints, responsibilities, and completion criteria for that stage. Each stage ends with the documentation of all activities in a report. This report then becomes the basis for deciding whether to proceed to the next stage. Completing all stages for a relatively small application may take several months. For large applications, such as the development of a comprehensive information system, the process may take several years. In some cases, the time required to develop a complex application is so long that the application is never completed before a redesign is considered.

An agency must complete all developmental stages for any application, but different approaches toward the development process do exist. The next section discusses several of these approaches, focusing on the tools, techniques, and skills needed in developing IT.

TOOLS, TECHNIQUES, AND SKILLS

Analysis and Design Techniques

Large system development efforts, such as automating a state child protective services or mental health department, can use analysis and design techniques that have been developed in business over many years. One group of techniques, called structured methodology, subsumes a variety of system development techniques (Yourdon, 1991). It organizes the systems analysis and conceptual design stages by using a series of increasingly detailed refinements.

Another group of techniques is referred to as *object-oriented design* (Yourdon and Argila, 1996). Object-oriented design views subsystems as independent modules of a system that can be reused in other applications. For example, one module might present the user with a series of multiple-choice questions. If object-oriented techniques are used and this module is developed as an independent subsystem, then it can be used in any application that presents multiple-choice questions.

Planning and scheduling are additional structured techniques. They help guide the development process from start to finish in an orderly fashion. Scheduling techniques include goals, objectives, and task statements, as well as scheduling charts, as in Figure 6.6. Writing skills are necessary to draft the clear, specific, and measurable objectives needed to guide and evaluate all processes involved. The specification of control and feedback points in the development process ensures that deviations are detected and corrected early in the process.

Another group of structured techniques involves graphic representation of the application design and the design process. Graphics allow hardware configurations, data flows, and decision processes to be reviewed quickly. One simple graphic representation technique for visually presenting the

FIGURE 6.6. A Simple Scheduling Chart for Completing a Two-Semester-Long Research Project

Task to be completed	Sep	Oct	Nov	Dec	Jan	Feb	Mar	Apr	May
Have research proposal approved	✓								
Literature review completed		✓							
Methodology section completed			✓						
Sample defined and measurement instruments developed			✓						
Data collected				✓					
Data analyzed					✓				
First draft of report submitted for input						✓			
Final draft of report to committee							✓		
Revisions made and report disseminated								✓	
Celebrate									✓

application hardware, its functions, and functional relationships is a block or *system diagram* (see Figure 6.7). A *data flow diagram* (see Figure 6.8) graphically illustrates the flow of data and decision logic in an application. Although the data flow diagram is easy to construct and read, it can present only limited information. A *system flowchart* (see Figure 6.9) uses standardized symbols to illustrate how data flows from one part of the application to another, the operations that are performed, and the data media being used. System flowcharts are relatively easy to construct and understand, but they tend to become lengthy and bulky.

Another useful graphic representation technique is a *decision tree*, in which the trunk represents a decision problem and the branches represent

FIGURE 6.7. A System Diagram

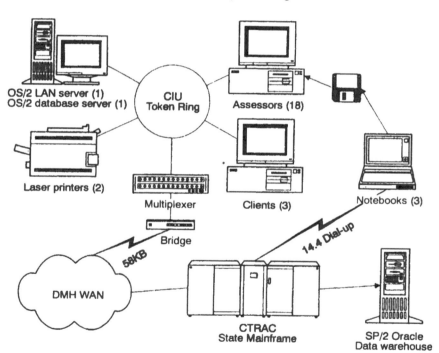

FIGURE 6.8. A Data Flow Diagram

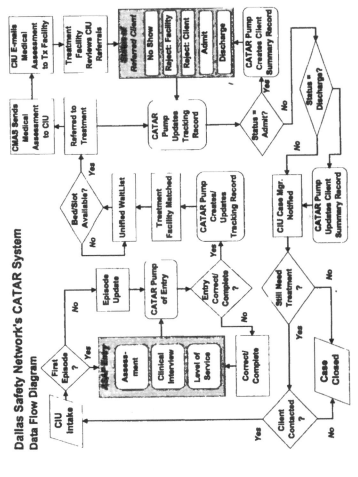

Source: From "Dallas Target Cities Safety Network Management Information System" by M. A. Krepcho et al., 1998, Computers in Human Services, 14(3/4), p. 36. Copyright 1998 by The Haworth Press, Inc. Reprinted by permission.

161

FIGURE 6.9. A System Flowchart

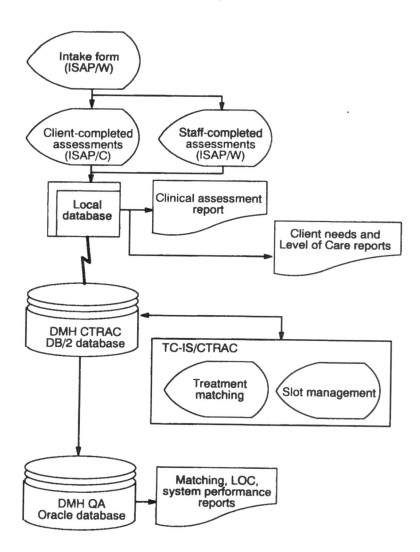

Source: From "St. Louis Target City Information System" by M. G. Hile et al., 1998, *Computers in Human Services, 14*(3/4), p. 123. Copyright 1998 by The Haworth Press, Inc. Reprinted by permission.

alternative solutions. Each major branch can have additional alternative or branching options. The decision tree in Figure 6.10 presents the decisions that occur at a telephone information and referral service. As each decision is made, the logic branches out to more-detailed considerations. A similar technique for graphically representing a decision situation is a *decision table*, often called a logic table. Decision tables present the rules for combining the conditions tested and the actions taken (see Figure 6.11). Rule 1 of Figure 6.11 states that if a caller's condition is a serious human service problem requiring help, and natural support groups exist, then the worker should discuss the support group option, while providing reassurance and follow-up. Rule 5 states that if the caller meets none of the conditions, then the worker should reassure the caller and terminate the call.

This section presented a few of the many techniques and tools used in a structured approach to analysis and design. Other applications are available that help the user apply structured techniques. These applications guide an agency through CASE (computer-aided software engineering) methodologies (Perrone, 1997; Topper, Ouellette, and Jorgensen, 1993). They can provide the application development and implementation expertise, rigor, and techniques that many agencies lack.

The Request for Proposal and Vendor Contract

Buying an application can be compared to marriage, since the agency and vendor are entering a long-term arrangement. This is especially true if the application solves a large agency problem. Several skills, tools, and techniques are available for structuring the communications and agreements between an agency and a vendor.

The request for proposal (RFP) provides a format for communicating application requirements and ensuring comparable proposals. Figure 6.12 outlines the contents of a typical RFP. At least three vendor responses are recommended. If the application is large and complex, a bidders' conference can allow vendors to tour current operations and ask questions about the potential application. Figure 6.13 presents some "conventional wisdom" that improves the chances of choosing and working with a vendor/consultant successfully. The guidelines for choosing an outside vendor or consultant are similar to those for selecting any outside consultant.

The formal signed vendor contract is an important document in developing an application. It helps remove excessively optimistic promises and "sales talk" from the proposal. The vendor contract reduces misunderstanding and becomes the agency's only assurance that it will receive the specified application. It states the responsibilities of both parties and describes the job, the price, and the contingencies should things not go as

FIGURE 6.10. Decision Tree for Answering a Telephone Call for Help

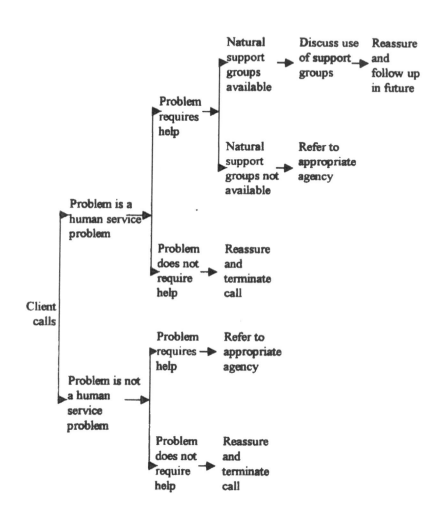

FIGURE 6.11. Decision or Logic Tables for Answering a Telephone Call for Help

Conditions and Actions	Rule				
	1	2	3	4	5
Conditions					
Problem is a human service problem	Y	Y	Y	N	N
Problem is serious enough to require help	Y	N	Y	Y	N
Natural support groups can provide help	Y		N		
Actions					
Refer to appropriate human service agency			X		
Refer to appropriate non-human service agency				X	
Discuss the use of natural support groups	X				
Reassure and follow up in future	X				
Reassure and terminate call		X			X

Y = Yes, N = No, X = action to take based on the conditions that exist

planned. The response to the RFP should become part of the contract with the chosen vendor. This ensures that both parties understand the nature of the arrangement and eliminates the reliance on general purpose contracts, which often can be confusing to the agency and generally do not contain details pertinent to the application. Some agencies demand the source code in situations in which the vendor defaults on the contract, fails to support the application developed, or goes out of business. This protection may be necessary because of the volatile IT market and its related vendor acquisitions and bankruptcies. Not having the source code can leave an agency stranded with a faulty application it cannot change.

Fact-Finding, Group Problem Solving, Planning, Training, and Communication

Since applications may generate fears over job displacement and power rearrangements, the development process requires sensitivity in people management skills and techniques. Good fact-finding techniques such as listening, observation, interviewing, document analysis, questionnaire construction, and sampling methodologies are essential. Good communication and training skills ensure that all affected staff have a chance to learn what is happening. Miscommunication or lack of information can lead to ru-

FIGURE 6.12. Contents of an RFP (Request for Proposals)

Introduction

- General information
- Overview of the agency
- Goals and objectives of the application

Information about the RFP and how it will be used

- Desired format of any submitted proposal
- Submission criteria, e.g., date of acceptance, maximum cost
- Vendor identification information required, e.g., evidence of experience, stability, and insurance, along with a list of previous similar customers
- Selection criteria and procedures

Requirements of the application to be developed

- Features desired
- Data/information/knowledge that the application should contain
- Processing that should occur on the data/information/knowledge
- Input forms, working screens and menus, and output reports desired
- Performance standards, e.g., processing speed, networking standards
- Compatibility with existing applications
- Training, documentation, maintenance, and support requirements
- Anticipated and maximum expected application growth/change

Contract conditions to be met

- Source code availability
- Delivery and installation deadlines
- Tests that will determine whether application is acceptable
- Ownership conditions or conditions of use and enhancements
- Payment terms and timetables
- Warranties
- Support services and special modifications

Attachments to the RFP for vendor use

- Descriptions, goals, objectives, specifications of existing applications
- Description of present hardware, software, and networking
- Forms, reports, and fields of existing databases

FIGURE 6.13. Conventional Wisdom on Choosing and Working with a Vendor

- Always choose from several vendors who have seen a written statement of your needs.
- Make the contract with vendors for "products delivered" that perform to a set of user specifications. Be willing to reexamine the user specifications and allow suggested improvements by the vendor and potential users.
- Avoid open-ended contracts. You may want to specify an estimated amount and an amount at which the contract will have to be renegotiated.
- Make sure you agree on the terms and time frames for application support and modifications.
- Have a professional with IT and legal expertise involved in writing, or at least reviewing, the contract.
- Retain the rights to modify and enhance any source code developed should the vendor go out of business or be unable to supply the needed enhancements.
- Team an in-house employee with any outside consultants as early as possible to train the consultant and to enhance agency learning.
- Never be intimidated by IT specialists, and do not expect them to be people oriented. Have them explain in language you understand and define and write down terms that are uncommon to either party.
- Ask colleagues to recommend a vendor with whom they are satisfied, because few formal qualifications or vendor vertifications exist.
- Request a list of ten to twenty customers. Contact several for an appraisal.
- If the consultant is part of a team, make sure that you know who will be doing the work and that you feel comfortable working with that person.
- Vendor may promote impressive, "gee whiz" hardware or software features. Before agreeing to purchase these features, make sure they relate to your needs analysis and application objectives.
- Vendors may sell hardware along with application development. Have someone familiar with hardware determine that the proposal represents a good and current solution rather than being convenient for the vendor's software. For example, can you use the hardware for other purposes if you decide to discontinue your agreement?

mors, fear, and resistance. Computer technicians, systems designers, managers, and direct service providers often use jargon that is peculiar to their jobs. To help agency staff and system developers communicate, the jargon of both groups should be defined in writing and circulated. A cardinal rule in organizational communication is "no surprises." People should have easy access to information as it becomes available, unless a very good reason for withholding information exists. A Web site is an excellent way to make this information available and accessible.

Application development usually involves task-oriented groups, so committee management skills are crucial. Some important committee management techniques are planning, brainstorming, nominal group process, Delphi techniques, and conflict resolution. Researchers have found that good supervision techniques, especially team building, social support, and work incentives, are helpful when integrating human skills with IT (Dorsey, Goodrum, and Schwen, 1993; Yang and Pascale, 1993).

DEVELOPMENT ISSUES

Developing an IT application is typically a difficult process. For example, see Figure 6.14 for a list of lessons learned during one application development process. Some key issues in developing an application include how the agency is going to approach the development process, secure the needed expertise, and structure the expertise within the agency.

Development Approaches

Three common approaches are top-down, bottom-up, and prototyping. Rarely do agencies use these three approaches in their pure forms. Agencies often use a continuous mix of the three approaches.

Top-Down Approach

In a top-down approach, an agency first designs a model of the entire system and then develops subsystems as integral parts of the total application. This is the traditional, logical approach. For this approach the person in charge of the development effort proceeds through a very structured process of identifying needs and application specifications before contacting vendors. The agency publishes the RFP and selects one vendor only after a thorough analysis of all vendors' abilities to meet the specified criteria.

FIGURE 6.14. Lessons That Have Been Reinforced in Implementing an Application

- Don't pioneer. If a "canned" program is available, use it. Careful reading of Western history indicates that, statistically, the pioneer lost his scalp more frequently than the settlers following him. So, if you get the pioneering spirit, check the statistics on who has lost their scalp.

- If your manual system is not working, don't try to upgrade to a computer. It will only compound your problems.

- If you don't have the full backing and support of the executive director and board, you won't survive.

- Feedback is essential. Upload the information that will be most beneficial to staff first so that it can be relayed back to them.

- Simplify rather than sophisticate. KISS (keep it sweet and simple).

- Don't put other demands on your staff when trying to implement the system.

- Always assume hardware and software will be LATE—LATE—LATE.

- Never assume that programmers know more about your finances and management than you do. They should only write the programs and run the hardware.

- Train clerks and secretaries first and involve them from day one. A stable support staff are the heart of the agency.

- Be prepared during the implementation stage to work seven days a week, fourteen hours a day, to get the system running. Our experience is that staff are more than willing to make this kind of commitment if they understand how the system will work for them.

- In a parallel implementation, you will always assume that your tried-and-trusted manual system is correct and the computer has erred. It takes experience to learn that the manual system has its errors too.

- Don't expect help from peers or funding agencies. They are more likely to be betting on your losing your scalp than succeeding.

Source: Adapted from "Lessons That Have Been Reinforced in Implementing a Computerized MIS" by J. Newkham, 1982, University of Texas at Arlington: *Computer Use in Social Services Network, 2*(2), p. 3.

Bottom-Up Approach

In a bottom-up approach, an agency develops small, well-focused applications based on immediate requirements. Agencies combine applications into a total system only when the need arises. Typically, in this approach, a worker or middle-level manager finds available hardware, software, and networking capabilities and starts to develop and implement an application that addresses an immediate problem. The activities are not formalized and receive minimal sanction and attention from superiors. After several bottom-up approaches are taken, coordination and compatibility problems force the agency to take a more top-down approach.

Prototyping

In prototyping, an initial "quick and dirty" application is developed and given to key personnel for testing and evaluation. It is a technique similar to building a test model of an automobile. The application specifications are determined through repeated cycles of quick analysis, development, use, evaluation, and refinement. The emphasis during prototyping is on quickly programming a trial solution. Conventional wisdom and standard practices are ignored for "what works." Prototyping allows users to agree on the look and feel of the application before developers fully define the specifications. The final application may not resemble the original information needs or the initial design. Prototyping allows users and system development specialists to educate each other about their respective needs and capabilities.

Developing a prototype need not be a major undertaking. Many inexpensive authoring systems allow one to develop a "shell" in hours or days. The objective is to have a three- to five-minute demonstration that will illustrate the look, feel, and function of the final product. The prototype should illustrate various options, such as types of media.

Comparison of the Approaches

Each approach has its advantages and disadvantages. In the human services, traditional top-down development is more appropriate for applications that address the routine and well-structured problems of middle management. In top-down development, the tendency exists to address only well-defined information needs. This tendency should be recognized and openly discussed. If necessary, agencies should develop ways to address less-defined information needs. Prototyping may be combined with top-down development to overcome this tendency. Prototyping is especially useful when a top-down approach is taken with applications that support the nonroutine and ill-structured problems at the top management, policy, and direct service levels.

One problem with a top-down approach is that it is difficult to adequately specify a solution for intricate processes in complex organizations. Often the process of designing a solution creates additional problems that need to be addressed. Consequently, controlling the scope of a project is challenging. If the scope of a project is not controlled, projects can grow bigger and bigger, eventually becoming so large that they are not feasible. Examples are the Internal Revenue Service's multibillion-dollar, multidecade tax application and the "promised" Federal Aviation Administration's air traffic control application.

Controlling projects by contract specifications that are too rigid can also cause problems. For example, one statewide networked information system gave each worker a computer that was set to display only sixteen colors. Everyone knew that the computers would eventually be used for multimedia training and Internet access, both of which require more than sixteen colors. However, the vendor would not listen to any ideas beyond the scope of the contract and refused to make the changes.

An organization may advocate a bottom-up approach when it has the opportunity to implement several needed applications but does not have the time or expertise to develop an overall IT strategy. The agency may establish a policy not to interfere with the applications developed unless overall coordination is necessary. After a learning period, those involved with the application could become the nucleus of a top-down steering committee. The rapid increase in interest and learning that occurs with the bottom-up approach may be worth future coordination and incompatibility problems. An additional problem with the bottom-up approach is developing an application that has a narrow scope. The application may incorporate "work-around fixes" for problems that require reengineering or larger applications. Often, these larger solutions could not be foreseen because a thorough systems analysis was not completed. For example, a bottom-up approach may result in a great services management application that is scrapped when experience with the system reveals that a total redesign of service delivery is possible and necessary.

An organization may advocate a prototyping approach when it is interested in IT but has little idea where to begin. Time and failure should not be major concerns, and the need for experimentation should be acknowledged. Learning and discovering an effective solution should be more important than efficiently building an application. Prototyping is most useful when the decisions supported are novel and not well structured, such as during counseling. Care must be taken when using a prototyping approach that short, "quick and dirty" solutions do not lead to a lack of integration. In addition, continual change and lack of a definable product should not be allowed to exhaust staff morale and enthusiasm.

For complex applications, it may be desirable to combine all three approaches. For example, initial top-down analysis could develop long-range agency IT objectives and general information requirements throughout the agency. The results of the top-down approach could provide guides and constraints for a bottom-up development strategy. Such a strategy may involve the development of independent applications that are later integrated. The most complex applications could follow prototyping techniques. This prototyping process could result in detailed application specifications that become part of the overall agency strategy. Eventually, all applications would be integrated into a total system.

Securing Expertise

Agencies have three options for obtaining expertise when developing applications: (1) develop and rely on internal expertise, (2) purchase expertise from outside consultants, and (3) use some combination of internal and outside expertise. Use of internal expertise alone may produce an application that is useful, but technically limited and difficult to support. Use of only outside consultants may produce an application that is technically appropriate, but has limited usefulness.

Moyer (1997) advocates placing outside consultants under the control of internal staff as the best option for handling the technical proficiency versus usefulness issue. This combination is especially good at controlling the scope of an IT application. Outside contractors, with the proper incentives, are able to curb users' and managers' appetites for expanding the application and users are best able to define the scope. Moyer suggests that consultants are needed to interpret IT for users, perform highly technical tasks, and train users how to approach the more basic tasks.

Structuring Expertise Within the Agency

To develop and manage information, an agency must create the appropriate organizational structure and assign the necessary responsibilities and tasks to key people. The following seven groups are involved in information management:

1. Agency management
2. Agencywide IT committee

3. Application steering committee
4. IT manager/department
5. Those impacted by the application, including client representatives
6. Technicians and specialists
7. Users

If one of these groups is not involved, the potential for successful information management decreases. In nonprofit agencies, members of the parent organization, funding sources, client advocate groups, and board members may also be involved through an IT advisory subcommittee. The following section presents the responsibilities and tasks of each of these groups.

Agency Management

Top management appoints the steering committee, approves contracts with vendors and consultants, adjusts workloads, establishes and maintains open lines of communication, and balances the conflicting needs of all agency components requiring IT resources.

Agencywide IT Committee

The IT committee performs in an advisory role to top management. The IT committee includes representatives from all departments of the agency. This ensures that the overall IT effort is consistent with agency plans and coordinated across departments. The major task of the committee is to develop an information management plan that contains (1) IT goals and priorities; (2) IT policies and procedures; (3) hardware, software, networking, and training budgets; and (4) coordination and integration standards. Committee members are also responsible for maintaining open lines of communication between themselves and staff regarding IT information and concerns. (The book Web site links to an example of an IT strategic plan.)

Figure 6.15 presents several ways to structure the agency's IT committee. Committee structures 1 and 2 may appear bulky and time-consuming, especially in a small agency, but is because we often fail to separate the assignment of responsibilities from the tendency to have long and unproductive meetings. Forming an IT committee establishes formal responsibility. The committee may meet only if it has business to conduct, and meetings may last only a short time—they could even be via e-mail. Poorly managed meetings should not be an excuse for failing to establish the appropriate committee structures and allocate responsibilities.

The IT committee may appoint task forces to work on special projects or issues, such as confidentiality. When the agency develops a new applica-

FIGURE 6.15. Ways to Structure the IT Application in an Agency

Structure 1

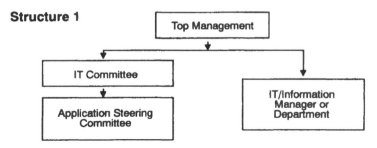

In structure 1, a balance of power exists between the IT committee and the IT/information manager. Top management settles disagreements.

Structure 2

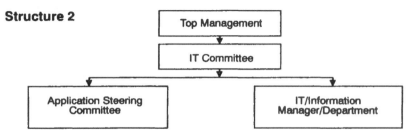

In structure 2, the application committee and IT/information manager report directly to the IT committee. This structure is recommended.

Structure 3

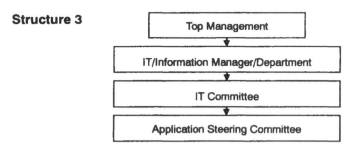

In structure 3, all IT committees are under the IT or information management department. This structure is not usually recommended because it gives too much control to the IT/information manager and makes access to top management by user representatives more difficult.

tion, the IT committee appoints an application steering committee. For organizations with one application, the application steering committee may be the agency IT committee. However, the IT committee has the responsibility for overall system planning and coordination, not just the planning of one application.

Application Steering Committee

An application steering committee represents all affected parties in the development process, sets overall policy, and monitors the development process. It helps foster communication, reduce resistance, and improve the chances that the application developed will meet the needs of all involved. The steering committee must ensure that communication channels are established and open and that feedback is obtained from all levels of the organization. If conflicts arise, the committee should help resolve them or refer difficult matters to top management for resolution. In agencies with several applications, each application steering committee may be a subcommittee of an agency IT committee.

The composition of the steering committee depends on the nature of the application and those whom the application will impact; for example, the development of a client information system would involve practitioners. The steering committee may appoint task forces to work on special problems or issues. For communication and coordination purposes, the person in charge of the application development effort may be a voting member of the committee. Factors such as the agency's management style, the amount of resistance anticipated, and the amount of learning required by steering committee members determine the tasks and power of the steering committee.

The IT Manager/Department

The IT manager is sometimes called a data administrator, information manager, or a management information system (MIS) director. This person is responsible for application development and documentation, managing and coordinating information on a day-to-day basis, and providing user training and support. The IT manager should understand all departments of the agency, as well as technology and application development. The role is primarily that of development, maintenance, coordination, control, and liaison. Therefore, the IT manager needs managerial, technical, and communication skills.

For communication and coordination purposes, the IT manager should be a member of the IT committee. The IT manager receives valuable input from the IT committee, which sets the overall policy and guidelines and sees that the IT manager's decisions are meeting the needs of its constituent users. Whether the IT manager chairs the IT committee or has voting privileges is a top management decision that is based on the power arrangements of the organization.

Those Affected by the Application

Experience has shown that one of the most important groups to be involved in IT development is those affected, especially the application users. Many techniques to involve users have already been presented, e.g., creating an IT committee, forming an application committee, teaming users with consultants, and using approaches such as prototyping.

The people affected by an application can vary substantially. An information system may impact almost every group and department in an agency. However, a performance support system that focuses on one process or body of knowledge can be designed and implemented with little effect on other parts of the agency. If possible, clients or client representatives should be members of the IT committee or application committee. They provide a perspective that cannot be obtained inside the agency.

Technical Specialists

Technical specialists supply the hardware and software expertise needed to develop and manage computer applications. The technical specialists may be in-house personnel, outside consultants, or a combination of both. The introduction to this book presented the assumption that human service specialists can more easily understand IT than IT specialists can understand human services. At present, IT personnel have many employment opportunities and often experience sudden job changes. Thus, training in-house personnel for the less technical tasks may be a satisfactory solution to the expertise problem. Review Figure 6.13 and the guidelines on vendor contracts for an additional discussion of using technicians.

The Agency Board

Since human service organizations are highly accountable to their boards and funding sources, both may play a role in agency information management. For example, an agency board member may have computer, networking, or information management expertise, or a funding source may require an agency to use its service definitions or information system.

Outside sources can be involved in agency IT through a special agency advisory committee, through participation on the IT committee, or through an application-specific committee.

Both internal and external needs may influence application design. However, rarely should an application be designed based on outside information needs. An application should primarily contain information and processes that model what occurs in the agency. This information should then be translated into reports for those outside the agency. For example, a funding source may ask for the number of clients served by age categories. The agency should collect date of birth and then have the computer process date of birth into age categories. Computerizing basic agency information offers flexibility because it can always be combined into categories. However, categorical information can rarely be broken down into smaller fields.

CONCLUSION

This chapter presented information for formulating an overall development strategy and designing and implementing an IT application. The suggestions presented are not prescriptive; instead, they outline alternatives within a developmental framework. Some of the problems that arise in developing applications are presented in Figure 6.16. The most appropriate strategies are those which combine the general guidelines in this chapter with the real-world situation an agency faces.

FIGURE 6.16. Problems in Developing Applications

I. Inadequate overall planning

Indicators:

- Lack of long-range IT goals and objectives or an IT strategic plan
- Lack of specific application and implementation plans
- Overreliance on nonintegrated applications
- Outgrowing the agency IT applications in one to two years

II. Inadequate communication, involvement, and user preparation

Indicators:

- Lack of well-established communication channels
- Missing a well-functioning, representative steering committee

FIGURE 6.16 *(continued)*

- An active rumor mill exists about the IT application
- Isolation of developers and designers from users
- Fear that information collected will be misused
- Lack of training for all potential users
- Thinking the IT development process will be easy
- Developers think the applications are great, but users hate them

III. Lack of top-level commitment and involvement

Indicators:

- IT function housed in financial department rather than in a separate high-level department
- No management control over application developers
- Top management unwilling to make the tough IT decisions
- Unstable funding and lack of needed resources
- Lack of quality personnel to develop and manage the application
- Blaming IT for management problems
- Budgeting for hardware, software, and communications, but not for training and implementation
- Overinfatuation with IT while ignoring use of application outputs
- Power politics played by withholding access to IT or information
- IT not integrated in agency policies and procedures, e.g., use not part of performance evaluation criteria

IV. Inability to determine the cost benefit of an application

Indicators:

- Lack of rules of thumb on when to use IT
- Lack of model to determine IT cost-benefit
- Lack of national norms on IT expenditures
- Lack of definitions of IT success

V. Inability to support the practitioner-client interaction

Indicators:

- Inadequate measures of client outcome and "good practice"
- Little consistency in terms and in the content of clinical records

- Social work practice not seen as information based
- Practitioners supply information, yet rarely receive useful outputs

VI. Rapid changes in IT

Indicators:

- Hardware and communications will be less expensive if one waits
- Lack of hardware/software standards
- Frequent acquisitions, mergers, and bankruptcies of IT companies
- Frequent job changes among IT personnel

VII. Difficulty in obtaining unbiased information

Indicators:

- Abundance of testimonials, lack of research
- Research is outdated before it is disseminated
- Most reliable information comes from vendors
- Professional associations offer little guidance

VIII. Inadequate documentation

Indicators:

- Lack of written information on the design, use, repair, etc., of IT
- Postponing organizational changes because no one knows how to change the IT involved
- Inability to function when the "system" crashes
- Panic when the application developer/programmer quits

REVIEW AND DISCUSSION QUESTIONS

1. How does planning for the changes associated with IT differ from planning for other agency changes, such as moving to a new office location?
2. Is the statement "the process is product" true of all stages of IT development?
3. Discuss when you would use the various approaches to IT development.
4. What agency staff are typically involved with application development and what tasks do they perform?

5. Specify an application and list the tasks that an IT consultant would perform and the tasks that agency staff would perform.
6. Should consultants report to agency staff involved with IT application development, or vice versa?
7. What would be the advantages and disadvantages of involving clients in the application development process?
8. How does a human service agency gain IT experience from the business community without incorporating business assumptions and values?

Chapter 7

Applying Systems and Decision-Making Theories

INTRODUCTION

Theories add to our basic understanding. For example, landing a person on the moon would not have been possible without theories of how the universe worked. Since IT applications are systems that model decision making, an understanding of human service systems and decision making is essential for their development and implementation. We often assume that systems and decision-making theories are commonly understood. This assumption may not be correct, for few can answer questions such as the following:

- What is it about systems thinking that is important for understanding, developing, and using IT applications?
- What characteristics of a system enhance a system's functioning?
- Is the client part of the delivery system or part of the system's environment, and what difference does it make?
- What can we do to improve our decision making?
- How is human service decision making different from the decision making of other professions?
- How does human service decision making impact computing system design?

This chapter presents two theories basic to IT systems and decision making. Although the chapter treats systems and decision making separately, the concepts are integrally connected. IT applications become information models of the decisions they support. For example, for an application to assist an information and referral (I&R) worker, it must provide the right information, at the right time, and in the right format. To develop an I&R application requires constructing a model of the decisions the worker makes and the information needed for each decision. Another example is that information systems tend to model the level of decentralization in an organization. If an organization's decisions are made by geographically decentralized program directors, then a loosely connected network of computers is typically more functional than a centralized system.

SYSTEMS

Human service professionals have had ample experience with systems, since they work in the human service delivery "system" (HSDS). Experiences gained from working in the HSDS can illustrate some basic system concepts and the problems in applying them. For example, one practice to improve the HSDS has been to place many agencies or their intake components in one location. The idea was that interagency coordination would occur as a result of agencies being in the same location. Clients could save time, effort, and confusion and be better served because the system would ensure that appropriate services were provided. However, all too often, this system of human service agencies became simply a "collection" of human service agencies. Service coordination and integration generally did not occur. Clients were required to move physically through multiple agency intakes and multiple delivery systems. For the integration of services to occur, additional staff time and effort would be required to standardize procedures, coordinate efforts, and process the additional paperwork. Reducing client time and effort would require additional involvement by other parts of the system, or time-saving IT and techniques must be employed.

Experience with multiservice centers taught us that understanding the nature of systems is important in their design. Multiple agencies in one location constitute a better system only if the following features exist:

- Systemwide goals and objectives
- Common or compatible definitions of services
- Uniform intake procedures
- Data sharing across services
- A central planning, managing, and controlling entity

Similarly, placing all agency information in a computer does not automatically create an integrated agency information system. To design and develop systems requires an analysis of their components and how the components interact. The following material presents a closer look at the nature of systems and how they work.

Basic Concepts and Definitions

Fundamental to the application of systems concepts is an understanding of how systems thinking differs from traditional thinking.

The Systems Perspective

Systems theory is a perspective or way of looking at complex phenomena such as organizations. Systems thinking is often contrasted with the traditional way of thinking, as illustrated in Table 7.1, shifting our focus from a reductionistic, deductive analysis of parts to a holistic, inductive synthesis in which the whole becomes the important focus.

During traditional investigation, all motion is stopped and the parts are isolated and divided until the smallest units are found. During systems analysis, the parts are examined as they interact as a whole with their environment. Systems thinking supplements the traditional concepts of cause and effect through theories of multiple causation and probabilistic causality. That is, rarely will only one condition or factor produce a given effect. Rather, the "dynamic interaction of multiple causes" leads to the overall condition in which the effect occurs.

TABLE 7.1. Contrast Between Systems and the Traditional Approach

Characteristic	Traditional Thinking	Systems Thinking
Overall view	Reductionistic	Holistic
Focus	On the parts	On the whole
Key processes	Analysis	Synthesis
Basic assumption	Cause and effect	Multiple, probabilistic causality
Type of analysis	Deduction	Induction
Focus of investigation	Attributes of objects	Interdependence of objects
State during investigation	Static	Dynamic
Operation of parts	Optimal	Suboptimal
Problem resolution	A static solution	An adaptive solution or dynamic model

In systems thinking, static solutions cannot resolve problems. By the time the solution is adequately developed, the problem has changed. In addition, in devising the solution, one often must interact with the system. This interaction changes the nature of the problem so that the solution may no longer apply. For example, an agency audit may result in many changes being made before auditors complete their report. Thus, solutions from a systems perspective are dynamic strategies that produce adaptive systems.

The health care system can illustrate the difference between the traditional way of thinking and systems thinking. The primary goal of the health care system is for people to live long and productive lives. For centuries, medical investigation involved dissecting the body into smaller and smaller parts to discover how the human body became ill. With more powerful analysis, the causes of more illnesses could be isolated and cures found. The electron microscope is an investigative tool of this analytic, reductionistic approach. The traditional approach carries over into health care solutions. When a person becomes ill, the person is placed in bed, labeled a patient, and isolated in a hospital. Then, the illness is diagnosed, classified, and the appropriate cure implemented. If the patient recovers, the patient is declared well, stripped of the patient label, and returned to his or her environment.

The traditional approach has much to offer, but systems thinking points to many areas where the traditional approach fails. The practice of holistic medicine typifies the systems approach to health care by including other related systems as factors in health. An instance in which traditional medicine neglects these factors is when a gunshot victim is taken to the hospital, cured, and returned home, only to be shot again during another argument. The concept of multiple causation reveals that, although the gunshot wound is the primary health problem, other problems produce the overall circumstances in which the shooting occurs. If we eliminate only one cause, the cure or solution may be inadequate. The gunshot victim's physical system may be functioning optimally when he or she returns home, but the victim's mental state, social support systems, and stressful environment may result in similar conditions, allowing the shooting to reoccur.

Another failure of traditional thinking is the optimization of one health care subsystem at the expense of others. When I first began working as a health planner, I found that the major treatment subsystem, the hospital, had been optimized to the point that many other health care subsystems were neglected. For example, although the minutes following an injury were known to be critical, the emergency medical subsystem consisted of a funeral home hearse. The funeral home had little incentive or money to improve this subsystem. Similar neglect still exists in the health care prevention subsystem.

These health care examples illustrate the systems theory focus on structures, processes, relationships, interdependence, and the whole within its environment. One applies systems theory by studying the dynamic flow of energy, resources, and activity as a system moves toward its goals within its environment. Using systems concepts, we can map a system's behavior and make changes to produce a system that more consistently meets its intended goals. Although systems thinking is primarily descriptive, it is ultimately concerned with prediction and control (Van Gigch, 1978).

System

A system is a *group* of *related elements* in *interaction*. Each term in this definition of a system is important. Elements are parts or components, such as stars in the solar system, people in a family, or ideas in a treatment system. *Elements* may be a combination of objects, people, and concepts, as are elements of the human service delivery system. *Group* implies that more than one element is necessary to form a system. An element not *related* to another element is not part of the system; for example, a stranger is not part of a family system. We can define the relatedness of two or more elements in numerous ways, such as by space (two feet apart), time (two hours apart), and function (a precipitating factor). The relationship can be expressed using words, diagrams, logic, or formulas. In a system, the elements are not only related; they *interact*. The distinctive properties of a system result from this interaction. A physically related but noninteracting collection of elements, such as a collection of people, is not a system. Only when the elements in a collection interact do they become a system. For instance, when a group of people react to a tragedy, they become a support system.

The interaction of system elements consumes energy and resources. This results in the natural tendency of all systems to move toward a state of decay, disorder, and uncertainty known as *entropy*. Systems survive by maintaining a *steady state*, called *equilibrium* or *homeostasis*, or by growing toward higher levels of adaptation. To preserve equilibrium, systems continually extract energy and resources from their environment. An expansion of the original system may result when the acquired resources are not necessary for survival. Therefore, systems usually grow more stable, more sophisticated, more adaptive, and often into larger versions of themselves. This tendency to grow and elaborate explains why systems change readily, but only when the change retains the existing balance or homeostasis of the system.

The previous discussion suggests that we can generalize from one system to another, as all systems work in a similar fashion. This book frequently makes generalizations from a transportation system to a computing system. Later sections of this chapter discuss properties and behaviors generalizable to all systems.

The Nesting of Systems

Russian nesting dolls illustrate the different levels of systems. Each doll is a separate unit, although all but the largest are part of a larger unit. In addition, all but the smallest contain a smaller unit. Similar to nesting dolls, systems are nested within larger units and comprise smaller units. We refer to the unit under investigation as the *system*. The larger unit in which the system resides is the *environment*. The smaller units that make up the system are called *subsystems*. The level of the unit under investigation determines which units are labeled the subsystem, system, and environment.

The area that separates a system from its environment is the *boundary* of a system. Identifying boundaries is the first step in an investigation of the system. In many human service systems, the boundaries are not precisely defined borders, but regions. For example, the board of directors of an agency may be part of the agency system or the environment, depending on one's perspective. Boundaries point to another systems concept, that of the interface between two systems or between a system and its environment. The *interface* is the area of contact or overlap of systems, as illustrated in Figure 7.1. Boundaries are high friction areas, so often boundary-spanning mechanisms are used to relieve the friction (for example, oil to lubricate gears). Since most boundaries in the human services are imprecise or fuzzy, the interfaces are areas of high interaction, interconnection, and contention. Boundary-spanning activities, such as public relations, are often necessary.

Types of Systems

We can distinguish systems by characteristics such as their size, complexity, and abstractness. The ordering of systems into levels by certain characteristics creates a hierarchy of systems. The intrinsic nature of systems is the basis of one common hierarchy. This hierarchy, derived by Kenneth Boulding (1956), defines levels of systems, ranging from nonliving static structures such as rocks through complex living systems such as societies to transcendental systems of the unknown. Systems at the higher levels of Boulding's hierarchy display self-correcting, adaptive, and learning properties.

FIGURE 7.1. The Interface Between Systems

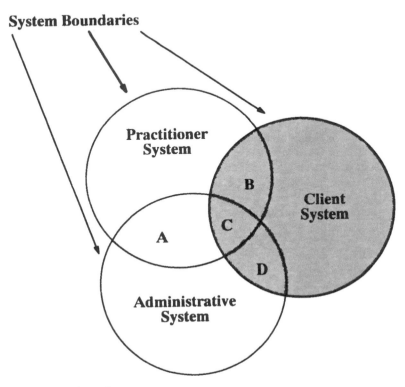

System Boundaries

System interfaces:

A = Staff meetings
B = Therapy sessions
C = Fund-raisers
D = Program evaluations

Another typology separates open from closed systems. A *closed system* has little or no interaction with its environment; a person in solitary confinement is an example. An *open system* is in constant interaction with its environment. Since all human services and computing systems are open systems, all future uses of the term system will refer to an open system.

Input, Process, Output

Another characteristic of systems is that they are dynamic; that is, interaction occurs among the elements. We can view this interaction as a series of inputs, processes, and outputs (see Figure 7.2). Process is an activity synonymous with terms such as conversion, transformation, or throughput. Inputs are the resources or start-up elements that are transformed into outputs, or elements leaving the process. Outputs may cycle back into inputs, be directly reprocessed, or exit the system into the environment. Inputs and outputs may be ordered or haphazard. Haphazard inputs result in random outputs, as when one flips a coin. Since random systems behavior is rarely desirable, control is a key concept in systems design.

Feedback and Control

To increase the likelihood of desired results, selected outputs must be channeled along a feedback loop to reenter the system as control inputs. The study of feedback and control is called *cybernetics*. Cybernetics stems from the Greek terms for governor (kubernētēs) and to govern (kubernan).

FIGURE 7.2. Input, Process, Outputs, and Control in a System

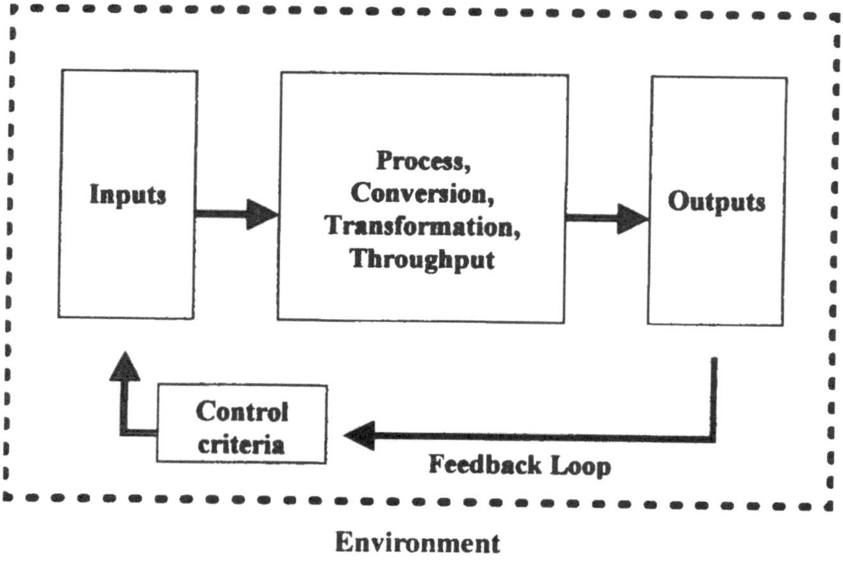

Environment

Feedback is a powerful form of control. However, control information can enter the system from sources other than the feedback loop. Behavior modification is a familiar human service process in which we change client behavior in the desired direction by using feedback.

Goal Seeking and Optimization

Systems move in directions expressed by the system's purposes or goals. One factor adding complexity to human service systems is that they often have multiple conflicting goals. If agreement on the overall system goals is not clear, subsystems may suboptimize. When systems *suboptimize*, they use more than their share of system resources to achieve subgoals at the expense of overall system functioning. The previous example of the hospital optimizing its goals at the expense of the health care system illustrates suboptimization.

Suboptimization usually prevents synergy from occurring. *Synergy* is a state in which the total system output is greater than the sum of the outputs of all subsystems. The importance of synergy can be seen when one sports team works synergistically during a match while the other team functions as a group of individuals. To obtain the synergistic or "team effect," all players must put team goals above individual goals. Concerted suboptimization is when all subsystems interact according to an overall design (synergistically) to optimize the total system.

Viewing Transportation from a Systems Perspective

The familiar characteristics of a city transportation system can illustrate systems concepts. A city transportation system is an open system with strong environmental influences, such as government funds and regulations, and other influences such as the weather, the price of oil, and transportation technology. Many subsystems make up a city transportation system, including the highway, mass transportation, traffic policing, and emergency routing subsystems. The interface of these subsystems is an area of constant concern and turmoil. For example, coordinating the roles of the police, firefighters, and medical personnel during an emergency is difficult.

A transportation system is characterized by a variety of inputs, processes, and outputs (see Table 7.2). Inputs include natural resources, such as wood and oil; human resources, such as the engineers, construction workers, and traffic police who design, build, and control the transportation system; and

TABLE 7.2. Input, Process, Output, and Control Elements in a Transportation System

Inputs	Process	Outputs
Financial Resources		
Money ⇨	Funding	⇨ Resources purchased
People Resources		
Traffic police ⇨	Controlling	⇨ Orderly travel
Drivers ⇨	Driving	⇨ Destination reached
Mechanics ⇨	Repairing	⇨ Reliable vehicles
Engineers ⇨	Designing	⇨ Maps and plans
Workers ⇨	Construction	⇨ Roads and bridges
Natural Resources		
Oil ⇨	Lubrication	⇨ Friction reduction
Material Resources		
Gasoline ⇨	Combustion	⇨ Movement, pollution
Rubber ⇨	Traction	⇨ Steady movement
Asphalt, iron, concrete ⇨	Construction	⇨ Roads and bridges
Manufactured Resources		
Automobiles ⇨	Travel	⇦ Location change

material inputs, such as gasoline, concrete, and rubber. These inputs are transformed into outputs such as a change in one's location, pollution, and wear on the system.

The goal of the transportation system is to move people in an orderly, safe, and efficient manner. To accomplish this goal, inputs, process, and outputs must work synergistically. Only then can they create a dynamic equilibrium whereby traffic moves as planned and traffic problems are minimal. A system must be well integrated to ensure optimal system functioning. For example, roads must be well connected and without dead ends or narrowing sections that create traffic jams. To keep a well-designed system functioning optimally requires that constant feedback and controls be built into the system. During periods of high activity, such as rush hour, traffic flow is often too complex for automatic mechanical controls such as traffic lights. In this situation, traffic police may override the automatic controls at problem intersections. Also during rush hour, traffic monitors on the ground and in airplanes report control information. These monitors create a feedback loop through which system performance can be observed and evaluated, and inputs adjusted, for optimum functioning, as when an accident requires traffic rerouting.

System problems such as traffic jams result from multiple conditions: some are primary conditions, such as accidents, and some are secondary or contributing conditions, such as the emergency vehicles called to the accident scene. Since traffic problems are constantly changing, the solutions must be dynamic. Some solutions become outdated even as they are developed. For example, a city map in a fast growing area is outdated before it is printed. The optimum state is a system that prevents accidents and traffic jams through the use of learning mechanisms, such as signs that read "slick when wet" or "ice on bridges."

Viewing a Human Service Agency from a Systems Perspective

Since most human service agencies are more complex and less controlled than a transportation system, they often exhibit fewer organized system characteristics. Figure 7.3 presents a generic organization systems model that is useful in analyzing a human service agency. The internal elements are technology, task, purpose, people, and structure. The environmental influences are political, sociocultural, economic, and technological. Table 7.3 presents some key inputs, processes, and output elements at the various levels of a human service agency. Chapter 8, which analyzes human service information needs, further develops Figure 7.3 and Table 7.3.

Applying systems theory to the HSDS is helpful in many ways, such as focusing our attention on the importance of the agency environment. Also, focusing on system goals, inputs, transformation processes, outputs, and feedback loops encourages the exploration of tangible and measurable resources and results.

Viewing Computing from a Systems Perspective

The application of systems concepts to IT applications will only be discussed briefly because it is the focus of several remaining chapters. Table 7.4 presents the inputs, processes, and outputs of an IT application.

The "hardware subsystem" of an IT application contains precise inputs, processes, outputs, and control elements. As the hardware subsystem combines with the people and procedures subsystem, a more complex IT application forms. The IT application has inputs, processes, and outputs that are much less precise than the hardware subsystem alone due to the complexity of human and organizational behavior. Because IT applications require specificity, they work best in well-defined areas of a human service agency, such as accounting. Many human service processes, such as family therapy, are too imprecise or complex for present IT applications to address.

FIGURE 7.3. A General Systems Model of an Organization

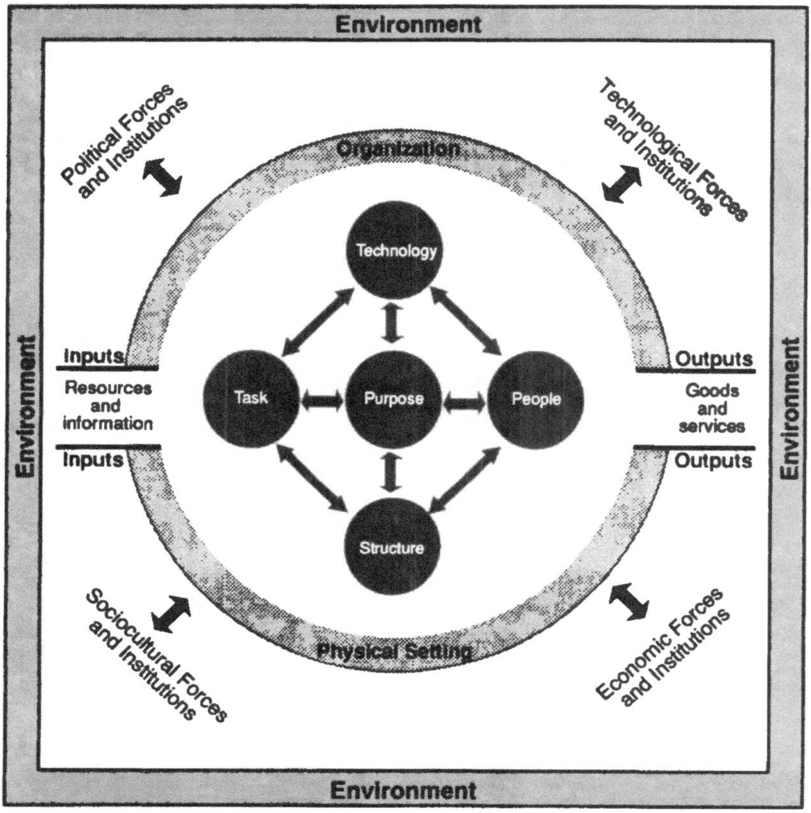

Note: From *Management Concepts and Situations* (p. 61) by H. M. Carlisle, 1976, Chicago: Science Research Associates, Inc. Copyright by H. M. Carlisle. Reprinted by permission.

The systems thinking associated with computers is based in the tangible, industrial age, whereas the thinking about networks typifies the conceptual, information age (Kelley, 1997). Kelley lists twelve rules that apply to network systems but not to traditional systems. Computers are parts and networks are links. A system of parts behaves differently than a system of links. For example, as the numbers of network parts increase slightly, the number of links increase exponentially. This behavior accounts for the difficulty of keeping a well-linked Web site up to date.

TABLE 7.3. Key Inputs, Processes, Outputs in a Human Service Delivery System

Inputs	Process	Outputs	Feedback
Policy Level			
Public opinion and values	Representation and lobbying	Legislation	Opinion polls and elections
Law and precedent	Legal interpretation	Court rulings	Laws obeyed
Legislation and laws	Interpretation, policymaking	Policies, rules, and regulations	Legislative intent satisfied
Community Level			
Citizens in need	Assessment	Services	Reduced needs
Other agencies	Cooperation	Joint ventures	Coordination
Management Level			
Funding	Purchasing and contracting	Services, staff, facilities	Accounting
People, agencies	Staffing, leading	Motivated staff	Evaluations
Regulations	Accountability	Goals achieved	Audits
Practitioner Level			
Client problems, practitioner expertise	Assessing, advising, counseling	Behavior changes, problems solved	Treatment plans
Theory, technology, values, ethics	Application of theory and ethics	Effective and ethical services	Professional certification and licensing

Another example is that parts that are the most scarce are more valuable, whereas links that are most plentiful have the greatest value.

DECISION MAKING

The previous discussion points to the benefit of viewing an IT application within the context of the decisions it supports. The use of processed information to improve decision making is fundamental to all human service activities. This section discusses the elements of decision making, their interactions, and their influences on whether decisions will be difficult or easy to support.

Decision making is often a synonym for problem solving. However, decision making may be only one small step in the long process of solving a problem. The term problem solving in this book indicates a process involving many separate decisions.

TABLE 7.4. Inputs, Processes, and Outputs in an IT Application

Inputs	Process	Outputs
IT Resources		
Hardware	Logical, mathematical, and I/O operations	Processing capacity
Energy	Electron flow, motors turning	Power provided and energy consumed
Software	Instructing	Data processed according to instructions
Communication links protocols	Networking	Linked systems operating as a unit
Information Resources		
Data, information, and knowledge	Processing	Reports, decisions, and predictions
People Resources		
Users with information needs	Information processing	People with information needs met
Systems designers	Systems analysis	Solution design
Programmers	Writing instructions	Software developed
System managers	System operation and control	Smoothly running system
Procedures		
Standard operating procedures	Guidance	Well-functioning system
Staff training	Learning of system	Accurate data and use
Evaluation criteria	Employees evaluated	Compliance, rewards

The Decision-Making Process

The process by which decisions are made is the subject of increasing study. Dewey (1910) suggested that decision making addresses three questions:

- What is the problem?
- What are the alternatives?
- Which alternative is best?

Rubinstein (1975) summarized a less rational, four-phase model of scientific inquiry:

1. *Preparation:* You go over the elements of the problem and study their relationship.
2. *Incubation:* You "sleep on" the problem. You may be frustrated at this stage because the problem has not yet been solved.
3. *Inspiration:* You feel a spark of excitement as the solution (or a route to a solution) suddenly appears.
4. *Verification:* You check the inspired solution against the desired goal.

Simon (1977, 1997) postulated that managerial decision making involves four phases:

1. *Intelligence,* or searching the environment for conditions calling for a decision. Simon's use of the term intelligence is similar to its use in "military intelligence."
2. *Design,* or inventing, developing, and analyzing possible courses of action.
3. *Choice,* or selecting a particular course of action from those available.
4. *Review,* or assessing past choices.

Simon expanded on Dewey's concept of finding the best alternative during the choice phase by distinguishing *maximizing* from a concept he called *satisficing.* Maximizing involves finding the best solution, while satisficing involves finding an acceptable alternative. Simon indicates that managers rarely have the time and resources to maximize by examining all the alternatives. They usually *satisfice* by examining only enough alternatives to say that the major options have been considered. Maximizing requires an exhaustive search, whereas satisficing requires only a selective search of limited alternatives. An example of satisficing relates to the hiring of a new employee. Typically, all potential candidates are not interviewed. Instead, managers interview only enough candidates to find several good potential employees.

Etzioni (1968) analyzed the policy development process to create a more complex decision-making process known as mixed scanning, which includes the following phases:

1. On strategic occasions, list all the relevant alternatives that come to mind. Briefly examine the alternatives, rejecting those with "crippling objections."
2. Repeat this process, each time studying the alternatives in greater detail. Stop when only one alternative remains.

3. Divide implementation, the resources to implement, and the commitments of others into sequential steps, with costly and less reversible steps appearing later in the process.
4. Review while implementing by continuously scanning the results, especially for steps that, although taken in the right direction, result in deeper difficulties.
5. Formulate a rule for the allocation of assets and time among the various levels of scanning.

Lewin (1947), and later Schein (1961), developed a different approach to decision making. They view decision making as a three-phase process of unfreezing, movement, and refreezing. Lewin's model assumes equilibrium and then postulates that unfreezing must create the conditions for a change to occur. Change can occur only after we prepare the climate for change. After change, the system will again refreeze or reach a new state of equilibrium. Lewin's three-stage model of decision making is the basis of many more-recent theories, as illustrated by the following quote:

> The decision-making process consists of *predecision, decision* and *postdecision* stages. These stages are interdependent, the postdecision phase often coincides with the predecision preparation for the next decision. Each decision stage is itself composed of a series of *partial decisions,* characterized by their own pre- and postdecision stages. (Zeleny, 1982, p. 86)

Although more complex decision-making models exist, most are elaborations of the previous models rather than new views. Most models stress that the decision-making process involves phases such as disequilibrium, solution seeking, analysis, choice, and equilibrium. All authors indicate that the phases occur repeatedly throughout decision making, as when the choice calls for new, more detailed analysis.

The differences in decision-making models occurred partly because researchers studied different decision situations. For example, Rubinstein analyzed scientific discovery; Simon analyzed managerial decision making; Etzioni analyzed the policy development process; Lewin analyzed individual and group decision making. Thus, we must study more than the decision-making process to understand decision making. Other important elements to study are the decision, the decision maker, the information available to make the decision, and the environment in which the decision is made.

Influences on the Decision-Making Process

Figure 7.4 illustrates a decision-making model. The model involves four influences on decision making, the decision, the person, the information, and the environment. This section further develops this four-element model.

The Decision

The nature of the decision to be made is an important decision-making input, for example, making a trivial decision about what to eat or making a life-threatening decision about whether to have high-risk surgery. We can

FIGURE 7.4. Elements in the Decision-Making Process

Environment

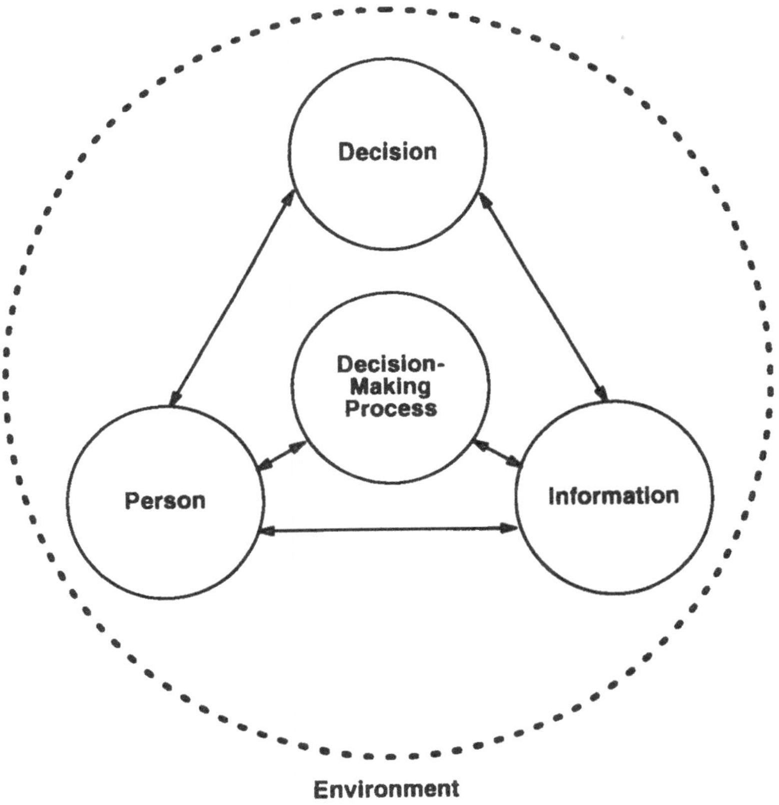

analyze the nature of the decision by examining three groups of decision attributes: complexity, consequences, and resources (see Table 7.5).

The first group of attributes, complexity, can be associated with the understandability, predictability, routineness, programmability, familiarity, chance of success, and structure of a decision. Table 7.5 presents the continuum of these attributes. Most of the terms describing the attributes in Table 7.5 are common to human service professionals, but structure and programmability may be new. *Programmable decisions* are those for which we can establish detailed procedures, such as determining service eligibility. *Nonprogrammable decisions* are those for which it is difficult to develop detailed procedures, for example, whether one should marry. A *well-structured decision* is completely specified in advance, such as deciding the amount of a payroll check. An *ill-structured decision* is one for which it is impossible to specify the appropriate course of action, for example, what salary bonus will retain an employee. Structure and pro-

TABLE 7.5. Attributes Involved in Decision Making

Complexity of the Decision		
Low Complexity		**High Complexity**
understandable	⇔	incomprehensible
predictable	⇔	unpredictable
routine	⇔	nonroutine
programmable	⇔	nonprogrammable
familiar	⇔	unfamiliar
high chance of success	⇔	low chance of success
well-structured	⇔	ill-structured
Known Consequences of Making the Decision		
Low Consequences		**High Consequences**
unaccountable	⇔	accountable
hard to measure success	⇔	easy to measure success
low agreement on success	⇔	high agreement on success
reversible	⇔	irreversible
uncertainty	⇔risky⇔	certainty
Resources Available		
Low Resources		**High Resources**
low funding	⇔	high funding
little time	⇔	much time
little expertise	⇔	much expertise
few technologies	⇔	many technologies
few people	⇔	many people

grammability are closely related concepts. Structure refers to the organized nature of the decision and programmability refers to the ease of establishing procedures for a decision. IT applications work best with decisions that are routine, programmable, repetitive, and well structured.

Success is another term often used to describe the complexity of a decision. Although success sounds like a useful attribute, it is often difficult to determine, even with hindsight. For example, in one marriage counseling situation, seeking a divorce may be a successful decision. In another, it may be considered an unsuccessful decision. Some criteria exist for examining decision-making success, including cost benefit, cost-effectiveness, satisfaction, and improved quality of life. However, these criteria often require more information than can be obtained. Therefore, human service practitioners are often concerned about the appearance of having unsuccessful results, for example, bad publicity and reporting errors. Since most practitioners are highly trained professionals, they are given considerable discretion in deciding whether their decision outcomes are successful. However, with the privatization of human services and managed care, this discretion is being severely limited. More pressure exists to measure and document successful client outcomes as the primary means to justify any intervention.

The second group of attributes in Table 7.5, consequences, focuses attention on our knowledge and confidence about what will happen after a decision is made. Consequences can be described by the attributes of accountability, measurability, agreement, reversibility, and certainty. Certainty has acquired a specific meaning in decision-making literature. A *certain decision* is one for which we know the likelihood of all outcomes. A *risky decision* is one that allows us to assign probabilities to the outcomes. An *uncertain decision* is one with no information about the outcomes. Deciding to attend a movie is of low consequence. Typically you are not held accountable for others' enjoyment of the movie, enjoyability is hard to measure, little agreement exists on what is an enjoyable movie; you can easily see another movie if your first decision is bad; you have little idea of what the outcome will be. In contrast, the decision to move abused children from their parents' home into foster care is of high consequence. The agency is legally accountable for the decision; most people agree on and can distinguish between a successful and unsuccessful outcome based on future behavior; the decision is almost impossible to totally reverse; and some things are fairly certain, such as that the mandates of the state are satisfied.

Since consequences concern knowledge about the future, they are often difficult to ascertain. For example, a seemingly inconsequential decision may actually have a high impact on one's life, as when the decision to drive to the store results in a severe accident. Any eventual tragedy resulting from a decision does not alter the fact that the decision was inconsequential at the time it was made.

The third group of attributes in Table 7.5 resources, can consist of money, time, expertise, technologies, and people. Resources are an important element in human service decision making because donations or taxes fund most human services. Given scarce resources, agencies must determine at what resource level the quality of decision making begins to decline. For example, agencies should know the optimum number of clients or cases that they can assign to a therapist or child welfare worker. A caseload level may exist so that reducing the caseload has little impact on decision making, yet increasing the caseload detrimentally affects decision making.

People are perhaps the most important resource in human service decision making. Highly trained people are typically required for human service jobs. Also, practitioners often consult with other experts about their decisions, for example, during case conferences or agency staff meetings.

The people continuum in Table 7.5 suggests that many of the other continuums there and in later figures, may be not as linear as illustrated, but curvilinear. That is, many people may not always be a resource. The old saying "Too many cooks spoil the broth" illustrates the curvilinear nature of the people continuum. Keen and Morton (1978) point out another complicating factor: the attributes of the decision may change as the decision-making process progresses. For example, the decision to add a controversial new service may have little structure at the intelligence phase of the decision, yet be well structured at the design and implementation phase. Obviously, the nature of the decision needs additional research to expand and refine the attributes presented here.

The Information

The information used in making the decision also influences the decision-making process. The three groups of attributes that describe information are measurability, time, and adequacy (see Table 7.6).

The first group of attributes in Table 7.6, information measurability, includes the ability to establish dimensions, magnitudes, relationships, and capacities by comparing something to known standards. Since much human service decision making defies traditional measurement techniques, we need to develop new ways to quantify and manipulate complex human

TABLE 7.6. Attributes Describing the Information Involved in Decision Making

Measurability of the Information

Hard to Measure		Easy to Measure
summary	⇔	detailed
low accuracy	⇔	high accuracy
low verifiability	⇔	high verifiability
prone to error and bias	⇔	free of error and bias
qualitative	⇔	quantitative
probabilistic	⇔	deterministic
unreliable	⇔	reliable
invalid	⇔	valid

Time Frame Associated with the Information

One End of Continuum		Other End of Continuum
frequent	⇔	infrequent
current	⇔	old
past	⇔	future
presented on time	⇔	presented early or late

Adequacy of the Information

Adequate		Inadequate
comprehensive	⇔	fragmented
appropriate	⇔	inappropriate
clear	⇔	unclear
right source	⇔	wrong source
accessible	⇔	inaccessible
available	⇔	unavailable
flexible	⇔	inflexible

service phenomena. The human brain is a model for working rapidly with hard-to-measure information; thus, neural networks may be one useful measurement technique. Another technique might involve working with digitized pictures and video.

The second group of attributes in Table 7.6, information time frame, involves characteristics such as the following:

- Number of times information is presented (frequent or infrequent)
- Age of the information (current versus old)
- Time horizon (past, present, future)
- Timeliness (when the information is presented)

Large IT applications in the human services have been criticized for their inability to meet the information time frame requirements, often providing practitioners with information that is outdated, not presented when needed, concerned with past events, and presented too infrequently to be useful. A somewhat different time problem occurs with information overload, in which a large volume of potentially useful information is presented all at once, thus hindering its effective use in decision making.

The third group of attributes in Table 7.6, adequacy, can be defined in many ways, including the following:

- Comprehensiveness (all versus part of the information)
- Appropriateness or relevance
- Clarity of form (mode of presentation)
- Source (right or wrong, internal or external to the organization, etc.)
- Accessibility
- Availability
- Flexibility or multiple-use potential

The correct combination of measurability, time frame, and adequacy is needed if information is to be fully used in the decision-making process. The correct combination is determined not only by the decision being made and the information available but also by the decision maker.

The Person

Since different decision makers use different mental processes and abilities to make the same decisions, the characteristics of the person deciding should be considered when developing computer systems that support decision making (see Table 7.7). Decision makers vary in how they define the problem, as well as how they filter, analyze, and integrate the information associated with a decision. Agency IT applications designed for one type of user will be less successful than systems that recognize the decision-making styles of a variety of users.

Decision makers vary in their aptitudes and attitudes. *Aptitude* is a combination of natural abilities, such as inherent physical, emotional, and intellectual talents and capabilities acquired through education and training. A person's aptitude for making decisions can be affected by excitability, attention span, memory, intelligence, intuition, and analytic abilities. Traditional job analysis takes a more applied approach. It considers aptitudes in working with people, numbers, and objects as most relevant to a task. *Attitudes* are ways of thinking, feeling, or acting. Attitudes may be general, such as when one is an optimist, or they can also be situational,

TABLE 7.7. Attributes Describing the Decision Maker

Aptitude

Low Aptitude		High Aptitude
poor at working with people	⇔	good at working with people
poor at working with numbers	⇔	good at working with numbers
poor at working with things	⇔	good at working with things

Attitude

Negative Attitude		Positive Attitude
pessimistic	⇔	optimistic

(too many relevant attitudes exist to be listed)

Cognitive Style

Low End of the Continuum		High End of the Continuum
low cognitive complexity	⇔	high cognitive complexity
low need for achievement	⇔	high need for achievement
low risk-taking propensity	⇔	high risk-taking propensity
thinking	⇔	feeling (Jungian model)
analytic	⇔	intuitive (learning style model)

Hemisphere Dominance

Left Hemisphere		Right Hemisphere
verbal	⇔	perceptual or nonverbal
linguistic	⇔	visual or kinesthetic
logical, analytical	⇔	spatial, analogical, holistic, global
rational	⇔	intuitive, metaphoric
Western thought	⇔	Eastern thought
intellectual	⇔	intuitive
convergent	⇔	divergent
deductive	⇔	imaginative
discrete, concrete	⇔	continuous, abstract
realistic	⇔	impulsive
directed	⇔	experiential
sequential, historical	⇔	simultaneous, timeless
objective	⇔	subjective
systematic	⇔	heuristic

such as when one has a "bad day." Physical characteristics such as size and attractiveness may influence one's aptitude and attitudes, as well as the receptivity of others to one's decision making.

Attitudes and aptitudes may be encompassed in cognitive style. Cognitive style is a consistent characteristic of functioning that individuals show in their perceptual and intellectual activities (Witkins, 1971). Several factors affecting cognitive style are cognitive complexity, need for achievement, and risk-taking propensity. Some researchers see cognitive style as the basic element determining how individuals define decisions and gather, filter, interpret, analyze, and integrate information (Schkade and Potvin, 1981). One extreme of the cognitive style continuum is typically described as thinking, analytical, logical, or deductive. The other extreme is feeling, intuitive, holistic, or inductive. Researchers often relate cognitive style to brain hemisphere dominance (Kettlehut and Schkade, 1991; Springer, and Deutsch, 1981). Some researchers suggest that IT applications should supply information to allow practitioners to use both inductive and deductive approaches to decision making. Open-ended, inductive analysis is necessary to complement the use of indicator-based, deductive performance measures (Cohen and Auslander, 1996).

The Environment

Decision making is also strongly influenced by the environment in which the decision is made. Many individual decision-making models fail to take into account the other people in the decision-making process. A funding source or supervisor may dictate that a certain decision-making style be followed. Group rules and norms may state that junior group members consult with the senior member who is ultimately responsible for the decision. Situations may exist in which no member is responsible for a decision and all group members must reach a consensus. A group may function harmoniously or choose several conflicting solutions, as when majority and minority opinions are part of the same debate.

Since human services are typically organization based, the organization is also a powerful environmental influence on human service decision making. One organizational factor is the level at which the decision is made, that is, the policy, management, or practitioner level. Other organizational factors include corporate image or style, for example, innovative, aggressive, or reliable.

IMPLICATIONS OF SYSTEMS
AND DECISION-MAKING THEORIES

Systems and decision-making theories can help to assess, explain, predict, and control. They offer a framework for examining problems and their solutions that may not be foreseen by examining practice alone. They have many implications for human services IT. Several of the most important follow.

Planning Parts with the Whole in Mind

The tendency when building IT applications is to begin by solving a small problem. As more problems are addressed, additional IT applications are built and added. Using such an approach can produce IT applications that have problems due to the development of a subsystem without prior examination of the total system.

The systems perspective focuses our analysis on the larger system and helps us to understand why building a subsystem without considering the whole system can be problematic. For example, an agency that does not have an IT plan may buy an application that is too narrowly focused or that cannot expand to meet future demands. Another example is when an agency builds an application without involving other parts of the agency. No matter how well one application is performing, it may have to be changed when merged with the overall system. Thus, considerable analysis and planning are critical in understanding the whole before we design any of the parts of a system. Agencies often neglect analysis and planning because they are the most difficult, unrewarding, and seemingly unproductive tasks in systems development. Overall planning is especially difficult in large organizations; yet the success of any application is highly dependent on systematic planning.

Information Is the Easiest Decision-Making Element to Change

Having examined the four elements in the decision-making process, it becomes apparent that the element most easily changed is information, one reason being that substantial IT tools exist for this task. Thus, a general principle for developing an application is to first change the information to the extent possible before changing the decisions or the decision makers. The chance of application failure increases when people and organizations must change substantially.

We often restructure decisions so paraprofessionals make the less complex decisions and highly trained professionals make the most complex decisions. However, systems theory warns that grouping decisions may prevent practitioners from taking a holistic and synergistic view of a client's situation. Restructuring decisions simply to enhance an IT application should be approached with caution.

Learning Systems

Systems that use technology to store information can be designed to learn from the past. The key to learning is a well-developed feedback loop, control mechanisms, and success criteria. Adding learning to a system is often neglected because time is required for the design and data collection. However, the payoff from developing learning systems is great. Hile (1998) reviewed Target Cities Projects that developed multiagency information systems for drug and alcohol programs. One of the design requirements was that:

> Systematic monitoring and evaluation provide the tools necessary for self-correcting systems. In the real world, things change and those changes need responses. Only by monitoring continuously can systems be sufficiently cognizant of those changes to make the necessary adjustments. (p. 3)

The Target Cities Projects' developers indicated that feeding back continuous improvement information improved the success of an application.

Consistent with this finding, Berlin and Marsh (1993) suggest that clinical practitioners who make better use of information know what to look for, have fewer preconceptions, derive useful inferences from observations, consistently keep track of important configurations so that small changes can be discerned over time, and have a system for organizing and remembering the emerging facts of a case. They state that a formal system for organizing, remembering, and tracking small changes is important: "it is important for clinicians to have a relatively explicit sense of what things to watch for and what these things mean, as well as the ability to adjust their thinking and actions on the basis of what they see" (p. 14).

Taking the extra time to developing continuous learning into IT applications pays off in the long term.

The Importance of Measurement and Mapping

Measuring complex phenomena has always been a struggle. Mathematics is the field in which measurement technology has developed and flourished. However, even definition of a simple phenomenon often requires a complex set of mathematical formulas. Mathematics works best representing phenomena that are measurable on standard scales, such as one's age. When we cannot make precise measures, we often use probabilities and statistical analyses to help express the imprecision. For example, we say an opinion poll is accurate within plus or minus three percentage points. Mathematics and probabilities are less useful in mapping human service phenomena such as ethnicity, anger, suffering, abuse, and depression. Human service IT applications could benefit from techniques that allow measurement, codification, and mapping of complex information, such as that contained in the following statement:

> Based on my experience, I find this home environment to be very risky for the child, but I am not very confident of this conclusion given the information I have now.

One solution to the measurement problem is to avoid analysis and instead focus on the arrangement of inputs that are associated with a specified output. We characterize this as the *black box approach* because the processes that change inputs into outputs are considered unobservable, unexplainable, and unknowable, as if concealed in a black box. Behavior modification often uses a black box approach. Behavior modification postulates that treatment should focus on input behaviors that consistently result in the desired output behaviors. The reasons a client's problems exist or how the behavioral treatment works are less important than results.

The black box approach suggests we can associate precise manipulations of inputs with measurable outputs with a degree of predictability, regardless of whether we understand the processes involved. The weakness of the back box approach is that the associations between inputs and outputs must be highly suspect, even if they are strong. Agency information systems coupled with neural networks and case-based reasoning techniques typify the black box approach. Care must be taken that such applications are only used to flag exceptions, match similarities, or tally relationships that practitioners can consider as second opinions.

To compensate for the inability to measure a phenomenon, we often use general principles, procedures, artificial taxonomies, rules of thumb, and ethical codes. The *Diagnostic and Statistical Manual of Mental Disorders* (DSM) is a good example of a set of terms and procedures for working with mental illness. DSM classifications provide a direction to the practitioner seeking complex solutions with imprecise information. The DSM also helps practitioners communicate about knowledge and practices. However, classifications such as the DSM should be used with caution. Insurance company payment may influence practitioner DSM classification more than the assessment of the client's problem.

Another implication of systems and decision-making theories is that measurement and mapping must take into account the contingencies under which the decision making occurs. Tables 7.5 to 7.7 summarize the elements of decision making and the attributes of each element. Research frameworks are beginning to appear that examine the interactions of these elements. For example, Table 7.8 presents one analysis of the interactions of two of the elements in Table 7.5, information and environmental context.

TABLE 7.8. Interaction of the Information and Organization-Level Components of Decision Making

Information Characteristics	Organization Level		
	Direct Service	Middle	Top Management
Source	largely internal	⟺	external
Scope	well defined, narrow	⟺	very wide
Level of detail	detailed	⟺	aggregate
Time focus	present	⟺	past/future
Currency required	very current	⟺	quite old
Accuracy required	high accuracy	⟺	moderate accuracy
Frequency of use	very frequent	⟺	infrequent
Type	quantitative	⟺	qualitative

Source: Adapted from "Human Service Workers As the Primary Information System User" by D. Schoech and L. L. Schkade, 1981, in R. R. Schmitt and H. J. Smolin (Eds.), *Urban, Regional, and Environmental Information: Needs, Sources, Systems, and Uses—Papers from the Annual Conference of the Urban and Regional Information Systems Association,* Washington, DC, Urban and Regional Information Systems Association (URISA), pp. 71-81.

Table 7.8 also illustrates the difference between the needs of managers and practitioners. The common practice of selling management oriented information systems as beneficial to practitioners fails to consider the analysis of Table 7.8. Robey and Taggart (1982) have attempted to develop a model of decision making by combining three decision-making elements: cognitive style, the decision, and the information. Their research suggests that analytical persons operating with structured data reports perform structured tasks best. Nonanalytic, intuitive problem solvers using flexible, nonlinear, graphic data reports perform less-structured tasks best. Although we need more complex models, these are a step in the right direction. Flexibility in such areas as data formats, timing, and data presentation will let users define models that take into account the realities of decision making.

The Construction of Dynamic Models

As mentioned in the previous discussion, one way to handle imprecision and complexity is to construct models. A *model* is a simplified replication of reality that aids understanding and/or prediction. Several types of models exist (see Table 7.9). IT provides excellent dynamic modeling tools because it allows complex feedback loops and rapid calculation of

TABLE 7.9. Types and Classifications of Models

Type	Distinguishing Features	Example
Verbal models	Verbal descriptions of phenomena	A story
Schematics	Two-dimensional drawings	Diagrams, pictures, charts, and graphs
Iconic model	A small-scale three-dimensional physical replica or representation	An anatomically correct doll used in child abuse investigations
Analog models	Based on analogous relationships	Action in a wind tunnel is analogous to movements in flight
Mathematical models	Uses symbols and mathematical formulas to represent reality	The mathematical formula for poverty
Deterministic	Lack the capacity to represent chance events	Computer playing chess
Stochastic	Take chance events into account	Payoff schedule for a slot machine
Static models	Represent reality at one point in time	City map
Flow models	Inputs, processes, and outputs can be ranges rather than points	Model of how floodplains work
Dynamic models	Can change course based on model-generated feedback	A thermostat, a mock battle

the relationships between complex phenomena. To develop an IT application that supports the human service practitioner, one must develop models of the information practitioners use in their work with clients. If the understanding of a problem is too poor to allow us to build an appropriate model, then a smaller phenomenon should be selected.

CONCLUSION

This chapter provided an overview of systems and decision making and showed that IT applications become information models of the decisions they support. Thus, an understanding of systems and decision making helps develop IT applications. The next chapter builds on this analysis by examining the information needs associated with human service decisions.

REVIEW AND DISCUSSION QUESTIONS

1. View your educational institution as a system. What are the goals of the system? What are the inputs, processes, and outputs? What feedback loops and control information ensure that the system will achieve its goals?
2. Answer the questions in number one for a human service agency with which you are familiar.
3. Why is the systems perspective important for IT? That is, what does it offer IT development that nontheoretical approaches do not?
4. Why is knowledge of decision making important for IT?
5. Describe two non-technology-based and two technology-based models in the human services. What processes do they model? How are they used in practice?
6. Name two non-technology-based and two technology-based human service decision-making tools. What types of decisions do they support? How are they used in practice?
7. What is your personal cognitive style? (use the dimensions in Table 7.7)
8. What capabilities does IT add to our attempts to improve decision making?

Chapter 8

Assessing Human Service
Information Needs

INTRODUCTION

The discussion on change in Chapter 6 pointed out the importance of conducting a thorough assessment of information needs before designing IT applications. Chapter 7 presented theoretical concepts that are helpful in this assessment. This chapter uses several approaches to analyze human service information needs. The first section discusses the organizational influences on human service decision making, contrasting human service organizations with business production organizations to better understand these influences. The second section examines the processes and decision making at each level of the human service delivery system. It also presents the information needed to support these processes and decisions. The final section discusses the implications of human service information needs for designing and developing IT applications. This analysis is a beginning attempt to determine the information base of human service practice from an IT perspective.

ORGANIZATIONAL INFLUENCES ON HUMAN SERVICE INFORMATION NEEDS

External Organizational Influences

External organizational influences on information needs will be discussed in terms of sociocultural, economic, political/legal, and technological aspects. Table 8.1 summarizes this discussion.

TABLE 8.1. External Influences on Information Needs

Area of Difference	Human Service Agency	Production Organization
Social and Cultural		
Right to service	Services seen as society's responsibility	Customer's rights to products are limited
Competition	Little competition in a service area	Marketplace is open and competitive
Economic		
Accountability, efficiency, and effectiveness	Accountability is most important	Efficiency is most important
Customer impact on survival	Grants and contracts sustain agency	Sales to customers sustain business
Political and Legal		
Influence of outside forces into internal operations	Outside forces may heavily influence internal operations, e.g., the press	Outside forces have limited direct impact on the internal organization
Composition of board	Citizens, consumers, and providers with no financial ties to agency	Business influentials with a financial interest in the organization
Tax incentives to adopt technology	Technology purchases offer no tax advantages	Technology purchases are tax deductible
Technological		
Incentives to develop technology	Adopting new technology can be risky	Adopting new technology is necessary to be competitive
Profitability of developing new technologies	New technologies are rarely sold to other agencies	New technologies are often sold to other businesses

Sociocultural Influences

One sociocultural force influencing human service information needs is the view that society has an obligation to care for its members in need. Thus, clients are often seen as having an inherent right to human services. The support for this view is constantly fluctuating in our society. This fluctuation results in the unstable and conflicting goals and mandates so often found in human service agencies. Given this unstable support for goals, many agencies do not specify exactly which objectives, tasks, and processes achieve these goals. By not translating societal wishes into precise information, an agency avoids recording information about actions taken against society's wishes. An IT application containing information based on goals, processes, and decisions that have fluctuating community support may be a liability if controversy surfaces. Managers learn that verbal directions are more flexible and less subject to scrutiny than advice written in software or available over the Internet. Verbal directions permit ad hoc handling of situations based on professional judgment and the unique facts of the immediate situation. For example, one mental health intake and assessment application was designed with a suicide prediction scale. However, administrators did not have the policies and resources to handle the suicide assessment. Consequently, the agency deleted the suicide scale until it could determine how to adequately respond to this.

In contrast to human service organizations, production organizations produce goods and services in response to market demands. With profit as an overriding goal, production organizations rarely experience the dramatic shifts in ideology found in the political system. Customers have only those rights associated with the purchased product or services. In production organizations, consumer demands and rights can be more easily translated into quantifiable organizational goals and objectives. Consequently, the processes, decision making, and information needs are more precisely defined, especially in the area of management control. This sociocultural influence is reflected in IT applications. Applications that track, predict, and influence market forces are considered essential for production organizations. However, similar applications are rarely found in human service organizations.

Economic Influences

The second category of environmental forces that influences human service information needs concerns the organization's economic environment. Profits from sales sustain production organizations, whereas human service organizations derive most of their funds from multiple government and private sources. Human service funds are not always related to the quantity of service needed or provided. Thus, agencies are often more inclined to satisfy funding sources rather than clients, who cannot go to a competing agency for services. For example, many hospitals can deliver your bill quicker than they can deliver your medical record.

The reliance by human service agencies on multiple, changing, external funding complicates information collection. One problem is that all funding sources rarely agree on what information agencies should report. The various funding sources of an agency may represent many different constituencies, which together place conflicting demands on the agency. Meeting client needs efficiently and ensuring client satisfaction do not always result in funding source satisfaction and agency survival.

Ideally, information needed for service delivery is similar to that demanded by environmental forces, but this is not always the case. In agencies that serve involuntary clients, the conflict between funding and client information requirements is obvious. For example, an abusive parent rarely wants data collected about the abuse. In agencies that serve voluntary clients, the conflict between client and funding source influences may be equally extreme. For example, many funding sources demand information on cost per service hour, yet consider details on service outcomes as too complex for their citizen boards to understand. Cost per service hour has little meaning to a practitioner treating a client in need.

The difference between information needed to serve clients and information needed by funding sources can be seen by comparing the information collected by publicly funded agencies with that collected by private practitioners. The amount of information collected by a counselor in a mental health or family service agency is typically much greater than that collected by a counselor in private practice.

In summary, when funding sources provide conflicting influences, establishing clear goals, processes, decisions, and information support is problematic. Reporting to multiple, changing funding sources requires IT application flexible enough to manipulate and format the data for many different reports.

Political and Legal Influences

The third category of environmental forces that impact human service information needs concerns political and legal influences. In production organizations, outside forces intrude into internal management only if gross negligence has occurred or the "public good" is at stake. In human services, external groups such as funding sources, legislatures, courts, and agency boards often intrude into the detailed operations of the agency. In private, nonprofit human service organizations, the agency board of directors, not the executive director, is legally responsible for debts and other organizational liabilities. Developing IT applications may be a riskier effort for a human service executive than for an executive of a production organization. Human service managers with little control and responsibility for internal operations may be reluctant to computerize information unless long-term support is assured. For example, a change in political parties due to an election may result in rapid and dramatic changes in human service delivery practices. Newcombe (1997) details the disastrous effect of federal and state policy shifts on California's statewide welfare information system (see Table 8.2).

TABLE 8.2. Environmental Influences on the California Statewide Automated Welfare System (SAWS)

1979	First attempt to develop SPAN, the Statewide Public Assistance Network.
1983	State legislature defunds SPAN and spending $15,000,000.
1984	Legislature decentralizes welfare automation with five demonstration projects.
1985	Federal government agrees to supplement costs only if one system, SAWS, is developed.
1989	State develops SAWS and two pilot systems, (1) MAGIC, a client/server system, and (2) NAPAS, a mainframe system.
1991	State stops all SAWS activities to evaluate the NAPAS and MAGIC systems.
1993	State decides that NAPAS will be the sole system for SAWS and federal supplemental funds are terminated.
1994	Unisys receives a controversial sole source contract for piloting SAWS in 14 counties. $800 million spent on SAWS to date.
1995	State auditor declares SAWS will not work. Governor moves SAWS management into another department and SAWS broken into four systems to come online in 1996, 1998, 1999, and 2002. Total cost for SAWS since 1979 is approximately $1 billion.

Source: Adapted from "Prodigal System: California's SAWS" by T. Newcombe, 1997 *Government Technology, 10*(13), pp. 1, 126-130. Copyright © *Government Technology* magazine. Reprinted with permission.

A legal factor affecting hardware acquisition is that human service agencies cannot depreciate capital expenditures. In production organizations, incentives exist to keep IT applications current, since fully depreciated equipment offers no tax advantage. In contrast, IT equipment represents a greater financial investment for a human service agency and a longer-term commitment. This factor is especially important given the rapid change in IT.

Technology Influences

The fourth category of environmental forces influencing human service information needs is technology. The incentives for the adoption of technology are different for human service organizations than for production organizations. Skillfully adapting technology in most production processes is crucial to delivering a quality, competitive product. Adopting innovative technologies is often a prime factor in organizational survival. In human service agencies, the adoption of technology may have little influence on agency survival. Making large organizational changes, such as those associated with an IT application, can cause disruption, raise controversy, and produce few rewards.

In-house research and development of new production technology for industry is often beneficial to individual employees. Scientists can become wealthy from high salaries and royalties from patented inventions. In contrast, in-house development of human service technology is uncommon. IT usually involves a joint effort of academic researchers, funding sources, and agency personnel. Research and development in the human services is rarely profitable for individuals or the agency.

Internal Organizational Influences

A second group of influences on human service information needs stems from the internal components of goals, people, structure, tasks, and technology. Table 8.3 summarizes these influences.

Goals

Goals translate external and internal influences into agency directions and guide the setting of objectives and work plans. A major difference between goals in human service and production organizations is the degree of measurability. Most production organizations can measure goal achievement by products sold, dividends to shareholders, expansion, or customer satisfaction. Human service goals usually concern total clients seen or hours of service provided rather than client change or client satisfaction. Even if client change is measured, those measures can rarely be translated into agency goal achievement. For example, many agencies have goals that concern improving the mental and social well-being of clients, but consensus rarely exists on what behaviors constitute mental and social well-being.

Another problem with goal measurement is that few criteria exist to determine an acceptable rate of success. For example, overcoming an addiction is a very difficult process. What success rate should an agency strive to achieve for persons with addictions? An agency that reports a client success rate of "15 percent of clients drug-free after one year of treatment" may have an excellent or poor success record. Agencies often avoid collecting information about success because they fear funding sources will favor programs promising better success. When success measures are established, agencies often practice "creaming," or taking the easiest clients, to show greater success. Developing success measures is also problematic because good measures require follow-up after the intervention has ended. Clients may see this continued agency involvement as an invasion of privacy.

TABLE 8.3. Internal Influences on Information Needs

Area of Difference	Human Service Agency	Production Organization
Goals		
Setting of goals	Goals often mandated by external forces	Goals usually set internally by managers
Goal consistency and stability	Goals may be conflicting and unstable	Goals are consistent and relatively stable
Measurability of goal achievement	Difficult to quantify, e.g., well-being	Relatively easy to quantity, e.g., profit
People		
Most numerous employees	Highly trained professionals	Blue-collar workers
Influence of employee associations	Influence how tasks are performed, e.g., through values and ethics	Influence what and how many tasks are performed
Consistency of approach	Approach to similar problems varies by discipline	All workers handle similar problems the same way
Structure		
Number of hierarchies	Professional and managerial coexist	Managerial predominates
Tasks		
Complexity of decisions	Usually very complex decisions	Usually routine decisions
Repetitiveness of task	Each client is considered unique	Most tasks are repetitive
Nature of problem addressed	Problems are crisis oriented and concern major problems of living	Problems concern people's everyday needs
Technology		
Basis of technology used	Person-to-person interaction	Person-machine interaction
Products of technology	Complex intangible services	Tangible items

One common method used to measure goal achievement is to ask clients if they are satisfied with services. Clients typically report satisfaction levels of 60 to 80 percent, even when services are inferior (Franklin and Thrasher, 1976). Various explanations are given for this high satisfaction rate, such as fear of being denied future services. Also, client satisfaction may not be an indication of client change. For example, student satisfaction may not be a good indicator that learning has occurred.

Because of the problems with optimizing human service goals, feedback loops and control mechanisms are relatively weak and imprecise. Goal achievement information at one level may be of little use at other levels in an agency. For example, policy information, such as the number of clients served, does not help a practitioner who is struggling to resolve a family crisis, and feedback that is valuable to the practitioner may be too detailed and complex for use at the policy and management levels.

Until goal measurement problems are resolved, human service goals will not provide adequate direction for human service decision making and information needs.

People

People are another influence on human service information needs, since highly trained professionals usually deliver human services. Practitioner education requirements are often higher than those for their managers. Practitioners learn theories, skills, and a scientific approach to decision making, along with professional values and ethics. Values and ethics often influence practice in complex situations in which theory and data fail to provide guidance. In contrast, production workers typically are less educated than their managers and have fewer professional ties. Labor unions and professional trade associations influence *what* and *how many* tasks are performed, whereas human service associations have more influence over *how* tasks are performed.

Another people-related influence is that human services contain a variety of professions and specialties that may require different types of information for approaching the same problem. For example, the processes, decisions, and information required by a Freudian practitioner may be different from those required by a behaviorist.

Structure

Structure concerns the arrangement of people to achieve organizational goals. Organization charts and job descriptions illustrate the formal agency structure. Major structural differences exist between human service organizations and production organizations.

Production organizations have a managerial hierarchy that defines and monitors efficiency and effectiveness. In human service organizations, a professional hierarchy usually coexists with a managerial hierarchy. For example, the chief psychiatrist in a mental health agency may have more power and receive a higher salary than the executive director. The professional hierarchy typically stresses effectiveness, while the managerial hierarchy stresses efficiency. In other human service organizations, the managerial hierarchy may predominate. The hierarchy that predominates impacts IT applications. For example, it is not surprising to find a hospital's management information system more sophisticated than its patient information system, because management holds the dominant position.

Task

Tasks reflect the nature of the work an organization performs. Production and human service tasks differ primarily at the bottom levels of the organization. The bottom level in production organizations often involves relatively simple, repetitive decisions and tasks that are easily supported by IT. In human service agencies, tasks at the service level frequently involve unique problems and complex, nonrepetitive decision making, for example, therapy and child maltreatment assessment. Many human service tasks are very difficult to support with IT. Also, human service tasks often involve the tragic aspects of the human condition. They can have a major, often irreversible, impact on the lives of clients.

Technology

Technology concerns the application of science to tasks and processes. Production technology is based on human-machine interactions that transform natural resources into products or services. Human service technology is based on person-to-person interactions that use information to provide services. Human service technology is typically less measurable and more complex than production technology.

Technology is perhaps the key difference between human service and production organizations. Many of the distinctions in Tables 8.1 and 8.3 diminish as technology changes from manufacturing to service provision, regardless of profit or nonprofit status. Contrasting a human service organization with a consulting firm using Tables 8.1 and 8.3 would result in many of the differences disappearing.

This comparison of production and human service organizations indicates that many organizational forces influence human service information needs. Consequently, human service information needs are complex, ill-defined, imprecise, and often subject to disagreement. Specifying the information needed to support human service decision making is difficult, especially at the bottom levels of the agency.

INFLUENCES OF HUMAN SERVICE PROCESSES
AND DECISION MAKING ON INFORMATION NEEDS

This section investigates human service information needs by examining the processes and decision making that occurs at various organizational levels, including policy/community planning, top management, middle management, direct service, client, and education levels. Applications capable of supporting the processes and decisions at one level may not support other levels as well. Developing an application to support all levels can be a complex and risky task.

Policy/Community Planning Level

The processes for policy and community planning differ somewhat. A typical policy process includes the following steps:

1. Search for theories, models, and data.
2. Use brainstorming and analysis to form policy ideas.
3. Develop policy options.
4. Choose the preferred policy option.
5. Develop details of chosen policy.
6. Monitor and evaluate policy implementation.

A typical planning process involves the following elements:

1. Sensing (getting the lay of the land, making contacts, establishing trust, assessing resources)
2. Clarifying overall direction by establishing a vision and guiding principles
3. Assessing and prioritizing needs and capacities
4. Intervention planning through goals and objectives
5. Developing immediate activities and recommendations
6. Implementing
7. Monitoring and evaluating

The key decisions at the policy/planning level involve the allocation of resources (who gets what), delivery methods (how services are delivered), and reimbursement mechanisms (who pays). Both policy and planning use group decision making where professional staff support nonprofessional citizen groups. Although citizen groups and professional staff follow similar processes and make similar decisions, their information needs vary considerably. For example, professional staff typically can assimilate much more detailed and complex data analysis than citizen groups.

Throughout the policy/planning process, decision makers need information such as the type and number of existing services, perceived and documented service needs, physical and psychological barriers to utilization, and demographic information. The format of needed information varies from raw data required by staff to easily understood summaries required by citizen groups. Some useful summarizing techniques are stories, pictures, graphics, statistical analyses, models, and simulations. Although the timing of information delivery to citizen groups is important, staff continually accumulate information that has potential for future analysis.

The decision making typical at the policy/planning level can be analyzed by plotting a decision using the categories outlined in Chapter 7. In Figure 8.1, the "p" rankings characterize professional staff policy decision making, the "c" rankings characterize citizen policy decision making, and the "x" rankings characterize both professional and citizen policy decision making. Although these rankings are not research based, they illustrate that policy/planning information needs for citizen groups and professional staff are similar in many ways, yet they can be quite different. Consequently, information systems to support policy decisions are difficult and expensive to conceptualize and design. Service providers often collect voluminous information simply to meet the complex and varied information needs of planning, policymaking, and funding bodies. The Internet seems a more effective tool for supporting policy and planning decisions because it provides easy continuous access to synthesized information in easily understood formats.

Top Management Level

Top management processes involve the following:

1. Leadership and setting the organizational climate
2. Designing and monitoring goals, objectives, and work plans
3. Negotiations within and between internal and external forces
4. Representing the agency to the community

FIGURE 8.1. Characteristics of Policy Decision Making

The complexity of the decision

understandable	|_____x__|	incomprehensible
predictable	|_____x_|	unpredictable
routine	|_____x__|	nonroutine
programmable	|_____x_|	nonprogrammable
familiar	|_____x__|	unfamiliar
high chance of success	|_____x__|	low chance of success
well-structured	|_____x_____|	ill-structured

The consequences associated with making the decision

unaccountable	|___p_____c__|	accountable
hard to measure	|____c_____p___|	easy to measure
low agreement on success	|_____p____c__|	high agreement on success
reversible	|_____x__|	irreversible
uncertainty	|____x_____|	certainty

The resources typically available to the decision maker

low funding	|_____x_____|	high funding
little time	|_____x___|	much time
little expertise	|___x_____|	much expertise
few technologies	|___x_____|	many technologies
few people	|_____x_____|	many people

The environment in which the decision is made

democratic tradition	|__c_____p__|	autocratic tradition
confrontational atmosphere	|__c_____p__|	appeasement atmosphere

The measurability of the information typically available

summary	|__c_____p_|	detailed
low accuracy	|_x_____|	high accuracy
low verifiability	|_x_____|	high verifiability
error/bias prone	|_x_____|	free of error and bias
qualitative	|_x_____|	quantitative
probabilistic	|_x_____|	deterministic
unreliable	|__x_____|	reliable
invalid	|_____x_____|	valid

The time frame associated with the information available

frequent	|_____x__|	infrequent
current	|_____x__|	old
past	|___x_____|	future
presented on time	|__c_____p_|	presented early or late

The adequacy associated with the information

comprehensive	|_____x___|	fragmented
appropriate	|_____x_____|	inappropriate
clear	|_____x_|	unclear
right source	|_____x___|	wrong source
accessible	|_____x_|	inaccessible
available	|_____x__|	unavailable
flexible	|_____x_|	inflexible

The characteristics of the decision maker

poor at working with people	|____p_____c_|	good at working with people
poor at working with numbers	|__c_____p_|	good at working with numbers
poor at working with objects	|__c_____p_|	good at working with objects
low cognitive complexity	|_____x_____|	high cognitive complexity
low need for achievement	|___p_____c_|	high need for achievement
low risk-taking propensity	|___p_____c_|	high risk-taking propensity
left brain	|___p_____c_|	right brain

Note: Ratings are not based on research.

Top management decisions concern setting agency policy, hiring key personnel, allocating resources, and structuring staff duties and responsibilities. Policy guidelines inherent in legislation, regulations, grant requirements, and citizen committees can lessen the complexity and risk of top management decision making. One can also argue that vague policies can result in top management decision making being similar to policy-level decision making. This argument is true if top management's role includes making policy, as in nonprofit organizations where executives often receive little guidance from their volunteer boards of directors. It is not true if top management's role is primarily policy implementation, as in government departments that are heavily controlled by legislative oversight and law.

Thus, depending on the organization, top management decision making and information needs are similar to those at the policy/planning or the middle management levels.

Middle Management Level

Middle management processes have been traditionally described as planning, organizing, staffing, directing, coordinating, reporting, budgeting, and evaluating. Middle management decision making is more detailed than that of top management in areas such as job monitoring, budgeting, and staffing. Collected information is often the basis of quality assurance programs, program evaluation efforts, and accountability reports to funding sources. At the middle management level, decision making becomes less risky, more quantifiable, routine, and procedural. The decisions with which agency evaluators, accountants, and supervisors must contend are less complex and more predictable than those at higher or lower organizational levels. The information needs of top and middle management are presented in Figure 8.2.

FIGURE 8.2. Characteristics of Management and Worker Decision Making

The complexity of the decision

understandable	I___■_____w__t__I	incomprehensible
predictable	I___■_____t_w_I	unpredictable
routine	I___■_____w___t__I	nonroutine
programmable	I___■_____w__t__I	nonprogrammable
familiar	I___■_____w_t_____I	unfamiliar
high chance of success	I_____■___t__w___I	low chance of success
well-structured	I___■_____w_t__I	ill-structured

The consequences associated with making the decision

unaccountable	I_____■__w__t_____I	accountable
hard to measure	I___w_t____■_____I	easy to measure
low agreement on success	I___t___w____■____I	high agreement on success
reversible	I_____■____t_w__I	irreversible
uncertainty	I____t_w_____■____I	certainty

The resources typically available to the decision maker

low funding	I___■_w_t_____I	high funding
little time	I__w___x_____I	much time
little expertise	I____t___w_____■___I	much expertise
few technologies	I__t_w_____■____I	many technologies
few people	I__t__■____w_____I	many people

The environment in which the decision is made

democratic tradition	I_____■_t__w___I	autocratic tradition
confrontational atmosphere	I_____w_t_■__I	appeasement atmosphere

The measurability of the information typically available

summary	l__w_t_____m___l	detailed
low accuracy	l__w_t_____m___l	high accuracy
low verifiability	l____t__w_____m___l	high verifiability
error/bias prone	l__w_t_____m___l	free of error and bias
qualitative	l__w_t_____m___·l	quantitative
probabilistic	l___w_t_____m___l	deterministic
unreliable	l_____w_t_____m___l	reliable
invalid	l_____w_t_____m__l	valid

The time frame associated with the information typically available

frequent	l_____m_____w__t__l	infrequent
current	l_w____m_____t__l	old
past	l__t__m_____w_____l	future
presented on time	l_w_t___m_____l	presented early or late

The adequacy associated with the information

comprehensive	l_____m_____t_w_l	fragmented
appropriate	l_____m_w_t_____l	inappropriate
clear	l_____m___t_w_____l	unclear
right source	l_w___m___t_____l	wrong source
accessible	l_____m___t_w_____l	inaccessible
available	l_____m___t___w___l	unavailable
flexible	l_____m___t_w_____l	inflexible

The characteristics of the decision maker

poor at working with people	l_____m_t____w_l	good at working with people
poor at working with numbers	l__w_t_____m__l	good at working with numbers
poor at working with things	l__w_t_____m__l	good at working with things
low cognitive complexity	l_____m____w_t_l	high cognitive complexity
low need for achievement	l_____m_w_t__l	high need for achievement
low risk-taking propensity	l___m_____t_w__l	high risk-taking propensity
left brain	l___m_____t_w__l	right brain

t = top management; m = middle management; x = both top and middle management; w = worker

Note: Ratings are not based on research.

The Direct Service Level

The direct service level involves the most complex and undefined processes because practitioners are interacting with people in trouble or facing crises. Management provides the structure, atmosphere, and basic performance objectives while professional practitioners are responsible for work details. How well practitioners perform their work is determined by professional education and experience, as well as by professional values and ethics. The interfaces between professionally prescribed behavior, management-prescribed behavior, and environmental forces are often troublesome areas. For example, practitioners have been arrested and charged with crimes while following standard operating procedures (see Figure 8.3).

The following processes typically occur during service delivery:

1. Client identification
2. Client needs and capacities assessment
3. Eligibility determination
4. Client intake and establishment of case
5. Detailed assessment
6. Case planning
7. Case management
   a. Delivery of service
   b. Service arrangement with another agency
   c. Purchase of services
8. Case monitoring
9. Case evaluation
10. Case closure

However, not all practitioners' time is spent in direct client contact. Surveys of public agencies typically find that practitioners spend 30 to 60 percent of their time in direct client contact; the remaining time is spent in activities that support client contact and in documenting their work. Thus, practitioners' information needs differ if they are managing their work or interacting with clients.

The information practitioners need to manage their work is similar to that of midlevel managers discussed previously. The remainder of this section will focus on the decision making and information needed during the professional practitioner-client interaction. The decisions made as professionals interact with clients should be distinguished from the more routine and structured decision making of paraprofessionals such as food stamp workers and institutional care workers.

Decisions at the professional direct service level can be characterized as nonroutine and ill-structured. Dire consequences can result from making a wrong decision. The information available is often incomplete, qualitative, and unverifiable. The decision-making process is often characterized by incomplete information, educated guessing, judgments, and consultation among peers or between practitioners and their supervisors. Successful

FIGURE 8.3. Workers' Arrest Illustrates Conflicting Influences on Practice Behavior

On June 22, Judge McClung ordered the arrest of four Texas Department of Human Resource (TDHR) employees: The Regional Director of Children and Family Services; The Dallas County Foster Home Director; the TDHR Attorney; and a caseworker. The four state employees were arrested, handcuffed, and escorted from the courtroom while television cameras recorded the event.

At the time he ordered the arrests, McClung said he was taking action because state authorities had failed to shut down a foster home for teenage boys after discovering the foster parents kept sexual devices and pornographic literature in their bedroom closet.

The legal cost of the four TDHR employees reached $17,000. Because the allegation at the time of their arrest was that the workers had committed a criminal offense, the state could not pay for their defense, said the TDHR commissioner.

In the end, no charges were brought against the TDHR employees. The foster parents disappeared shortly after publicity about the incident for which they face no criminal charges.

Source: Excerpted from *The Dallas Times Herald*, Saturday, February 2, 1985, p. a-33. Reprinted with permission of *The Dallas Morning News*.

decisions are expected despite the limited guidelines, time, and resources available to the decision maker.

Two steps in the service delivery process outlined earlier require complex decisions: (1) need and capacity assessment and (2) service delivery. If the client's problem is complex, case planning and case evaluation can also involve complex decision making. Table 8.4 illustrates the types of activities that occur during the service delivery process. The difficulty of defining the information needed for key direct service decisions is obvious when trying to establish data to support activities such as reflection and problem exploration. This complexity explains why a bachelor's or master's degree is required, even though practitioners spend much of their time on low-skill tasks such as monitoring and paperwork.

The job of a child protective service worker can help illustrate the information needs of professional practitioners at the direct service level. The information needed could be characterized as follows:

- The risk of harm and injury to a child for intervention options ranging from doing nothing to permanent removal
- Factual data, key activities, and events of similar cases, as well as some indication of whether the similar cases were successfully handled

- Knowledge of laws, agency rules, procedures, and how they affect the present case
- Knowledge of applicable theory and research
- Knowledge of the foster care and child care systems and the chances of the child or children progressing better in these systems than through treatment at home
- Knowledge of community standards and norms to anticipate or avoid a decision that may outrage the community
- Knowledge to monitor stress, burnout, and to protect personal safety.
- Capacities to rearrange, analyze, and synthesize information to answer "what if" types of questions

Ideally, workers should have abundant time and resources to make the correct decision rather than just an acceptable decision.

The crucial sources of information are usually supervisors, peers, experience, education, and case records. Case records may be a source of information, but they suffer from many problems. Among them are the time required to enter and retrieve information and the inconsistent quality and reliability of the information. Records are often used for quality assurance, accreditation, legal protection, and funding justification. Record contents often support those activities at the expense of supporting practitioners. For example, since insurance companies may pay only for certain mental health diagnoses, misinformation may purposely be entered into the client's record to obtain payment for services. Also, if workers do not use the information in their decision making, the tendency is to enter information that is the simplest rather than the most accurate.

TABLE 8.4. Activities During the Practitioner-Client Contact

Technique/Activity	Proportionate Use of Technique
Person-situation, personality, and early life reflection	40.0
Exploration-description-ventilation	39.9
Direct influence	6.4
Structuring the treatment relationship	6.0
Sustainment	4.1
Other	2.4

Source: From "Communication Processes in Social Work Practice" by A. E. Fortune, 1981, *Social Service Review, 50*(1), p. 100.

From the discussion in this chapter, we can conclude that practitioners need continuous access to the following resources:

- Data, information, and knowledge about agency activities and service outcomes
- Work reduction tools, such as applications that minimize routine paperwork, check meeting schedules for possible meeting times, or distribute information to selective groups
- Education that enhances understanding of a concept or topic
- Advice, such as that from (1) stored expertise, (2) examples that illustrate successful and unsuccessful practice, and (3) interaction and communication with experts
- Procedural help, such as (1) schematics of the current task, (2) software "coaches" that explain and work one through a procedure or through "models" of good practice, or (3) instructions that summarize complex processes or review previous training, for example, a short computer-controlled video simulation
- Self-assessments that monitor the user's proficiency with the current task or decision and that recommend help if needed
- Resources and reference materials, such as definitions of terms, interactive agency manuals, bibliographic listings, agency news, and community resources
- Emotional support, such as opportunities to vent emotions, remember pleasant experiences, or play games that distract and amuse

Client Level

The processes and information needs at the client level can be similar to those at the direct service delivery level. Clients need the following information:

- A thorough assessment and documentation of their problem
- An analysis to determine whether their problems require services
- An analysis of their strengths on which services can be based
- A description of all relevant services
- Information to evaluate the appropriateness of relevant services given the client's problems and strengths
- Information to monitor client progress and to know when to terminate services or reassess for different services

Education/Training Level

Decision making at the education/training level varies by the subject and teaching method. An instructor using the Socratic method would make different decisions and use different information than one using video-based methods. Also, the purpose of education influences the education process, for example, educating someone to think and learn independently requires a different process than training someone how to perform a particular task. Educating on how to learn involves teaching how to locate information, determine its importance, analyze and apply the information, and evaluate whether the appropriate conclusions were made. Training on a task involves learning to incorporate agency processes and procedures into practitioners' decision making. However, whatever the purpose of education, most teaching involves learner assessment, communication, and feedback to ensure that learning has occurred.

IT can change some teaching processes considerably. Easy access to electronic information allows educators to focus on processes associated with the integration and use of information rather than its acquisition. Two-way video can structure the delivery of curriculum materials. CAI can require very detailed presentation of curriculum because human flexibility during delivery is eliminated.

IMPLICATIONS OF INFORMATION NEEDS ON IT DESIGN AND DEVELOPMENT

Technology Transfer from Business

In the past, human service agencies have implemented IT applications patterned after those in production organizations, often using business technology specialists. The contrast between human service organizations and production organizations illustrates the distinct nature of human service information needs at various agency levels. Table 8.5 shows that business and human service decision-making characteristics are only the same at the middle management level. They are somewhat similar at the top management level and vastly different at the worker level.

This analysis suggests that the traditional business concept of an information system does not translate well into most human service organizations. Applications designed for top-level managers and policymakers may not be useful for middle managers. Corporate information system developers with no human service experience are likely to encounter problems designing human service applications. Therefore, they should work with someone who understands the information needs of various agency levels.

Applications based on management information concepts and implementation strategies may be successful at the middle management level,

TABLE 8.5. Decision Making in Business and Human Service Organizations

Organizational Level	Key Decision-Making Characteristics				
	Routine-ness	Quantity	Risk	Quantification	Environmental Complexity
Worker level					
Business	high	high	low	high	low
Human service	low	high	high	low	high
Midlevel management					
Business	med	med	med	med	med
Human service	med	med	med	med	med
Top-level management					
Business	low	high	high	low	high
Human service	low	med	med	low	high

Source: Adapted from "Human Service Workers As the Primary Information System User" by D. Schoech and L. L. Schkade, 1981, in R. R. Schmitt and H. J. Smolin (Eds.), *Urban, Regional, and Environmental Information: Needs, Sources, Systems, and Uses—Papers from the Annual Conference of the Urban and Regional Information Systems Association,* Washington, DC, Urban and Regional Information Systems Association (URISA), pp. 71-81.

but frustrating to top managers, and especially to workers. Promises that information systems will help workers should be made with caution and special attention should be paid to involving workers in the design and implementation process. Finally, transferring business applications to human service agencies may be problematic, especially at the bottom and policy levels of the organization. The business decision-making processes supported by the application should be compared with the human service decision-making processes before attempting application transfer.

Information Support for All Human Service Levels

Ideally, information generated during the client-practitioner interaction should be captured, stored, processed, and reported back to practitioners to support their decision making. Less detailed summaries should be reported to middle management for planning, controlling, and budgeting purposes. Middle management information should eventually be combined with information about the organization's environment and used to support top management decision making. As Figure 8.4 illustrates, each organizational level should collect only the information required by its level, but each should have access to the information collected at other levels (Hile, 1989). The assumption is that most management and policy information can be extracted from the information generated during client-practitioner interactions.

It is debatable whether the overlapping information needs, as presented in Figure 8.4 actually exist. The overlap illustrated in Figure 8.5 is more likely. That is, information needed to support the practitioner-client interaction has little management use. The overlap of the practitioner and management circles may be much smaller than anticipated. However, the overlap of the policy and middle management circles may be sizable. Agencies with a flexible information system have found management data extremely useful in policy/planning decisions. For example, quickly projecting what will happen to clients if funds for a program are reduced has saved many programs during the budget allocation or legislative processes.

FIGURE 8.4. Ideal Overlap Between Information Needed for Policy, Management, and Practice Decisions

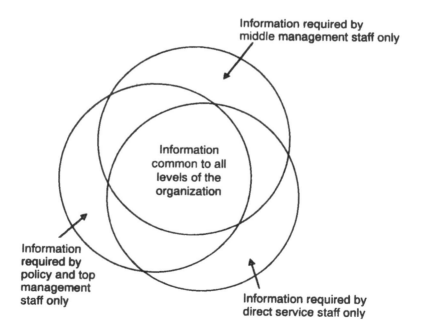

FIGURE 8.5. Probable Overlap Between Information Needed for Policy, Management, and Practice Decisions

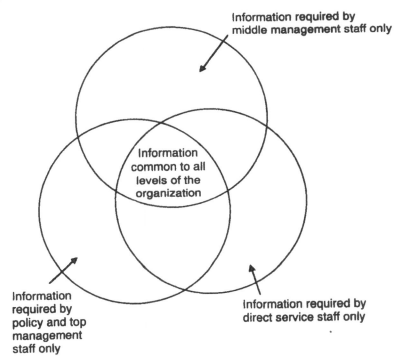

Information required by
middle management staff only

Information
common to all
levels of the
organization

Information
required by
policy and top
management
staff only

Information required by
direct service staff only

Although information collection, storage, and retrieval occur at all levels of delivery, the ideal situation of Figure 8.4 rarely occurs in practice. Most agency IT applications collect management information with little regard for the information needs at the direct service level. One reason that the policy and direct service levels receive so little support is that middle management processes are easier to quantify and computerize. Another is that managers, who are more familiar with their own needs, design and control most human service IT applications. Typically, the only other persons involved in designing and implementing these applications are technical consultants specializing in business systems. The comments of policymakers, practitioners, or clients are too infrequently a force in application design. Another reason is that IT applications that can provide practitioners with quick and easy access to the large amounts of information they need are difficult and expensive to develop. Consequently, the usual role of practitioners and clients has been to collect and record the information required to drive management-oriented applications. Overall, these management-oriented IT applications have resulted in more paperwork for practitioners, with few outputs supporting their decisions. This disparity between IT support and information needs explains the negative attitudes most non-management personnel have toward many applications.

Addressing the Needs of the Direct Service Level

Many human service decisions, especially those at the direct service level, have traditionally not been based on processed information. One reason is that processed information has not been available; another is the belief that practice is so complex and intuitive that supporting information cannot be determined. However, IT now offers the capacity to capture, sort through, and comprehend information that was once considered beyond integration and simply forgotten. With IT widely available, the information base of practice is undergoing reexamination. Although challenging and difficult, it may be possible to define and model many practitioner interventions sufficiently to develop IT applications that provide support.

Although practitioners can expect IT applications to focus initially on managerial and policy support, eventually, many applications will be available for the direct service level because the majority of agency information transactions and personnel are at this level. The direct service level has previously had so little information support that each new application may dramatically affect how services are delivered. As such, we can expect IT applications at this level to require the most organizational change.

IT support at the practitioner level is especially of interest to those wanting to improve service quality and lower cost. For example, estimates suggest that twenty-four months of experience is required for a new child protective services worker to become proficient (Arthur Young and Company, 1983). Yet, job-related stress and inadequate pay and working conditions result in the average tenure in this position being as low as nine months in some inner-city areas. It makes sense for policymakers to spend scarce resources developing permanent IT applications to support the less experienced practitioner. Once computerized, support systems can be refined and upgraded, eventually becoming an integral part of practitioner intervention.

Although the potential is great, the research and development needed is also great (Berlin and Marsh, 1993). Previous discussion pointed out that practitioners need quick access to information that:

- justifies, documents, and manages professional actions;
- presents the latest practice guidelines, research, experience, and policy considerations;
- guides actions with clients; and
- helps query, integrate, and present the vast quantities of information that influence decision making.

The first two functions are the most amenable to IT support. Applications that support the third function currently focus primarily on problem identification and clarification, structuring problem situations, and following procedures. The fourth function requires a variety of rapidly available information in easily understood and manipulable formats. No matter what information needs an application addresses, it must be able to present the underlying assumptions, rationales, statistics, models, and decision rules that are used.

Modeling of Direct Service Processes

Attempts have been made to develop models of direct service decision making in many human service settings, including child welfare and psychiatric diagnosis. The typical models developed involve cookbook, or logical, approaches or mathematical-statistical approaches. Although these models bring structure and thoroughness to the decision-making process, they experience difficulties in the following areas:

- Storing practice experience and wisdom in a format that enables easy manipulation by IT
- Addressing the interdependence of information
- Handling uncertain information and confidence in information
- Synthesizing aspects of the problem nonsystematically (for example, using nonlinear thinking, such as hunches)
- Exploring hunches by jumping from one knowledge base to another

IT applications may never be able to simulate emotions such as caring, guilt, and love and behaviors such as denial and self-destruction. Yet these and other aspects of personality may be the key to interpreting and integrating facts and experience when making complex decisions. The discussion of cognitive style in Chapter 7 describes how many other hard-to-model aspects of personality may influence practitioner decision making. In addition, group decision making may add another level of complexity that present models are unable to address.

Models, even if fully developed, may only be able to represent a portion of practitioner decision making. The typical direct service decision is based on the recall of facts of similar situations, synthesized experience, and intuition, in the following proportions:

Recall of facts	Synthesis of experience	Intuition
33.3%	33.3%	33.3%

Although present IT applications are capable of rapidly providing facts, few applications exist for quickly synthesizing previous experiences with the facts of the case at hand. Debate exists over whether IT support for intuition is possible, or even desirable.

Since most practitioners often describe intuition as a factor in their decision making, the meaning of intuition deserves more attention. Intuition is often described as the feelings that result from sensing, gut reactions, and listening to one's emotions. For example, child protective services workers often say you can "smell abuse" in a home. Intuition may not involve information processing as it is currently conceived.

New Tools, Tasks, and Skills

As applications begin to address nonroutine, ill-structured, and complex decision making, we need better tools and techniques for codifying, capturing, and disseminating information. For example, midlevel managers can accurately explain what information they use, although practitioners rarely can. The process of asking practitioners what information they use is rarely beneficial because much of their decision making is automatic. The situation is similar to asking an experienced driver what to do if an automobile starts to skid; it is easier for an experienced driver to show someone what to do than to explain what information is needed and how it is processed. An important task in developing direct service IT applications will be to categorize the direct service processes into key decisions and the outcomes that result from each decision (Stein and Rzepnicki, 1983). An example of this type of research is the Wisdom Project whose goal "was to conduct a comprehensive and integrated study that could assist the field of child welfare through advancement of its understanding of the Decision Making Ecology and lead to a more developed framework to aid future research" (Texas Department of Protective and Regulatory

Services, 1997, p. 12).* The Wisdom Project developed predictive models for staff burnout, staff turnover, whether an abuse/neglect case should be opened for treatment, and the priority assigned to an open case. Future modeling efforts of the Wisdom Project include predicting which children are at the highest risk for abuse/neglect recidivism. Another essential task for developing direct service IT applications involves determining the criteria for measuring decision-making success. A related task is determining the contingencies and validity associated with a recommendation. Practitioners must understand the validity and circumstances of data or the advice of an IT application before they will use it.

Since research is inadequate and practitioners have difficulty expressing their information needs, new application development approaches are needed. One approach is to provide practitioners with tools and technical support, and then observe how they use IT to collect, process, store, and present information. This approach to building an information model of practitioner decision making is inefficient and expensive. However, it allows practitioners to experiment with the application before it is rigidly defined and developed. One example of this approach, *The Digital Social Worker,* found that mental health practitioners need the following four types of information to support clinical decisions:

1. Treatment descriptions, syndromes, and client information
2. Guided searches for similar cases to determine what has been effective in the past
3. Decision rules from acknowledged experts
4. Models to describe and interrelate parameters to predict treatment outcomes (de Groot, Gripton, and Licker, 1986)

This discussion suggests that IT applications which support the practitioner-client interaction should be developed with caution. Sizable applications may be classified as research efforts if the promise of success is low. Prototyping or small modular efforts will lessen the risk of failure. Potential users and top-level managers should understand and accept the risk associated with these efforts. New technologies, such as the Internet chat and neural networks, should be explored to determine their potential. National associations can aid in defining potentially promising technologies, helping secure funds, and disseminating the results and lessons learned. Research universities can become involved in experimenting and demonstrating the feasibility of these applications to the business community. Given the difficulty of developing IT models, it might be wise to let researchers develop models and have agencies focus on prototyping small support applications. Small performance support systems may be more beneficial than decision support systems, given current technology. For example, Schwab, Bruce, and McRoy (1985) developed several sophisticated statistical models to match children with residential care assignments. Although these models were found to produce significantly better placements (Emmert and Schoech, 1991), they were not used in their sophisticated form. The models evolved into a simple matching process that is available over the Internet.✱

CONCLUSION

This chapter is a first step in an analysis of the information base of human service practice. Human service processes and decisions must be continually reexamined in light of new research and new technology. The task is difficult because few professionals have a detailed understanding of many types of IT and their use in human service practice. In addition, since top management and direct service are often not seen as information based, discovering supportive information is difficult. As technology continues to rapidly develop, discovering the information base of practice will be a key task for the human service professions.

REVIEW AND DISCUSSION QUESTIONS

1. Would several professional practitioners who used different methodologies (cognitive or behavioral) need the same information to work with the same client? Should they be consistent in their information needs?
2. In direct service with clients, does a best decision typically exist, or are many decisions equally good in most cases?
3. Why are novices often better than experts at explaining what they do?
4. How would you define intuition? What role does processed information play in intuition? What role does intuition play in practitioner and top management decision making?
5. What added complexities for IT exist when a decision is made by a group rather than by an individual (for example, in a case conference)? What IT tools exist to support group decision making?

Chapter 9

Hardware and Software Influences on IT Development

INTRODUCTION

This chapter examines hardware, software, programming, and language influences on IT development. These influences come into focus particularly during the feasibility and design stages, during which information wants and needs are matched with current and future IT capacities. This chapter presents many of the terms technicians commonly use when discussing IT. It's purpose is to help the reader communicate about the basics of hardware, software, programming, and languages and to understand their influences.

HARDWARE BASICS

Chapter 2 defined hardware as the physical, tangible components of IT, comparing the computer's function to that of an automobile's motor. This automobile analogy will help us further explore hardware basics in this chapter.

Hardware and Transportation System Analogy

Although the internal combustion engine is complex, the concept of how engines turn gasoline into rotary power is easy to understand. Similarly, although the computer is a very complex component of IT, the concept of how computers process data is relatively easy to understand. An understanding of elementary mechanical concepts helps when driving an automobile (motoring) and in communicating to automobile mechanics. An understanding of elementary computer concepts helps when using a computer (computing) and in communicating with technicians about applying computers to human service problems. This section presents many analogies between an IT system and a transportation system (see Table 9.1). Many analogies focus on the key hardware device, the computer, and are illustrative rather than a precise description of a one-to-one relationship.

TABLE 9.1. Hardware and Transportation System Analogy

Function/ Characteristic	Transportation System	Computing System
Basic Components and Measures		
Overall concept	Motoring or transporting	Computing or processing
Medium of movement	Vehicle	Electronic pulse
Source of power	Motor	CPU
Unit to receive action	Human being	Bit of data
Larger number of units	Group of people	Byte (8 bits of data)
One path for movement	Street	Circuit, data line, data path
Multiple paths	Multiple lane highway	Bus structure, motherboard
Process		
Process	Moving people (put person on road system riding in vehicles)	Processing data (put byte on bus structure riding on pulse)
Measures of process	Persons transported per day or vehicle miles per hour (MPH)	Bits per second transferred (BPS) or millions of instructions per second (MIPS)
Speed of process	Revolutions per minute (RPM)	Megahertz (MHz)
What controls process	Police, laws, and customs	Control unit and programs
Retention		
Long-term retention	Long-term parking lot	Disk or tape storage
Short-term retention	Short-term parking lot	Random access memory chip (RAM)
Immediate retention	On-street parking space	Register
Flow regulation	Toll booth area	Buffer

When comparing an IT application to a transportation system, a person is analogous to the smallest piece of data (a *bit* in computer terms). Several persons constitute a group, as eight bits of data constitute a *byte*. A vehicle is analogous to an electronic pulse that transports data.

Both transportation and computing systems exist to solve user problems. Consider the following user transportation problem. A subordinate is told to travel to a neighboring city, meet with a list of potential clients, and return with the names of interested clients. The subordinate is given an envelope containing the necessary information, told not to waste time, and urged to get back as quickly as possible.

The subordinate may take the following actions to carry out the executive's command. First, the subordinate calls the automobile department to request that a company vehicle be obtained from the long-term parking lot. The parking lot could be considered sequential long-term storage or mass storage. Each vehicle is given a parking space number, and vehicles are parked sequentially according to the number listed on the parking space. The person retrieving the vehicle must pass all vehicles with lower numbers to get to the desired vehicle. In a computing system, a tape drive is a sequential long-term storage device.

Vehicles are moved from long-term parking to short-term parking to await the driver. Short-term parking is analogous to the random access memory (RAM) of a computer. Data in RAM is not accessed sequentially, but according to a storage scheme designed for quick access. The speed at which the employee can get a vehicle in and out of long- and short-term parking influences how efficiently that subordinate can carry out the commands. Similarly, the speed at which computers access data from storage devices influences computer system efficiency. Access time is a critical factor because applications repeatedly perform input/output (I/O) functions that move data to and from storage.

The checked-out automobile must be driven on roads to find its destination. A road is analogous to a computer circuit or data line. The overall layout of roads is analogous to the bus structure of a computer. In a city center, roads are concentrated and referred to as streets. Streets in a city center are analogous to integrated circuits in the central processing unit (CPU) of a computer. The movement of a vehicle on a street is analogous to the manipulation of data in the CPU. Just as many actions are taken as a vehicle travels from its initial position to its end destination, many operations occur as data are processed. However, unlike a vehicle, for which many actions are taken internally by the driver, actions in a computer are not taken by the data but by the CPU.

A computer's central processing unit has (1) an arithmetic-logic unit, (2) a control unit, and (3) high speed memory registers. The arithmetic-logic unit performs mathematical operations such as addition and subtraction. It also performs logical operations such as determining whether something is equal to or greater than something else. These are core computer processes, just as spark plugs firing and valves opening are core motor processes. The movement of data through the arithmetic-logic unit is under the supervision of the control unit which functions similar to traffic police. Traffic police direct and sequence vehicles to maintain an even flow of traffic. Similarly, the control unit of the CPU directs and sequences data to ensure efficient processing. Registers in a CPU are analogous to parking spaces on both sides of a street; they provide temporary stopping locations that do not interfere with other movement through the system.

Continuing the analogy, several factors influence system performance or how quickly the executive's command can be accomplished. One factor is the speed at which a vehicle can potentially travel. Vehicle speed is usually measured in kilometers or miles per hour (MPH). MPH is analogous to the number of instructions a computer can process in one second. This speed is usually measured in millions of instructions per second (MIPS). Another measure of transportation system performance is the number of persons transported per day, which is analogous to the number of bits transferred per second (BPS). A factor that determines vehicle speed is the number of revolutions per minute (RPM) a motor is capable of turning. RPM is analogous to the clock speed of the CPU, which is specified in megahertz (MHz). A hertz is a frequency measure of one cycle per second. Theoretically, a CPU with a speed of 400 MHz will process data twice as fast as a CPU with a clock speed of 200 MHz. However, as in vehicle movement, other factors play an important part in overall processing speed. One example is the input/output speeds of the registers.

The number of traffic lanes on each road also determines the performance of a transportation system. Road lanes are analogous to the data lines or paths of the CPU. Personal computer CPUs typically have 16-, 32-, or 64-bit-wide data paths. The width of the data path determines how many bits of data can be processed simultaneously.

A factor similar to the number of road lanes is the number of lanes on the entrance ramps leading to the road. Entrance ramps are analogous to the data access paths of the CPU. Personal computers typically have 16-, 32-, or 64-bit-wide access paths. The number of access paths does not always coincide with the number of data paths. For example, some CPU chips, such as the Intel Pentium, have 64-bit data paths and 32-bit access paths to external RAM.

Other factors involved in system performance are the efficiency of the route and traffic flow. Where traffic flow is not steady, such as before and after a toll area, multiple lanes are often created. These help provide temporary stopping places for vehicles as they move past the toll booths. In a computer system, a buffer, such as a RAM computer chip, is used to compensate for differences in the rate of data flow; for example, a buffer is often used with a slow printer. One final factor that determines overall system performance is the number of detours and accidents encountered. Accidents and inoperable streets can be compared to computer hardware malfunctions.

The preceding analogy presents the major hardware functions and components that will be discussed in this chapter. The analogy will be continued later in the chapter when nonhardware factors are presented.

The Silicon Chip

A basic IT hardware component is the silicon chip. Silicon is the element from which glass is made. Silicon chips are designed for specific purposes, such as information storage, input/output operations, and data processing. A silicon chip is a reduction of many complex electronic circuits that are etched in silicon. These electronic circuits are many lines or pathways along which electrical current travels. Large drawings of numerous computer circuits are transferred to thin slices of silicon or wafers. The process used is similar to that used in black-and-white photography, whereby large scenes are reduced to small silver lines on the film negative. Blueprints of some computer chips would occupy several football fields if the smallest feature of the chip were blown up to a tenth-of-an-inch scale. To use the transportation analogy, a chip is like having the transportation system of the United States, with all its roads, intersections, and parking lots, etched on a small piece of glass the size of your thumb. Computer chips are expensive to design but inexpensive to produce, once the manufacturing process has been set up.

Representing Information in an IT Application

Another basic hardware concept is how numbers, alphabetic characters, and symbols are represented. The following material examines numbering systems, data coding schemes, and data quantities. A *number* is a mathematical concept that denotes how many items or entities are in a group. A *numeral* is a symbol or group of symbols that represent a quantity or number, for example, the Roman numeral III. Numbers can be manipulated mathematically; numerals cannot. That is, you cannot multiply Roman numeral III by Roman numeral VIII.

Numbering Systems

Computers use several different number systems. We are familiar with the base 10, or decimal numbering system, that uses a combination of ten unique numerals (0 through 9) to represent all possible numbers (see Table 9.2, column 1). For example, the quantity 34,168 is represented by an appropriate combination of the numbers 0 through 9. The decimal numbering system is relatively easy to understand, possibly because humans often use ten fingers when counting.

TABLE 9.2. Common IT Numbering Systems

Decimal Numbers (base 10)	Binary Numbers (base 2)	Hexadecimal Numbers (base 16)
0	0000	0
1	0001	1
2	0010	2
3	0011	3
4	0100	4
5	0101	5
6	0110	6
7	0111	7
8	1000	8
9	1001	9
10	1010	A
11	1011	B
12	1100	C
13	1101	D
14	1110	E
15	1111	F

Computers count as if they had two fingers; that is, they use the binary or base 2 number system. In the *binary number system*, two numerals, zero and one, are combined to represent all possible numbers (see Table 9.2, column 2). The binary numbering system is used with computers because the two binary states are easily represented in electronic form using positive and negative electric charges. *Hexadecimal (*base 16) is another common IT numbering system (see Table 9.2, column 3).

A *bit*, or binary digit, is the smallest unit for representing data. A bit represents one of two states—a light switch could be considered a bit switch—it is always on or off. In the binary number column of Table 9.2, different arrangements of bits in four columns are used to represent the numbers 0 through 15. Although the base 2 or binary numbering system is easy for a computer to read and manipulate, it is a difficult system for humans to grasp. For example, adding, multiplying, or subtracting the binary numbers 101010111101100 and 1101111010101011 is difficult.

Coding Schemes

Most people are familiar with Morse code, which uses a long and a short signal to represent characters. Since computers only process binary code, all data and characters to be processed must be translated into binary code using a coding scheme. The coding scheme that computers use is similar to Morse code. In computer code, typically 7 or 8 bits or 1 byte of information is used to designate any letter or number. Table 9.3 presents several letters and numbers in Morse Code, and in two common computer coding schemes, EBCDIC (Extended Binary Coded Decimal Interchange Code) and ASCII (American Standards Code for Information Interchange).

Data Quantities

Since computers are able to process large quantities of data, the term byte is preceded by prefixes to indicate the number of bytes. For example, the term Kbyte is often used. It is similar to the standard notion of kilo, or 1,000, as in kilogram. Besides Kbyte, two other designations are in common usage: megabyte (1,000,000 bytes) and gigabyte (1,000,000,000 bytes). To visualize storage in bytes, consider that this paragraph contains 720 bytes of information. A double-spaced typewritten page of information contains approximately two Kbytes of information. This chapter contains approximately 70,000 bytes of information or 70 Kbytes. This book is approximately one megabyte in size.

HARDWARE FUNCTIONS

As the introductory analogy pointed out, a computer consists of hardware that perform the following functions:

1. Execute data processing operations
2. Input and retrieve data from short-term memory
3. Input and retrieve data from long-term storage
4. Transfer and receive data from other components and other computer systems

These functions are graphically depicted in Figure 9.1. Each function will be further discussed in this section. The IT components that perform these functions will be discussed in the following section.

Data Processing

Data processing is performed by the CPU using arithmetic/logic, control, and input/output operations.

TABLE 9.3. Examples of ASCII, EBCDIC, and Morse Code

Letters and Numbers	ASCII	EBCDIC	Morse Code
0	0101 0000	1111 0000	-----
1	0101 0001	1111 0001	.----
2	0101 0010	1111 0010	..---
3	0101 0011	1111 0011	...--
4	0101 0100	1111 0100	....-
5	0101 0101	1111 0101	.....
A	1010 0001	1100 0001	.-
B	1010 0010	1100 0010	-...
C	1010 0011	1100 0011	-.-.
D	1010 0100	1100 0100	-..
E	1010 0101	1100 0101	.

FIGURE 9.1. The Functions of a CPU

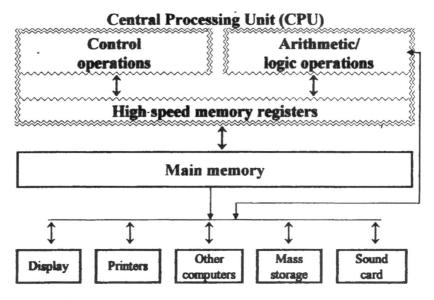

↔ = Both input and output flow
→ = Either input or output flow

Arithmetic-Logic Operations

The four arithmetic capabilities of a CPU are addition, subtraction, multiplication, and division. The logic capabilities of a CPU involve both logical expressions and logical relationships. Figure 9.2 provides illustrations of a CPU's logical capabilities. Examples of logical expressions are AND, OR, and NOT.

FIGURE 9.2. Logical Capacities of a CPU

Logical (Boolean) Expression	Illustration
A	Process if A, e.g., if client is male
B	Process if B, e.g., if client is Caucasian
AND	Process if A AND B, e.g., if the client is male AND Caucasian
NOT	Process if NOT B, e.g., if the client is NOT Caucasian
AND NOT	Process if A AND NOT B, e.g., if the client is male AND NOT Caucasian
OR	Process if A OR B, e.g., if the client is either male OR Caucasian
NOR	Process if neither A NOR B, e.g., if the client is neither male nor Caucasian
XOR	Process if A AND NOT B, OR B AND NOT A, e.g., if the client is male AND NOT caucasian, OR if Caucasian AND NOT male

Logical Relationship	Illustration
Equal to ($=$)	Process if A is EQUAL TO B, e.g., if age $=$ 40
Not equal to ($\neq$)	Process if A is NOT EQUAL TO B, e.g., if age is ($\neq$) 40
Greater than ($>$)	Process if A is GREATER THAN B, e.g., if age is ($>$) 40
Less than ($<$)	Process if A is LESS THAN B, e.g., if age is ($<$) 40
Less than or equal to ($\leq$)	Process if A is LESS THAN OR, EQUAL TO B, e.g., if age is ($\leq$) 40
Greater than or equal to ($\geq$)	Process if A is GREATER THAN OR EQUAL TO B, e.g., if age is ($\geq$) 40

An example of a logical operation is the process of selecting the name of all male service recipients who are between the ages of thirty and forty. That is, selecting first name AND last name if sex is *equal to* male AND age is *equal to* OR *greater than* thirty AND *equal to* OR *less than* forty.

Control Operations

Computers process data under the supervision of the CPU's control unit. The control unit operates similarly to a human supervisor. It determines what work needs to be done, how it is to be done, and what to do with the results. The instructions for the control unit are contained in computer software. The control unit determines which instruction to execute, retrieves that instruction from memory, interprets it, and executes it. If data are required for the execution, the control unit accesses the data. It then tells the arithmetic-logic unit which operations to perform on what data, where the data can be found, and where to store the results.

Input/Output and Data Communications

Input/output (I/O) operations involve the transmission and reception of data and instruction. Input/output is a function that occurs throughout IT applications. For example, under the supervision of the control unit, data are input directly from the keyboard to the arithmetic-logic unit of the CPU. Once processed, the data are output to memory, and possibly to the display, or across a network to a printer. A complex application, such as a statistical analysis, involves thousands of input/output operations. Data transmission is often referred to as *data communication*. Data communication across telephone lines is called *telecommunications*.

Storage/Memory

Storage refers to the retention of data and instructions. The terms storage and memory are often used interchangeably, although memory usually refers to a shorter period of retention. Storage varies primarily by length of retention, access time, and cost of storage media.

Storage retention length is usually divided into short-term memory (RAM chips), long-term mass storage (hard disk), and archival storage (backup tape). *Access time* is the time lapse from when a call for data is made until the data are delivered. Access time is frequently measured in milliseconds, or one-thousandth of a second. As the introductory analogy pointed out, access time is a crucial variable in computer system efficiency. Typically, the faster the access time, the more costly the storage device. Technicians will be able to examine an application's specifications to determine the most efficient memory and storage components. Table 9.4 presents different types of storage and a money analogy.

TABLE 9.4. Terms Describing Information Storage

Storage Concept	Definition	Function	Money Analogy
Registers	High-speed memory locations inside the CPU	Provide temporary, very high-speed storage of information	Cash register
Main memory	Storage that is directly accessible by the central processing unit	High-speed storage to service the workings of the CPU	Safe
Buffers	A temporary storage area	Keep the computer system operating efficiently as data move at different times and at various speeds	Purse
Mass storage	Storage that cannot be directly accessed by the CPU without first being loaded into main memory	Allows for inexpensive retention of large volumes of data	Vault
Virtual memory	A combination of main storage and fast mass storage	Allows data to be very rapidly and efficiently moved between main memory and fast mass storage; thus, users have the impression they are working only with the main memory	Debit card
Archival storage and backup	The least expensive storage, often slow and involving sequential access	Inexpensively keeps duplicate and infrequently used data	Safe-deposit box

HARDWARE COMPONENTS

Many hardware components or devices accomplish the computer hardware functions described previously. They are often divided into devices associated with the CPU and peripheral devices. A *peripheral* is a hardware component that is physically separate from the CPU and main memory, but connected to it. Peripherals perform functions such as storage, input/output, and telecommunications.

Only the most important hardware devices will be discussed here. In describing these devices, this section uses personal computing illustrations because the PC is more common than other systems. Nevertheless, the components discussed apply to any size computer system.

Processing Components (the Central Processing Unit)

The central processing unit performs data processing. The CPU is often described as the "brain" or "engine" of a computer. As stated previously, the central processing unit has three parts. They are the control unit, the unit that performs mathematical and logical operations, and memory registers. These three units may all reside on one computer chip, called a microprocessor, or in a variety of small components.

Input/Output Components

Hundreds of different I/O devices are available. Most IT applications require only the most common devices, which are discussed in the following material.

Displays and Keyboards

Displays or terminals allow human input and computer output of information. A common type of terminal is the remote bank teller machine. It allows customers to input an identification card and control codes along with their cash request. A video display terminal (VDT) is a TV-like screen for displaying computer outputs. This screen is sometimes called a monitor or cathode ray tube (CRT). A blinking marker called the cursor marks the user's position on the CRT. Some displays have an attached keyboard for generating input; others use a separate keyboard or number pad.

Printers

A printer is a common output device. Two types of printers exist, nonimpact and impact printers. Impact printers produce characters by physically hitting the paper. They are used primarily for printing multiple-copy forms. *Dot matrix* impact printers form images using a print head made up of many pins that form characters and symbols by firing an arrangement of pins onto a ribbon that moves between the print head and the paper. Nonimpact printers provide more versatility in printing, especially graphics and pictures. An *ink jet printer* sprays images onto paper. *Laser printers* use a process similar to a copying machine, in which paper is rolled against a drum to receive characters that are electronically arranged on the drum and coated with a dark powder called toner.

Other Input/Output Devices

Many other I/O devices exist. The *mouse* and the *trackball* allow the user to move the cursor to a designated location on the screen and to press a button to select an item displayed at that location. A *joystick* is a hand-held control for manipulating the cursor and providing other inputs. A *scanner* could be considered a reverse printer because it converts pictures and text on paper into computer-usable text, graphics, and pictures. A *microphone* inputs speech to control the computer or to convert speech into text. Other input devices include video and digital *cameras*, which input moving and still pictures. Networking I/O components are covered in Chapter 11.

Storage Components

Information storage has advanced rapidly from the early days of punched paper tape and computer cards that held only eighty characters of data. The following are some of the most common storage devices used today.

Semiconductor Memory Chips

A semiconductor is a silicon chip that contains thousands of tiny memory cells. Each cell contains a capacitor capable of storing a charge and a transistor that helps determine whether the charge exists (binary 1) or not (binary 0). Several types of semiconductor chips exist.

RAM stands for random access memory. RAM chips store data that the central processing unit can rapidly write to and access. Memory locations on a RAM chip can be addressed without sequentially accessing other memory locations. RAM chips are volatile; that is, they lose all their contents when the electricity powering them is turned off.

ROM stands for read only memory. ROM chips only release the information etched in circuitry during the manufacturing process. A computer cannot write to, or store information in, a ROM memory chip. ROM chips are nonvolatile. They do not lose their contents when electricity is unavailable. An example of the use of ROM memory chips is providing initial instructions to a computer when it is turned on.

Storage Disks

Disks offer random access to data and have become a popular mass storage device. Disks are typically divided into concentric circles called tracks and pie-shaped sections called sectors (see Figure 9.3). An index, sometimes called a file allocation table (FAT), is stored on the disk to keep track of the location of all files stored. Some disks can be removed from the drive that accesses them. A removable disk can provide a computer with extensive mass storage. However, the data access time is typically slower for a drive with a removable disk.

A *hard* disk is a large capacity storage disk. A hard disk is a thin, rigid, rapidly spinning metal platter coated with ferrous oxide. Ferrous oxide is the material covering the surface of cassette tape. It is often called iron oxide and has the same chemical makeup as rust. The iron filings in ferrous oxide can magnetically store bits of information.

Optical disks are high capacity, removable plastic platters, for example, *CD-ROMs* (compact disk-read only memory) and *DVD-ROMs* (digital versatile disc-read only memory). Some optical disks are rewritable, offering substantial archival storage.

Another older, rewritable, and removable storage disk is the *floppy disk*. Floppies are constructed of thin, flexible plastic coated with ferrous oxide. The read/write head of the floppy disk drive unit actually touches the slow-spinning floppy disk to read and write data, whereas the read/write head of a hard disk floats above the disk surface.

Magnetic Tape

Magnetic tape is one of the oldest mass storage technologies. Magnetic tape is a thin, flat plastic ribbon coated with ferrous oxide. Tape has the disadvantage of allowing only sequential access. Since tape is a relatively inexpensive, removable, slow-access storage medium, it is primarily used for backup and archival storage.

Other Hardware Components

A variety of other computer hardware components exist.

FIGURE 9.3. Sectors and Tracks of Storage Disk

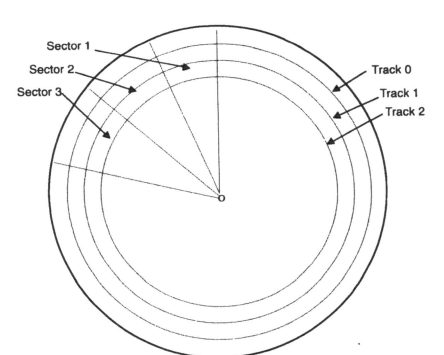

The *case* is the container or chassis that houses and protects the compo-nents of the computer. The chassis frequently appears too large for the spacing of the components inside. The extra space separates the compo-nents and allows for the ventilation of the heat that many of the compo-nents produce.

The *power supply* converts electrical current into the many different voltages and amperages needed inside the computer. Some portable com-puters are powered by battery packs.

A *bus* is typically a group of parallel wires or circuit lines encased in rigid plastic to which components are attached. A bus connects most of the internal components of the computer.

A computer *card* is a thin, flat, plastic rectangle on which electronic components are encased or soldered, for example, a sound card or modem. Cards plug into receptacle slots on the bus.

A *port* is a connection for joining computer components together. Two computers can be connected by wires running from the port of one computer to the port of the other. A *serial port* allows data to be transmitted across a single wire one bit at a time. A *parallel port* allows multiple bits of information to be transferred simultaneously.

A computer can have various other components, for example, a sound card or fans to reduce the heat generated by the computer components.

By now, all the bits, bytes, RAMs, and ROMs probably have your head spinning. Remember that knowing all the terms is not as important as obtaining a basic understanding of the concepts involved. When someone begins using terms such as megabytes, you should think "large storage of information" and not lose the meaning of the conversation. The next section will illustrate how software uses the bits, bytes, RAMs, and ROMs to solve user problems.

SOFTWARE BASICS

Applications combine hardware with software, procedures, and people. *Software* consists of computer programs and the accompanying documentation. Programs are computer instructions in languages that the computer can understand. This section presents the basic concepts concerned with software, programming, and languages.

Software and Transportation System Analogy

In an earlier section, a hypothetical scenario developed analogies between computer hardware and a transportation system. This section extends the analogies into the area of software programming and computer languages (see Table 9.5). In the scenario, an executive gave the following commands to a subordinate: "Travel to the neighboring city. Meet with this list of potential clients. Return with the names of clients who are interested in our project. This envelope contains the necessary information. Don't waste time. Get back as quickly as you can."

Instructions in a transportation system are analogous to computer programs. The process of designing and engineering instructions in a transportation system is analogous to the process of outlining and programming a solution to a computing problem. People from several disciplines develop instructions. For example, city designers and traffic engineers develop transportation system instructions, and systems analysts and software engineers develop computer instructions. For instructions to be understood,

TABLE 9.5. Software and Transportation System Analogy

Function/ Characteristic	Transportation System	Computing System
Basic Concepts		
Overall purpose	Solving user transportation problems	Solving user data processing problems
Development process	Designing and engineering a transportation system	Outlining and programming a problem solution
Communication rules	Human languages	Computer languages
Instructions	Directions	Programs
Personnel		
Designers	Traffic engineer	Systems analyst
Builder	Construction worker	Software engineer
Processing modes		
Scheduled	Ferryboat river crossing	Batch processing
Continuous	Bridge river crossing	Interactive processing
Performance measures		
Error free	Not getting lost	Bug-free program
Appropriateness	Correspondence of directions to street layout	Match of programs to hardware
Efficiency	Good travel instructions	Well-written programs
Types of Instructions		
Communication agreements	Traffic symbols	Protocols
System controls	Traffic police	Operating system
System aids	Stoplight	Utilities
User solution	Route plan	Applications software
Custom-made instructions	Taxicab tour	Custom software
Prepackaged instruction	Bus tour	Software package
Documentation		
Written descriptive information	Manuals and road reports	Computer manuals
Continuously available information	Traffic-oriented radio station	Interactive help files

the instruction giver and receiver must agree on common terminology and its use. In doing so, they develop a language. In the communication between people and the automatic transmission of an automobile, an agreement exists that P = Park, D = Drive, and N = Neutral. Instructions to computers are communicated using languages such as C and BASIC.

Travel instructions can be simple commands, such as start, stop, or turn, or they can be more complex commands, such as "if traffic looks heavy, take the bypass or the main expressway." Computer languages allow for the expression of simple commands, such as load, save, and run. They also allow for complex statements, such as "if X is greater than Y, then execute line 100." Efficiency of action depends on how well instructions are written. For example, efficient travel according to the executive's instructions depends on the executive's envelope containing clear, straightforward instructions to all offices. Similarly, computer instructions must be clear and direct. When traveling, the correspondence between the instructions given and actual street patterns determines how many wrong turns are made. In computing, the correspondence between computer programs and computer capabilities also affects performance. A similar performance factor involves errors in the instructions, or programming errors. Faulty instructions are considered bugs or errors in a computer program. Bugs often result in the problem being solved inefficiently or not being solved at all.

Vehicles cross a body of water by several means. If a ferryboat is used, all vehicles are stopped and sorted by type, for example, large freight trucks versus passenger vehicles. When the boat arrives, vehicles are loaded by type and transported to the other side. This is analogous to batch data processing in which similar types of jobs are grouped and then processed. If a bridge exists over a body of water, all vehicles can cross the river as they arrive. This is analogous to interactive processing in which the data are processed at the time they are requested by the users.

Several types of instructions exist. One type of instruction helps manage the system. Computer programs concerned with internal performance of the overall system are called system software; and several types exist. The operating system is the most important system software. The transportation analogue of an operating system is a traffic officer who maintains efficient system operation. The officer performs functions such as keeping track of the locations and destinations of vehicles, directing and supervising traffic movement, and sequencing vehicles into traffic lanes. In a computer, the operating system manages efficient program execution by performing functions such as controlling input/output processes and maintaining files as data are retrieved, used, processed, and stored. Utilities are another type of system software. Computer utilities help perform a frequently used function, such as file sorting or program testing. A transportation analogue is a stoplight that provides instructions for no single user, but ensures that the system operates smoothly for all users.

Another type of instruction helps users solve their problems. A route plan is a transportation example because it helps the user reach the desired destination. Computer programs that solve user problems are called application software. A word processing program is an example of application software. Since users have a variety of needs, thousands of application software programs exist.

Application programs can be custom designed or packaged. Similarly, transportation routes can be custom designed, such as when one hires a taxi for a tour of a city. They can also be packaged, such as when one takes a prearranged tour of a city on a tour bus. Application programs often make use of the capabilities of system software, just as route plans may follow routes designed to help manage traffic.

Descriptive information about an IT application, its use, and maintenance is called documentation. Transportation system documentation exists as road specifications, maps, vehicle operator manuals, and special radio channels that constantly report traffic conditions. IT documentation can be internal to a computer program, printed in computer manuals, or readily available through the interactive help files of a software program.

Basic Software Concepts

Software is divided into three overlapping categories: system software, application software, and documentation.

System Software

System software primarily solves problems related to the computing system itself. Examples of these problems are helping the computer work as an efficient system, providing standard tools and user interface, and providing a platform from which to run user applications. Ideally, system software should be invisible or transparent to the naive user. The following material covers some of the most common system software.

An *operating system* is the integrated group of computer programs that supervises the actions of a computer. Several of the most common operating systems in the small computer market are trademark names such as Windows and UNIX. Windows and OS/2 were designed for personal computers; UNIX was designed for larger systems. The following are some of the most important functions of an operating system:

- Manage files by helping to create, store, retrieve, add, delete, copy, back up, and list the status of files.
- Sequence and monitor tasks or jobs to maximize efficient use of computer components such as the CPU or a sound card.
- Provide a set of basic functions and a standard user interface that a variety of applications can use.
- Initialize or format the tracks and sectors of storage media.
- Provide "windows" for viewing multiple concurrent operations.
- Standardize functions so a program written on one computer can operate on other computers that run the same operating system.
- Link many computers together to operate as an integrated computing network.

The choice of an operating system for an application is a critical decision, especially if software packages are used because all software runs on the operating system, and not all software is available for all operating systems.

Utilities and programming aids are another group of system software. They help the user perform diagnostic tests on the computer system, debug programs, keep track of file characteristics and use, and perform other similar chores. Utilities are considered programmers' tools.

Application Software

Application software solves problems users encounter at work or play, for example, statistical software or recreational games. The distinction between system and application software is primarily for clarity. Software often falls somewhere between these two types, having applications that can perform major system tasks as well as major user tasks.

Application software can be custom designed or commercially packaged by vendors. *Custom-designed software* can better address the user's problems. However, it typically involves more initial design and future maintenance costs. To use the automobile analogy, a custom-designed car is expensive to maintain, whereas a standard car can be taken to almost any mechanic for parts and repair. A *software package* is a self-contained product that requires little or nothing of the user before the software is used. Typically, users are required only to install the software by selecting the installation options that correspond to their hardware and use needs. Packaged software exists for solving most common user problems. Packaged software allows the vendor to spread out development costs to many users. However, it may not address the user's problem as effectively as custom software.

Some software is available as *freeware,* or a gift from its owner. Other software is *shareware* and distributed free for trial use. A registration fee is requested from those who use the software after the trial basis. Small vendors often use the shareware alternative because of problems with marketing and distributing their products through commercial companies. The Internet provides a software distribution system whereby almost anyone can participate in the shareware market.

Documentation

Documentation is descriptive information explaining the rationale and logic involved in the development, use, operation, and maintenance of a computing system. Documentation serves the following essential functions:

- Helps control the development and operation of an application by providing the system's overall purpose and intended performance specifications
- Makes the complexities of an application comprehensible to those not involved with its design and development
- Provides a communication mechanism during the process of developing an application
- Aids in testing and debugging all parts of an application
- Helps make an application transportable, that is, transferable to another agency or computer
- Lessens the trauma caused by the high job turnover associated with IT employees
- Provides information useful in longitudinal and historical analysis of an agency's IT effort
- Provides valuable information if application redesign is necessary

A system will operate without documentation, but good documentation enhances the ability to use, repair, or modify a system.

Documentation has several different audiences: (1) the organization housing the application; (2) application users; (3) those who develop, maintain, and enhance the application; and (4) those who operate and control the application. Each group's technical understanding and reasons for using documentation are different.

The organization needs documentation such as the application's purpose, the performance specifications, and the format of the database, input forms, and output reports. Users need to know how the application can meet their information needs and what to do if it does not work as desired. System developers need to understand the detailed workings of the system and the rationale behind its construction (see Table 9.6). Operators need to understand the system and its components, file names and storage location, how to manage the system, and what to do in special circumstances, such as when the system fails.

TABLE 9.6. Documentation Needed by Application Developers

Information	Description
Title	Application name, unique identification number, and date.
History	List of each version, their programmers, dates of programming, and time required. Revisions should include a brief description of the revision.
Application Specifications	General description of the application, its basic purpose and features, frequency of use, and input, output, and processing performed. It can include a system flowchart, description of the record layouts, input forms and output reports, and hardware and software requirements.
Description	Description of the application, including error checking, any table used within the application, special forms used, special operating instructions, and detailed program logic, for example, flowcharts and/or decision tables.
Details	The source code of each program should be listed, including a description of all files used and their contents.
Testing	Testing procedures should be specified and the test data provided.

Documentation may take several forms. It may exist internally within an application, printed in accompanying manuals, or supplied as a separate program module for interactive access by users.

Documentation internal to an application is not necessary for program execution. It is included for communication, testing, debugging, and maintenance. Written manuals that accompany an application should reflect the different ways people learn and retain information. They should be constructed keeping in mind that some people read all instructions thoroughly before using an application; others read instructions only after trial and error results in failure. Some people prefer lists, diagrams, and illustrations over text. Often, documentation includes a short introductory section to be read before application use. Other sections are referenced when questions or problems arise. Interactive documentation may contain the same information as manuals, but it is organized and accessed differently. It may also be context sensitive, that is, help specific to the user's situation is presented upon request. The Internet can deliver interactive documentation, thus ensuring that the latest information is readily available to all users.

Documentation for packaged software has significantly improved in recent years. Especially important are wizards and guides that lead the user through the problems encountered. Good documentation is characterized by the following:

- Structure or organization (grouping of similar ideas and logical transitions between ideas)
- Sequencing or a progression of ideas, for example, from simple to complex, known to unknown, and general to specific
- Consistent terms and style
- Frequent examples, diagrams, and illustrations keyed to the text and close to the associated ideas
- Easy to follow schemes for section, page, and paragraph numbering
- Tables of contents, introductions, reviews, summaries, indexes, FAQs (frequently asked questions), appendixes, glossaries, and headings that are consistently organized and structured

Good documentation is expensive to develop. Users are often disappointed by the interactive help available in human service applications. Although human service application vendors do not have the volume of use to pay for sophisticated documentation, they should provide adequate documentation, given the nontechnical nature of human service professions. Weak documentation is especially a problem in custom-developed applications.

System designers and programmers often see documentation as something to do after the application is working well. In addition, programmers have little incentive to document well, as it makes them easier to replace. This low priority often results in poorly designed or incomplete documentation. Users often only discover documentation problems when the application does not work as expected. Correcting documentation at this stage can be difficult.

Basic Programming Concepts

Programs

A *program* is a sequence of instructions. A *computer program* is a sequence of instructions written in a computer language that directs the computing system to perform one or a group of operations.

We frequently encounter programmed instructions in everyday life. The selector dial on a washing machine is a mechanical program. Once the selector dial is set, the selector mechanism sends a series of predetermined signals to the washing machine. Figure 9.4 presents a simplified sequence of instructions for a washing machine. An example of a human-oriented program is a behavior modification program. In the behavior modification program of Figure 9.5, the instructions are less detailed than the washing machine instructions. This is because people are involved, and most people can break general instructions into detailed steps, for example, they can praise and describe without requiring detailed instructions.

A computer program is constructed similarly to a program for a mechanical device or a human. The English instructions in Table 9.7 illustrate the construction of a computer program that adds three numbers. By rapidly processing many instructions, computers perform tasks so complex and sophisticated that they exhibit humanlike intelligence, for example, playing chess. Complex programs, such as Windows, require millions of lines of instructions.

A *transaction* is one data processing operation. The term's use in computing is similar to its use in banking to denote an exchange of money, that is, a financial transaction. A data processing transaction could involve the execution of a complete computer program, a module of a program, or a single instruction that accomplishes one result.

Processing Modes

Processing modes concern the way in which computers handle transactions. They impact system performance and how users interact with an application.

Batch and interactive are two common terms associated with processing modes. *Batch processing* is a data processing mode in which similar transactions are held and then processed simultaneously. If the holding queue (waiting area) contains many batch jobs, users must wait for the computer to reach their job. A computing example of batch data processing is many people using the same printer: the computer controlling the printer places all jobs in a queue and prints one job at a time.

Batch processing of similar jobs is contrasted with interactive processing, which takes place as the transactions occur. *Interactive processing* exists if each user entry elicits a response from the computer. In an interactive environment, the user provides the computer with instructions and data and then waits for the computer's response. Almost all processing today is interactive. Some programs may provide an interactive interface while queuing the tasks for later batch processing, for example, running monthly budget reports or answering e-mail off-line from the Internet.

FIGURE 9.4. A Programmed Set of Instructions for a Washing Machine

Module A. WASH

1. Open hot water valve.

2. Close valve when water in tub reaches level corresponding to load size.

3. Agitate at medium speed for fifteen minutes.

4. Pump water out of tub.

Module B. RINSE

1. Open cold water valve.

2. Close water valve when water reaches level corresponding to load size.

3. Agitate at medium speed for five minutes.

4. Pump out water.

5. Spin tub slowly while opening cold water valve every thirty seconds.

6. Stop spinning tub after ten minutes.

Module C. SPIN DRY

1. Spin tub slowly for three minutes.

2. Spin tub rapidly for five minutes.

Module D. END

1. Stop all operations.

2. If extra wash cycle set, repeat modules A, B, and C.

3. Sound beeper five times.

Another term related to processing modes refers to how the CPU executes programs. *Multitasking* is the interactive processing of several jobs at one time, whereby the computer concurrently processes many different jobs in very small time slices. Through split-second sequencing, a computer can simultaneously calculate a payroll, sort a mailing list, search for a client's record, and print a monthly report.

An additional mode of processing refers to the number, location, and interaction of the processing units it a computing system. In a *multiprocessing*

FIGURE 9.5. A Behavior Modification Program

Lesson 1: Praise and Attention

Skill Description* [Overall description of module]
Praise and attention should follow your child's good behavior to encourage it to happen more often. Praise and attention includes positive statements, descriptions of behavior, encouragement, touching, and physical affection.

Skill Rationales [Conceptual design of program]
1. Your praise and attention encourages your children to behave well and to do the good things more often.
2. Praise in a positive way to help your children learn what you expect from them.
3. Your recognition helps your children feel good about themselves.
4. When you are teaching your children, your praise for correct performance can help them learn faster and remember better.
5. Praise helps you build strong positive relationships with your children.

Key Points to Remember [Detailed design specifications]
1. Praise immediately to increase good behavior.
2. Describe what you like.
3. Don't give attention for misbehavior.
4. Praise everyday good behavior.

Goal [Performance specifications]
During a ten-minute checkout, you must give ten descriptive praises.

Suggestions [Program statements, although not complete]
1. Remember to praise the small good things your child does.
2. Use positive words such as great, good, fine, excellent, and beautiful to show approval for your child's behavior.
3. Be descriptive. Descriptions are simply made by telling what you see. For example, "Joanie, you took your dishes off the table and put them in the sink."
4. To be most effective giving praise, use many different combinations of positive words and descriptions. For example, one time you can say "Billy, you're doing a great job of hanging up your clothes when you come in from school." The next time you might say, "Your room looks so neat now that you're hanging your clothes up after school. Billy, you're really starting to act responsibly."
5. Remember to praise during or immediately after good behavior.
6. Use physical affection, hugs, pats on the back, touches on the arm, and kisses, with your praise.
7. Don't pay attention to minor annoying behavior.

---

* The corresponding computer description of each module is enclosed in brackets

---

Source: From *Winning! Specialist Handbook* (Second Edition) by R. F. Dangel and R. A. Polster, 1984, Arlington, Texas: American Children's Foundation.

TABLE 9.7. English Equivalent Statements of a Computer Program That Adds Three Numbers

1. Set all registers (memory locations) in the CPU to 0.
2. Load the three numbers to be added from RAM memory into registers A, B, and C.
3. Fetch the number from register A.
4. Fetch the number from register B.
5. Add the two numbers.
6. Store the results in register D.
7. Fetch the number from register C.
8. Fetch the number from register D.
9. Add the two numbers.
10. Store the results in register D.
11. Fetch the number from register D.
12. Send the number to the display.
13. Stop.

Source: Compliments of Joseph Zeevi.

mode, two or more processors in the same geographic location simultaneously execute instructions. An example is several small computers connected to a large mainframe.

Distributed data processing (DDP) is the concurrent execution of instructions by a system having computers in separate locations. In a DDP environment, a system of computers acts as one computer system. The processing is distributed throughout a network of separate computers. In a DDP environment, users need not care which computer is processing their data or on which storage device the data physically reside.

A final processing mode is *parallel processing*. Parallel processing involves two or more CPUs simultaneously handling separate parts of the same problem while sharing all other computing resources. During parallel processing, computers break a problem into many parts and all computers process their parts simultaneously. The human brain is believed to solve problems through parallel processing. For example, one can drive a car while carrying on a conversation.

Modularity

One accepted programming technique is modularity. A programmer may break the problem solution into independent modules that perform separate functions. Program modules are executed according to the order specified when the user interacts with the program. Modular program design helps break programs into logical units that are easy to manage and simple to understand. Each module has well-defined entry and exit points. When the program runs, no module will ever be exited before it is completed. In addition, no module will ever enter or intrude into the middle of another module. Thus, modules can be added, deleted, or changed without problems arising from unexpected module interaction. With a modular approach, several programmers can simultaneously code portions of the solution to a problem. Modular design helps confine errors to a single module, making them easier to trace. Thus, modularity helps make a program easier to read, debug, understand, maintain, and modify.

Object-oriented programming is an extension of modularity. With object-oriented programming, everything is considered an object that has its own independent program code. For example, all parts of the display, clickable buttons, etc., are objects that can have associated programs.

Routines and Subroutines

Programmers use previously validated series of instructions called *routines*. Routines solve a frequent or general problem such as sorting a list or finding a file. A library of routines may accompany a programming language. Routines that are not stored as independent entities, but are set apart in a computer program, are called subroutines. The use of proven routines and subroutines makes a program more accurate, less complex, and less expensive to develop.

Bugs

Bugs are errors in computer programs. Debugging is the process of finding and correcting errors. The term debugging originated with ENIAC, one of the first computers. ENIAC failed when a moth was smashed between the contacts of a switching unit and prevented electronic current from passing. Subsequently, the process of laboriously checking every detail to find a computer error was called debugging, and the error, a bug. The carcass of the first bug is taped in a log book at a Navy Museum in Virginia.

Basic Computer Language Concepts

A *language* is a set of characters, conventions, and rules for conveying information. Computer languages provide the mechanism for person-machine communication just as human languages provide the mechanism for person-to-person communication. Computer languages provide for communication between the programmer and the computer, between the programmer and other programmers, and between the programmer and the user. The communication between the programmer and the computer consists of statements that are translated into code using ones and zeros.

Learning a computer language is similar in complexity to learning a human language. With several days' work, one can learn basic statements that accomplish basic tasks. However, being a proficient programmer of computer language requires an effort similar to that required to become proficient in a human language.

Language Level

One typology of languages refers to the level of a language or how closely it resembles the binary code required by the computer. *Machine language* is the lowest-level language. It is written in binary code unique to the circuitry of the CPU on which the language runs. *High*-level languages are more similar to human languages in structure and content. They require less knowledge of computer-specific codes on the part of the programmer. Programs written in a high-level language allow complex manipulations with brief English-like statements and allow programs to be machine independent. Figure 9.6 presents a machine language program that adds two numbers and its high-level-language equivalent.

Although several hundred high-level languages exist, only ten to fifteen are in widespread use today. Although all languages can be used to solve simple problems, each language is designed to optimize a specific programming approach or address a type of problem. Table 9.8 contains some of the major high-level languages and their original focuses. Newer versions of these languages are continually being developed, since they are robust enough to address a variety of problems. In addition, new languages are continually being developed. For example, the World Wide Web, a relatively recent phenomenon, spurred the development of HTML (HyperText Manipulation Language) and Java.

FIGURE 9.6. A Machine Language Program and Its High-Level-Language Equivalent

Machine language program (adds two numbers)

```
11AB010EO9CDO5000E01CDO500FEO3CA
000032A601112C020E09CDO5003AA601
DE30FEOODA3201FEOAD2320132A601C3
3DO10E0911F501CDO500C3000111C801
OEO9CD05000E01CDO500FEO3CA000O32
A7010E09112CO3CDO5003AA701DE30FE
OODA6901FEOADA740111F501OEO9CDO5
OOC33DO132A70111E701OE09CD05003A
A701473AA60180FEOADA9BO1DEOA32A6
O1OEO21E31CD05003AA601C6305F0E02
CD0500C300000000456E746572206120
73696E676C6520646563696D616C2064
67676974203A2024456E746572206120
7365636F6E6420646967697420706C65
617365203A20245468652073756D2069
73203A202454686174206E756D626572
206973206E6F742062657477656E20
2020616E6420392E20506C6561736520
74727920616761696E2E2E2E2E0A0D24
```

Source: Compliments of Joseph Zeevi.

BASIC language program that adds two numbers and displays the results.

```
10 PRINT "ENTER THE FIRST NUMBER:": INPUT A#
20 PRINT "ENTER THE SECOND NUMBER:": INPUT B#
30 PRINT "THE TOTAL IS:" A# + B#
40 END
```

The basic program as it runs. The OK indicates BASIC is ready. User entered information is italicized.

```
OK
RUN
ENTER THE FIRST NUMBER:
? 2
ENTER THE SECOND NUMBER:
? 3
THE TOTAL IS:  5
OK
```

TABLE 9.8. Some Common Languages and Their Focuses

Language and Approximate Date	Focus of the Computer Language
FORTRAN 1957	FORTRAN (FORmula TRANslator) was designed for efficient manipulation of numbers. It is widely used for scientific, mathematical, and statistical problems.
COBOL 1960	COBOL (COmmon Business-Oriented Language) was designed for the Department of Defense for military applications. It is commonly used in business data processing.
LISP 1962	LISP (LISt Processing) was developed by the artificial intelligence community for symbolic manipulation and list processing.
BASIC 1965	BASIC (Beginner's All-purpose Symbolic Instruction Code) was designed for multitasking and education.
Pascal 1971	Pascal is a general purpose language named for the French mathematician Blaise Pascal who built a digital calculating machine in 1642. Pascal was developed to teach structured programming techniques and efficient programming.
C 1972	Designed as a systems language for the UNIX operating system. C programs are relatively easy to adapt to different hardware.
Ada 1980	Named for the Countess Ada Augusta, considered the first programmer. Ada was designed for the Department of Defense to handle large-scale, complex applications.
SQL Mid-1970s	SQL (Structured Query Language) is a standard language for gaining access to data in database management systems.
VRML 1994	VRML (Virtual Reality Modeling Language) is used for creating integrated three-dimensional graphics and multimedia, for example, in 3-D virtual-reality worlds.

IMPLICATIONS FOR SYSTEM DESIGN AND DEVELOPMENT

The discussions of hardware and software allude to the many ways they influence application design and development. For example, the advice in IT development is to select applications that meet user needs first and then select the appropriate hardware, software, and networking on which those applications run best.

Developing custom software should be avoided, if possible. Purchasing commercially available software packages provides sophisticated computing power for fractions of the cost of hiring the expertise to custom develop an application. Another advantage of packaged software is documentation and support. Software companies often provide technical assistance, voice mail, Internet sites, newsletters, and training sessions to keep the user proficient and current. Good software vendors continually upgrade their product based on the latest technology. These upgraded versions are available to customers at a fraction of the development cost and usually can work with files generated by the old version. However, software packages can be problematic if a user's application differs considerably from the application for which the software was designed. Modifying packaged software is difficult and rarely recommended.

When a computing solution is not available from commercial software vendors, users must custom design their own software. This situation frequently exists in human service agencies. For example, tracking client progress is a common function, but progress indicators vary by client problem to the extent that few generic tracking software packages are available. Given this situation, an agency often chooses to develop custom software.

The risk when developing custom software is high because the complications involved are rarely anticipated before software development begins. In addition, obtaining good advice is difficult. We all understand that a Ford salesperson will not recommend a Buick and that a car buyer with several children might be persuaded to purchase a small, expensive sports car. Similarly, IT personnel may use the hardware, software, and languages they know best rather than the best tools for the application. Errors can be avoided by having well-defined information needs and consulting several vendors who are familiar with a variety of systems. Risk can be lowered by using standard hardware, software, and networking to build an application.

Because agencies have limited resources, they often neglect simple software development items, such as documentation. This can result in costly future system maintenance and modification. Once an agency decides to develop custom software, reversing that decision is difficult. Although agencies should cautiously consider the decision to develop custom software, many have developed custom applications successfully. The increasing capacity of software development tools, such as database form and report generators, is making custom development a safer option.

Since most software packages often solve a single problem, an agency may require several different packages for an IT application. Using many different software packages requires knowing the unique interface of each. Another limitation of using several separate software packages is the difficulty of moving from one software package to another. Files written by one software package may not be usable by other packages or may require translation.

Because of these compatibility problems, many companies have developed generic software packages that integrate the most common applications, such as word processing, drawing, data management, spreadsheet analysis, and data communications. Some human service vendors have integrated applications such as client data management, services tracking, and billing. These integrated packages use a similar interface and have compatible files. The sacrifice for software integration may be that one of the packages is weak or not well suited to the agency. By selecting several separate packages, an agency could develop a more powerful overall application than by selecting an integrated package. Nevertheless, integration is a desirable goal because it simplifies use and support.

Another consideration of software is its perceived friendliness. Although no formal definition of *user friendly* exists, user-friendly software adapts to human ways of doing things rather than requiring humans to adapt to the computer. Some user-friendly techniques are dividing the display into smaller areas, called windows, and using mouse-clickable menus and icons. Friendliness can also be achieved by making a system conversational. A *conversational* system achieves interaction through a dialogue between the user and the system. Voice processing allows the user-machine interface to be more conversational. The movement toward user-friendly software is especially important to the human services field because professionals often are not keyboard proficient or technically trained. A similar phenomenon occurred with the automobile. Early automobiles were not user friendly. They required a hand crank and had difficult gear-shifting mechanisms. User-friendly developments, such as the electric starter and automatic transmission, made the automobile more usable and, hence, more commonly used.

CONCLUSION

One need not be concerned with how an automobile works every time you drive it. Similarly, one need not be concerned with how an IT application works each time you use it. However, most people realize that taking their car to a mechanic and saying, "It doesn't run right; fix it," is not sufficient. The better the driver can describe the nature of the problem to the mechanic, the greater the chance of getting satisfactory results at a reasonable price. Similarly, unsatisfactory results may result if human service professionals give system developers only a brief description of their needs. They must be able to communicate intelligently about the many decisions that will be made in the process of developing an IT application.

This chapter presented the basics of computer hardware, software, programming, and languages to achieve the following:

- Help take the mystery out of IT applications
- Present the concepts and terms necessary to understand IT applications

- Enhance communication between human service professionals who know their information needs and the more technically oriented systems designers and computer programmers who must translate those needs into hardware and software applications
- Provide human service professionals with an understanding of how IT applications are influenced by hardware, software, programming, and languages

REVIEW AND DISCUSSION QUESTIONS

1. What hardware components can you identify? What contribution does each hardware component make to the overall computer system?
2. A CPU is often called the "brains of a computer." Do you consider this a good comparison?
3. The human body is often compared to a computing system. What computing system functions and components do you feel are analogous to the parts and functions of the human body?
4. What is the difference between hardware and software?
5. What are the two main types of software? Give an example of each.
6. What do you consider good computer documentation? Give some examples.
7. This chapter provides a behavior modification example of a programmed set of instructions that human service professionals use. What other programmed instructions do practitioners use?
8. Compare and contrast a computer language with a human language.
9. What are some computer languages that have been developed within the last three years?

Chapter 10

Database Management Influences on IT Development

INTRODUCTION

Production organizations transform natural resources, such as oil and iron, into products. Information organizations process data resources, such as numbers and symbols, into information and knowledge. Failure to manage natural and data resources wisely results in lost opportunities and needless waste.

This view of organizational data as a valuable resource to be processed to the fullest extent is a change from the traditional human service view. In the traditional view, data are collected and processed for use by only a few people. For example, traditionally, accounting data had little relevance for practitioners and client progress notes had little relevance for managers. However, many decision questions are asked frequently by managers, planners, evaluators, supervisors, practitioners, and funding sources that involve data from throughout the agency. In this new way of thinking, an organized and easily accessible pool of agencywide data supports all agency decision making, but this new view is only possible if database technology exists. Consider the potential if a counseling agency's database contained client progress notes that were codified according to client problem, level of functioning, and client outcome. The agency could answer questions such as "What outcomes are associated with an intervention strategy for a typical set of client problems?" If data on service costs were integrated into the database, questions about treatment efficiency could also be examined. With sophisticated database management tools and practices, all agency staff can make decisions based on better information.

This chapter presents the terms and concepts associated with data and database management. It begins with a discussion of data constructs, relationships, and views of data organization. A historical perspective on data management is then presented along with a discussion of database management software. In the final section, and throughout the chapter, implications of database management for IT applications development are presented.

To manage data requires precise definition and description. One difficulty is that database concepts are new and still evolving. As a subject evolves and more becomes known about it, the number of ways to describe the subject increases. For example, Eskimos have a large variety of words to describe snow. Where snow falls infrequently, only a few descriptive words exist. A similar situation is found with data and data management. As data are more complexly explored and managed using technology, more precise forms and meanings are required to describe what occurs. The distinction between these concepts is not always consistent in current IT literature. New terms are sometimes used without regard for overlap with existing terms. This chapter attempts to organize, clarify, and simplify the terms and concepts related to data and database management. For ease of understanding, the definitions and organization in this chapter represent a simplified view of these complex concepts.

DATABASE MANAGEMENT BASICS

This section introduces the concepts of data and database management by expanding on the transportation analogy introduced in previous chapters.

Database System and Transportation System Analogy

The previous analogy between an IT system and a transportation system can be extended to help understand data and their management (see Table 10.1). The original instructions given by the executive in the analogy were as follows: "Travel to the neighboring city. Meet with this list of potential clients. Return with the names of clients who are interested in our project. This envelope contains the necessary information. Don't waste time. Get back as quickly as you can."

Some basic terms are necessary to begin the analogy. The analogy assumes that a human being is analogous to a bit of data and transporting is analogous to processing. An entity is something about which data can be stored, for example, a car or a client. Attributes are properties of entities, for example, the color of a car or the age of a client. A value is the specific identity of one attribute, for example, a yellow car or a sixteen-year-old client. Fields are the attributes in which we are interested, for example, a person's address. Fields can be elementary or nonelementary. A nonelementary field can be divided into smaller fields; for example, an address can be divided into street address, city, state, and zip code. City and state cannot be further divided so they are elementary fields.

TABLE 10.1. Database System and Transportation System Analogy

Function/Characteristic	Transportation System	Database System
Unit acted on	Human being	Bit
Action	Transporting (moving vehicles)	Processing (manipulating data)
Basic terms: entity attribute value	Examples of basic terms: car color of car a yellow car	Examples of basic terms: client age of client 16-year-old client
Constructs	group crowd neighborhood city metropolitan area	byte, character data information knowledge concept
Groupings	Vehicles car car and trailer caravan of vehicles vehicles in traffic line vehicles at rush hour	Data elementary field nonelementary field record file database
Relationships: one to one one to many many to many	car:motor car:tires cars:passengers	1:1 1:N N:N
Views/models: physical logical conceptual	street layout city design user image of transportation system	storage locations database design report from a database
Viewing tools: for display for definitions	maps map scale and symbol definition	schemata data dictionary
Complexity simple intricate	Address street address skyscraper office address	Data structure flat file database
Access guides	street indexes landmarks map edge coordinates	database indexes pointer relational tables

Another group of analogies involves the terms used to describe humans and data as they are transported or processed. Various collections of humans are described by different terms. Several humans gathered together constitute a group, more constitute a crowd, and still more constitute a neighborhood, city, or metropolitan area. Similarly, as bits are combined, terms such as character, information, knowledge, and concept are used to describe what is processed. The change in terms not only represents a change in quantity but also a change in the nature of what is processed. For example, crowd behavior is not simply a combination of individual behaviors and knowledge is not simply an aggregate of data.

Various types of entities are used for processing just as various types of vehicles are used for transporting. If only one human is transported, a car is typically used. For transporting vacationers over a long distance, a car and travel trailer may be used. A car-trailer combination is analogous to a nonelementary data field, often simply called a field, because it can be divided into two separate parts, a car and a trailer. An elementary field cannot be divided further and still retain its original characteristics. For example, a car cannot be divided further and still be a car. Another example of an elementary field is the name of a city.

Thus far, the discussion has concerned categories to describe data, for example, a field. The actual data that correspond to these categories are called data items. A data item is one piece of data. The city-name field could contain the data item Dallas, Berlin, or any other city name of interest.

As more entities become involved, different terms are needed to describe the increasing complexity of the relationships. Returning to the analogy, a caravan of vehicles is analogous to a record (several related data items), vehicles in a stream of traffic are analogous to a file (many related records), and vehicles in rush-hour traffic are analogous to a database (many data items in complex relationships).

In transporting humans and processing data, the relationships between things become important. For example, a family of four will usually get into one taxicab. A group of four strangers rarely will. Several types of data and human relationships exist. In a one-to-one relationship (1:1), both entities have a single relationship to each other. For example, a car has only one motor and a motor is only in one car. In a one-to-many relationship (1:N), one entity is related to many entities, and the many entities have a single relationship to the one. For example, a car is attached to several tires, but a tire can be attached to only one car. In a many-to-many relationship (N:N), many entities may be related to many other entities. For example, many cars may carry many different passengers and many different passengers may be carried by many different cars.

Having presented key terms that help describe data, the efficiency and effectiveness part of the executive's instructions can be discussed in relation to the management of data.

In traveling, one's view of the transportation system is important for reaching a destination with minimum time and cost. This view can take a physical, logical, or conceptual perspective. The physical view of a transportation system is the location and arrangement of buildings, streets, and vehicles. The physical view of a database is the actual storage location of data.

Often, the physical view of a transportation system is not as useful as the logical view. For example, cities such as Salt Lake City, Utah, are designed as a grid with streets emanating from the center of a north-south, east-west axis (see Figure 10.1). This grid design helps the traveler easily learn the transportation system. It is relatively simple for a newcomer to map a route to the address 2025 West Street, 1508 North Street. One would go to a block that is twenty blocks west and fifteen blocks north of the city center. Although the grid system simplifies the locating of addresses, the physical path to any address is not direct. One cannot drive diagonally to an address. Other city designs can solve the problem of inefficient routes. Cities such as Washington, DC, are designed as a grid with major avenues radiating outward from the city center (see Figure 10.2). This grid-and-spoke design provides efficient diagonal access through the city. However, it often makes it difficult to find an address, especially if it is on a diagonal. Many other logical views of a city are possible. Each has advantages and disadvantages for finding an address and minimizing travel time and distance. Similarly, many logical views for organizing data exist in a database. Three common logical views are hierarchy, network, and relational. Each has implications for efficient and effective data management.

Users of a city's transportation system often have an image of how the transportation system operates. For example, the transportation system of San Francisco evokes an image of steep hills, cable cars, and BART (Bay Area Rapid Transit). In data management, the user's view of the system consists of how data are combined into records and files. For example, an accountant may view the attribute "total client visits" as part of a financial report. However, a therapist may view it as part of a client progress report. This overall user image of how data are organized is the conceptual view of a database. A database designer's conceptual view would be a model of how entities are related to one another and the attributes of these entities.

Maps, which graphically present physical and logical layout, help one travel efficiently and effectively. Maps include a small section that defines the transportation symbols used and a distance scale. In databases, the schema is a map of the logical structure of the database, and the data dictionary contains information such as data definitions and relationships.

FIGURE 10.1. A Grid Transportation Layout of a City

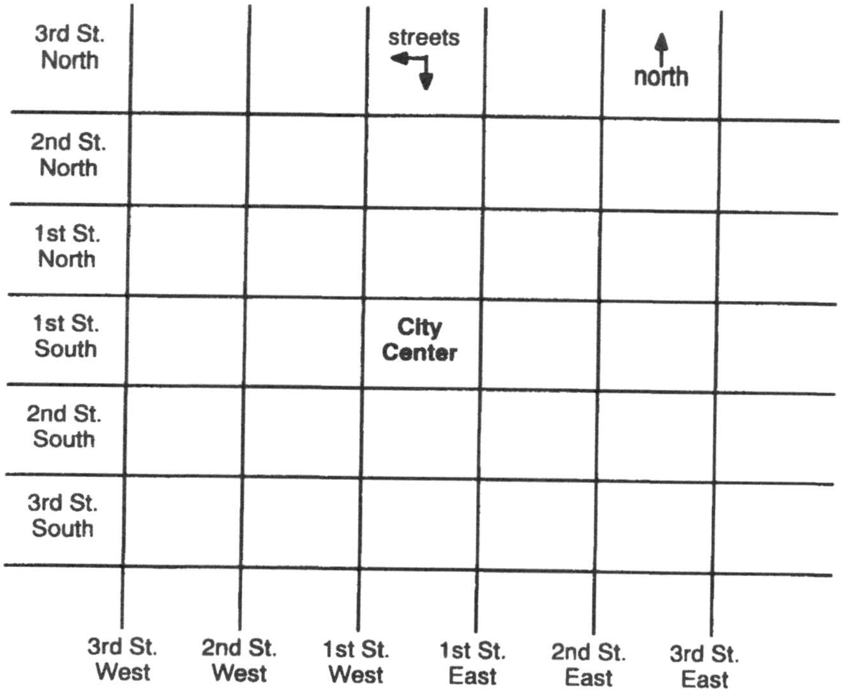

3rd St. North			streets		↑ north
2nd St. North					
1st St. North					
1st St. South			**City Center**		
2nd St. South					
3rd St. South					
3rd St. West	2nd St. West	1st St. West	1st St. East	2nd St. East	3rd St. East

Another factor in efficient and effective transportation is the simplicity of getting to an individual's address. Individuals who live in suburban houses that have unique street addresses are the easiest to find. However, if frequent contact among many individuals is required, as when people work together, the suburbs are not efficient. Housing assignments in a suburb are usually on a first-come-first-serve basis. City centers are designed to be more efficient in proximity than suburbs. Skyscrapers, which add a vertical dimension to an address, provide greater proximity than houses. Height allows the distance between individuals to be shortened; it also adds address complexity. Thus, the location of an office building and the assignment of offices are based on the communication and transportation needs of employees. Similarly, data management systems can be designed as flat, two-dimensional files or complex, multidimensional database structures for storing data.

FIGURE 10.2. A Spoke-and-Grid Transportation Layout of a City

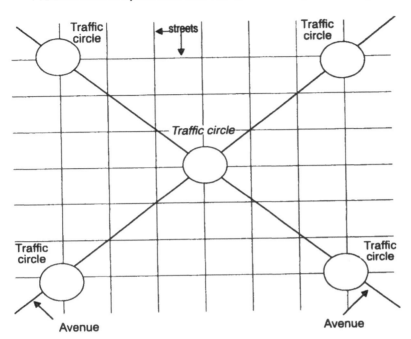

In a transportation system, street indexes, landmarks, and map coordinates help one access locations efficiently and effectively. In a database, indexes, pointers, and relational tables are often used to aid access. Database indexes are analogous to the street index on a map. Pointers are analogous to landmarks that help one locate the next correct turn on a route. Relational tables are somewhat analogous to the map edge coordinates that divide the map horizontally and vertically into sections, such as section A-1 or J-6.

In this analogy, many other factors affect how efficiently and effectively the executive's command is carried out. One important performance factor is how many people must be met at how many different locations. For example, if five individuals must be met, each of whom works in a different office building, traveling to the five locations consumes considerable time. Similarly, if a computer software program must access data from many files, then additional time will be required to (1) locate each file, (2) access, manipulate, and store the necessary data, and (3) exit the file. As the number of places to travel increases, so too do the chances of making a wrong turn or getting lost. The chance of failure or a programming error in a computer program also increases with the number of files being accessed.

Basic Terms

The terms entity, attribute, and value are essential to the management of data. *Entities* are objects or events about which data can be stored. Thus, entities are things we are interested in keeping track of, such as a person, an agency, or a client visit. *Attributes* are characteristics or properties of one or more entities, such as a person's age or address. A specific occurrence of an attribute is called a value. Fifty-two may be the value of age for a specific person.

A single attribute of interest is called a *field*. Other names for a field are data item, data element, or element. The field level of data is often divided into elementary fields and nonelementary fields. Elementary fields are those which cannot be divided, such as a city name. Nonelementary fields are those which can be divided. For example, the attribute "client address" can be divided into four fields, as indicated below in the address 1311 West Lavender Lane.

Elementary fields of attribute "street address"	Value of each field
building number	1311
directional designation	West
street name	Lavender
street type	Lane

An advantage to dividing information into elementary fields is that more processing potential exists. For example, a mailing list comprised of the fields name and address is impossible to sort by last name or zip code. A mailing list file is most useful when divided into the six fields of first name, last name, street address, city, state, and zip code.

A *record* is a group of related fields. A record in data management has a meaning similar to the traditional concept of a physical record. A physical record is a collection of client information such as age, gender, marital status, and problem. In data management, a record is a grouping of the values that are treated as a single unit, for example, a client record.

A *file* is a group of similar records. In database terminology, a *file* is similar to the traditional use of the term in "file cabinet." For example, the clients file may contain the records of all agency clients.

A *database* is a group of files, an organized collection of interrelated or interdependent data items stored together to serve one or more applications. All the files of an agency or the files of one program could constitute a database.

The terms describing the groupings of fields form a hierarchy, as illustrated in Figure 10.3. Our traditional concepts of records and files are the basis for the concepts in data management. However, no traditional concepts apply to a database. One way to visualize a database is as a glass goblet filled with multishaped beads of data (see Figure 10.4). The shape of the beads distinguishes different fields. All the data in the goblet (database) can be logically grouped into records and groups of records into files (see Figure 10.5). A bead may be part of many records and files, since records and files are arbitrary linkings of beads. Using the goblet conceptualization, database management involves three separate tasks: (1) designing forms for data collection, (2) storing the data for efficient access and minimum redundancy, and (3) designing reports for displaying the data to users.

Data Constructs

In computing, many terms describe the meaning associated with one or a combination of symbols. Some examples are characters, data, information, knowledge, and concepts. These terms can be considered data constructs because each is a constructed form, or subform, of data. Each term conveys a slightly different meaning. Table 10.2 defines and provides an example of these constructs. The terms in Table 10.2 form a hierarchy, with those at the bottom of the figure conveying more complex meaning than those at the top. For example, a concept can convey more meaning than a character.

Character

The simplest item for representing meaning is a character. A *character* is any number, alphabetic letter, or other symbol that, when used alone or in combination, has an agreed-upon meaning. Examples of characters are the number 1, the letter A, a punctuation mark, or a symbol. Chapter 9 indicated that a character is typically represented to the computer by a combination of 7 or 8 on/off states (bits) called a byte. Review Table 9.3 on ASCII and EBCDIC codes.

Data

Data consist of one or a group of characters (letters, numbers, or other symbols) that are assigned to a fact or event. For example, 5 is a commonly recognized character. On a five-point Likert scale, 5 often designates the

FIGURE 10.3. Hierarchy of Data Groupings

Data item, data element, or field:
A label given one small unit or piece
of information, for example, client
last name, age, or date of birth.

Record: A set of related
data items, for example,
a client record.

File: A grouping of similarly constructed records
treated as a unit, for example, a master file of
client records.

Database: A collection of data, consisting of multiple records in multiple
files, where the data are stored and managed to minimize redundancy and
to allow for easy manipulation and access. An agency database usually
consists of fiscal, client, services, and staff lines.

---

response "strongly agree." When the character 5 designates "strongly agree," it is a piece of data. The character 5 may assume other meanings; for example, it may mean the number five as in $1 + 4 = 5$. Thus, although characters have common meaning, the meaning of data is determined by the intended use.

Data can be of several types, such as alphabetic, numeric, date/time, currency, picture, sound, and video. Data types have implications for data manipulation and data error checking. For example, one cannot multiply alphanumeric data, and alphabetic data cannot contain a number. The data type "date" illustrates the importance of data type. If a database has the capacity to manipulate dates, a user could request the total clients served between December 1, 1999 and March 31, 2001. The user would not have to know the number of days in each month or whether February 2000 contained twenty-eight days.

Information

Information is the meaning associated with data through processing. Information is data processed according to a set of procedures or rules to enhance

FIGURE 10.4. Visualizing Data As Beads in a Goblet

FIGURE 10.5. Grouping of Fields into Records, Files, and Database

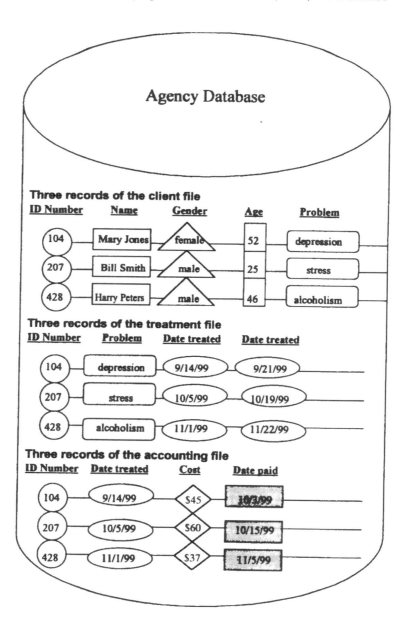

TABLE 10.2. Data Constructs, Definitions, and Examples

Construct	Definition	Example
Character	A letter, number, or symbol used alone or in combination to represent data	A e 15 121 * @
Data	The assigned characters that represent facts, entities, or events	15 (represents age)
Information	Data processed to add additional meaning	15 percent error rate
Knowledge	Information in the form of descriptions and relationships	Description: a divorced person is not married but can have children. Relationship: previous abusive behavior increases the likelihood of subsequent abusive behavior.
Concept	A generalized idea or model formed on the basis of knowledge or experience	Feedback, child abuse, poverty

its meaning. Structuring, ordering, or manipulating can change data to information, as when data on individual client achievement are combined to produce a client success rate. The character 5 conveys information when used in the statistical sense of 0.05 level of significance. Table 10.3 illustrates how processing gives additional meaning to data collected during an interview.

Knowledge

Knowledge consists of descriptions and relationships. Descriptions are statements that identify, define, and differentiate phenomena and classes. An example of a description is "Child abuse consists of physical abuse, and/or sexual abuse, and/or emotional abuse, and/or neglect." Relationships are statements that express the association between phenomena and classes. A relationship between previous abuse and later abuse might be "If previous abuse is verified in a household, then subsequent abuse is 40 percent more likely to occur."

TABLE 10.3. Changing Data into Information

Interview Question	Data Collected	Information for a Human Service Worker
Please type in your age:	55	This fifty-five-year-old male client entered treatment with a presenting problem of depression and alcohol abuse. The client was divorced in 1978, after three years of marriage. He has one child, a girl, named Kathy.

Please indicate your gender:
   (1) = male
   (2) = female
	1	

Are you?
   (1) married
   (2) divorced
   (3) remarried
   (4) single—never married
	2	

Enter the date of your marriage:	5/30/75	
Enter the date of your divorce:	2/30/78	
How many children do you have?	1	

Is this child a boy or a girl?
   (1) boy
   (2) girl
	2	

Type in your child's name:	Kathy	
Type in your major problem:	Depression	
Enter other problems you have: etc.	Drink too much	

Concept

A concept is knowledge combined to form a generalized idea or image, such as mental illness. Currently, it is extremely difficult to represent concepts to a computer. However, as more generalized knowledge bases become available, it may be possible to combine knowledge into a concept and to work with that concept in other applications.

In general, the more meaning conveyed by a data construct, the more difficult it is to manipulate. For example, it is usually easier to work with data than with knowledge. One reason is that errors can occur as complex meanings are combined and manipulated. Many mathematical theorems and formulas can be used to work with data, but few theorems and formulas exist for working with knowledge. Middle-level managers, accountants, planners, and evaluators typically work with data and information. However, top-level managers and practitioners typically work with knowledge and concepts. Thus, a database containing only data and information may provide little support to them.

Although this section distinguishes among data constructs, when the term data or information is used in the remaining sections of this chapter, typically all the entities are denoted.

Relationships of Data to Aid Storage and Access

Another group of basic data management concepts concerns how efficient and accurate access is achieved by relating data. A library analogy helps to illustrate the concepts associated with the relating of data to aid access. In a library, books are not randomly stacked; they are arranged according to a system. These book classification systems specify the relationships among books. For example, books by the same author, or on the same subject, may have similar Library of Congress numbers. The Library of Congress number on a book is analogous to a key in database terms. A key is one or more characters within a set of data that contains information about that set. For example, the attribute "client ID number" may be designated a primary key in a database. Once the ID field is designated as a primary key, all client ID numbers in the database must be unique. Designating a primary key prevents duplicate records from being entered in the database. It also allows more powerful data manipulations, such as when several databases with last name as a primary key are merged into one unique list.

For efficient database design and data manipulation, the relationships among fields are often important. Three basic types of data relationships exist: one-to-one (1:1), one-to-many (1:N), and many-to-many (N:N). Each relationship, its abbreviation, and a human service example appear in Table 10.4.

Views of Data Organization

Another basic group of data management concepts relates to how data organization is viewed. Data organization can be viewed from a physical, logical, or conceptual perspective, as illustrated by Figure 10.6. The physical view concerns how data is actually stored on a storage device. The logical view of data is the abstract mapping of data relationships regardless of physical location. The conceptual view of data organization involves the user's perspective. A library can again be used to illustrate these views of data organization. In a library, examining where books reside on shelves provides a physical view; examining the card catalog and floor indexes provides a logical view; asking users how they find what they need in the library provides a conceptual view. Just as the design of libraries has produced a body of knowledge known as library science, the design of databases is becoming a well-defined IT science.

TABLE 10.4. Three Basic Data Relationships

Relationship and abbreviation: one-to-one (1:1)

   Definition: Each entity has a single relationship to the other.

   Entities: Worker, Social Security number

   Nature of the relationship: Possesses

   Example: A worker possesses only one Social Security number and a Social Security number is possessed by only one worker.

Relationship and abbreviation: one-to-many (1:N)

   Definition: One entity has relationships to many (two or more) entities while the many entities have a single relationship to the one.

   Entities: Therapist, client

   Nature of the relationship: Work with

   Example: A therapist can work with many clients, but a client works with only one therapist. (This may not be true of all agencies.)

Relationship and abbreviation: many-to-many (N:N)

   Definition: Many entities have relationships to many other entities, and the many other entities have relationships to many other entities.

   Entities: Clients, service programs

   Nature of the relationship: Involvement

   Example: A client may be involved in many different service programs, and service programs may involve many different clients.

Database users are concerned with ease of entering, manipulating, and retrieving data; they are not concerned with where on the storage medium the data physically reside or how the data are logically organized. Consequently, complex logical data organization allows users many conceptual views of the data, although the data's physical storage allows only one view. A map of the overall logical structure of a database is called a *schema*. The *data dictionary* of a database is the listing of all the fields, their characteristics, and their relationships.

Many logical views exist for organizing data for efficient and effective management. The three basic logical views for organizing a database are the hierarchy, network, and relational structures. A comparison of these is beyond the scope of this chapter. However, since users often hear the term relational database or see diagrams of a relational view of a database, this structure will be briefly defined.

In a *relational database*, records or fields are structured in two-dimensional tables of columns and rows called a relation. In a relational table,

FIGURE 10.6. Physical, Logical, and Conceptual Views of Data Organization

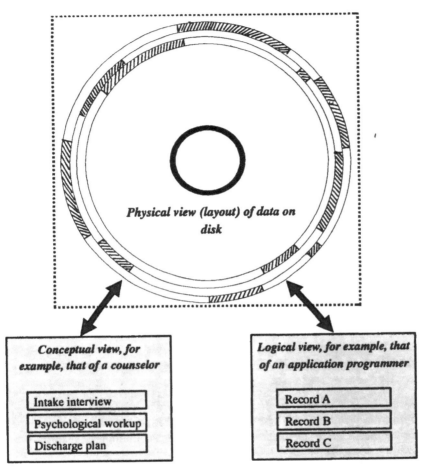

the horizontal rows represent records and the vertical columns represent fields. Figure 10.7 shows three relational tables in an agency database. Any field in the database can become part of a new record by defining a new table. Thus, 1:1, 1:N, or N:N relationships can be created easily.

FIGURE 10.7. Relational Database Structure

Relation #1. Monthly payroll file

Worker first name	Worker last name	Monthly salary	Days worked	Deduc- tions
Chris	Jones	$3,000	20	1
Saraj	Milles	$4,000	18	3
Etc.				

Relation #2. Client demographic file

Client first name	Client last name	Client ID #	Worker last name	Problem #1
Sonny	Day	0842	Milles	alcoholism
Ophelia	Blues	1784	Jones	depression
Etc.				

Relation #3. Client services file

Client ID #	Date of visit #1	Service codes	Date of visit #2	Service codes
0842	15 Nov 99	3, 7, 21	22 Nov 99	3, 7, 14
1784	8 Dec 99	7, 21, 14	22 Dec 99	7
Etc.				

All agency data stored in one database and related

MANAGING DATA

Objectives of Data Management

Management requires developing goals and objectives. The goal of data management is to have accurate data available where needed, when needed, and in the format needed. Achieving this goal requires many data management objectives. Some of the most important are multiple concurrent use, security, integrity, limited redundancy, relatability, data independence, and ease and speed of access. Since data management and library management have much in common, database management objectives will be explained using a library example.

Multiple Concurrent Use

Multiple concurrent use means that many users can have simultaneous access to the same data in the database. In a library, putting frequently used books on reserve and purchasing multiple copies of books result in multiple concurrent use.

A database system uses programming techniques to ensure that when two users require data at the same time, one is locked out until the other transaction is complete. In addition, if two users are simultaneously updating different parts of the same record, the database system will not overwrite one user's updates with the updates made by the other. Providing multiple concurrent use by storing duplicate data is not usually recommended. It can hinder the achievement of other data management objectives, such as having minimum data redundancy and maintaining data integrity.

Security

Security as a data management objective means ensuring data protection against accidental or willful unauthorized access or destruction. Often in a library, a library card must be shown before a book can be withdrawn. Inside a library, staff members are often placed in highly conspicuous locations to hinder destruction and theft. Carrying a book out of the library without checkintg it out can activate an alarm or lock an exit door.

A database system has similar mechanisms to assign, control, and remove the rights to use data. *Passwords* are a unique group of characters that a user must supply to satisfy security requirements before gaining access to a database. Passwords prevent unauthorized access. They also allow associated user activities to be monitored and linked to an account number. Various levels of access to data can be associated with each record or field. These levels involve the ability to read, add, delete, or change data. For example, therapists may read, add, or change information in their clients' records. However, they may be locked out of the client-identifying fields of name and address for other therapists' clients, while still being able to read non-client-identifying fields.

Integrity

Integrity as a data management objective means having the ability to maintain a high degree of data consistency and correctness. In a library, the card catalog is kept current and shelves are frequently scanned to ensure that books are in their proper locations.

Data integrity requires that all related fields be updated concurrently. For example, changing a client's address in one file means that the exact same change should be made immediately to all files containing the client's address. A computer failure during record updating should not result in the loss of data or in having to update the same data twice. Programs that check for errors when data are entered can help maintain data integrity, for example, by not accepting a client's name if it contains a number.

Limited Redundancy

Limited redundancy as a data management objective refers to having limited duplicate data in a database. In a library, multiple book copies waste shelf space and reduce the efficiency of locating books. To help limit redundancy, infrequently used duplicate books are discarded. However, sometimes it is necessary for a library to store multiple copies of a book as in the case with popular books, which may be placed on short-term reserve to ensure maximum use without having to shelve multiple copies. The objective is to manage redundancy, not to eliminate it.

Unnecessary redundancy in a database wastes storage space, hinders data integrity, and may lessen efficient access. Since data management software uses different techniques to store and access data, the acceptable level of redundancy in a database may vary. Data redundancy can be reduced through complex design techniques, which are beyond the scope of this book, for example, normalization (Dutka and Hanson, 1989).

Relatability

Relatability as a data management objective refers to having the ability to easily connect related fields. In a library, relatability is accomplished by the card catalog, which links books by author and subject. In addition, each card in the card subject catalog usually contains a list of related topics.

A database system must accommodate complex relationships among data to reduce redundancy and to store, access, and manipulate data efficiently. For example, a client's name may be part of a client file, an accounting file, an evaluation file, and a fund-raising file. The schema and data dictionary explain some of the underlying relationships in a database.

Data Independence

Data independence as a data management objective refers to having the ability to store data independent of the programs used to access and manipulate them. In a library, data independence means that books can be physically added, removed, or moved without affecting other systems, such as those for lending and returning books. In addition, the organization of books in the library remains unchanged regardless of changes in library staff or management techniques.

In a database system, data independence means that minimum changes occur in input forms, data manipulation procedures, and output reports when new data are added or old data are changed or deleted. The converse should also be true. Users may add or change input forms, manipulation procedures, and reports without affecting the data or other existing programs. Data independence is very important in the human services because data on services frequently change.

Ease of Access

Ease of access as a data management objective refers to ensuring that data can be obtained from the database quickly and easily. In a library, the information desk facilitates easy and speedy access. At the information desk, a librarian can interpret user needs into the terms and concepts the library uses. Other methods are the on-line catalog and floor indexes.

A database system uses storage techniques, such as indexes and pointers, to provide speed and ease of access. It may provide software that translates user data requests made in common English into commands the database system can use.

It is not possible to achieve all data management objectives, since achieving one objective may adversely affect another. The goal is to understand which objectives are important for an application and to achieve a balance of the desired objectives. In human service financial applications, integrity and limited redundancy might be important objectives. In applications that support practitioners, relatability and security may be important objectives. Those developing new data management applications should be aware of the compromises that must be made when optimizing one or several objectives.

DATA MANAGEMENT SOFTWARE

Many software packages exist to help achieve the previous objectives. This section discusses the characteristics of data management software packages. Some packages are simple enough for beginning users to solve basic data management problems, such as managing a mailing list and a simple tracking system. Other database software is so complex that experienced programmers have to customize the software.

Historical Perspective

Data management has been a chore throughout history. Only with the recent advent of IT has the capacity to manage data taken a quantum leap in sophistication. The history of the movement from manual to computerized data processing helps one to understand database management systems (DBMS).

In the late 1950s, IT applications for handling data were essentially computerized versions of existing manual and mechanical data processing systems. Applications, such as payroll, bookkeeping, or client data, were essentially self-contained. Their files, although physically located in the same electronic storage device, were separate. The originating department considered the applications their property and responsibility. The computer programs that managed the data were unique to each file. The physical and logical organization of the data, as well as the method of accessing data from the files, heavily influenced these programs. Processing efficiency was important because hardware was expensive.

As computers processed more agency files, the integration of information across files became an increasing problem. Each additional application required a new file, but much of the data in the new files were already present in existing files. Redundancy of data and computer programs not only wasted scarce computer storage space but also caused inconsistencies among reports derived from different files. Inconsistencies existed because any change in one file had to be made simultaneously in all other files, and some needed changes would invariably be missed.

Throughout the 1960s, declining computer hardware prices made computing power more accessible. The increasing number of applications made the problems of data connection, redundancy, and inconsistency more acute. Computers processed data within files; top management needed processing across files.

Database management concepts were a major advance in data processing technology in the 1970s. Database management software distinguished the programs that input, processed, and reported data from the programs that specified database organization and data access methods. With data in the database independent of the programs designed to work with them, expanding a database had little effect on existing data and programs. Because one database, rather than separate files, stored the data, data redundancy was minimized and agencywide reports were more easily produced. The change from multiple separate files to database integration in the 1970s has been followed by database management systems with user-friendly interfaces that allow nonprogrammers to design, manipulate, and report data.

Features of Database Software

This section discusses the features that are typically found in database management systems (DBMS). These features can be called functions, modules, or programs.

Database

The database is the core module that stores data, with which all other modules interact. Agencies that use pictures and video in records should ensure that the DBMS can handle these data formats.

Data Dictionary

The data dictionary helps define and document the contents of the database. Its functions are similar to those of an ordinary dictionary. It provides a listing of fields, their size, type, error check upon data entry, relationships with other fields and records, security considerations, and other basic descriptive information. Users can change the descriptions in the data dictionary without affecting the computer programs that manipulate and report the data.

The data dictionary helps maintain, document, and standardize the database in several different ways. New fields are added and old fields are changed or deleted by changing the data dictionary. Users can determine what data are available and who controls and uses the data. Terms used to describe data are clearly defined, along with the precise formats of the data, records, and files. Inconsistencies and redundancies can be spotted easily.

Passwords

The password module allows the person in control of the DBMS to set up and maintain user passwords to prevent unauthorized access. Some password modules control only entry into the DBMS. More sophisticated password modules enable each user to add, read, change, or delete any field. Since data privacy is essential for client records, a sophisticated password module is desirable for human service applications containing confidential information.

Data Encryption

The data encryption feature scrambles and unscrambles data for security purposes using techniques such as formulas and algorithms. An encryption module may store the last name Smith as &%{n*. When access is authorized, the encryption module interprets &%{n* as Smith. Because agencies work with sensitive client data, a data encryption module can ensure data confidentiality and protect client privacy. Encryption is especially useful if client-identifying data leave the agency, such as during transfer over a network to another location. If data are transferred over telephone lines or over the Internet, data encryption of all client records should be mandatory.

DBMS Language

DBMSs often have a unique set of commands for working with the database. These commands are called the DBMS language. DBMS languages resemble other computer languages in structure, commands, and use. However, they rarely contain the sophistication and capabilities of general purpose languages. These special DBMS languages can be more efficient and easier to use than general purpose languages. They offer the nonprogrammer a tool for working with the database. A DBMS language may be useful for agencies that allow staff to set up small databases to support their work, for example, mailing lists or tracking systems.

General Purpose Language Interface

DBMS packages may allow users to interact with the database using one or more general purpose computer languages, such as BASIC. Thus, experienced programmers can use a common computer language to write programs that input, manipulate, and output data. A computer language interface extends the power of a DBMS by allowing programmers to construct forms, queries, and reports that would not be possible with the DBMS language.

Query Language

The query feature allows users to easily manipulate and retrieve data without writing a special DBMS language or a general purpose language program. For example, the query might help the user display all clients between the ages of thirty and forty who reside in a certain zip code. A sophisticated, yet easy to use query language is important for agencies that need frequent one-time reports, have limited database expertise, or have high turnover in staff who query the database. It is also important if the vendor requires extensive time and money to design special reports. If an IT application will involve many DBMSs from different vendors, it is necessary for the databases to accept queries in a standard format. Structured Query Language (SQL) is a popular standard language that allows queries to retrieve data from many different databases.

Forms and Report Generators

Forms are computer screen templates designed by users for collecting data that are input into the database. Reports are standard formats for retrieving and presenting data from the database. Form and report generators allow users to design and modify input forms and output reports without costly programming. They also provide experienced programmers with a tool to quickly design forms and reports that can be customized later using the DBMS or general purpose language.

Form generators can provide methods to check for simple data entry errors, such as letters in numeric fields and improper ranges, for example, when year of birth is entered as 1853 instead of 1953. Report modules often allow the construction of complex formats, such as crosstabs or pie charts.

Databases may also provide the capacity to link all forms and reports into a menu system for easy access. Agencies without access to a programmer should select a database with a powerful form and report generation capability. Agencies needing special formats, such as crosstabs with row and column totals, should ensure that the database has these capabilities. Similarly, graphics output is often desirable in the human services, since practitioners tend to be visually oriented. A database with a wide selection of graphic output or one with a special graphics package can save substantial programming time and increase data use. Agencies using the Internet as a network should ensure that the features they need will run over the Internet.

Other Modules or Features

DBMSs can include an assortment of other features. For example, some DBMSs allow the user to record all transactions to the database. If an error is made or the hardware malfunctions, the transaction log allows the database to be reconstructed. Another useful feature allows the database to import and export files in standard formats such as ASCII code. This feature allows the DBMS to share data with other software packages, such as a nonprofit accounting system. Typically, DBMSs can import and export data in ASCII format or in formats used by spreadsheets and other popular DBMS software. Although DBMSs can import and export data, they usually cannot import or export queries, forms, and reports. Therefore, switching from one DBMS software package to another may involve substantial reprogramming.

The preceding discussion illustrates that DBMSs have many features that determine their suitability to human service applications. Since changing DBMS packages can be difficult and time-consuming, choosing the DBMS software that meets present and future needs is crucial. If a large or complex database is part of an IT application, a specialist with a wide knowledge of DBMS software is desirable to help select the proper DBMS.

DESIGNING A DBMS

Since database design is a complex process, this section only provides a brief introduction. Designing a database involves more than specifying the needed fields and designing input screens and output reports. It involves determining the most efficient arrangement of the fields. This arrangement is not always obvious, as illustrated by a system that tracks donors along with the amount and date of the donation. The donation system might contain the following fields:

1. first name
2. last name
3. title
4. organization
5. mailing address
6. city
7. state
8. zip code
9. donation amount
10. donation date

If one record contained all the fields, a file of twenty donors would look similar to Table 10.5.

Several problems exist with this file. First, there is no way to determine whether Bill Smith, the first entry, is the same person as B. Smith, the last entry. If the file was used to send year-end thank-you letters, Bill Smith may receive several duplicate letters, giving the impression of a disorganized agency. A similar problem is that two entries exist for Pete Latta, each with a different address. Another problem is that May Bril appears to be donating twice a month; thus, she has six separate records in a three-month period.

TABLE 10.5. A Simple Donation File

First name	Last name	Title	Orga- nization	Mailing address	City	State	Zip code	Dona- tion	Donation date
Bill	Smith	Mayor	City	Harvey Rd	Ely	TX	74321	5,000	1/14/99
May	Bril			523 West	Ely	TX	74322	300	1/15/99
Sam	Howe			401 Hazel	Baum	TX	75043	1,000	1/21/99
Pete	Latta			911 Forest	Baum	TX	75043	500	1/22/99
May	Bril			523 West	Ely	TX	74322	200	1/30/99
Mary	Able			2456 Oak	Baum	TX	75043	1,000	2/05/99
Mike	Coch	Director	A&P Inc	21 1st St.	Baum	TX	75043	2,000	2/10/99
Alice	Ball	Manager	IBM	44 W. Pine	Ely	TX	74322	800	2/14/99
May	Bril			523 West	Ely	TX	74322	300	2/15/99
Glen	Jones	Owner	G.J. Inc	34 Center	Ely	TX	74321	1,000	2/22/99
R. C.	Colla			#33 Pearl	Ely	TX	74321	750	2/35/99
May	Bril			523 West	Ely	TX	74322	300	2/28/99
S. B.	Howe			401 Hazel	Baum	TX	75043	500	3/02/99
Pete	Latta			22 Angle	Ely	TX	74323	500	3/10/99
May	Bril			523 West	Ely	TX	74322	300	2/15/99
Kathy	Hally	Owner	IP Corp	502 Rose	Baum	TX	75041	1,000	3/18/99
Lyle	Pils			561 River	Baum	TX	75041	200	3/22/99
Molly	Bogon	Director	SSI	43 Fallow	Ely	TX	74322	2,000	3/25/99
May	Bril			523 West	Ely	TX	74322	200	3/31/99
B.	Smith			Peach St.	Ely	TX	74321	5,000	3/29/99

Assuming many donors follow similar patterns as May Bril, the file would contain substantial redundancy by the end of the year. This redundancy would waste data input and computer storage resources and hinder data relatability. A more efficient design would require entry of only new information for additional donations, that is, the amount and date of donation.

Adding a new field containing a unique identification number would solve much of the confusion over duplicate names. Upon entering the last name of a donor, the DBMS could present the data entry person with the records of entries with similar names. The data entry person could then determine whether the donor is a current contributor or a new donor and enter the information accordingly.

Dividing the donor file into two files, as illustrated in Table 10.6, could reduce data redundancy. One file would contain mailing list records; the other file would contain donation records. Only three pieces of information would need to be added for current contributors who gave a new donation. Since a unique ID number connects the files, reports could contain fields from both files. Although a new ID field was added, the amount of stored data was reduced. The two changes mentioned reduced the number of data items stored from 200 in Table 10.5 to 168 in Table 10.6. In a database with thousands of records, the reduction in redundancy and increase in efficiency could be dramatic. However, the input screens and output reports to work with data in multiple files may be more complex.

This example illustrates that database design requires training in design techniques. Although a discussion of these techniques is beyond the scope of this book, one should understand that the construction of complex databases is difficult, even with user-friendly software. Database construction involves the application of design principles and techniques that are not based on common sense. Training and experience is required. The 80/20 rule presented in Chapter 6 applies to database design. Developing a well-functioning application often requires four times the effort of developing the initial prototype. Agencies designing a database should consider hiring an expert to assist during the design process. As the following quote illustrates, even sophisticated vendors fail, especially with large applications that link existing databases:

Is it a law, or only reality, that government and high-tech don't readily mix? California's failed attempt to create a statewide system to track deadbeat parents is the latest public-agency computer flop to raise the question. On Thursday, the state announced that after spending US$100 million over the past five years to set up the Statewide Automated Child Support System—and implementing it in only 11 of California's 58 counties—it pulled the plug on the project. . . . Who's to blame? California points to contractor Lockheed Martin Information Services Corp. . . . The company has acknowledged difficulties, but says that the wildly different technical requirements from the state's counties created insuperable obstacles. ("California Computer System Bites the Dust," 1997. Copyright © 1994-99 Wired Digital, Inc. All rights reserved.)

TABLE 10.6. A More Efficient Database Design for the Donation System

Mailing List File

ID #	First name	Last name	Title	Mailing address	City	State	Zip code	Orga-nization
1	Bill	Smith	Mayor	Harvey Rd	Ely	TX	74321	City
2	May	Bril		523 West	Ely	TX	74322	
3	Sam	Howe		401 Hazel	Baum	TX	75043	
4	Pete	Latta		22 Angle	Ely	TX	74323	
5	Mary	Able		2456 Oak	Baum	TX	75043	
6	Mike	Coch	Director	21 1st St.	Baum	TX	75043	A&P Inc
7	Alice	Ball	Manager	44 W. Pine	Ely	TX	74322	IBM
8	Glen	Jones	Owner	34 Center	Ely	TX	74321	G.J. Inc
9	R. C.	Colla		#33 Pearl	Ely	TX	74321	
10	Kathy	Hally	Owner	502 Rose	Baum	TX	75041	IP Corp
11	Lyle	Pils		561 River	Baum	TX	75041	
12	Molly	Bogon	Director	43 Fallow	Ely	TX	74322	SSI

Donation Log File

ID #	Donation amount	Donation date
1	5,000	1/14/99
2	300	1/15/99
3	1,000	1/21/99
4	500	1/22/99
5	200	1/30/99
6	1,000	2/05/99
7	2,000	2/10/99
8	800	2/14/99
2	300	2/15/99
9	1,000	2/22/99
10	750	2/35/99
2	300	2/28/99
3	500	3/02/99
4	500	3/10/99
2	300	2/15/99
11	1,000	3/18/99
12	200	3/22/99
13	2,000	3/25/99
2	200	3/31/99
1	5,000	3/29/99

IMPLICATIONS OF DATA MANAGEMENT
FOR IT DESIGN AND DEVELOPMENT

Many implications of data management for IT application design and development have already been presented in the previous sections. However, data management has larger implications than those concerning database design and development. In this larger view, data management involves linking the information in an organization and making that information available to all for goal achievement. Many define this role of integrating and connecting organizational information as knowledge management. *Knowledge management* involves the systematic, on-line capturing of what the organization knows about what it does and disseminating it to the right people at the right time. Knowledge management is supported by a *data warehouse*, that is, historical data stored to optimize query, analysis, and decision making. *Data mining* is the process of digging through tons of warehoused data to discover knowledge in the form of patterns and relationships. In this view, IT provides the tools to create and disseminate an organization's "intelligence." This intelligence is available to employees through their desktop technology and allows them to be more productive, cost-efficient, timely, and effective. That is, each employee has instant and easy access to the accumulated knowledge of the agency and the capacity to use that knowledge to improve job performance (Ikujiro and Hirotaka, 1995).

Organizational intelligence implies that training workers to be intelligent information producers is just as important as training workers how to be intelligent information consumers. It should be just as important for employees to publish their intelligence for others as it is for them to use the intelligence published by others. This dependency on original sources makes workers more responsible for collecting accurate and reliable data. Having more pervasive, reliable, and accurate information allows more decisions to be made closer to the bottom of the organization. This improves decision making while eliminating multiple layers of management. As these changes occur, information becomes a living, pulsating, lifeline through which workers learn together, improve together, and create a more intelligent agency.

Although this view of data management is far from what often occurs in many agencies today, it is useful to think of applying IT to build organizational intelligence. Developing agency intelligence goes beyond the task of setting up a DBMS. Chapter 11 on networking and Chapter 12 on managing IT will expand the concept of data management to include the realm of organizational intelligence.

CONCLUSION

With IT applications that provide more sophisticated data management, our concepts about data and its management are becoming more complex and more precise. This is particularly true when examining the software that performs data management functions. DBMS software is one of the most important packages that allows human service agencies to develop the applications they need.

REVIEW AND DISCUSSION QUESTIONS

1. What is the difference between data, information, knowledge, and concepts?
2. What is a database?
3. What are some examples of manual databases?
4. How does a computer and DBMS software change a manual database system?
5. What are the objectives of data management?
6. What are the differences among logical, physical, and conceptual views of a database?
7. What are the typical features of database software?
8. When would an agency use a DBMS that was linked to the Internet?
9. What considerations would a multiagency DBMS entail that a single-agency DBMS would not?
10. How does IT change data management?
11. Explain the concept of organizational intelligence.

Chapter 11

Networking, Telecommunications, and Internet Influences on IT Development

INTRODUCTION

Although the automobile was a significant invention, its impact on society occurred only after a system of roads was built. In the United States, the interstate highway system is often credited with changing American lifestyles because it allowed people to travel long distances by car. Interestingly, the interstate highway system was built by the Department of Defense as a way to quickly transport military personnel and equipment in case of attack.

Similar to automobiles, computers in isolation had less of an impact on society than their connection via networks. The Internet, which allowed computers throughout the world to easily connect and communicate, is having substantial impact on society. Not surprisingly, the Department of Defense initially developed the Internet as a way to distribute computing power to survive in case of a nuclear war.

This chapter discusses IT connectivity, or networking. It continues the transportation analogy developed in previous chapters and then presents basic concepts. Next, the types of networks and network activities are discussed, along with the nature of cyberspace. The implications of networking for IT application development and design are mentioned throughout the chapter and discussed specifically in the final section.

NETWORKING BASICS

Most people understand that the telephone network consists of wire lines, radio relay towers, and communication satellites that connect devices such as telephones, FAX machines, and answering machines. Similarly, IT networks consists of wire lines, relay towers, and communication satellites that connect computers and peripherals all over the world. As with the technology introduced in previous chapters, networking involves new concepts and substantial jargon. These are introduced using the transportation analogy developed in previous chapters.

Networking and Transportation Systems Analogy

Table 11.1 applies the transportation analogy to networking. In this analogy, travel is analogous to data transmission, as expressed by slang such as hitting the road or surfing the net. Travel is from one house or office to another, while data transmission is between two nodes on a network. Travel is over various types of roads, from small country roads to large highways. Similarly, data is transported over various links, from slow twisted-pair cable to coaxial cable and high-speed fiber-optic cables. Humans often travel in groups. Similarly, bits are typically grouped and transported in packets.

Several measures of movement exist. Miles per hour (MPH) is a measure of vehicle speed, just as bits per second (BPS) is a measure of data transmission speed. Another measure of speed refers to roadway capacity or the maximum number of vehicles a roadway is capable of handling per hour. In communications, the baud rate is the name given to data line capacity.

Universal agreements are important in vehicle and data movement. In a transportation system, traffic signs have internationally recognized colors and shapes to aid understanding. In data communications, the agreed-upon conventions are called protocols. In a transportation system, many different techniques help manage the flow of traffic. Stop signs and stoplights not only allow cross traffic; they help space vehicles. Stop signs evenly space vehicles within the flow of traffic, while stoplights group vehicles to allow alternate traffic flow. Similarly, asynchronous and synchronous are two common methods for separating and reconstructing the stream of bits during data transmission. Asynchronous transmission breaks the data stream into single bytes, whereas synchronous transmission breaks the stream into similarly sized groups of bytes. Another universal agreement concerns the direction of movement. One-way traffic flow is analogous to simplex mode in computer communications and two-way traffic flow is analogous to duplex mode.

All systems need control mechanisms. In urban transportation systems, vehicle movement is often restricted during periods of high air pollution. To enforce this restriction, vehicles may only be allowed to travel on certain days. Vehicles traveling on the wrong day are in error and a mechanism exists for traffic officers to check for these errors. One method of detecting such violations uses vehicle license plate numbers. Vehicles with license

TABLE 11.1. Networking and Transportation System Analogy

Function/ Characteristic	Transportation System	Computing System
Basic Terms		
Basic activity	Travel	Data transmission
Slang	Hitting the road	Surfing the Net
Accumulations	Groups of people traveling together	Packet of information sent as a unit
Residence	House/office on a road	Node on a network
Type of links Low speed Medium speed High speed	Roads Country roads Highways Interstate or Autobahn	Data links Twisted-pair wire Coaxial cable Fiber-optic lines
Action Terms		
Direction of movement	One- or two-way traffic	Simplex or duplex modes
Basic measures Speed Capacity	Traffic flow Miles per hour Vehicles per hour	Bandwidth Bits per second (BPS) Baud rate
Periodic sequencing	Stop sign	Asynchronous
Continuous sequencing	Stoplight	Synchronous
Agreements		
Universal agreements	Traffic sign shapes	Protocols
Error checking	Odd/even license plate restriction technique	Parity checking
Internet		
System of systems	National transportation system	The Internet
Separate sophisticated system	Interstate highway system	The World Wide Web
Address	Home street address	Uniform Resource Locator (URL)
Easy to find address	Main street location	Easily remembered URLs, e.g., books.com
Entryway	The entrace room of your home	Homepage on the World Wide Web
Access tools	Vehicles that can use the interstate highway system	Browser that lets people travel the World Wide Web
Private use	Toll roads	Intranets
Safety and Hazards		
Physical hazards	Crashes and gridlock	Crashes and gridlock
Human hazards	Reckless driving and road rage	Flaming and spamming
Access control	Border checkpoint	Fire wall

plates ending in an even number may be permitted to travel on even-numbered days, whereas vehicles with license plates ending in an odd number would be allowed to travel on odd-numbered days. Computers use a similar method, called parity, whereby an even or odd "parity" bit is added to each byte of transferred data. This parity bit is checked to determine whether data were accurately communicated.

Another final group of concepts related to the Internet is the information superhighway. Systems sometimes have subsystems that operate according to a special set of rules; for example, the interstate highway system has uniform speed limits and standard signs. Similarly, the World Wide Web is a system of Internet sites that uses a common language, called HTML (Hypertext Markup Language) or XML (Extensible Markup Language), to display information. The Web also uses a common site identification system. Each site has a uniform resource locator (URL) address similar to the street address of a house. Web sites with easy to remember URLs are considered main street locations on the Web. Just as a home or office has an entryway or reception area, each Web site has a home page that greets users and channels them to the remaining areas of the site.

For people to use certain transportation subsystems such as interstate highways, they must have a vehicle that meets interstate requirements, for example, capable of moving at a minimum speed. Similarly, for people to use the subsystem of the Internet called the World Wide Web, they must have a browser software program that has certain capacities. Just as private toll roads exist on the interstate system, private use of Internet technology, called intranets, exists within organizations.

Hazards and safety are concerns in transportation as well as on a network. Just as vehicles crash and are stuck in gridlock, networks crash and users become stuck in gridlock. Reckless driving and road rage are analogous to flaming and spamming on the Web. Border checkpoints are used to protect one road system from another, for example, to check for overweight trucks. Similarly, fire walls channel communications between two networks so that they can be examined for privacy and security threats.

Just as fast highways and inexpensive and reliable vehicles spurred our use of the transportation system, the WWW and graphical browsers have opened the Internet to people with limited computer ability and spurred the development of WWW sites.

Basic Terms and Concepts

An isolated computer or peripheral has limited use. When IT is connected, applications can become more robust and focus more resources on user problems. A collection of computers and peripherals that works together as one system is called a *network*. Each computer on the network is called a *node*. *Data communications* is the transmission of data between computer nodes or peripherals. *Networking* is data communications between computers and peripherals. Data communications within a computer, for example, between the processor and hard disk, are not considered networking. *Telecommunications* is networking across telephone lines.

Communication between computers requires that the sending device and the receiving device are synchronized on the format of the data and the method of data transfer. *Protocols* are predetermined communication conventions for the format and timing of communications between IT devices. Two Internet communication protocols are TCP/IP (Transmission Control Protocol/Internet Protocol) and HTTP (HyperText Transfer Protocol). *Handshaking* is the process whereby computers automatically exchange protocols. Based upon the protocol selected, the information is broken into *packets* that contain addresses and other pertinent information, such as error-checking data.

Data communications often involves an error correction method that adds a "parity" bit to each byte of transferred data. *Parity* refers to whether the total number of ON bits in one byte of transferred data results in an even or an odd parity bit being added to the byte. When transmitting data using even parity, the parity bit is set to 1 if the total of binary ones in a byte results in an even number. In odd parity, the parity bit is set to 1 if the total of binary ones in a byte results in an odd number. Parity checking only finds transmission errors that impact byte structure, such as telephone line interference. Parity does not control for improperly transmitted data, such as a misspelled word.

Asynchronous and synchronous are two common methods for separating and reconstructing the stream of bits during data transmission. *Asynchronous transmission* of data breaks the stream of data into single bytes. *Synchronous transmission* breaks the stream of data into similarly sized groups of bytes. Asynchronous and synchronous are also used to describe user interaction. Synchronous refers to users interacting in real time; asynchronous refers to users interacting on their own schedule, for example, using voice mail.

Three basic modes exist for describing the direction of data transmission (see Figure 11.1). In *simplex mode*, data are transmitted in one direction, such as from a computer to a printer. In *half duplex mode*, data can be transmitted in both directions, but only in one direction at a time. In *full duplex mode*, data can be simultaneously transmitted in both directions, as when a computer communicates with the Internet.

FIGURE 11.1. Data Transmission Modes

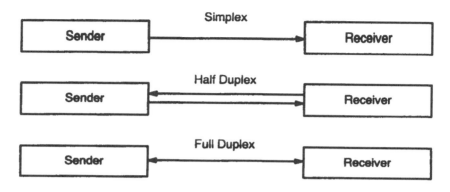

Bandwidth refers to the amount of data that can be transmitted in a specified time. Several measures of bandwidth, or data transmission speed, exist. *Bits per second* (BPS) is a measure of the number of bits that flow across a data link. *Baud rate* is the data transfer measure that is named after the nineteenth-century French communications pioneer Baudot. Baud rate refers to the number of times per second the line signal can change states. Baud rate is often confused with BPS because with some older communication devices, the baud and BPS rate were the same.

Networking Architecture

Networking architecture refers to the configurations of components in a network. In *client/server* networking architecture, each device is either a client or server. Clients run applications and rely on servers for network resources, such as common files, devices, and processing power. Servers handle communications among all client computers and peripherals and with any device outside the network. Servers manage disk drives (file servers), printers (print servers), or network traffic (network servers). Client/server networks exploit inexpensive hardware but require more sophisticated application design and resource management. One advantage of the client/server configuration is that each network is a self-contained unit that can easily be linked to other networks. Massive computer networks can be built by linking many client/server networks together. Since each client/server network is independent, the failure of one network has little impact on the total network.

Another architecture type is the peer-to-peer network. In a *peer-to-peer network,* each node has equivalent capabilities and responsibilities, unlike client/server architectures that dedicate some nodes to serving others. Peer-to-peer networks are usually simpler and less expensive than client/server networks and are primarily used for the sharing of files.

Networking Hardware

Several hardware components are involved in networking. Data are transmitted over communication lines or channels called *data links.* Data links can be made of several types of materials at varying costs. *Twisted-pair wire* contains two inexpensive insulated wires twisted around each other. One wire carries the signal; the other wire is grounded and absorbs signal interference. *Coaxial cable* consists of a center wire coated with insulation and surrounded by a grounded, braided wire shield to minimize electrical and radio interference. It is used in cable television and inexpensive computer networks. *Fiber-optic cable* is comprised of many strands of hair-thin glass threads that allow signals to be transmitted over light passing through the strands. Wireless data links are frequently established using radio waves transmitted by *microwave* dishes or *satellites.*

Computers must have a port to connect to the data link. A simple network may use the standard parallel ports of personal computers. Networks that exchange substantial information and programs may require a special computer board with a networking port, for example, an Ethernet card.

Data links are connected to a communication control unit. A *communication control unit* (CCU) is a peripheral device that handles the data communications function of a network. Communication control units are sometimes called *routers, communication processors,* or *front-end processors.* The CCU performs functions such as checking user passwords, controlling transmission errors, and sequencing the communications of multiple users. In some networks, the CCU may be a small computer specifically designed to relieve the CPU of some networking functions.

Telephone lines are a common means of connecting computers and networks. However, computers use digital signals, which can be only one of two states, and telephones use analog signals such as the human voice, which can take a wide range of frequencies and tones. Consequently, before standard telephone lines can be used for networking, a device that changes digital to analog and vice versa must exist between the computers and the telephone line. Modulation is the process of changing a digital signal to an analog signal; the reverse process is demodulation. A *modem (modulation-demodulation)* is the device that connects a computer to a telephone line and makes signal conversions. Since residential telephone lines are of low quality with a small bandwidth, modem speeds are relatively slow. Consequently, modems are used primarily for home connections to the Internet or when the cost of a high-speed data link is prohibitive.

TYPES OF NETWORKS

Local Area Networks

A *local area network* (LAN) connects computers and peripherals in the same physical location. Each LAN node can execute programs locally as well as use the data and resources of any connected device. A LAN allows users to send messages to another networked computer, to work with applications stored on another networked computer, and to work with devices of another networked computer, such as hard discs or a printer. Most IT applications will run on a LAN. When LANs in nearby physical locations are connected, they form a *metropolitan area network* (MAN). If the LAN connects locations separated by large distances, they form a *wide area network* (WAN).

The characteristics of a LAN or WAN determine the number of computers and peripherals that can be connected and the distances between nodes. LANs differ in the topology, cabling, and protocols used. The protocols determine whether the network uses a peer-to-peer or client/server architecture. Many types of LANs exist, token-ring networks, Ethernets, and ARCnets being the most common for PCs.

Topology refers to the geometric arrangement of devices on a network. The three principal LAN topologies are ring, star, or straight line (see Figure 11.2). In a *straight line topology*, a central cable, called a bus or backbone, connects all devices. Straight line networks are relatively inexpensive and easy to install. In a *ring topology*, all devices are connected to one another in the shape of a closed loop, with each device connected directly to devices on either side. Ring topologies are relatively expensive and difficult to install, but offer high bandwidth and can span large distances. In a *star topology*, all devices are connected to a central hub. Star networks are relatively expensive and easy to install and manage, but bottlenecks can occur because all data must pass through the hub.

Commercial Networks

Commercial networks are operated by organizations that sell many networking features, for example, America Online and Usenet. Specialty

FIGURE 11.2. Network Topologies

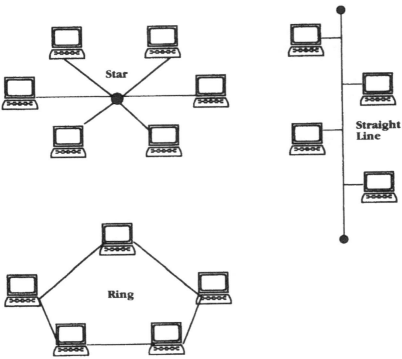

commercial networks exist in the human services, for example, HandsNet. Commercial networks may provide their users with Internet access, as well as with many of the activities described in the next section. Some of the features of commercial networks may be available only to their members. For example, people connected directly to the Internet cannot access many of the chat rooms of America Online.

The Internet

The Internet is a worldwide network of networks. The *Net*, as it is often called, overcomes some of the barriers of other networks, such as LANs. Most networks require special hardware and software for networking to occur. Computers on one network are rarely able to communicate with computers on another network. However, the Internet uses a universal set of communication protocols called TCP/IP (Transmission Control Protocol/Internet Protocol). Therefore, the Internet can link most networks, and all computers can easily link to the Internet. With the Internet, a personal computer using an inexpensive modem and telephone line can become a node on the same network that links corporate and military supercomputers around the world. Any Internet-connected computer potentially has access to the information and the information manipulation capacity of all the other connected computers. Access at each node is not limited by technology, but by each node's security settings.

Nodes on the Internet are identified by their address, called a URL (Uniform Resource Locator). A typical URL is http://www.uta.edu/cussn/cussn.html, where http stands for hypertext transport protocol; www.uta.edu indicates it is a World Wide Web site at the University of Texas at Arlington (UTA), an educational (edu) institution. At UTA, files are stored in a computer directory named CUSSN. The address contains the name of the executable HTML program: cussn.html. URLs on some computers are case sensitive; that is, the computer interprets capital and small letters differently.

Although many Internet resources are free, you usually must pay for Internet access. Agencies often connect internal computer networks to the Internet using high-speed telephone lines. Most individuals connect to the Internet using a modem, a standard telephone line, and a SLIP/PPP (Serial Line Internet Protocol/Point-to-Point Protocol) connection provided by a local telephone company or a specialty ISP (Internet Service Provider). However, even fast modems result in slow Internet access because the bandwidth and quality of residential telephone lines cannot handle the large data transfers required for text, graphics, pictures, audio, animation, and video. To solve the bandwidth bottleneck, cable television companies, which have high bandwidth wire running to residential homes and businesses, and others are beginning to offer faster Internet access.

The *World Wide Web* (WWW *or* Web) is a subset of Internet nodes that provide access to sites that use a standard graphical protocol (HTML) and hypertext linking of resources. On the WWW, sites contain pages of text, pictures, and graphical information with clickable buttons and images. The Web allows one to click on "hot words" or hyperlinked text and images and jump from topic to topic or from site to site. A special page on a Web site is the home page. A *home page* is the initial page that users see when visiting a site. It usually contains introductory information or graphics that help the user understand what the site is about and what links are available. By selecting links, users can be transferred to another part of the same page, another page of the site, another site, or to a specific file or other resources.

Many vendors offer Web site authoring tools that make it easy to create home pages. Most popular word processors have HTML authoring capabilities for designing simple Web pages. In addition, most browsers provide authoring tools and wizards that guide one through the process of constructing a simple home page. Using these tools, nontechnical novices can set up a simple Web site using text, documents, pictures, agency logos, and other useful information. However, as with most IT, a Web site can quickly become complex and require the services of a specialist called a Web master.

Gopher

Gopher is an older, menu-based tool for browsing the Internet. Gopher menus allow the user to perform tasks such as displaying documents or automatically connecting to another Internet site. Usually, the first file on a gopher menu is a read-me or index file, which when clicked displays the descriptions of the other files. A gopher site's URL begins with the word gopher rather than http.

Intranets

An *intranet* is an internal organizational network based on Internet tools and communication protocols. An intranet could consist of a single network or several networks tied together using Internet technology. An intranet is readily accessible only to members of the organization. An intranet may be connected to the Internet through a fire wall. A *fire wall* is a software or a software-hardware barrier between two networks on a computer. A fire wall is often compared to the moat and drawbridge of a medieval castle (Tanenbaum, 1996). The moat channels all castle visitors through the drawbridge where they are inspected to see if they are a threat to internal security. Similarly, all users are channeled through a fire wall, which can be programmed to allow specific users and functions.

Extranets are extensions of intranets to key stakeholders outside the organization. An example of an extranet would be judges having access via the Internet to child protective service agency files on foster care children in their jurisdictions.

Intranets allow agencies with little networking expertise to develop networks because the Internet service provider manages the network and many standard internet tools can be used. Intranets made it possible for staff to use a local Internet connection to record and access client data using a handheld computer and cellular telephone. Therefore, intranets are especially attractive for small consortiums of agencies, dispersed partnerships of practitioners, or workers who need access to agency IT from their car or a client's home. Security and confidentiality should be a concern if the agency intranet is linked to the Internet or uses an external Internet service provider.

NETWORK ACTIVITIES

The type of activity that can occur on a network is influenced by the hardware, operating system, utilities, and IT applications available. A simple, inexpensive network may only share files between hard disks and printers. A sophisticated network may manage file sharing, route internal and external e-mail, maintain commonly used software, protect files from unauthorized use, log network use, and maintain backups for easy recovery. Most of these activities are unseen by the network user.

This section focuses on network activities from a user perspective. Since the Internet is the most robust and widely used network in the human services, it will be used to illustrate these activities (Grant and Gorbman, 1998). The following are some of the most common user network activities:

- Sending and receiving messages (e-mail, voice mail, video mail)
- Searching for information and resources (browsing, database searches)
- Conferencing with like-minded people (lists and newsgroups)
- Real-time interaction with others (chat rooms, games, virtual worlds, Internet telephone)
- Distributing information and products (electronic publishing, Internet commerce)
- Transferring files (FTP)
- Using another computer (Telenet)

Each of these activities is explained in more detail throughout the remainder of this section.

Sending and Receiving Messages

Messages sent electronically over networks are called *e-mail,* or electronic mail. E-mail messages can be simple text or a complex, interactive document that, when clicked, links to Web sites, runs internal programs, presents a survey, or plays a video message. E-mail software allows users to not only compose, send, and receive messages but also to include the original message in the reply, attach files, broadcast a message to one or a group of recipients, and maintain an e-mail address book. As Internet bandwidth improves, e-mail will involve more voice and video.

To send a message, you must know the electronic address of the recipient. An Internet e-mail address looks like the following: schoech@uta. edu. The first part of the address contains the user's initials, name, or nickname. The name is followed by an @ sign and the name of the organization. The final part of an address contains a period followed by the type of organization. It is easy to recognize some types of organizations; for example, .gov stands for government, .edu stands for education, and .com stands for commercial. E-mail usually reaches its destination within minutes of being sent. However, if delivery is important, precautions should be taken, just as with postal service mail, by requesting verification of delivery from the recipient.

E-mail is probably the first-implemented and most-used networking function in the human services. It primarily offers practitioners the opportunity to easily communicate with colleagues. If the agency network is connected to the Internet, practitioners can communicate with anyone globally. Therefore, e-mail is useful for client advocacy, influencing legislation and regulations, consulting with others, and communicating with clients. As with all technology, avoiding the risk associated with powerful features requires additional caution. One colleague, when e-mailing a fellow worker, made complaints about his boss. Instead of choosing the colleague's private e-mail address, he mistakenly chose a group address and sent his message to colleagues all over the world, including his boss! Almost everyone using e-mail has a similar embarrassing story to tell.

Searching for Information and Resources

Another popular networking activity is searching for information and resources, such as IT applications. *Browsing* or *surfing* is the name given to the unplanned, casual search of the Internet for anything of interest. Browsing is similar to casual shopping in a worldwide mall. On the Internet, you can go from viewing federal regulations, to pictures of Thai temples, to children available for adoption, to viewing the world of a child through a home-page constructed as part of a school assignment. What makes Internet searches useful is that you can do many things with the information you find, such as print it, save it to a file, mark it for later use, or e-mail it to others. Since Internet information is easily copied, special attention must be given to copyright. Under U.S. copyright law, information on the Internet is copyrighted unless stated otherwise.

Some Web sites contain a search program or engine that allows a key-word search of the site or of every Internet site around the world, for example, Yahoo. These companies have software programs that continually travel the Internet, record the contents of each Web site, and create an index of site contents. Before using a search engine, reading how search operators can combine key words is useful. Search operators, such as AND, OR, NOT, are important because they limit and focus the searching activity. This is especially important when conducting a search of the Internet that could result in thousands of key-word matches.

An emerging use of the Internet is to tap into large databases that are maintained by a variety of organizations. This differs from standard Internet access, whereby the user views linked pages of information. The home page of the National Center for Missing and Exploited Children is an example of a searchable database.✽ Some Internet databases allow the user to enter, as well as search for, information. Such databases are also useful in intranets, for example, entering case notes on clients or getting specific information on clients.

Special programs are becoming available that help users in the search process. *Agents* are software programs that automate many networking tasks based on the specifications of the user. Overnight, your agent could connect to a local newspaper on the Net and search for information about local issues of interest. It could then check various electronic networks for your e-mail, download an electronic journal, and accumulate a listing of new computer programs that have your key words in their title. When you wake in the morning, you would consult your agent for the personalized information it had accumulated.

Conferencing

Another popular networking activity is the organized discussion of topics within groups. These discussion mechanisms are called *conferences, newsgroups, listservs, lists, threaded discussion forums,* or *bulletin board systems (BBSs)*. Conferencing is also called *asynchronous interaction* because participants can join the conference at any time to interact with others. Some conferences are simply public e-mail areas. Others offer the user sophisticated tools to locate, browse, and reply to one or several messages on a selected subtopic. Conferences often post previous discussions on topics and conference rules in an FAQ (Frequently Asked Questions) file.

Discussion of a popular conferencing software program, LISTSERV, illustrates how conferencing works. To become a member of a LISTSERV conference, a user sends an e-mail to the LISTSERV's software with the message "subscribe," followed by the conference and the user's name. The LISTSERV then forwards to the user every message that subscribers e-mail to the LISTSERV. LISTSERV software performs other related functions, such as archiving e-mail for easy downloading, screening messages that seem unintended for the list, probing users to see if their e-mail address is correct, and preventing unauthorized messages in private conferences. Since each message is sent to all subscribers, LISTSERVs are network intensive. For example, if a mailing list has 10,000 subscribers, each message must be sent 10,000 times. Even for a computer network, this is not a trivial task, especially if the messages are long or contain attached files. In addition, conference messages take up storage space on the subscriber ISP and eventually on the subscriber's computer. On popular LISTSERVs, the volume of e-mail messages can be overwhelming, with message quality ranging from very useful to a waste of time.

Usenet is a worldwide network that uses a different format to distribute thousands of conferences. Usenet is separate from the Internet, but well integrated into most Internet browsers. Usenet is sometimes referred to as *Internet news* or *newsgroups*. Comparing newsgroups to LISTSERVs will help in understanding Usenet. As discussed previously, LISTSERV messages take up communication bandwidth and add to the Internet gridlock. Newsgroups alleviate this problem by storing their e-mail messages on a single computer so that anyone who contacts that computer can read them. Similar to classified advertisements, newsgroup messages are stored according to the type of information they contain, and navigational aids between messages and replies are available. Similar to LISTSERVs, newsgroup messages vary in quality.

Conferencing is a very important activity in the human services, especially for managing client self-help groups. These virtual groups function similarly to face-to-face (F2F) groups, although users can post and read messages at any time. Practitioners use conferences when setting up community networks that allow clients or agencies to establish the equivalent of an interactive community newspaper. As with a newspaper, these community networks convey news and information as well as advertise projects of interest, jobs, and services.

Real-Time Interaction

In contrast to conferencing where users' interactions are separated by time, another popular use of networks is to interact with people in real time. Interaction in real time is often referred to as *synchronous* network-ing activity. Several tools exist for real-time interaction.

Chat software allows the simultaneous typing and viewing of all inter-actions by two or more persons connected electronically. Chat rooms are virtual spaces where participants type to one another about a similar topic. Chat rooms exist for almost any topic; for example, many human service-oriented chat rooms concern client self-help. Most distance education courses offered over the Internet include a chat room where the teacher and students interact. Text-based chat is problematic, however, because people type slower than they think or talk. Fortunately, voice and video chat rooms are overcoming this limitation and expanding the nature of chat.

Groupware, or teamware, is another real-time application. Groupware helps geographically dispersed colleagues to organize and manage their activities over a network, allowing them to function as a F2F work groups. Groupware allows participants to e-mail, manage individual schedules and appoint meeting times, hold synchronous and asynchronous conferences, use a common white board, and simultaneously use standard software such as a word processor or spreadsheet. In communities, groupware allows for virtual town meetings for discussing many community issues. Given the pervasiveness of work groups in the human services and the difficulty of getting work group members in one location, groupware is becoming popular and its related features are maturing rapidly.

One real-time use of networks is as a telephone system. Using special hardware and software, Internet users can make a telephone call anywhere in the world. This hardware and software can be cost-effective since they allow one to make free calls to colleagues or clients worldwide.

Other forms of real-time interaction involve games and virtual worlds. Internet-based, multiplayer, interactive *games* for recreation and competi-tion are a popular form of entertainment, especially among youth. Some graphical action games involve forming on-the-spot virtual teams that compete. Games may use *virtual worlds,* or three-dimensional graphic spaces, created with VRML (Virtual Reality Modeling Language). Games and virtual worlds are important, for they invent, explore, and bring new interactive technology into the mainstream.

Diversity University (DU) is a human service example of a text-based virtual world.* DU uses concepts and terms associated with a physical university campus. DU has virtual "buildings" and chat-based classrooms. The Social Work Department of DU has courses, workshops, and other common trappings, such as a virtual AIDS quilt. DU uses Multi User Domain (MUD) virtual world technology.

Distributing Information and Products

The exchange of information and products is a basic function of any network. The Internet allows this exchange to occur worldwide. *Electronic publishing* is the posting or sending of anything from articles to music in electronic form. Often, a plug-in is needed for users to view what is distributed.

In the past, commerce required a large number of "middlemen" to link producers and consumers. However, with the Internet, anyone can distribute information or products directly to anyone else. Thus, the Internet is similar to a global marketplace, with sites replacing stalls. What becomes popular in this global market is often surprising. For example, some Internet nodes simply consist of a video camera that sends a picture to a Web site every few minutes. One historic video-cam Web site simply provides a video of the coffee pot at Cambridge University.✿

Since the Internet provides a more direct producer-consumer marketplace, many believe its real potential is the commercial selling of products and services. The rapid growth of some Internet businesses, such as the bookstore amazon.com, and the high value placed on these businesses through public stock offerings fosters the frontier mentality. Net commerce is rapidly expanding the tools available on the Internet. Many of these new tools will be important for agency intranets and human service Internet use. One problem with Internet commerce is finding a safe and trusted way for people to conveniently purchase products. One innovative human service solution is the Shareware Psychological Consultation Web site, where users pay for counseling only after trying it and finding it valuable.✿ Additional human service Internet commerce problems, such as professional, ethical, and legal concerns, will be discussed in Chapter 13.

Transferring Files

Electronically transferring files involves the sending (uploading) and receiving (downloading) of files between one computer and another. On the Internet, file transfer is called FTP (File Transfer Protocol). With the introduction of Web browsers, transferring a file is often as easy as clicking on a button labeled "download software." Some FTP sites require that users have an account and password. As the Internet becomes more integrated with desktop software, the transferring of files will become an unnoticeable background activity.

A good Internet download site is located at the Washington University Archive.✿ This site stores nearly 72 billion bytes of information, or the equivalent of the information contained in 150 copies of the Encyclopedia Britannica (Butterfield and Schoech, 1997).

Using Another Computer

One traditional use of the Internet is to remotely access another computer and use it just as if you were physically there. *Telnet* is a tool that allows remote connections to other computers. Researchers often Telnet to a computer that contains the specialty software or processing capabilities they need. Telnet is also convenient when you are away from home and want to read your e-mail. With Telnet, you can connect via the Internet through a local ISP and access your mail using a mail reader configured to your account.

Although the activities in this section give an idea of networking, their combination results in a phenomenon that is bigger than all possible activities combined, a synergism known as cyberspace.

CYBERSPACE

The global village becomes a reality when the majority of people in a society own a computer linked to the Internet. Traditional ways of interacting change in the global village and new ways to interact emerge. *Cyberspace* is the term often used to describe this new virtual world. Cyberspace is the nonphysical place where people meet and share resources using telecommunications. This section presents a brief travel guide to cyberspace. As with most travel guides, some information will be outdated before it is printed.

Nature of Cyberspace

Cyberspace is slowly developing its own culture. Internet culture is fast-paced, freewheeling, and terse. People in cyberspace quickly move in and out of chat rooms and virtual spaces. In cyberspace, people compose e-mail messages as they type and rarely edit. This process brings to mind a quote attributed to Mark Twain: "Forgive my lengthy letter. If I had had more time, I would have written a shorter one." In cyberspace, people are bombarded with an overwhelming amount of poorly written and formatted information, often containing slang. People may sift through hundreds of e-mail messages each day to find the information they require.

One current problem is that cyberspace is primarily text based. Thus, few visual emotional cues exist when people exchange information. This lack of visual cues makes it easy for misinterpretation to occur. People new to cyberspace are often shocked by the bitter exchanges that occur in on-line conferences of human service professionals. Newsgroups and lists often develop customs, norms, and techniques to make up for the lack of emotional cues. Text formats are used to help express emotion, for example, TYPING IN ALL CAPITALS IS EQUIVALENT TO SHOUTING. Acronyms are often used to add emotional content, for example, IMHO (in my humble opinion) and LOL (laugh out loud). Another technique to quickly express emotions is to use *emoticons*. When viewed sideways, emoticons represent common facial expressions, for example:

- :-) happy
- :-(sad
- ;-) wink/sarcasm
- :-o shouting/shocked

New members of a newsgroup or list can be treated harshly if they transgress the group's social norms. See Figure 11.3 for the reaction of someone who transgressed the norms of a group. In another example, one vendor sent an unsolicited advertisement to 7,000 conferences. In some Internet areas, unsolicited commercial messages are as offensive as evening computerized sales calls to one's home. The volume of hate replies crashed the sender's local network. New members of newsgroups, lists, or chat sessions are encouraged to observe or "lurk" for a while to discover the unhidden rules and social norms.

Unlike an F2F environment, where one's gender and age are difficult to change, in cyberspace, anyone can easily change gender, age, and other personal characteristics. Menon (1998) describes the dramatic changes

FIGURE 11.3. The Reaction of Someone Flamed in a Discussion Group

HAH!!!

    I lurk for months, finally got my nerve to post (what was to me, important) about ways to take an ethical stance, do advocacy for clients, etc., and I got blasted. I was called a megalomaniac, stupid, a damn fool, arrogant, etc., etc. (I also got many more replies that were of a positive nature.) But hey, who needs the crap and insults and flames?! I get enuff!!!! in my job all day, and I would like to think of this group as supportive. So I will be back to lurking again for another 6 months.

that occurred in a personal chat room when he changed from thirty-year-old "Pops" to nineteen-year-old "Betsy." Although everyone ignored Pops when he entered the chat room, everyone personally greeted Betsy.

Using electronic communications, people construct mental pictures of others that are incomplete and often inaccurate. Reports from F2F meetings of people who have networked via e-mail for years revealed that one's physical presence and virtual presence can be quite different. Communicating electronically also has some unexpected benefits. On one project, I communicated on-line with someone for months, only to find during a face-to-face meeting that he was nonvocal. We could not interact in person, only in cyberspace. I had made a friend and colleague in cyberspace that I could not have made in a normal work environment.

The Internet has pranksters and troublemakers similar to the F2F world. One common way to cause trouble is to send an irritating message to an individual or a group. Sending "flame bait" to get others stirred up is equivalent to hurling an insult in an F2F situation. Some users take pride in entering a group and starting flame wars or e-mail shouting matches. Others, with a lot of time on their hands, can dominate a conference conversation indefinitely. Figure 11.4 could be considered flame bait, since it was posted to a professional group having a serious discussion of the rights of local jurisdictions to regulate Internet therapy. Luckily, only a few sent angry or defensive replies; the list owner quickly posted the rules of the list, and the topic returned to the issues and not a defense of the list. Table 11.2 contains standard "netiquette," or net etiquette.

Cyberspace also contains people who view on-line communities as similar to neighborhoods (Rheingold, 1993). These communities link virtual and F2F events, have on-line celebrations, on-line marriages between participants, and many other aspects of a real community.*

FIGURE 11.4. Section of a Flame Bait E-Mail

Subject: The Paranoid Style of Psychological Services

The entire dialogue regarding the licensing and regulating of any psychological service seems absolutely bereft of any interest other than the therapist. It is extremely apparent that very, very few participants on this list have much concern for this patently obvious professional standard, which exists separate from and well above any legislated mandate in any jurisdiction. First, do no harm.

TABLE 11.2. Net Etiquette or Netiquette

Advice	Rationale
DO NOT USE ALL CAPITAL LETTERS	Text in all capital letters is hard to read and suggests SHOUTING.
Check out conference FAQs and keep instructions	When you join a conference, see if an FAQ (Frequently Asked Questions) file exists, so you do not ask questions that have been answered repeatedly by others. A rule of thumb is to read two weeks of postings, and then follow the norms.
Separate personal e-mail from conferences	Sending personal e-mail to someone via a conference is rude and may cost some conference members who pay for Internet access by the amount of time on-line. Also, always get permission to forward a personal e-mail message to someone else or to a conference.
Make messages meaningful	Messages such as "me too" typically do not add anything to the conversation, are unnecessary, and require others to do extra work to read and delete them.
Keep instructions and separate types of messages	Keep initial conference messages explaining how the conference works. They explain the address for sending e-mail to subscribers and the address for changing a subscriber's status. They are especially important because e-mail addresses change and unsubscribing with an outdated address is difficult. A frequently annoying message in conferences is "tell me how to get off this list."
Use formatting to enhance readability	Terminal screens read differently from the printed text. Help readability by formatting. For example, separate paragraphs with a blank line.
Always sign your e-mail with your e-mail address	Often it is difficult to identify the sender from the message header. Signing all e-mail with your e-mail address allows people to contact you, no matter where your message is forwarded.
Use one subject per message and use meaningful and accurate subject titles	Subject titles on messages help users skim through the volume of mail they receive. To keep conference discussions on track, use the same subject title of the original message, unless you change the topic significantly. Also, limit each message to the subject specified in the title.

TABLE 11.2 *(continued)*

Quote original if replying	If replying to a previous message, quote a small part of the message or the relevant parts of the message so your reply is put into context of previous discussion. Save bandwidth by sending only the parts of the original message that are necessary.
Warn of long messages	Readers should be warned if a post is over several paragraphs, e.g., "long message" or "20 pages follow." This allows users to download the message and read it later.
Warn of cross-posting	If you post a message to several lists, indicate at the beginning which lists will receive the post so that readers will know to avoid the message on the other lists once they read it.
Stick to facts and try not to interpret emotions	E-mail carries few emotional cues. People can easily become offended by misinterpreting e-mail. Try to state positions without attacking positions different from yours. Be very clear if you are using subtle humor, sarcasm, or irony.
Avoid flaming	Flames are messages intended to provoke a response or hostile reaction in the recipient or others. Small provocations can easily get out of hand with e-mail and are difficult to correct.
Avoid spamming	Spam is unsolicited e-mail, often sent to many people with no working return address. Spamming congests mailing lists, clogs mailboxes, and costs money for those paying for access by the minute.
Be careful if advertising	Most lists have norms that forbid advertising and self-promotion. Ask before promoting or advertising.
Download large files during off hours	Downloading takes away resources from those performing more interactive tasks. Downloading during evening or night hours is courteous to others.

Issues in Cyberspace

Cyberspace continually raises issues for which no precedents have been set. Some of the more commonly raised issues are discussed in the following material.

Privacy and Confidentiality

A serious issue is the lack of privacy in cyberspace. The potential for privacy abuse is greater for electronic information than for paper-based information because electronic information is easily searched and linked

in creative ways. For example, many users assume that e-mail and conference messages are as private as regular mail. Unfortunately, people in
cyberspace should operate on the assumption that whatever you do in
cyberspace is public. If someone wants to know what Internet sites you
have accessed or the contents of the mail you send and receive, they can
generally find a way to get that information. A few examples may help
highlight the lack of privacy that exists on the Internet.

In the United States, employers have a legal right to read employee
e-mail even though they do not have a right to open employees' Postal
Service mail. Employers also have the right to install computer programs
that record what employees do on their work computer. When anyone
accesses an Internet site, the user's computer and the node contacted
record the connection and often the site from which the user came. Individual usage patterns are often marketed to businesses with few or no
safeguards. No laws require that users be notified that this information is
being gathered, and few restrictions exist on its use or sale. Furthermore, it
is typically more difficult to totally erase electronic information from a
computer. As Oliver North, a controversial figure in the Iran-Contra scan-
dal during the Reagan Administration, discovered, even when you erase or
delete computer files, technical experts may still be able to retrieve them.

Since global privacy laws do not exist in cyberspace, the limits on
privacy seem to evolve based on consensus. For example, many Web sites
send your computer a short program, a cookie in Internet jargon. The
cookie typically is used to track your use and provide site use data. However, the cookie could record many things about your computer and its use
and then upload the information periodically when you access the Internet.
Questionable practices such as these generate hate mail, and hackers often
punish the offending site. However, few individual protections exist in
law, so users must take precautions to protect themselves. The lack of
laws, and norm enforcement by hackers and a massive amount of hostile
e-mail, reinforces the concept that cyberspace is in its "frontier days."

Although individuals may be willing to risk their privacy for the benefits of cyberspace, human service agencies and practitioners must not be
willing to submit their vulnerable clients to such risks. For example, agencies using a public Internet service provider for an intranet or to communicate client information through e-mail should ensure that all information is
encrypted. Agencies with internal networks that are connected to the Internet should spend the time and money to develop a secure fire wall between
the internal network and the Internet. Even fire-wall technology is not
foolproof. Many government and corporate WWW sites, including the

U.S. Central Intelligence agency's WWW site, have been hacked and pornographic links added.✱

Offensive Materials

Anyone with children who use the Web should know that offensive materials exist in cyberspace just as they exist in any city. Hate groups, pedophiles, and pornographers use the Internet along with churches and charities. Fortunately, downloadable applications exist that will help block objectionable sites from reaching your computer. Some Internet service providers cater to users with children by blocking objectionable sites. Still, adults should treat the Internet as they do cable TV and discuss and monitor their children's use. Agencies connected to the Internet should address the appropriate use of the Internet by employees in their personnel policies and training.

Viruses

Viruses are computer programs designed to annoy the recipient or damage hardware and software, and they are capable of quickly spreading and multiplying during common computer operations. Viruses can be transmitted over the Internet, however, not as easily as through the sharing of floppy disks. A virus can be crippling to an individual or agency. An interesting exercise is to calculate the time and effort required to recover if a virus destroyed your agency's computer files. This cost can then be balanced with the cost of efforts to protect the system from infection. The adage "an ounce of prevention is worth a pound of cure" applies to IT and viruses.

A personal story can illustrate how destructive viruses are. While working at night, I received a virus attached to a student paper e-mailed from a government agency. Upon notification by my virus scanning software, I put the virus's name into an Internet search engine. The search engine presented several sites that explained the virus, its destructive potential, and how to remove it from my system. Due to early detection and the wealth of information on the Internet, the virus was safely removed before it could do damage. However, it took the university and government agency countless hours to eradicate this same virus from the hundreds of computers that had been infected. There are many sites where you can download Internet virus-scanning shareware.✱ Although the offender in this example was a student, I have received viruses from colleagues and even editorial board members of computer journals.

Internet Addiction

Cyberspace can be addicting. Users can lose all sense of time when surfing, chatting, or answering e-mail. People will often neglect face-to-face contact to spend time in cyberspace. A "Cyber Addict's Prayer" has even been composed: "Almighty Web master, grant me the serenity to know when to log off, the courage to know when to check e-mail, and the wisdom to stay away from chat rooms, Ctrl,Alt,Del". People argue whether cyberspace communications and relationships are as socially beneficial as person-to-person communications. Others argue that spending time in cyberspace is no different from watching TV or being absorbed in a book.

IMPLICATIONS OF NETWORKING FOR IT DEVELOPMENT

Since individuals in organizations rarely function in isolation, pressure exists to install networks. However, networking many hardware components to perform as one system is still a difficult task. The larger the network, the more complex and risky is the design and maintenance. The Internet adds another level of potential benefits, complexity, and risks.

Considerations in Setting Up an Internal Network

Most human service agencies, even small ones, have complex operations that involve information flowing from many departments. Since an information system models the organizational structure of the operations it supports, most agencies eventually become networked. At present, the biggest problem with agency networking is the increased complexities involved in designing and maintaining the network. Employees who can set up and run networks are currently in demand, and human service salaries are not competitive. Small agencies, especially, have a problem obtaining technical expertise. Obtaining networking capacity from an intern or volunteer is risky because the intern or volunteer typically moves on and system maintenance may suffer.

Given the risks, agency networking should be a slow evolutionary process. The agency can begin by establishing a LAN (local area network) for internal e-mail and file transfer. Those in the agency who have some technological sophistication and like to experiment can debug the network before requiring its use by reluctant staff. If staff take the trouble to change a work pattern, they need to receive useful information and positive feedback. A successful experience can create the knowledge and impetus to expand the use of the network in core agency work. The network can then be connected to the Internet and other networks. The agency can develop a Web site and begin to provide information and services using the Web.

Throughout the development, the agency can establish a training mechanism such as peer training, whereby each trained user mentors and trains a new user. The agency can also develop the policies and resources to make networking a rewarding experience. Most Web sites are like gardens; they cannot be left alone for any length of time without dire consequences.

Considerations on Multiagency Networking

Since networking is powerful and well accepted organizationally, it seems a logical next step to develop multiagency networks. However, this simple logic has caused much unnecessary work and grief. Many human service networks have failed due to lack of use, support, and maintenance.

Electronic networks must be distinguished from face-to-face communication networks. Face-to-face networks exist when a group of people shares information and resources. Electronic networks build on face-to-face communication networks; they cannot create them. Many associations or organizations mistakenly hope that electronic networks will cause their members to communicate better. If face-to-face communication or the need to communicate does not exist before the electronic network is developed, the electronic network will have a higher chance for failure. The slogan "build it and they will come" has not worked in electronically networking human service professions.

If networking with other agencies reflects a personal work style and not an advantage for completing one's job, a multiagency network may not be worth the investment. If networking with other agencies is not valued, then it becomes additional work rather than an integral part of doing one's job well. In addition, networking is a personal activity that is most successful when staff have personal computers at work and home. Training is an essential factor in success; however, training is often overlooked and not budgeted.

Multiagency networks work best with agencies that have mature internal IT systems. Many agencies are currently developing management information systems and do not have the expertise or work patterns that support multiagency networking. The Internet and intranets provide a standard, low-cost option with many features for linking community agencies. However, agencies need to come together to plan multiagency networks by going through the application development process described in Chapter 6.

CONCLUSION

Our world is changing as we move from the Model T Ford period of IT (see the book's introduction) to the supersonic jet airplane period of IT. The Model T period of IT was based on stand-alone personal computers and stand-alone organizational networks. The Model T period focused on evolutionary improvements to traditional ways of doing business. Data-based management systems were the workhorses of the Model T period. The major challenge was slowly building the organization's information system so that it served the total organization.

Network technology is rapidly closing the door on the Model T period of IT. Networking has been slow to develop, but a milestone occurred when the Internet arrived to provide an inexpensive, standard, worldwide communications system. Since the Internet is in its infancy, we should consider ourselves as early motorists who could only cross the country by driving slowly on roads of questionable quality. When inexpensive hardware and unlimited bandwidth can support applications such as video conferencing, society will enter the jet period of IT. We can then expect many revolutionary IT applications that are as different from today's IT as flying is from driving across the country.

The jet period of IT will be based on all applications sharing information locally and globally. The jet period will see incremental change often overtaken by completely new ways of thinking and working. The workhorse in the jet period will be the network, that is, IT applications working together. The virtual office will be one possible example. Many current traditional IT activities focus on building an office, yet offices may not exist in cyberspace. The rethinking involved in the virtual office involves having well-trained practitioners continuously interacting with the knowledge base of the agency, no matter when or where they are working. The reasons to physically collect employees in one location may not exist in the future.

A challenge for human service managers and IT application developers is to continue evolutionary progress, while integrating revolutionary developments, without brutalizing and burning out employees. The next chapter discusses the task of managing technology.

REVIEW AND DISCUSSION QUESTIONS

1. What are the distinguishing characteristics of the various types of networks?
2. How would you distinguish between an information system and an intranet?

3. What design and development problems and capacities are added by networking an agency?
4. Compare the impact of the Internet on the human services to that of the personal computer.
5. How can a human service IT application, with which you are familiar, be enhanced by Internet connectivity?
6. Discuss the impact on services when clients are networked with agencies.

PART IV:
MAINTAINING INFORMATION
TECHNOLOGY

Chapter 12

Managing, Supporting, and Evaluating IT Applications

INTRODUCTION

Management is a series of activities that promotes the accomplishment of goals. A typical listing of management activities includes planning, organizing, staffing, controlling, reporting, budgeting, and evaluating. Accomplishing these activities from an IT perspective was introduced in Chapter 6, with a discussion of change and the IT development process. Chapter 6 focused primarily on planning, organizing, and staffing activities. This chapter focuses on controlling, budgeting, reporting, and evaluating activities.

Several ways exist to categorize the organizational resources that are to be managed. One categorization is the management of people, things, money, and information. The more formal terms are personnel management, facilities management, financial management, and information/knowledge management. Information and knowledge are the latest organizational resources to be formally identified and managed.

Managing other organizational resources is good preparation for information management, but new learning and experience are also required. A similar situation exists in transportation. Driving a car and a bus may be similar, but the ability to drive a car does not guarantee that one can drive a bus. However, knowing how to drive a car helps in learning to drive a bus.

This chapter examines the management of both the technology and information resources of an organization. Managing the IT resources is different from managing the agency's information because information management tasks are not always technology based, for example, the task of training users. Also, technology can be used for more than information management. For simplicity, the term information in information management will refer to computerized data, information, and knowledge, and the term technology will refer to IT unless otherwise noted.

BASIC CONCEPTS

Information As a Resource

Information is the primary resource used in delivering human services. Essential to managing agency IT is viewing information as a resource capable of being managed. Managing information is an organizational process as important to agency success as managing money, personnel, and property. Failure to manage information is wasteful. It causes poor decision making and results in low goal achievement. The management of information implies that someone is responsible and that the appropriate technology is used to collect, store, manipulate, and distribute information.

The information resource is different from other resources that must be managed. Information is relatively easy to generate, but very difficult to use to its maximum potential. Although the use of resources, such as money, is relatively easy to observe, the use of information is not, especially during complex decision making. For example, in policy setting, multiple studies of the situation may exist; however, policymakers may subtly ignore all research and base their decision on individual values and personalities. Books even exist on how policymakers lie with statistics (Huff, 1993).

A second characteristic of the information resource is its durability. In contrast to most resources, information does not wear out; it grows in importance. Old information is useful in trend analysis, modeling, and research. Since information does not wear out, we must manage it or purposefully destroy it whenever practice dictates or when storage costs are greater than future worth. The warehousing of legacy or archival data is a critical IT management task.

A third characteristic of information is that it increases in value the more it is connected and shared. The more we can connect systems and share information, the smarter our applications will be. Thus, the more plentiful information becomes, the more valuable it becomes. This is in contrast to natural resources such as oil and gold for which scarcity equates with value. However, information pervasiveness and sharing involves losses as well as gains. Information management involves a clearinghouse function that causes individual departments to no longer have complete control of their information. With information management, information becomes a resource for all levels of the organization to share. If departments ignore this sharing, agencies may collect redundant information and produce inconsistent reports. A variation of this problem is when departments collect information in different formats; for example, one department may collect age categories, another actual age, and yet another may collect date of birth. Information can also be collected with insufficient precision, for example, using address as one category rather than separating by street address, city, state, and zip code.

A fourth characteristic of the information resource is that those who collect and manage it can easily sabotage it. The "garbage in, garbage out" syndrome illustrates this problem. Although entering faulty information into an application will not result in computer failure, it will result in a questionable application output. The legal convictions of disgruntled employees and hackers who destroyed information illustrate its vulnerability.

These characteristics make information a difficult resource to manage. Since information has only recently been considered a resource, most organizations have limited information management experience. Also, more experience and tools exist for controlling physical property and money than for controlling information. Inventory control techniques can help control physical property and audits can help control money. However, with information, few guidelines, tools, and mechanisms currently exist to prevent, control, and audit for errors, misuse, and abuse. Constant forethought and vigilance are needed to detect unintentional and deliberate errors before they result in wrong decisions.

Technology adds complexity to the management of information. For example, IT applications rapidly perform thousands of instructions and typically only display limited results of the processing. Detecting errors is difficult because applications generally provide few details on how the information was processed. Programming bugs may only show up years after the applications are completed and then only in rare circumstances, for example, the year 2000 problem, also known as Y2K or the millennium bug. In some applications, the manipulation is so complex and lengthy that the results would take years to check manually. Since IT applications detect only errors that they are programmed to detect, IT errors can be unexpected, large, stupid, and embarrassing. In addition, users often give information more credibility simply because it is computer generated. Even with these limitations, computerized information is probably more accurate than the paper-based information it replaces. Many agencies discover how error laden their manual system is only after computerizing.

Information Management As a Basic Organizational Function

Information has value when it is accessible to the right person, at the right time, and in the right format. Managing information involves maximizing its value given the resources and constraints that exist in the organization. In some human service areas, this task is difficult. Agreement may not exist on the right information, the right person to use it, or the right formats. Ideally, users should be able to control the timing and format of the information they need. However, IT costs prevent users from having easy access to all the information they need in the format they desire.

Another critical task of information management is ensuring that people have the attitudes and skills necessary to use processed information. Changing work habits and attitudes along with developing new skills may be more important than choosing the most appropriate application. To use the transportation analogy, having a properly operating vehicle is important, but trained personnel to operate the vehicle and navigate the road may be more important. Professionals build habits when working with clients. It takes time and training for a new application to become part of staff work habits.

The preceding discussion indicates that the goal of information management is to provide the right information in the right format to the right person at the right time along with training to use the information effectively. Industries such as banking and airlines spend roughly 8 to 10 percent of their overall budget on IT. The human services may need to spend a higher percent due to the complexity of the information they collect and the sophisticated processing it needs.

The IT Department

For information to become a fundamental resource and receive the required attention, the information management function must have a separate identity in an organization. Clear lines of authority and responsibility should accompany this identity, which is often housed in a top-level department. The information management department might be a better name than the IT department because the department's responsibilities involve manual systems as well as networks and IT applications.

We can view the information management department as an organization within an organization. The information management "organization" has its own budget, products (reports and documents), and clientele (end users). The information management committee is its board of directors, and the information resource manager, its executive director. In small agencies, it may be necessary to assign information management responsibilities to one person, such as the financial manager. However, the executive director must treat the information management role as a separate function that can be easily isolated as the agency grows. For example, the financial manager may be given a dual title, such as director of finance and information. This title allows both functions to be more easily separated, and the department divided, if the agency grows.

The Director of Information

The person responsible for information management has various titles, for example, the information resource manager or the director of information. The director of information is preferred because it parallels other top-level managers, such as the director of finance or the director of personnel. The director of information performs the following *managerial* tasks:

- Understands and plans for the information needs of the organization
- Assigns responsibility to staff for data collection, manipulation, dissemination, and use
- Ensures standardization of data definitions, software packages, communications, etc.
- Supervises IT personnel and contracts for outside IT expertise
- Updates agency technology on a cost-effective basis
- Complies with the growing number of laws concerning information confidentiality and citizens' rights to records and privacy
- Ensures feedback loops are providing continuous improvement information to the right people

The director of IT performs the following *technical* tasks:

- Develops, coordinates, and maintains organizational databases
- Combines legacy data with current information to accumulate and distribute the organization's intelligence
- Selects, acquires, develops, and maintains hardware and software
- Ensures that all individual applications are coordinated and functioning as a network
- Keeps all applications running smoothly by preventing viruses, maintaining backups, etc.
- Preserves information integrity, confidentiality, and security by designing error-checking safeguards and passwords

The director of IT performs the following *communication* tasks:

- Disseminates information about IT developments and potentials
- Listens to and negotiates disagreements among users
- Involves users in the application development process
- Provides training on the use of applications and how to use IT outputs in decision making

The director of information must perform several specialized functions. Probably the most important of these functions is database administration. This involves optimally structuring the database, maintaining data definitions, and coordinating the use of the database. The director of IT must also develop and maintain the data communications network. As with database construction, data communications requires a high level of technical expertise that may only be available from specialized staff or outside consultants.

INFORMATION MANAGEMENT ISSUES

Information managers face many controversies. This section highlights additional issues the information manager faces that were not mentioned in previous chapters.

Maintaining the Right Balance of Distributed and Centralized IT

IT is evolving just as other forms of power have. The first uses of mechanical power involved a large centralized waterwheel or one steam engine to run a factory. However, centralized mechanical power was soon replaced because of the complexity of channeling power to many small users. Today, factories use a mix of large and small motors to distribute mechanical power where it is needed. With powerful mobile computers and cellular telephones, IT can also be distributed where it is most needed. However, IT distribution is not a goal. The goal is to have a mix of centralized and distributed IT that provides the information necessary to support decisions throughout the organization.

Distributed data processing (DDP) is the traditional term to describe arranging the IT resources of hardware, software, network, and personnel to provide IT power where it is needed. DDP implies dispersed IT that is linked as one integrated network rather than many isolated applications. That is, the distributed applications will function as one large system irrespective of where data are entered, processed, or stored. Users should be unconcerned about the physical location of hardware or information. They need only know what information they need and in what format they need it. For example, if a practitioner wanted to know what community resources are available for a client, he or she should be able to enter the proper security codes, followed by the nature of the client's problem. The application would then provide the community resources, with the practitioner being unaware that the information was gathered using a common query language from many different local, regional, and state computers connected to the Web.

The economics of IT favor distribution. Hardware costs have continually declined as a percentage of total IT cost, and other costs, such as personnel and software, have risen. However, the economics that favor distribution also have limitations. The increase in complexity of a distributed environment may lead to overall higher personnel and software development and maintenance costs. It is difficult to make the distribution/centralization decision based on cost alone. The true cost of maintaining a distributed environment often remains hidden because a variety of personnel may be devoting some of their time to IT. Although this involvement is not cost-effective, it may address the critical IT goal of making staff more knowledgeable about IT. Although distributed IT has made the information manager's task of controlling and justifying IT costs more difficult, a key understanding is that centralization and distribution are not always opposite choices. A distributed environment implies connections between the decentralized IT to allow the decentralized network to function as one system or as an integrated group of systems.

A DDP issue is on what basis to distribute IT. Two options exist: one is to distribute IT based on geographic area, for example, national, regional, and local offices; the other is to distribute IT based on functional areas, for example, financial services, adult services, and children's services. A rule of thumb is that high levels of communication and processing activity should take place *within* distributed systems, with much lower levels *between* distributed systems. In addition, a powerful and flexible distributed system is only possible if the organization builds a common, integrated, yet distributed database. However, an agency cannot achieve both a distributed database and an integrated database without strong central planning.

Eventually, the distribution of IT will match the distribution of other agency resources that IT supports, such as funds, personnel, and services. Therefore, the centralization-distribution mix that supports a centralized office would be much different from the mix that supported a consortium of practitioners contracting their services.

Balancing Centralized Management with End-User Planning and Control

One of the most significant management challenges is controlling end users who have a tendency to develop and operate applications independently of the IT department. The IT department must exercise control without stifling innovation and learning by end users.

It may seem paradoxical at first, but the best route to a properly functioning distributed environment is through centralized control. To avoid
the protectionist attitude of many distributed IT groups and applications,
top management, via the IT committee, must first establish the distribution
strategy. It must then provide central staff with the authority necessary to
implement this strategy. The intent is not to create an adversarial relationship between distributed IT units and the central unit. Rather, the intent is
to administer the entire distributed network as one integrated system. This
will remove some of the advantages of distribution, for example, complete
independence of end users. However, the gains far outweigh the losses.
Without central control, many systems may compete and avoid interaction
and information sharing.

Two primary techniques for achieving centralized control exist. First,
centralized approval can be required for major improvements to existing
applications to keep individual distributed units from acquiring hardware,
software, or personnel on their own. Second, common standards can be
developed to maintain system compatibility and common taxonomies,
ease system maintenance, control privacy and security, and increase the
transferability of software, personnel, and equipment among distributed
sites. One key to distributed IT is the development of a master plan by the
IT committee. The master plan establishes the IT environment for a two-
to four-year time horizon and shows how distributed sites achieve organizational goals. Also important is clarifying the roles of the IT department
and the end users

How to Provide End-User Training and Support

One complicated IT management task is end-user support and training.
One way to accomplish this task is to have all organizational units share
technical specialists; for example, system programmers can help maintain
software and system analysts can help in the design of applications
throughout the organization. Another aspect of end-user support is the
arrangement of IT training. This training can take many forms, ranging
from on-line training packages to in-house seminars and programs. External sources can also provide training.

The concept of a help desk addresses user support and training. A help
desk is a virtual or physical place where users can get IT information and
services (Sharon, 1996). Help desks often use a variety of techniques to
lessen the cost of face-to-face assistance. Some of these techniques are
e-mail technical support, automated faxing of documents, an FAQ infor-

mation page, and a Web site that contains documents, downloads of the latest software, and computer conferences.

REVIEWING IT PERFORMANCE

Systematically reviewing the performance of an application is an important, yet often overlooked, step in information management. It is as important as inventory monitoring, personnel evaluation, or client outcome evaluation because it periodically refocuses attention on the appropriate use of IT resources. After discussing different types of performance reviews, this section presents indicators of IT success.

Types of Performance Reviews

Three common types of performance reviews help evaluate IT: (1) postimplementation audit, (2) periodic monitoring, and (3) IT audit.

Postimplementation audits are usually performed three to six months after the implementation of a new IT application. The audit determines whether:

- the application was completed within the budgetary and time limits,
- the application is performing as designed (goals and objectives are met),
- the forecast benefits have materialized, and
- application use is as expected.

The postimplementation audit is based primarily on the specifications in the initial feasibility study and plan. A sample survey to obtain user input on a postimplementation audit is shown in Figure 12.1.

Periodic performance monitoring is closely related to the postimplementation audit. Periodic monitoring tracks performance on repeated success measures for an application. Periodic monitoring can be performed by the information management department or a senior manager who is not involved with the IT application being reviewed. It can be performed every six months or yearly, depending on the difficulty of collecting the measures being monitored.

FIGURE 12.1. User Survey for a Postimplementation Audit

Instructions: Your department is seeking feedback on the [application name]. Please answer the following questions. Do not sign your name. Your answers will be kept confidential.

Your position or type of work: _____

Number of years working for organization: _____

Number of years working in present position: _____

Indicate your agreement with the following statements by circling the appropriate number on the 1 to 5 scale, where SD = strongly disagree, D = disagree, N = neutral, A = agree, and SA = strongly agree.

Statement	Agree—Disagree
The application was well planned.	SD D N A SA
I know what the application is designed to do.	SD D N A SA
The application is meeting its objectives.	SD D N A SA
My opinions were sought as the application was developed.	SD D N A SA
Someone on the application development committee represents my point of view.	SD D N A SA
I have received adequate training about the application.	SD D N A SA
Documents exist to explain the application and how to use it.	SD D N A SA
Top management is committed to making the application a success.	SD D N A SA
I know who to contact to voice my concerns about the application.	SD D N A SA
The application provides the information I need in my job.	SD D N A SA
Reports from the application are clear and easy to read.	SD D N A SA
Reports I get from the application are accurate.	SD D N A SA
Reports I get from the application help me make better decisions.	SD D N A SA
The application has improved the process I go through in making decisions.	SD D N A SA
I use the application reports as often as the application designers intended.	SD D N A SA
If I need information from the application, I can get it quickly.	SD D N A SA
The confidentiality of the information in the application is well protected.	SD D N A SA
The application can quickly produce any special requests for information I might have.	SD D N A SA
Fears I have had about the application have been put to rest.	SD D N A SA
My paperwork is more up to date because of the application.	SD D N A SA

The application has reduced the time I spend on paperwork and recording.	SD D N A SA
The application has increased the accuracy of the data I use.	SD D N A SA
The application has helped me stay in compliance with perfor-mance standards.	SD D N A SA
Our agency functions better because of the application.	SD D N A SA
I would not mind returning to the way things were before the application was developed.	SD D N A SA
The application has helped me to better perform my job.	SD D N A SA
The application has resulted in better services to clients.	SD D N A SA
I would recommend that colleagues develop similar applications.	SD D N A SA
Overall I am satisfied with the application.	SD D N A SA

Complete the following sentences on the back of this form:

1. I use the application reports most often to . . .

2. The application could be improved by . . .

The *IT audit* is a study to ascertain the performance of the agency's IT environment. It is wider in scope than the other reviews and usually performed every three to five years. An IT audit may include data from periodic monitoring and the postimplementation audit. The areas that de-serve scrutiny include application users, outputs, planning, control, per-sonnel, and development of new applications, hardware, software, and networking. Table 12.1 lists some questions that an IT audit might address.

Either an in-house or outside consultant can conduct an overall IT application audit. The chief concerns are expertise and objectivity. Usual-ly, IT expertise lies in the agency's information management department. However, it would be difficult for them to evaluate themselves objectively and impartially. A more objective, yet internal, approach is to appoint a task force consisting of a few senior managers with some IT knowledge. A third option is using outside consultants who can be more objective than in-house personnel and more knowledgeable than members of an agency task force. Consultants may be from universities or from consulting firms that specialize in review. One strategy is to hire outside experts to develop the review instrument and conduct the initial review. In-house personnel could conduct later reviews.

Direct Measures of Impact or Success

The impact of IT is the primary concern of any application performance review. Of specific interest are impacts that classify the IT as successful or

TABLE 12.1. Questions for an Audit of All IT Activities

Clientele (Users)
- Are they satisfied?
- Are they involved in the planning for new applications?

Outputs
- Are reports delivered on time, in the required quantity, and in the desired format?
- Can on-demand reports be produced?
- How easy is it for users to change outputs to more closely meet their needs?

Planning
- Is there a formal long-range plan?
- Is there a short-term plan?
- Do all applications tie in with the agency's long-range IT plan?
- Are all users represented in the planning effort?

Control
- Are cost-accounting procedures in place, and are budgeting controls rigorous enough?
- Are internal audits performed?
- Are application standards, e.g., documentation standards, enforced?
- Do backup procedures and disaster recovery procedures exist?
- Are passwords assigned and used appropriately?
- Is data encryption used when possible?

Personnel
- Are users and IT staff adequately educated and trained?
- Do career paths exist?
- Is morale high?
- Are turnover and absenteeism too high?
- Are formal performance evaluations conducted?
- Are job descriptions formally documented?

Maintenance and Enhancements
- How much time is spent keeping applications current versus implementing new applications?
- Are application changes properly documented?
- What selection and approval procedures are followed to determine which new application is developed?
- Are postimplementation audits performed?

Hardware, Software, and Networking
- Are hardware, software, and networking current?
- Are the latest technologies and tools being used? If not, should they be?
- How much downtime occurs?
- Is internal and external system performance being monitored, and are reports being reviewed?

Source: Adapted from "Approaches for Evaluating Information Systems" by S. Sircar, D. Schoech, and L. L. Schkade, 1982, *Information and Referral, 4*(1), p. 57.

unsuccessful. Although the literature contains numerous anecdotal accounts of the impacts of IT, it is noticeably vague on what constitutes IT success. Many business success measures, such as better cash management and production planning, are not directly applicable to the human services. In addition, success is viewed differently by users, managers, and technicians. Many technically successful applications are difficult for practitioners to use. Thus, success often rests on subjective judgment more than on objective data. Nonetheless, human service agencies must consider success measures such as system efficiency and effectiveness, cost benefit, use, satisfaction, and improved agency performance.

System Efficiency and Effectiveness

One well-established indicator of success is whether IT performs in an efficient and effective manner. IT efficiency can be maintained through the following activities:

- Removing slowdown points, for example data input, Internet access, or printing
- Redistributiing "peak load" jobs, for example, running system maintenance operations at night
- Finding hardware bottlenecks, for example, inadequate memory on a server, hard disks running close to capacity, etc.
- Increasing the overlap of data processing and the input/output of data whenever possible

Hardware and software monitors can help in the efficient use of computer resources. Hardware monitors are electronic devices attached to a computer. Software monitors are special applications housed in computer memory. Both methods generate performance information that helps identify bottlenecks and peak use.

One problem with reviewing the efficiency of a system is that hardware and software efficiency standards do not exist. Each application has its own computational and input/output characteristics. No two applications place identical requirements on the system resources. The efficiency of one IT application can be compared to that of another only if both perform the same functions and the systems have other features in common. Since programming continues to be more of an art than a science, complex applications developed by different programmers may differ widely in efficiency. The speed of most applications can be improved, but reprogramming requires substituting costly human resources for increasingly inexpensive hardware resources.

System effectiveness concerns whether the IT is performing as intended, that is, meeting the organization's goals. The following are some measures of effective system performance:

- Accuracy of system data
- System failure rate
- Total number of interactions and reports distributed per day, week, month, or year
- Average turnaround time to produce reports and total user waiting time
- User Interactions with the system to obtain additional information, for example, number of queries
- Fairness in providing applications to all users using priorities consistent with agency goals

Effectiveness measures often conflict with the measures of efficiency and with each other. For example, to increase the total number of reports processed per day, one would select reports with short run times. This would not be fair to users needing reports requiring long run times. On the other hand, maximum hardware utilization could be achieved by giving preference to the processing at intensive reports to the detriment of smaller requests. Obviously, each agency must find its own balance between system efficiency and effectiveness.

Cost Benefit

Cost benefit is an alluring measure for establishing the success of an IT application. Several difficulties exist with using cost-benefit analysis in IT. Costs before and after an application is implemented are difficult to measure. Often an application changes the information collected and the procedures used to collect the information. Comparing the cost benefit of a manual system with that of a computerized system may be similar to comparing the cost benefit of a horse with that of a car. A horse is less expensive, but no one would recommend using a horse to travel in today's cities. Thus, the increased costs after an application has been implemented may primarily reflect new ways of handling information.

Another difficulty is that most cost-benefit analysis techniques are designed for use in profit-making organizations and may have limited value in nonprofit fields. In addition, many costs and benefits are intangible, such as those listed in Table 12.2.

TABLE 12.2. Cost and Benefits Associated with an IT Application

Obvious Costs	Hidden Costs
Computer hardware	Disruptions during implementation
Computer software	Disruptions due to application failure
Space and storage of equipment	Personnel training and education
Expertise via staff/consultants	Displacement and retraining of staff
Connectivity, such as a link to the Internet	Loss of work effort and quality during development and implementation
Application planning, design, and programming	Time and effort needed to overcome conflict and resistance
Electricity	Running both new and old applications during implementation
Application maintenance	Enhancements to keep the application current, e.g., software upgrades

Obvious Benefits	Hidden Benefits
Increased timeliness and accuracy of data	Improved quality of service, e.g., allows workers to do a better job
Reduction in routine work of staff	Frees workers from routine tasks
Quick access to data and information	Possible revenue increased from improved paperwork, e.g., billing
Decision making based on more accurate data and information	Improved competitive position in seeking funds
Greater monitoring and control over agency planning and operation	May help integrate agency services to clients, e.g., better communication about services
Reports and special studies that previously were impossible to obtain	Better communications and relations with the community due to more current and accurate information
Better communication among staff	Higher morale due to a feeling of being on the cutting edge

Use and Satisfaction

Use and satisfaction are popular success measures. To use the automobile analogy, a car may be very efficient, effective, and cost beneficial, yet people may dislike cars and avoid using them because of the inability to find a parking space. The satisfaction of all who are affected by an application should be determined. Although intended users may be satisfied with the application, others may be frustrated by it. This often occurs with applications that provide data to middle managers while placing a heavy data entry burden on practitioners.

Figure 12.2 presents an instrument designed to measure the success of an application. It is based on the change in costs for collecting information, user satisfaction, and the usefulness of information for those collecting it. If the information collected changed due to an application, a different instrument would have to be used.

Improved Agency Performance

The overall goal of most IT applications is to improve client services at a reasonable cost. For example, some fund-raising applications have quadrupled collections in eight years while reducing administrative costs by 17 percent (Batchilder, 1997). However, in many human service areas, measures of improved services are difficult to obtain, and these measures vary by the type of service provided. In mental health, goal attainment scaling and problem-oriented records are often used to help measure goal achievement. With many applications, however, agencies must rely on the perceptions of administrators, direct service personnel, support personnel, and the agency board.

Table 12.3 presents a list of open-ended questions about improved agency performance. Since this questionnaire assumes no baseline information, the results provide only an impression of success. In addition, improved success may be the result of non-IT changes occurring at the same time the IT application was implemented.

Indirect Measures of IT Application Success

The previous discussion presented the more direct measures of IT application success. Previous chapters and sections described factors that improve the chance of IT application success, for example, following the development process in Chapter 6. These factors can be considered indirect measures of IT application success because their presence increases the chance of success, but the relationship between their presence and success is circumstantial.

Other Factors Impacting IT Application Success

The preceding discussion considered the application static rather than dynamic. However, applications have a life cycle that begins with the feasibility study and ends with the application's revision. In addition to the

FIGURE 12.2. Instrument for Measuring Cost Benefit, Satisfaction, and Use

General Information: Complete this instrument before and after a new application is implemented if similar data are collected. Once completed, the total costs for all forms can be calculated for the old and new applications. The usefulness of the information can be compared to costs using several of the statements.

Form #22 contains information I use in my agency? ___Yes ___No
(If yes, answer items below; if no, go to the next form.)

It takes me ___hours and ___minutes to complete each #22 form based on the data/information I work with in my agency.

If others are involved with this form, estimate how long it would take all involved to complete form #22. ___Hours and ___minutes

I suspect the information I provide on form #22 is accurate ___percent of the time (use a number from 0 to 100).

Indicate your agreement with the following, where SD = strongly disagree, D = disagree, N = neutral, A = agree, and SA = strongly agree.

Statement	Agree—Disagree
My colleagues and I agree on how to complete Form #22.	SD D N A SA
I am satisfied with how data on Form #22 are collected and processed.	SD D N A SA
The information on Form #22 is worth the time and effort required to collect and process it (general reports).	SD D N A SA
The information contained on Form #22 helps me make decisions.	SD D N A SA
The information on Form #22 is relevant to the decisions made in this agency.	SD D N A SA

In order to calculate the total cost of completing the forms above, we must know your salary. As with the rest of the information, your salary will be confidential and used only to calculate cost/benefit figures. Indicate your salary in the form you prefer.

___.__ per hour
___.__ per month
___.__ yearly

My work week is ___ hours.

Thank you for your cooperation.

application life cycle, an organization goes through various stages in IT use (Nolan, 1979) (see Table 12.4). Success may need to be measured differently at different stages of the application life cycle and of an organization's IT use. For example, when an application is introduced, practitioners may question its usefulness because of the changes in work patterns that are required. However, once the agency and staff have adjusted to the application, its perceived usefulness may increase. Bellerby and Goslin (1982)

TABLE 12.3. Open-Ended Questions to Help Determine Application Success

These questions are intended for all impacted by the IT application.

Were you involved in the planning of the IT application? If yes, how much time did you spend on planning activities? Were these activities useful?

Applications are often designed to change the way you work. Do you continue to work the way you did before the new application was implemented? Do others? How many hours a week are involved in doing things the old way?

When you first began to use the application, did you ever feel frustrated or alienated? If yes, how long did this feeling last? Did these feelings affect your job performance? Were you absent or late for work or unmotivated because of these feelings?

Were there disruptions in your agency due to the implementation of the application? Describe the disruptions. Did these disruptions affect your job performance?

Has the application ever failed? How did this affect your job performance?

Does the application provide more and better information, for example, information that is more relevant, useful, and up to date? Is this information helpful in your job?

Is it easier to obtain information using the new application than using traditional ways?

Does information exist in the application that would be helpful in your job, but that the application cannot provide?

Do you feel that the application requires the collection of too much information?

Has the application improved the accuracy of the information you collect and use?

Does the application provide information that is clear and understandable?

Do you feel that the application is as useful to you as it is to others in the organization?

Has the IT application resulted in more time or less time to spend on other aspects of your job?

Has your decision-making process changed because of the application?

Has the application improved the quality of your decisions?

Has the application made it possible for you to consider more alternatives before making a decision?

Has the application increased your ability to provide information requested by clients, organizations, or other agencies?

Has the application been helpful in publicity or fund-raising in the community?

How has the application affected our agency's image with clients and others in the community? In what way?

Has the application taken over tasks that agency staff consider unpleasant?

Has the application had any other effect on the services you offer?

TABLE 12.4. Stages in Organizational IT Use

Stage	Description of Stage
Initiation	Development of several low-level applications, typically accounting and client data.
Contagion	IT expands. Emphasis is on innovation and extensive applications. Overoptimism and overuse result in mistakes and applications that are overloaded, out of control, criticized, and inadequately designed.
Modification	Emphasis shifts from managing IT to managing the organization's data. Database concepts and internal planning and control are developed and enforced. The data management function is redesigned, formalized, professionalized, centralized, and elevated in the organization. User accountability is demanded.
Integration	Rebuilding is completed. IT grows rapidly as it moves out to the end users. Interactive use by end users increases. Control is initiated by setting user priorities.
Data Administration	Rapid growth again creates problems. A director of information is hired, or the current data manager moves higher in the organization. Distributed IT grows.
Maturation	IT matures; all basic IT applications are complete. A balance exists between use and control, central and distributed processing, and so on. The IT applications model the organization's information flow, decision making, and so on. Process is ready to be repeated with the emergence of radically new technology, e.g., intranets.

Source: Adapted from "Managing the Crises in Data Processing" by R. L. Nolan, 1979, *Harvard Business Review, 57*(2), pp. 115-126.

found that for each stage of development, success differed on factors such as documentation, involvement of the steering committee and users, and perceived usefulness.

Factors in the external and internal environments of an organization may influence application success and, therefore, must be considered. For example, organizational size and application scope have a large impact on application success. Kanungo (1998) found that organizational culture significantly relates to IT use and satisfaction. Task-oriented organizations were associated with positive use and satisfaction, whereas people-oriented organizations were associated with negative use and satisfaction. Table 12.5 presents a standard list of organizational context factors and dimensions that

TABLE 12.5. Organizational Context Factors and Measures

Factor/ Dimension	Dimension Measures
External Relationships	
Affiliations	Number of formal contractual arrangements impacting budgets and services
Agency Size	
Budget	Total yearly budget; personnel budget
Personnel	Number of employees (administrative, direct service, and support); ratio of staff to budget
Service area	Population of service area; ratio of clients served to geographic service area population; ratio of staff to service area population
Structure—Centralization	
Span of control	Number of subordinates who report directly to the executive, regardless of the hierarchical position of subordinates
Staff ratio	Ratio of administrators, direct service personnel, and support personnel to total personnel
Hierarchy of authority	Number of vertical levels in the organization; percent of budget spent for administrative versus direct service
Geographical distribution	Number of organization locations
Authority distribution	Number of subunits with responsibility for their own budgets
Structure—Formalization	
Procedures	Percent of service processes for which written procedures exist
Goals and objectives	Percent of agency goals and objectives that are measurable; proportion of agency activities related to agency goals and objectives
Service output	Percent of services that have measurable outputs
Psychological Climate of Agency	
Morale	Perception of high morale; perception of how innovative and adaptive the agency is
Fear	Fear of technology, job loss, status loss, or change
Trust	Perception that IT will be used for the benefit of staff and clients
Staff turnover	Percent of administrative, service providers, and support staff changing position or leaving the agency in the previous year
Culture	Task oriented versus people oriented
Job Content and Design	
Nature of job	Perception of (1) how routine or repetitive tasks are; (2) variety of tasks associated with each job; (3) autonomy and responsibility associated with each job; (4) percent of time spent working with people, information, and things

should be taken into account when measuring success. A more detailed discussion of these variables is beyond the scope of this book, but is available in the management literature (Savaya and Waysman, 1996).

A three-dimensional matrix helps examine IT success (see Figure 12.3). The matrix takes into account organizational and environmental characteristics and phases of development. Research may indicate that some measures are curvilinear. For example, user involvement may be important at an initial stage of application development, less important at a middle stage, and again important at a later stage. In addition, some variables may be necessary for avoiding failure, but may have little influence on system success.

FIGURE 12.3. A Three-Dimensional Approach to Modeling IT Success

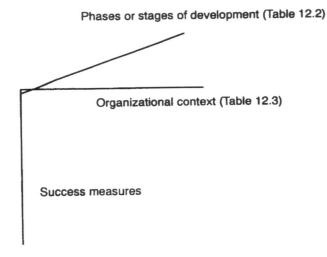

GUIDELINES FOR SUCCESS

The literature cites many indirect factors that can help IT application development be more successful (Hile, 1998; Kidd, 1995).✿ Models of IT success even exist in the management information system literature (De-Lone and McLean, 1992; Saunders and Jones, 1992; Garrity, 1998).✿ The problem is that most literature on application success is specific to one application or type of application. However, factors that are repeatedly cited will probably be important in the success of any application.

This section presents the frequently mentioned guidelines for IT success. It is a review of the last several chapters from a "dos and don'ts" perspective. If followed, these guidelines should help an agency to avoid disruption and to anticipate problems before they occur. The advice is summarized in Table 12.6. As with all advice, it must be customized to the current situation. For example, the advice presented in this section may need to be altered, depending on where an organization is in the stages of IT development, as described in Table 12.4.

Begin by Planning

Planning is consistently mentioned as a key factor in successful IT implementation. A three- to five-year plan should address how applications will be tied together to form an overall system that achieves agency-wide goals. Planning allows modular implementation, which lessens risks, increases flexibility, distributes costs, and provides time to react and adjust. An application plan is needed for each application development in the overall plan.

Agencies that are highly influenced by their environment should view applications as part of a larger community IT system. The IT plan should address how an agency will integrate its applications into this larger system. For example, case management applications that match clients to services may require continuous updating of available community services. Agencies could cooperatively update a community services database using the Web.

Place IT in a Separate Top-Level Department

Although differences between right and wrong organizational structures are seldom clear-cut (review Figure 6.13), one guideline concerning the IT department is widely held. Since information cuts across departmental and organizational boundaries, the IT department should be a separate high-level department. This advice is not often followed because the tendency exists to place the information management function in the department that first computerizes. Creating a separate high-level unit is considered only after an agency develops several applications. For example, since an accounting application is typically installed first, the budget officer is often responsible for information management. This evolutionary practice conceals a serious trap, as the following quotation indicates:

TABLE 12.6. Guidelines for IT Success

Factor/Dimension	Possible Dimension Measures
Planning	
Types of plans	Whether agency has a long-range plan (3 to 5 years) for agency IT and a plan for each application
Written specificity of plans	Whether the application effort has written, up-to-date, well-defined and clear purposes, goals, objectives, system requirements, and mechanisms for evaluation and revision
Application Characteristics	
Month of operation (maturity)	Months since IT application was purchased or developed
Sources of application	Developed in-house versus purchased from a vendor
Application scope	Number of agency departments or agencies the application spans
Application size	Number of subsystems developed and type; number of intended users
Accessibility	Ratio of input/output devices to targeted users; whether access is available during normal work patterns, e.g., mobile access with handheld devices
Flexibility	Estimate of the time and cost to change the database structure or add a new form or report to the application
Primary orientation	Whether application is designed to meet needs of administration, direct service personnel, or support personnel
Privacy protected	Formal written procedures used to ensure security and privacy; perception of security and privacy protection by user
Documentation	Whether formal documentation exists on each application for users, developers, and managers
Reflection of agency operations	Extent that application is an information model of the operations it supports
Implementation Strategies	
Separation of changes	Number of agency changes implemented at the same time as the IT application was developed
Implementation gradualness	Number of applications developed per year, adjusted by agency size
Formality	Extent to which the IT application is reflected in agency operating procedures

TABLE 12.6 (*continued*)

Factor/ Dimension	Possible Dimension Measures
User Involvement	
Steering committee	Existence and inclusion of key decision makers; representative of user groups and agency as a whole
Open communication	Number of written communications; number of communication-oriented meetings; whether jargon defined and circulated
Involvement in implementation	Estimated number of hours spent by administrators, direct service personnel, and support personnel in each stage of development
Training	
Money spent	Percent of total budget spent for IT training versus other training
Recipients	Hours of training received by administration, direct service personnel, support personnel, and agency board; extent IT is part of orientation of new employees
Results of training	Knowledge of development process, how to use applications, and realistic expectations of success
Top Management Commitment and Control	
Commitment	Adequate funds secured and budgeted; board support secured
Control of IT effort	Perception of top management control of IT application effort by administration, direct service personnel, and support personnel
Control by agency	Whether agency developed application on its own or application mandated by others, e.g., government; ability to control the application budget
Involvement	Time spent by top management in approving major decisions, assigning responsibilities, reviewing plans, ensuring documentation, and monitoring implementation progress
Incentives to use application	Perception of rewards and punishments for use of application by targeted users
IT Application Department/Manager	
Rank	Number of levels below the chief executive officer
Location	In its own department versus within another department
Stability of staff	Number of internal personnel changes per year
Expertise	Ratio of years of human services training and experience divided by years of IT-related training and experience of IT staff

The department that controls the resource becomes strongly protective of it, often because a manager or group within it wants to build up power and influence. When the time comes for computing to assume a broader role, real conflict arises—conflict that can be costly in terms of management turnover and in terms of lingering hostilities that inhibit the provision of computer services and applications across functional areas. (Gibson and Nolan, 1974, p. 80)

This problem is especially serious in the human services in which contracts and grants provide funds that are not tied to customer outcomes and satisfaction. Thus, an agency can quickly develop a strong information system designed around accounting and funding rather than client services. Since IT applications become information models of organizations, they should reflect the agency's mission, that is, client services rather than funding.

A separate high-level department helps achieve the following results:

- Management demonstrates their commitment to IT and information management.
- The information manager is able to cope with the power struggles and controversies that information management creates.
- The information manager can maintain high visibility within the organization and not be identified with one department.
- The department will attract top-quality personnel who have a management and a technical orientation.

Involve Stakeholders

Application success increases when all persons affected by the application are involved in its design and implementation. This is difficult advice to follow because involvement is time-consuming and "messy" and the payoffs are long term and hard to measure. Involvement is particularly important in agencies that quickly purchase and implement prepackaged applications. Purchasing IT bypasses much of the learning that occurs when an agency develops its own application. If the agency purchases sophisticated applications, it must substitute other learning experiences for those which occur with custom applications development; for example, staff could visit similar applications in other agencies. Planning and user preparation mean different things at different levels of the agency and for the total agency.

Agency

An agency should be prepared psychologically and financially for designing and implementing an IT application. The agency that will be the most successful in these tasks will already be functioning well, so it can take the time and risks associated with the required changes. An organization in crisis, or one barely surviving, may not have the necessary time, energy, or morale, although it will be highly motivated to change.

An agency should have formalized and stable goals, procedures, and operations because IT applications are information models of the operations they automate. An agency with frequently changing goals, structures, and procedures will find its IT applications quickly outdated and expensive to maintain. An agency unprepared for developing an application may go through a system development process similar to that in Figure 12.4. Wasted personnel and lost opportunities are the result.

Top-Level Decision Makers

The success or failure of most IT applications can be traced back to the presence or absence of clear, consistent, and visible involvement by a key leader. Top-level decision makers can demonstrate leadership by doing the following:

FIGURE 12.4. The "True" Application Development Process

🍷🍾	Unwarranted enthusiasm
	Growing concern
🚑	Unmitigated disaster
🚓	Searching for the guilty
🔒	Punishing the guilty
☞	Punishing the innocent
🤝	Promoting the uninvolved

- Become educated about IT so as not to be dazzled by technology and vendor promises.
- Ensure that the organization is reasonably stable.
- Maintain control over the development effort.
- Ensure that accountability for results is clearly assigned, openly understood, and that those accountable have the necessary authority to take initiatives and make decisions that impact results.
- Expend the extra time and energy required throughout the application development and implementation process.
- Ensure that those developing an application receive the necessary release time from normal duties.
- Guarantee that all users are provided education and training.
- Demonstrate that the information, data, and the power inherent in any application will not be used for personal gain or punishment of employees.
- Separate IT changes from other changes; that is, do not blame IT for organizational changes that management has been reluctant to make.
- Assume responsibility for resolving conflicts that arise during implementation.
- Openly demonstrate commitment and involvement by attending important meetings, assigning quality personnel to the development effort, and making timely and firm decisions. Employees will not support the application if the organization's leaders do not take it seriously.

An example will illustrate the importance of top management to the IT development process. The clinical training committee of a mental health provider sought the assistance of a consultant to help them integrate clinical IT applications into the organization. They brought in the consultant because they feared the accounting department was controlling and restricting the scope of clinical IT. The executive director took a hands-off approach because he did not understand the subtleties of technology and the control issues IT raises. However, major IT change could not move forward without this dispute being resolved.

The Users

Those who supply information or use the results of an application are crucial, yet their preparation is often neglected. Prepare users by involving them directly in the total development process or indirectly through representation on an agency steering committee. Figure 12.5 illustrates an application development process without user involvement. User involve-

FIGURE 12.5. Application Development Without User Involvement

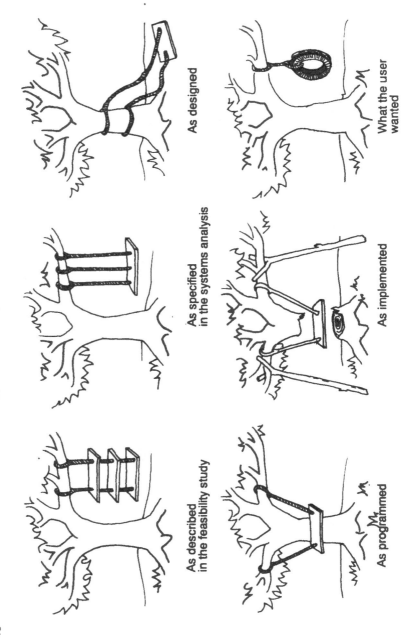

As described
in the feasibility study

As specified
in the systems analysis

As designed

As programmed

As implemented

What the user
wanted

ment also provides valuable training, opens communication channels, reduces unrealistic application design, lessens fear and resistance, and secures commitment and future use. The importance of user involvement is the lesson most frequently mentioned in the application development literature. Some literature even advocates strong user control over IT development and design (Moyer, 1997). The following steps help ensure user involvement:

- Design the application to fit user needs, such as reduced paperwork and improved data retrieval.
- Expose the user to a positive similar application as early in the process as possible.
- Provide adequate training for those uninitiated in IT.
- Be willing to commit funds for presentations, demonstrations, assistance to users in initial contact with the application, etc.
- Make application use easy, enjoyable, and nonthreatening.
- Reward use more than nonuse.
- Include the application and its use in agency standard operating procedures (for example, in employee training and evaluations).
- Provide for a few early payoffs from the application.

The following example illustrates the necessity of user involvement in every aspect of application development. A vendor developed twenty hours of computer-aided instruction (CAI) to train workers on a newly developed statewide information system. Workers had limited involvement with the CAI development. Although the training software performed as designed, statewide CAI training was a failure because the developers did not understand the work pressures and mentality of the workers. To gain acceptance, developers administered quizzes at the end of the CAI that were easy to pass. When this fact spread across the state, workers skimmed through the twenty hours of CAI, obtained just enough information to pass the easy end quiz, and went back to work. Consequently, workers were not sufficiently trained when the vendor implemented the information system, thus causing major problems.

Clients

Involving clients and client advocates in application development should be considered. Clients have the unique ability to continually focus applications on the bottom line, that is, better services. Their perspective is often ignored unless they have an active part in the process.

Consider Agency Sophistication

Since an application is typically more complex than its manual counterpart, it requires a higher level of sophistication on the part of agency operations and the user. One example of this sophistication is the standardization that accompanies any application. Standardization takes many forms, such as the definition of terms, common operational procedures regarding information, and centralized control and access to information. An agency generally must impose far more discipline throughout the organization when IT applications are used. This required sophistication has several implications for agency IT.

Extent of Pioneering

The history of technology contains many stories of pioneers who were first, but who failed in the long run. Success is most often reaped by settlers who follow close behind the pioneers, making substantial improvements while avoiding the pioneers' mistakes. Most human service organizations should avoid implementing the latest IT developments. Although being on the forefront of IT can be exciting, it is usually frustrating and costly in terms of agency time, effort, and morale. In addition, problems often plague newly developed applications. Also, learning a new application is difficult, and most users resist changing hardware and software even if a much better application exists. No agency should attempt developing IT applications without board, staff, and funding source support. Cautiously implementing "proven" applications is safer for agencies not capable of withstanding the pressures of pioneering. Agencies best able to withstand the stress of pioneering are those which are either successful or failing. Successful agencies can more easily weather the accompanying changes; failing organizations are often more open to large changes. Pioneering in IT is best left to those who can take risks, for example, university researchers and vendors.

An example will illustrate this point. One mental health agency, with federal and state support, contracted with a vendor to develop a sophisticated information system that included goal attainment scaling and problem-oriented records. A larger company purchased the vendor, leaving the agency owning the software. The agency eventually marketed the system to other similar agencies to help pay maintenance and upgrade costs. Meanwhile, the developers quit the vendor and formed their own company. The developers used what they had learned previously to create a more sophisticated and less expensive system. The developers then sold this new system, making it difficult for the agency to sell the initial system. The developers became a successful vendor, while the agency continually struggled with maintenance and upgrade. Numerous similar stories exist inside and outside the human services; for example, read any book chronicling the history of Microsoft and the many pioneers who paved Microsoft's way.

The Intended Users of the Application

Another consideration is whether IT should address the needs of agency directors, midlevel managers, workers, or a combination of these. Different levels of the organization have different information needs (review Chapter 8). The ideal is to design the application to support core processes and have the application collect information that serves other levels of the organization. One consistent finding is that clients resist technology much less than human service professionals. Whereas most clients are in need and seeking change, most practitioners are satisfied with their situation and prefer the status quo. Applications that allow client interaction and reduce practitioner paperwork have a high chance of success.

Another consideration is what type of application to implement first. Some suggest that an application which is very important to agency functioning should be first so the benefits will be more obvious. Others recommend a less crucial application in order to learn about IT.

Avoid Overreliance on a Few Isolated Technical Specialists

Reliance on one or several people for IT development and implementation presents serious risks for an agency. A consultant may change firms and leave an agency stranded. An in-house designer may quit and set back the IT effort. Agencies must ensure continuity for the two or three years a major application requires, regardless of the personnel changes that occur. A strong application committee helps reduce dependency.

One recommendation is to distribute the expertise on any application development effort. If outside consultants are used, they can be teamed with in-house staff. This practice ensures that consultants do not foster agency dependency. In choosing staff to team with outside specialists, select employees who will be with the agency for a long time. Training the brightest, most interested, and younger members of the staff may seem logical. However, these employees are more likely to leave the agency with their newly developed expertise.

Another way to lessen dependence is to have good documentation. Managers neglect documentation because its value is not immediately recognizable. In addition, documentation is a boring and time-consuming task for application designers. However, documentation is the basis for evaluating and controlling the IT effort, as well as for building additional applications. Documentation is also the key to continuity, especially when technology is changing rapidly and knowledgeable IT personnel change jobs frequently.

Agencies often have employees who are interested in systems design. They know the agency well, but do not have the technical expertise needed to develop professional applications. These employees and any beginning applications they have developed can be a valuable asset in working with vendors.

Application development requires a balancing act between the expertise of external vendors and internal users. Overreliance on external vendors can result in applications that work according to specifications, yet do not serve the needs of users. Overreliance on internal developers can lead to applications that meet user needs, but have technical and upgrade problems. Allowing vendors too much control over the development effort can result in applications that sacrifice usability for project completion. Allowing users too much control over the development effort can lead to applications that are constantly changing and never fully developed. For a useful discussion of this balance of internal and external expertise, as well as stories of success and failure (see Moyer, 1997).

Select Software Before Hardware

In developing an application, hardware is a less crucial factor than software. If hardware and software are purchased separately, choose software before purchasing hardware. This is not easy advice to follow, especially in the small computer market. One way to seek software is to obtain the names of comparable agencies that have similar applications. A telephone call to state and national associations or a site visit to an agency with a similar application can provide valuable information. The Internet contains numerous links to software and discussion lists that provide access to many people who use software packages. Software selection requires a well-designed assessment of agency information needs developed by key staff throughout the organization.

The tendency often exists to custom design a solution when a packaged solution could be purchased. Even if internal developments seem less costly, an outside package should be considered because the purchase/build decision can affect agency IT for many years. Once made, this decision and its consequences are difficult and expensive to reverse. This decision is similar to choosing an automobile. A customized one-of-a-kind car may fit the driver's needs best. However, a very common car will be easier and less expensive to repair and maintain. Even with custom-programmed software, the agency should encourage the use of generic tools such as database management systems and intranets. The money invested in these tools often results in less overall programming time and reduces dependence. The idea that programmers' time and effort cost little because they are salaried may encourage custom-programmed solutions that are more expensive in the long term. Also, application developers have little incentive not to custom develop every part of the application, since custom-developed applications ensure job security.

Working with vendors is not always easy. Vendors often use terms loosely and advertise products that are not currently available to attract buyers away from competing products. Venders commonly leave customers waiting for an essential piece of software that was promised months earlier. Vendors can change products and marketing strategies, leaving their customers stranded. A rule of thumb is that software does not exist until it is running on your computers. When considering software from vendors, ask for a list of organizations presently using the software and randomly contact several. Be sure that the vendor does not limit the potential list by recommending only a few well-screened possibilities. Also, ensure that the agency will have access to the application source code if the vendor goes out of business or is unable to support the product.

These comments are not intended to reflect negatively on vendors. Vendors are a much-needed part of the IT world. The human service field needs more vendors. However, human service professionals should not confuse the helping relationship between practitioners and their clients with the business relationship between vendors and their clients.

Safeguard Security and Confidentiality from the Beginning

Surprisingly, it is difficult to find good definitions of security, privacy, and confidentiality. *Security* usually refers to the protection of hardware, software, and data by passwords, restricted physical admittance, fire walls, duplicate storage, and protection from fire and electrical interruption. Back-up procedures should be established and rigidly followed (see Table 12.7).

Privacy refers to the rights of individuals to keep their possessions, including information about themselves, away from others. *Confidentiality* is a level of secrecy assumed or formally agreed upon by two or more parties with the expectation that shared information will be used consistent with this agreement. Confidentiality is a matter requiring proper levels of authorization, access codes, encryption, and other measures.

IT applications can be secure and protect the confidentiality associated with client information as well as any paper-and-pencil system. However, this is true only if security and confidentiality are part of the initial design

TABLE 12.7. Methods for Backing Up Computer Files

Backing up computer files is an important task that is often overlooked until a disaster occurs. It is important to implement a backup scheme during application installation and to follow it rigorously. Simply backing up a system every day on the same media, covering over the previous day's backup, could result in a problem if an error is not discovered for a week or a month. Backing up every day on a new medium may be too expensive. Methods of backing up files offer a compromise between cost and recoverability. The following are two typical backup methods.

Method A

This method requires at least twenty-two versions of backup media. In this example, the backup medium will be a disk, although any medium, such as a tape, may be used. Do the following:

1. Label four of the disks with the first four days of the week, i.e., Monday, Tuesday, Wednesday, and Thursday. Label four of the disks with the weeks of the month, and label twelve of the disks with the months of the year. Additional disks should be labeled by year.
2. Each day of the week is backed up on the properly labeled disk, with Friday's backup being on the disk labeled with the corresponding week.
3. The last day of the month backup is made on the disk marked for that month.
4. The last day of the year backup is made on the disk marked for that year.

This method allows you to go back one week for an exact daily backup, four weeks for a weekly backup, or twelve months for a monthly backup.

Method B

1. Each drive should have three disks associated with it. An "Odd-Day" disk is used for backup on odd-numbered days. An "Even-Day" disk is used for backup on even-numbered days. A "weekly" disk is used for backup at the end of the week.
2. Label each disk with the drive name and application name.
3. Keep a backup log near the computer. Record the date, the drive, and the disk used for the backup in this log. The person performing the backup should initial each entry.
4. Store the backup disks under lock and key when not in use.
5. Store the weekly backup disks off site in a secure location known only to the person in charge of the application and the agency director.

and if the agency establishes and follows appropriate policies and procedures. Establishing security and privacy safeguards after an application is developed can be expensive and time-consuming.

IT applications have a tendency to make private information public, and mistakes are often big. For example, a private e-mail may be accidentally displayed for all to see or staff may be obtaining gossip by snooping into computer files. The manager's task is to plan for security and privacy from the beginning of any application development and to justify the cost. Often security is lax until after a violation has occurred. The training of users on protecting security and privacy is equally as important as passwords, encryption, audit trails, and asking users to verify the last recorded use under their names. Training helps to avoid problems such as passwords taped on the display and spouses' names used as passwords.

Incorporate Continuous Improvement Mechanisms

Continuous monitoring and openly sharing feedback about key activities and results with stakeholders is beneficial, especially with complex applications (Hile, 1998). Many feedback measures can be derived from the application's goals and objectives. Other measures to track are efficiency, effectiveness, satisfaction, and application success. These measures and feedback mechanisms must be built into the application development process at the outset. Measures are more powerful if they are positive rather than negative and address application output rather than input. For example, they might concern the use of data in decision making rather than the reliability of data input. Once the agency is satisfied that a performance measure is valid, reliable, and meaningful, it can be used as part of individual and departmental reward and recognition efforts.

Continuous improvement is an iterative process. An agency must periodically assess whether the current measures are producing the desired results. Measures that become obsolete, contain little variation, or resist change can be deleted. In some cases, measures can be simplified or the number or measurement period reduced without sacrificing needed feedback. However, frequently changing measures can hinder improvement efforts. Employees may think they can ignore a measure because it will soon change. A hidden problem is that if not wisely used, performance measures focus attention on the measure rather than on goal achievement. For example, students can be so concerned with their careers that they focus on course grades rather than learning.

Expect the Development Effort to Be Frustrating and Time-Consuming

Designing and implementing IT applications is not an easy process. Problems multiply as the size of the application and the complexity of the tasks supported increases. Although routine applications also can be difficult, developing a complex application, such as an agency information system or Web site, can be a long-term process requiring many revisions. Estimates of the time and work involved are often very inaccurate. For example, when building a Web site, the number of tasks to be completed seems to grow exponentially, rather than geometrically, as the number of pages in the site increases.

Administrators sometimes expect that if they develop a better way of doing things, people will adopt the better way. As professionals who specialize in producing client change, we often forget how difficult change is and that the natural tendency of people is not to change. A generation of professionals who have worked with IT throughout their education may be required before human service professionals are comfortable using IT.

During development, a computer should be distinguished from an IT application and its implementation. Application failures often are inappropriately attributed to the computer rather than to the design or the implementation process. For example, an agency may experience problems when implementing a computerized client tracking system. The problems may occur regardless of whether a computer is involved, stemming instead from an inadequate implementation process and having little to do with the client tracking system or the computer.

Developing IT applications is similar to other complicated processes, for example, democracy or making sausage. The product may be beautiful, but the process can be very messy, time-consuming, and sometimes out of control. Those viewing the process from the outside should have early warning, enabling them to overlook the mess and to focus on a quality product.

CONCLUSION

Managing IT requires a shift in thinking that involves the following:

- Viewing practice as information based; that is, day-to-day decisions are based on processed information.
- Viewing information as a commodity; that is, using information costs resources; whereas failing to use information wastes resources.

- Viewing information as cumulative, interactive, and connected; that is, practitioners interact with the accumulated knowledge of the agency and the profession by examining trend data, synthesizing expertise, networking with colleagues, and querying predictive models.
- Viewing information acquisition, manipulation, presentation, and use as part of agency policies and procedures; that is, IT is incorporated into new worker training and performance evaluations.

Developing and managing IT to support this new way of thinking will continue to be a difficult process.

REVIEW AND DISCUSSION QUESTIONS

1. What is the difference between managing the agency's IT application and managing the agency's information resource?
2. How is managing an agency's information resources similar to, and different from, managing an agency's financial resources?
3. How is managing a manual information system similar to, and different from, managing a computer-based information system?
4. What general management skills are applicable to information management, and what new skills need to be learned?
5. Who are the different people involved in managing an agency IT application, and what role does each play?
6. Can you think of success measures other than those mentioned in this chapter? Do any of the success measures or indicators conflict with one another?
7. If you could select only one piece of advice on application development from this chapter, what would it be?
8. What do the following sayings mean?

    - In IT, it is acceptable to reinvent the wheel, but not to reinvent the flat tire.
    - You can tell the pioneers by the arrows in their backs.
    - When on the cutting edge, be prepared to be cut. Or, if you're in the lead, be prepared to bleed.

Chapter 13

Trends, Issues, and the Future

INTRODUCTION

This chapter speculates on the future to encourage critical and divergent thinking for today's applications. To use the transportation analogy again, when motoring first started, we did not need those who fought change and wanted to return to the days of the horse-drawn carriage. We needed futurists who could speculate about the benefits of our modern transportation system while helping to prevent smog-choked cities and traffic jams. Stretching our imagination about the future and examining issues will help to avoid the problems that will inevitably occur as we move into the information age.

Most thinking about the future is evolutionary and involves rational, linear, step-by-step extrapolation. More difficult and risky thinking is revolutionary and involves bringing things together in different ways or using new approaches. Evolutionary thinking invented the horseless carriage by replacing the carriage horse with a motor. Revolutionary thinking invented the airplane. This chapter presents both evolutionary and revolutionary thinking about IT for various levels of the human service delivery system. Each level includes future scenarios, trends, impacts, requisite skills, and issues.

SOCIETY

Future Scenario

Terri's "smart house scheduler" woke her up thirty minutes early because she had several urgent requests for a consultation from the Smith family in rural Alaska. She had programmed her scheduler to wake her up early if it predicted she needed the additional time to organize her day.

Terri was a thirty-five-year-old therapist employed by a virtual family counseling cooperative serving primarily Western countries. Her specialty was dual-parent households adjusting to victimization. Using her multi-purpose IT device, Terri reviewed her "to do" list and her overnight communications to determine how to dress and how to organize her day. Her scheduler indicated her pantry was well stocked for the family's customary eating habits and no essential shopping was necessary. The scheduler also noted that her children needed transportation to afternoon dance lessons and evening soccer practice.

One urgent communication was from the Smith family, requesting a quick teleconference. They wanted to discuss the recommendations from the Automated Diagnostics Network (ADN) in light of their daughter's threatened suicide last night. The Smith's daughter was a recent victim of a violent attack. The Smiths had spent several hours with the ADN assessing the threat and completing several educational sessions on suicide. Using research and previous similar cases worldwide, ADN provided the Smiths with a list of potential interventions, outcomes, and a monitoring routine. It provided Terri's agency with a suicide-potential score that indicated the threat was serious. Terri quickly requested her scheduler to telelink with the Smith family. Luckily, all family members were available for a fifteen-minute videosession to discuss the threatened suicide. During the thirty-minute session, Terri answered questions raised about the threatened suicide, the assessment, the education programs, the suggested outcomes, and the recommended interventions and monitoring. Based on this discussion, they selected several outcomes and agreed on the interventions and monitoring that ADN recommended. Terri immediately received a suggestion from her agency to set up a fifteen-minute follow-up session with the mother and daughter later that day. After the Smith's session, Terri went to breakfast hoping that her day would not be a series of client crises.

Trends, Impacts, and Requisite Skills

A continuing trend is the declining cost of hardware relative to total application development costs. We can look forward to a universal information device that consists of a voice-controlled, powerful CPU with unlimited RAM and a large, thin display. This device will be integrated with our computers, Internet, telephone, television, and entertainment systems with high bandwidth links to the Internet. With the shrinking size of components, this device will come in the size and shape required by the application. The biggest components of the device will be those required for human interface, for example, the display and printer.

Developing software will still be a long, tedious, risky, and expensive task that requires very specialized technicians. However, some new software applications may temporarily leap ahead. The Internet will link stand-alone desktop computers into one large network. Consequently, the number of linkages among applications will increase dramatically. The primary linkages will change from people interacting with computers to computers interacting with computers. Applications that entertain, save time, and allow people to be more productive will flourish. Personalized assistants that help people live in a complex world by performing routine tasks will be common.

As information becomes digital, people will work with pictures, graphics, sound, and video as they now work with numbers and text. Information will be the primary commodity bought and sold in the global village. In an information society, everyone is an information consumer and producer. People will no longer spend time tracking down information because smart applications will find the information and the people who need it. Collecting information for a few to access at relatively high prices will not be profitable. Rather, profit will be made by selling small pieces of information to millions of users at very small prices. Just as the value of travel was only understood as more people gained the ability to travel, the value of information will only be realized when most people are connected electronically.

Human robotics, memory implants, artificial intelligence, and genetic engineering may one day produce a biotech person or other new life form.✿ Such ideas are requiring human beings to rediscover themselves by asking questions about the nature of intelligence and the essence of human nature. It is ironic that the answers to some of these questions may be found in primitive societies that are being destroyed rather than being mined for their knowledge.

These predicted changes will:

- improve the quality of life worldwide, especially for the underdeveloped populations and disadvantaged in society;
- allow for virtual world governance structures and virtual village meetings;
- allow equal participation in global trade and competition, even from the smallest rural village;
- make governments more efficient and increase their accountability; and
- reduce income inequalities by opening the wealth of the world to developing countries, for example, making virtual world libraries and

universities available to even the smallest village, anytime and anywhere in the world.

Issues

Society views IT through rose-colored glasses. This lack of a large
thoughtful opposition to IT means that large mistakes can easily be made.

Gap Between the Haves and Have-Nots

Although IT is predicted to reduce information and education inequalities, it has exacerbated income inequalities worldwide. Since information
is a basic commodity of modern society, those who know how to use the
tools to access and work with information will gain power and those who
do not may be left out. People who are potentially disenfranchised in an
information society are those with mental disabilities, the uneducated, and
oppressed groups such as the poor, minorities, and women. Thankfully,
some groups who were disenfranchised in an industrial society will do
better in an information society, for example, people with physical disabilities.

The issues of the haves and have-nots will be a problem until electronic
skills and access become as common as the television and the telephone.
However, access to information may become an issue if governments
allow corporations to monopolize and sell information and the channels on
which it passes. The solution to these disenfranchisement issues involves
IT availability, education, and consumer-friendly policies. Human service
professionals must help educate the IT industry on the advantages of
resolving information disenfranchisement and IT's undesirable consequences. The effort on behalf of people with disabilities is a model for
others to follow. For example, guidelines and techniques developed by the
government, advocacy groups, industries, and researchers make technology more accessible to persons with disabilities.✤

IT is often linked to job loss and job displacement. Some speculate that
countries which have rapidly industrialized will experience massive unemployment when robots in developed countries can work less expensive-
ly and more reliably than laborers in underdeveloped countries. However,
it may be possible for agricultural/tribal societies to go directly into an
information society and bypass the painful industrial phase, for example,
Middle Eastern oil-rich countries. It will take time for the world to adjust
to employment and compensation for work in an information society.

Values Inherent in IT

IT is often presented as culture and value neutral. However, those making these assertions are typically from a high-tech culture. IT has an underlying cultural and worldview that is scientific, quantitative, mechanistic, rationalistic, linear, competitive, and primarily white male (Bowers, 1998). The view upon which IT is built has its roots in Western scientific culture. Basic software, such as operating systems and computer languages, contains American values and culture.

With IT, reality is filtered through the characteristics, limitations, and philosophies of hardware and software before it is presented to a user. For example, in developing some expert systems, knowledge that does not fit into if-then rules must be modified or discarded. This filtering of reality to fit hardware and software reinforces some values and discourages others. Therefore, applications are rarely value or culture free.

Taking a phenomenological view of IT can illustrate its inherent values. IT is a solitary experience. The user is generally sitting upright, staring at a display, and interacting with abstractions that do not exist outside the computer. There are few distractions; thus, eye and neck strain are common. Rarely is human-to-human communication as limited and concentrated for similar lengths of time. IT interaction is consistent, reliable, addictive, and engrossing. It is addictive in that the rewards are immediate, numerous, and variable in schedule. The reward schedule of IT interaction produces behavior that is difficult to change. On a similar reward schedule, pigeons will peck at a lever for a long time after all food rewards have stopped. We hear often of computer widows, of Internet addiction, and of the dangers of competitive and violent adolescent games. Altering the application changes the IT phenomenological experience very little. Surprisingly, applications that stop the user after a specific time and recommend that the user take a break to maintain perspective and peak efficiency are not common.

The values inherent in IT are important because practitioners work with problems that have cultural overtones, such as deviance. We need to take a very critical look at IT, as Joseph Weizenbaum, the inventor of ELIZA, states:

> What's needed . . . is an energetic program of technological detoxification. . . . we are intoxicated with our sciences and technology and . . . we are deeply committed to a Faustian bargain that is rapidly killing us spiritually and may eventually kill us all physically . . . (Long, 1985, p. 78)

Lack of Societal Control

IT defies control by society's traditional means. For example, controlling the Internet is difficult because it does not exist as a physical entity. The Internet has no corporate headquarters, no chief executive officer, no budget, and no strategic plan. Yet it continues to grow rapidly and will affect the lives of almost everyone on Earth. Governments find their traditional controls to be ineffective and too slow. When controls are imposed in one area, the Internet seems to immediately shift to bypass the controls and punish the controller. For example, the U.S. government tried to regulate encryption standards. Technological developments often overtook these regulatory efforts, and U.S. regulations hindered the ability of U.S. companies to compete in the global market.

IT affects other forms of societal control. In the physical world, identity is relatively permanent because it is based on one's gender, age, and residence. Identity helps society hold individuals responsible for their actions. However, in cyberspace, the basis of identity can change at the user's whim. Users can assume any gender, age, or location. Consequently, responsible parties are not as obvious and accountability for actions is more difficult to enforce.

POLICY FORMULATION AND ANALYSIS

Future Scenario

The on-line hearing on health disability benefits was looking like a Hollywood production. The instant opinion polling on the twenty issues that the congressional committee was addressing showed that both sides had rallied their constituents in an almost even battle. It seemed that almost everyone receiving disability benefits was connected via Internet-based discussion groups to the questioning of witnesses. A hacker even attempting to disrupt the testimony of the insurance industry witness by superimposing onto the screen the amount of money each committee member received from the insurance industry. The meetings were recessed until technicians were able to debug the hacker's tampering. Most witnesses made graphic presentations of numbers and facts. However, one witness had committee members wear virtual reality goggles to assume the body and lifestyle of a quadriplegic on disability benefits. The committee then went virtual grocery shopping. Most committee members had difficulty maneuvering the wheelchair, and several were unable to keep within the budget allowed by current benefits. Although IT allowed hearings to be held on-line and facts to be easily collected and immediately distributed worldwide, in the end, it seemed that the committee's decisions would be based on the political power of the constituent groups rather than the facts.

Trends, Impacts, and Requisite Skills

Use of IT to systematically collect, analyze, and disseminate information about citizens' needs and capacities has been limited. Without adequate information, policy is often based on ideology, political philosophy, or political power.

The Internet has greatly expanded the role of IT in policy formation and analysis. Independent information can be stored and linked together to form an easy-to-use resource reservoir on any issue. Other information collection tools can be added to policy Web sites, for example, instant polls, conferences, and chat rooms. The Internet can also make access to policymakers and elected officials much easier, especially for groups traditionally left out of the policy decision-making process.

Techniques will need to be developed to allow policymakers and elected officials to assimilate the massive amounts of information about a topic. Information synthesizing and communication skills will become increasingly important. Those with technical knowledge and resources will conduct better studies and produce more understandable presentations. Being able to organize and manage highly technical and diverse teams, both virtually and in person, will be another necessary skill.

Issues

Policy Leading Practice

One issue will be keeping policy current with technology to prevent problems. Figure 8.1 illustrated how financial incentives associated with federal policy destroyed the rational development of California's welfare information system. A lack of policy is preventing technology-mediated counseling on the Internet. Practitioners wanting to experiment are fearful of violating policies and ethical standards designed for face-to-face practice. Without sanctioned experimentation, it will be difficult to answer many questions about technology-mediated or technology-delivered counseling. For example, how are virtual relationships different from face-to-face relationships? Do certain problems lend themselves better to virtual counseling? Do certain forms of intervention work better during a virtual encounter? What virtual counseling procedures should clients expect to protect privacy and confidentiality? What additional liabilities and ethical standards should apply to virtual counseling? If the client lives in another state or country, which ethical standards apply—the standards of the practitioner's or client's jurisdiction? Currently, local standards are not consistent. For example, if a client reveals the inclination to commit a crime, in some states, the practitioner is ethically bound to report this information to law enforcement officials, and in others, the practitioner is ethically bound to respect the client's privacy.

Appropriate Use

A similar issue involves setting policies that encourage the appropriate use of IT. Promoting IT to solve one problem may create another problem. For example, an experiment in the United Kingdom on teleshopping for the elderly found that teleshopping benefited shut-ins, but also lead to the closing of small neighborhood stores that provided a social network for the mobile elderly. These neighborhood stores were unable to adopt technology quickly enough to compete with large stores for government programs. Another possible illustration is that virtual offices may ease car pollution, yet cause social isolation. Human service professionals need to help policymakers and the public see the unintended consequences of IT, plan services for problems that IT produces, and involve the IT industry in solving the problems that IT creates; for example, many IT companies have a well-paid core staff and a worldwide low-paid workforce of temporaries. IT companies should work with human service professionals to understand the social consequences of temporary employment, for example, insecurity, divorce, depression, inability to afford health care, and structural poverty. Since human service professionals see people's problems first, they must forewarn others to allow time for preventative action.

ADMINISTRATIVE PRACTICE

Future Scenario

The Family Behavioral Health Cooperative (FBHC) had been struggling in many ways since its formation three years ago. Many of the problems were due to rapid change, a lack of trust, and failure to unite around FBHC management initiatives. FBHC was founded due to agencies' fears of not being able to survive independently. FBHC IT staff were struggling to provide the hardware, software, connectivity, training, and support that member agencies needed. FBHC also had management problems. The cooperative was weak because agencies feared centralized control. Staff, many of whom had a human service background rather than business experience, lacked needed skills. Many had a bureaucratic mentality stemming from their experiences in government. They did not think in terms of virtual teams, teleconferences, continuous quality improvement, and IT support. Some staff felt it was acceptable to temporarily go into debt in order to provide essential client services. Lack of resources was the common thread running through FBHC's problems. FBHC had difficulty attracting qualified IT professionals because its salaries were too low. The cooperative was even struggling to pay its bills. Yet FBHC's board rejected help from a private vendor willing to provide cash for a controlling management interest. Although the cooperative was formed so that agencies could use technology to gain control over their future, the future was more uncertain than ever.

Trends, Impacts, and Requisite Skills

Most agencies are still in the process of networking all staff into a basic agencywide information system integrated with the Internet. Agencies with basic applications in place are struggling to maintain them while looking for off-the-shelf IT that can improve services to clients on a cost-benefit basis. IT is allowing big changes in human services management, such as privatization of services and the use of corporate management techniques. These changes are also spurred on by increasing service complexity, increasing demand for accountability, and increasing need for better services given shrinking resources. This same phenomenon happened to many industries. For example, fast-food chains employing redesigned work patterns supported by IT, put many low-tech "Mom and Pop" restaurants out of business. Also, health care has had a "bumpy ride" getting managed care systems working.

Many smaller agencies are finding that their survival depends on technology and management skills they do not possess. Interagency agreements and cooperative networks allow agencies to compete, but often agencies cannot make the radical changes as quickly as needed. IT encourages mergers and privatization because it enables large companies to invest the resources to design applications that can provide more efficient services. However, large companies have found that their management systems and principles have not been as successful in many human services as they anticipated.

Another IT trend involves user interaction with information. Tradition-ally, IT outputs were printed reports. Interaction was only possible with the help of an IT specialist capable of manipulating the database. In the future, users will be expected to interact with the information they are using. Consequently, the value of information changes from that inherent in the information to that associated with its interactive capabilities. The field "client address" can illustrate the power of interactive information. When client address is just a text field in a database or on printed reports, it has limited value. However, geographic information systems allow users to display clients' addresses as points on community maps along with other information such as income level or location of social service agen-cies. Thus, client address becomes a more meaningful piece of informa-tion. Another example is a treatment plan that can become interactively integrated with agency and community information. When agency staff can actually view how treatment plans vary, such as by diagnosis type or client address, then the value of the treatment plan greatly increases. A final example is a program evaluation. When managers can see how se-lected changes in staffing patterns or workload impact program outcomes, then the program evaluation becomes an important day-to-day decision-making tool within the agency.

Another trend concerns the evolving concept of an organization. IT changes the concept of an organization as a physical office to one of people communicating to achieve goals no matter where the people are located or with what technologies they communicate. Virtual teams and on-line meetings are new office tools. Although the virtual office may be new, for some human service professionals, it is a return to the older ways of doing things, as the following quote illustrates:

> Social work began from the home, and the first social workers did not have an office to go to. Many old child care officers and NSPCC workers will be able to recall from personal experience the filing cabi-net and telephone in the front room. Change the cabinet for a computer and the picture is much the same. (Glastonbury, 1985, p. 137)

Managers must increasingly address the changes resulting from IT. For example, IT allows hierarchical organizations to flatten into network-style organizations. Flattened hierarchies allow citizens, clients, practitioners, and managers to be more connected and to function more as equals. IT usually makes tasks more procedural. Workers must follow new regimens and specify that tasks are done. Another impact is job rearrangement. As IT improves information flow, many routine clerical and midlevel man-agement tasks decrease. Better information flow allows midlevel management positions to be reduced because decisions can be more easily made lower in the organization and monitored higher in the organization.

The previous discussion suggests that the following management tasks and skills are needed:

- Integrating IT with the overall organization, that is, strategic planning
- Building a responsive IT infrastructure that can design and maintain applications, manage IT contracts, improve data integrity and quality, integrate new technologies, justify IT investment, train and support users, and ensure security, confidentiality, and privacy
- Knowledge engineering to develop the complex applications that synthesize legacy data and generate organization intelligence
- Working cooperatively to develop common definitions and processes, synthesize information from diverse perspectives, and maintain a qualified and motivated IT workforce given shortages and scarce resources
- Applying change management skills to help people address their fear of change, develop new work habits, and implement and manage collaborative support systems

Issues

Chapter 12 presented application development, maintenance, and enhancement issues, such as determining:

- the balance between IT distribution and integration;
- the balance between end-user development and support versus central management and control;
- whether to use a formal top-down or a more bottom-up or prototyping development approach;
- how to balance the control various stakeholders have in IT development efforts;
- how much development should be done in-house and how much should be contracted out to vendors and consultants;
- how much of the IT budget to spend to protect security and privacy and to reduce computer-related strain and stress, for example, glare reduction screens, special lighting, specifically designed furniture, and frequent work breaks;
- how to price applications when enhancement and update costs are difficult to project;
- how to balance the need for application update and enhancement against new application development; and

- how to ensure that clients, who are exceptions, do not become "victims of the system," given that applications are often used for repetitive and well-structured tasks and exceptions are costly to program into an application.

Table 13.1 presents what business executives of 500 organizations consider to be the ten most critical issues for IT management. The results indicate that the important issues involve developing an IT infrastructure that is responsive to the organization as a whole and to end users.

TABLE 13.1. The Ten Most Critical IT Issues for Management

Rank	Issue	Mean	Std. Dev.
1	Building a responsive IT infrastructure	7.19	1.65
2	Planning and managing communications networks	6.93	1.92
3	Establishing effective disaster recovery capabilities	6.88	1.66
4	Making effective use of the data resource	6.87	1.63
5	Facilitating organizational learning	6.86	1.59
6	Facilitating and managing end-user IT	6.80	1.73
7	Educating senior management in relation to IT	6.73	1.96
8	Using IT for competitive advantage	6.72	1.91
9	Improving IT strategic planning	6.72	1.91
10	Aligning the IT organization within the enterprise	6.71	2.04

Source: Adapted from "Information Systems Management: An Australasian View of Key Issues—1996" by G. Pervan, 1997, *Australian Journal of Information Systems, 5*(1), September. http://www.cbs.curtin.edu.au/is/staff/Pervan/ajis96ki.html.

Appropriate Use Issues

One of management's major tasks is to see that IT applications are used to their full potential and not misused. The issues concern ways to overcome skepticism and resistance without creating the resentment that results in data inaccuracy and sabotage. Agency procedures can often contain incentives and rewards for use, but incentives could be viewed as manipulation. However, disincentives can be easily removed without this charge being leveled. Application use for new employees can be made a condition of employment and stressed during orientation.

Although lack of use is a problem, inappropriate use also occurs. Examples are computer dependency, overbelief in IT-generated information, and blaming the computer. As one employee stated, "Blaming the office computer works so well that I bought a home computer."

A final issue of use/misuse concerns information overload. To cite a personal example, during an agency board meeting following the change from manually processing budget reports to detailed computer printouts, many issues were raised. Board members shuffled through their packet of printouts looking futilely for familiar and understandable information. Although more and better information was available, decisions were based on less information than before.

COMMUNITY PRACTICE

Future Scenario

"It's 2 a.m. and we need more bandwidth and processing power to get this video finished," said Mary. Aaron quickly voicemailed back, "What about tapping into 'The European People's Grid' to find several experts and servers that can help us." "Great idea," said Mary. "I forgot that at this late hour, it is morning in Europe. I've had good luck getting help from some of the cooperative movements there." "I'll get right on it," said Aaron. "We can't let the company off the hook now. We've got to voicemail all managers in their corporate headquarters and attach the video that shows that the workers who clean their fancy offices cannot feed their families without a second job. However, that new fire wall has put a kink in our plans. We need people on the inside who can videomail our information and cover their tracks. Or, better yet, someone in Europe may have experience with their new fire wall and know how to get around it." "Good thinking," said Mary. "If we can get our message past their fire wall, they will know that we have the capacity to videomail their financial backers, business partners, neighborhoods, and customers. Then they'll have to take our demands seriously."

Trends, Impacts, and Requisite Skills

Computer technology has been important for community practice, primarily for managing mailing lists, agency information systems, word processing, and volunteer management. IT has not been used extensively due to cost, time, and the expertise needed to develop and maintain applications. However, the Internet offers community practitioners tremendous capacity for almost all their activities. The major limitation concerns the lack of access of community groups to the Internet.

For advocacy efforts, the Internet provides the opportunity to quickly communicate with large groups of like-minded people. Interested community members can quickly educate themselves using linked Web sites, advocate via on-line petitions and e-mail campaigns, and stage Internet-awareness-raising events such as virtual conferences and protests.

For community planning, virtual meetings can involve a more diverse group in the planning process. Face-to-face meetings can be video broadcast in real time or posted for future reference. The Internet also provides an easy way to conduct surveys and opinion polls and post draft plans for community input.

For coalition building, the Internet offers a way to develop common agency databases, share information about client needs, hold virtual case conferences, and connect staff on issues. IT might be able to remedy many of the problematic tasks associated with services integration, for example, record sharing.

For neighborhood building, the Internet offers a way to link people within neighborhoods. Virtual neighborhoods can easily distribute local news, share problems, work together on issues, and provide many other traditional neighborhood supports. Virtual neighborhoods may help regain the physical neighborhoods that existed when neighbors had no backyard fences, worked the same hours, attended the same social institutions, and required only one breadwinner and job per family. Virtual neighborhoods offer practitioners a way to again use the neighborhood as part of an intervention strategy. For example, news and progress on illness and injury can be automatically posted on a neighborhood home page as it is recorded in the hospital record. Local crime information can be made available by neighborhood with links on possible solutions. The adage "think globally and act locally" is advice with a new meaning as neighborhoods enter the information age.

To accomplish these tasks, community practitioners need the following skills:

- Develop indicators and measures of community well-being and need
- Run virtual meetings and work in virtual groups
- Use IT technology for building Web sites, Web publishing, on-line communications, conducting on-line surveys, and connecting independent databases
- Use GIS technology and monitor Internet tools for applications relevant to community practice

Issues

One of the biggest issues involving IT and community practice is access to IT, which was discussed previously. This issue should lessen as the television, computer, telephone, and Internet merge into a low-cost household appliance. Another issue is that the global society will exacerbate some urban problems and create new ones. Communities are good barometers of social problems. Having community indicators of well-being and potential problems will allow these negative impacts to be identified early and studied and interventions to be implemented monitored. The whole monitoring process can be disseminated to those impacted locally and to the global communities of concern.

Another issue involves the tendency for businesses and governments to optimize their own situations by shifting costs and problems to communities. Two business examples are moving profitable plants overseas and abandoning contaminated property. Governments, always trying to do more with less, use IT to push many of the tasks they previously performed onto the citizen, for example, searching for planning and zoning information or providing information about city services. Although some shifting is appropriate, communities must be organized and aware of this practice to combat shifts that are destructive to their citizens.

INDIVIDUAL, FAMILY, AND GROUP PRACTITIONERS

Future Scenario

"I have looked at the week's worth of data from your body monitors · and see some trends we need to discuss," said family therapist Rachelle. "But before we begin the discussion, could you all move into the same room so you have face-to-face contact. I am old-fashioned about my preference for families being in the same room, as I have found that televideo sessions with everyone in separate rooms is less effective. Thanks for moving," said Rachelle. "Now, let's first look at the points on the graph where the skin monitors and the brain monitors indicate very high and very low stress and examine what was happening within the family at those times. The very lowest stress was when the family was talking about the day's activities and petting the cats. I would like the family to increase low-stress activities, so I have requested the video system to pull together all the low-stress video into one file that we can watch later. The highest stress was recorded when Hanna asked about dating. Let me play the dating discussion along with the stress charts. Let's take it sentence by sentence to find what statements caused excess stress and what could have been said differently to avoid stress."

Trends, Impacts, and Requisite Skills

Practitioners have always felt limited by information systems that reduce the complexities of people's problems into numbers and text. IT now offers the capacity to provide supportive information in forms such as pictures, graphics, video, and audio. For example, if digitized client pictures were stored in a database, child protective services workers could highlight a bruise on the picture of the child they were assessing and search the database for pictures of children with similar bruises to determine what might have happened to this child.

New forms of intervention and supervision are being developed, for example, on-line two-way video for therapy, monitoring, supervision, or conferencing. Self-help and homebound intervention offers an attractive option. IT may provide new intervention techniques; for example, virtual reality has been used successfully to treat fear of heights (Lamson, 1995). Virtual reality could also be a training tool. For example, parents could be transported inside a virtual room with a virtual child that exhibited problematic behaviors. A virtual parenting specialist could guide and mentor as the parents improved their parenting skills.*

Human service delivery is often viewed as the practitioner imparting information to the client. However, the Internet gives practitioners and clients equal access to information. Clients will be able to examine the research and resources available and familiarize themselves with appropriate interventions before deciding to seek help. Clients can approach intervention more informed about their problem than the practitioner. Consequently, intervention will become more of a partnership, with the practitioner providing the wisdom of experience and the client providing the specifics of the problem and details on client progress. The following client e-mail from the NetPsy discussion forum illustrates this point:

> I virtually prescribe my own psych meds because the knowledge I have gained from the Internet and books/articles has outstripped my psychiatrist's. I've also diagnosed myself with mild hypothyroidism when my own doctor missed it. For me, the Internet has been a godsend. Today, with managed care, it seems that some doctors do not pursue problems that do not have straightforward answers, and do not necessarily know the up-to-the-minute information in their field. Unfortunately, I've learned that if patients do know a signifi-

cant amount about their own problem, it can cause an antagonistic reaction from the doctor. I do think the Internet provides an excellent way for patients to educate themselves, with the caveat that they teach themselves how to separate the valid research from the junk. (1998)

With on-line intervention, clients can evaluate and select a practitioner anywhere in the world. Specializations will proliferate as clients have more choice. To reduce costs, many routine intervention steps can be automated, for example, assessment and outcome monitoring. Monitoring of client progress will assume a more important role and treatment will be more focused and short term. The more common intervention tasks will be supported by evidence from codified information, procedures based in practice wisdom, and research.

The present state of IT-mediated intervention reflects an attempt to adapt IT to existing practices. However, technology allows new intervention formats and features. An example is a "smart" assessment that requests key facts from the client or practitioner, uses these facts to determine what test is appropriate, and "custom builds" the test with questions pertinent to the client's situation. Also, IT assessments can contain text, images, movies, and use a variety of input devices, including speech recognition. Although new assessments are not difficult to program, validation takes years, and acceptance by practitioners takes even longer.

Given these changes, practitioners need skills in the following areas:

- Understanding research and theories on human service problems and their solutions to increase practice skill levels
- Analyzing and synthesizing information into knowledge, that is, applying expertise and experience to information
- Educating clients to be wise consumers of human services
- Locating information on the Internet and evaluating its quality
- Understanding the IT of their specialty

Issues

Liability

Liability is important since the human services involve inexact and controversial decision making. IT applications can support practitioners' judgment in situations involving considerable risk, for example, suicide intervention. However, who is liable if an application fails—the vendor, knowledge engineer, programmer, researcher, or the practitioner/user? Liability issues will eventually be resolved in the courts; however, most organizations cannot afford the court costs and emotional strain caused by a precedent-setting lawsuit.

The other side of the coin is equally problematic. Consider a situation in which an IT application recommends that a child be withdrawn from the home, yet the child maltreatment worker uses professional judgment and leaves the child in the home. If the child is subsequently abused or killed, what is the liability of the agency and worker? Are the recommendations of the IT application confidential, or can they be used against the worker in a malpractice suit? Liability issues can result in agencies not implementing useful IT applications, as illustrated in the following quote:

> The legal implications of relying on computer reports for the prediction of behavior potentially dangerous to self or others are unclear, even when the automated reports are appropriately considered as just one source of data among many. This, combined with the fact that predictions of such behaviors are constrained by low base rates of occurrences, has resulted in a reluctance to use computer-generated predictions. It was concern with these issues that led to the suppression of predictive statements involving suicidal and assaultive behavior from output of the Missouri Actuarial Report System. (Hammer and Hile, 1985, p. 10)

Liability is an important consideration for application developers. One questionable area concerns the clinical backup necessary for self-help therapeutic IT applications. For example, what if the use of a self-help application evokes emotional responses that require help beyond the application's capabilities? One can envision a depressed person working with a self-help antidepressant program becoming suicidal. How should clinical backup be handled by this application? Must monitoring for adverse client reactions be part of the application? Must the developer include screening in the application and try to lock out users who potentially may have adverse reactions? Are the responsibilities and liabilities of the developer similar to those of the author of a self-help book? Or, since an IT application can be more encompassing than a book, does the developer incur responsibility and liability similar to that of the manufacturer of a new drug?

Quality and Regulation

Another issue has to do with traditional professional associations' and government agencies' ability to license practitioners and regulate quality in a global marketplace. Which regulations apply when the practitioner and client live in different countries—the regulations where the practitioner resides or the regulations where the client resides? Who has the responsibility and authority to protect clients from fraudulent practice?

Another aspect of quality concerns who can use human services IT. For example, should psychological assessments be restricted to human service professionals, psychologists, or to those trained to interpret them? Should a lawyer defending an alleged child abuser have access to an IT application that profiles an abuser, if the profile is used in the perpetrator's defense? Should the marketplace decide these issues, or should professional associations and governments become involved? These questions will become increasingly important as more human service expertise is stored and marketed using IT.

Skepticism versus Protectionistic Resistance

Another practitioner issue is the need to distinguish a healthy skepticism of IT from protectionistic resistance. For example, although practitioners are often hesitant about direct client-IT interaction, clients are not. This bias against technology needs to be replaced by research that validates practitioners' claims against technology.

Practitioners' biases manifest in subtle ways. For example, those selecting training CAI applications often require stringent evaluations to show that the CAI is effective. However, they rarely require the same evaluation results from face-to-face training. Some suggest that demands on IT applications are greater than on traditional methods, as the following quote suggests:

> One pertinent theme is that issues of reliability, time and cost efficiency, and client comfort have been far better dealt with than issues of validity. . . . Agreement among clinicians as to definitions, diagnoses, and interpretations is so low, . . . that computer-generated assessments could be at serious odds with those of the clinician and still be accurate—or indeed, could be seriously flawed. (Hudson, Nurius, and Reisman, 1988, p. 59)

Some feel that we should compare the validity and reliability of software to that of professional judgment:

> How many practicing clinicians have validated their clinical judgments when they interpret tests and make assessments? In fact, while many computer assessment procedures may be worthless, it may be

much easier to identify them as having little value than more traditional assessment practices. Because the parameters of a program are clearly outlined (in fact a computer program is totally specified), computer software, theoretically, can be easily demonstrated to be invalid. . . . However, it is true that a computer program will allow an incorrect procedure to be disseminated more easily than ever before. (Erdman and Foster, 1988, p. 78)

Mundt and colleagues (1998) point out that the bias in most research is that clinician assessments are assumed to be accurate and that observed differences with alternative methods reflect error and should be eliminated. However, since clients have been found to reveal more sensitive information to a computer than to a human, the computer assessments may reflect the client's "true" psychological state and clinician assessments can be assumed to contain error. If this is the case, work to bring computer assessments in line with clinical assessments may worsen the assessment instrument.

Given client acceptance and the scarcity of low-cost human services, practitioners must determine which tasks IT can do best and which tasks humans can do best. Table 13.2 presents a beginning analysis.

EDUCATORS

Future Scenario

"Has everyone played an hour as the planner, neighborhood activist, business leader, and elected official in the neighborhood simulation?" asked Professor Ling of the twenty students videoed onto his large computer display. All nodded. "Any reactions?" asked Professor Ling. "I must have done something wrong," said Jesse. "I felt more powerful as the community activist than in any other role, yet community activists aren't very powerful, are they?" "Project that portion of the video from the game where you experienced those feelings so we can observe what was happening," said Professor Ling. All watched as Jesse projected the video. "I think the issue, education equality, allows Jesse to feel powerful," said Tina. "If you have an issue where justice is on your side, you feel powerful. We felt very powerful at times during the struggle against apartheid here in South Africa during the 1980s." "Jesse chose an easy issue," said Mike. "I chose neighborhood destructive zoning as my issue and had the opposite feeling. I also couldn't get anyone to join me at the on-line zoning

TABLE 13.2. IT Performance versus Human Performance

Areas in which human beings tend to perform better

- Understanding nonverbal communication (reading between the lines)
- Divergent, synergistic, integrative and holistic thinking (making leaps in logic and associating diverse ideas)
- Exploring theoretical constructs
- Spontaneously expressing emotions such as joy, fright, sorrow, reverence, hate, and love
- Recreation, creativity, originality, humor, riddles, and paradoxes
- Understanding complex phenomena such as values, virtues, and vices (faith, hope, charity, hate, envy, jealousy)
- Expressing moods and emotions (happiness, anger, pain, loss)
- Developing interpersonal relationships and feelings (trust and love)
- Expressing caring, affection, mutual support, exchange of sentiment, warmth, empathy, concern
- Introspection and self-reflection
- Understanding dreams, daydreams, fantasies, and nightmares

Areas in which IT applications tend to perform better

- Meticulously searching through large volumes of information
- Using logic consistently
- Performing repetitive tasks consistently
- Being patient and always available, especially in soliciting information
- Performing calculations and data analysis
- Thoroughness
- Unbiased interaction
- Quickly executing millions of lines of instructions
- Performing tedious tasks without distraction
- Continuous performance without breaks or rest
- Consistently using pleasant dialogue
- Optimizing on a goal if information can be codified
- Pattern recognition
- Planning strategy, such as in playing chess

meeting. I felt alone and ignored." "Good, we have identified *the issue* as another variable to add to the model of organizing effectiveness that we are building," said Professor Ling. "Let's begin to define that variable and its measures and provide weights to use when we test the model on a real situation."

Trends, Impacts, and Requisite Skills

Learning will continue to change dramatically over the next ten to twenty years for several reasons. First, education costs continue to rise much faster than the cost of living. Second, learning has become a lifelong process; college students are older, part-time, and employed rather than full-time and directly out of high school. Third, education technology is rapidly changing. We now have multimedia training programs, virtual libraries, and video-conferencing over the Internet. This new technology supports education that is learner centered, collaborative, interactive, and location independent. Fourth, business practices are being used to restructure the education arena similar to how managed care restructured health care practices. IT allows universities to deliver courses without the expense of a physical building and with minimum administrative overhead. Corporate virtual universities will compete for students and offer more flexible ways to receive education and degrees.

Evaluation and achievement will be based on the student's portfolio rather than on grades and courses passed. Students will shop for courses and make selections based on specialized degree programs, portfolio needs, cost, and time available. Courses could contain students from all over the world. Faculty will need to specialize to attract students world-wide.

Interactive simulations of the human service delivery system may allow students to practice as policymakers, managers, or practitioners. Upon entering the simulation, students could interact with a simulated client and receive video monitoring and remedial demonstrations in the therapeutic modality chosen. The situation may become similar to today's airline pilots who must periodically practice in a simulator to remain licensed, with human service practitioners required to complete simulated counseling to be certified.

The skills needed by educators will change. Instructors will need very specialized expertise that is well integrated with other specialties. They will also need skills in designing courses that are largely self-delivered and assessments that give depth to students' needs and achievements as expressed in their portfolios. The teacher will be expert, leader, guide, facilitator, curriculum designer, monitor, coordinator, synthesizer, researcher, innovator, and evaluator. These changes mean that "the sage on the stage" turns into "a guide at the side."

Issues

Corporate Thinking versus Education

As education meshes with corporate thinking, instructors must find ways to protect the search for new knowledge and academic freedom from bottom-line thinking. A similar phenomenon occurred in managed care, requiring health care professionals to weigh profitability and organization survival against quality of patient care. Deprofessionalization, or the use of temporary and less expensive workers to perform tasks traditionally left to instructors, will also challenge the quality of education. Schools will struggle with what practice content should be delivered via computer-assisted learning, interactive distance learning, or face-to-face instruction.

Professional Credentials and Socialization

A quality issue stems from the difficulty of measuring the competencies that a beginning practitioner should possess. Complicating this issue is that human service education involves professional socialization. It may be difficult to instill and measure professional values and ethics under the new models of learning, especially if students are not required to be on campus, but receive most of their education through CAI and distance education. Alumni loyalty will be harder to develop as students select courses worldwide. New events or living situations may need to be developed to replace the college life that was once a common part of a young person's socialization.

Integrating IT into the Curriculum

Another issue concerns how to integrate IT into professional education. The issue becomes clearer if IT applications are viewed as tools similar to assessments and statistical tests. However, IT applications may be more basic than other tools because information is fundamental to practice and IT fundamentally alters information and its use.

Curriculum issues can be analyzed by examining the phases involved in integrating technology into the curriculum (see Table 13.3). These phases are based in history and on a natural progression of IT use. In each phase, educators must address the issues of IT integration philosophy, what to teach, who teaches, how to teach, and what resources are needed. Throughout all phases, questions need to be answered, such as those in Table 13.4.

Regardless of how IT is taught, the focus should be on information use, not technology. As Grebel and Steyaert (1993) point out, "we do not put the question how to introduce IT in the curriculum but how to stimulate teachers to think more explicitly about information and offer IT as a means to handle it." Teachers not only have the burden of knowing the IT in their specialty but also of giving students the capacity to understand the appropriate and ethical use of the technology.

TABLE 13.3. Phases of Integrating Technology into the Curriculum

	1. Research Course Phase
Philosophy	IT is primarily a research tool.
What taught	IT taught in research course with an IT elective established to tie IT to practice areas. IT elective varies substantially depending on instructor.
Who teaches	Research faculty, faculty who have an interest in IT, and adjuncts.
How taught	Traditional lecture with IT as homework or a small part of one or several classes.
Resources	Research courses complete computer assignments using university facilities.
	2. Lab Phase
Philosophy	Lab is used primarily for statistics courses. Some complain that lab content is not relevant for practice.
What taught	Same as above. Students like lab and use it for word processing. Student papers better formatted than faculty handouts.
Who teaches	Research faculty, faculty who have an interest in IT, and adjuncts.
How taught	Statistical software and a few human service practice applications installed in the lab.
Resources	A departmental computer lab is developed and a research instructor manages the lab. Lab takes substantial teaching and maintenance resources.
	3. Computer Literacy Phase
Philosophy	All faculty accept that IT is here to stay. Student computer literacy becomes a goal.
What taught	Literacy defined in terms of generic (word processing, spreadsheet, etc.) and statistical packages. Students want IT more relevant to practice.
Who teaches	Faculty interested in IT, adjuncts skilled in IT, and graduate research assistants.
How taught	Generic software taught in lab. Students can test out all, or part, of a course.
Resources	Faculty lab manager burns out and does not get tenure. Faculty manager replaced by technician or graduate research assistant.

	4. Internet Phase
Philosophy	Internet seen as an important IT application for human service practice. IT course begins to move away from IT research roots.
What taught	Specialty courses add content on resource sites and tools, such as e-mail, listservs, and chat rooms. IT finally seen as much more than a research tool. Student papers improve in quality/timeliness.
Who teaches	Faculty interested in IT, adjuncts skilled in IT, and graduate research assistants.
How taught	Web sites and listservs are used in practice courses.
Resources	Lab connected to Internet. Misuse of lab and Internet addressed only after disasters occur.
	5. Integration Phase
Philosophy	Faculty see computers and Internet as equally important tools for all human service practice.
What taught	Some IT (computer and Internet literacy) content taught in all courses.
Who teaches	Faculty who teach courses integrate computers and Internet into their courses.
How taught	Faculty use the Internet as a teaching tool, e.g., Web page, listservs, and chat room designed for course, e-mail of papers, etc.
Resources	Lab turned into student work area. Most students have PC and Internet access. Access is an issue for only a few students. Faculty training needs not well met.
	6. Pervasive phase
Philosophy	Entering students are IT literate and have access to PCs and the Internet. No technology access problems exist. Faculty teach about the IT of their specialty, e.g., technology-mediated therapy.
What taught	How to find, evaluate, and use appropriate IT to support human service practice at all levels.
Who teaches	Regular faculty.
How taught	Technology integrated into curriculum as another basic tool and concept for all practice areas.
Resources	Faculty given adequate training and IT resources to keep current.

Note: Phases may overlap or be skipped entirely.

TABLE 13.4. Questions and Possible Answers Regarding IT and Education

Question: How do you obtain support from faculty and administrators who may not be technologically literate?

Possible answers:

- Changes involving technology should be treated as any other organizational change.
- Use behavioral principles; make sure supportive behavior is rewarded.
- Do not try to force change.
- Make change enjoyable (play and reward with e-mail, chat, listservs).
- Use representative committees to involve those who will have to change.
- Involve students, as they are typically advocates of technology.
- Involve agencies that understand the need for technology.

Question: Should the school invest the time and energy in developing a computer lab?

Possible answers:

- To teach about IT, hardware, software, and Internet access should be readily available in a student work area or teaching lab.
- Although hardware is always welcome, it should not be the driving force behind the introduction of IT into the curriculum. A lab is artificial in that it requires the user to bring a problem into the lab for solution. The more natural situation is to bring IT to the problem. The proliferation of low-cost handheld computers with modems may make the computer lab obsolete.
- An IT lab poses many problems that can turn a good teacher into a burned-out technician. Among these problems are the following:
  1. Getting the hardware to work, especially a local area network
  2. Keeping the hardware running
  3. Continually finding money to purchase the software of one's profession
  4. Ensuring that hardware and software are not vandalized or stolen
  5. Keeping the lab from being quickly outdated
  6. Preventing viruses, pirated software, and inappropriate use of the Internet

Question: How do you prevent inappropriate, unethical, and illegal uses of technology while encouraging exploration and experimentation?

Possible answers:

- Be proactive rather than reactive; that is, have expectations written and clearly posted.
- Have a committee representative of practice areas and student groups prepared to handle problems.
- Get wider support and be consistent with the larger university.
- Include expectations in new student and faculty orientation.

Question: How do you define IT literacy and competency?

Possible answers:

- Replace the concept of computer literacy with that of professional IT competency, which involves knowing how to locate and use the IT of one's profession effectively and ethically.
- Focus on the informational components rather than on hardware and software. IT-competent professionals may know little about the computer or networking, but a lot about how to find and appropriately use human service applications according to professional standards and ethics.

RESEARCHERS AND IT DEVELOPERS

Future Scenario

"Load up the new VR (virtual reality) data analysis program," said Professor Tanya to Bill, her research assistant. Tanya had used 30,000 client records to develop a model for predicting client outcome. However, the model's accuracy was low. "It's loaded," said Bill. "Can you believe it took 100GB on the DVD?" "Put it into statistical VR viewing mode and lets put on the goggles to examine the models," said Tanya. Walking into the model, they saw balloon-shaped variables connected by arrows with formulas written on each balloon. "Let's move this variable over here," said Tanya as she grabbed *client positiveness about treatment* and moved it from the client characteristic to the treatment characteristic balloon set. The arrows connecting the balloons were quickly rearranged along with formulas and balloon sizes. "Did we violate any assumptions? We increased our predictive power by .3 percent," stated Tanya. "Can we import the data into neural network mode?" asked Bill. Tanya aimed the remote control and clicked the necessary buttons. The neural network mode was like being inside a human brain with neurons and synapses pulsing as the model was running. "The *client positiveness about treatment* node fired five times during that last prediction," said Tanya. "This VR model seems much better. I will come back when I have several hours to see if I can eliminate unexplained patterns." "See you later," said Bill as he floated upward for a bird's-eye view of several new model structures that he had not used before.

Trends, Impacts, and Requisite Skills

Researchers are often distinguished from IT developers. Researchers use IT primarily for statistical data analysis and communication and information dissemination. Developers use IT primarily for databases, information systems, and networking. However, research and IT development are now merging, as researchers develop practice models and advisory systems using new techniques, such as neural networks and performance support systems. Application delivery will increasingly be through the Internet.

Future knowledge and skills needed include knowledge development, measurement, model building, validation, evaluation, and outcomes research.

Issues

Information Quality

An important issue for researchers and other practitioners is how to determine the quality of information that is available via software applications and the Internet. With everyone an information producer, evaluating the quality of information becomes more important. Currently, the source of the information and the integrity of the publisher often determine quality. However, IT applications can be very complex, and their underlying rationales are less easily observed and more difficult to understand. Consequently, practitioners have a tougher time judging application quality. In the past, the marketing of substandard IT applications could be prohibited. Today, the Internet allows an application to be distributed worldwide, regardless of quality, via a server in a country where regulations are lax.

Professional associations could issue a "seal of approval" for IT applications. The fees for reviewing applications could be used to support reliability and validation efforts. In the medical field, the U.S. Food and Drug administration is using the Medical Devices Act of 1976 to review diagnostic and treatment expert systems. However, the FDA review process is time-consuming and expensive.

How to Stimulate and Reward IT Development and Research

Another issue concerns ways to encourage and fund IT development and research. One problem has been that instructors with IT interests are put in charge of the computer lab or given the tasks of developing school administrative systems. Little time is left for professional IT development and research. Another problem is that academics are rewarded more for using old technology (writing articles and books) than for using new technology (developing IT applications). Developing Web sites or software is more complex than writing books and articles, and IT applications require continued development and enhancements. The only incentive to develop applications is to sell them. However, market-driven research and development stimulates popular and profitable IT rather than basic research and long-term development. Until incentive issues are resolved, the lack of IT research and software development may continue.

CLIENTS

Future Scenario

"I found our discussion on manic depression in our last session very useful," said Kim to her therapist. "In fact, I spent the last several days on the Mental Health Network doing homework. I think your diagnosis is absolutely right. In the manic depressive support group, I found people from all over the world with exactly the same problems I have. From what they told me, I think I should be using the bio fluids monitoring application each evening. Version 4 of that application is just out, but I am sure you are aware of that. Also, I concluded that your statement about the biological cause of my problems is a little off base. I found research from Finland that seems to contradict what you said." "Hold on, Kim," said Dr. Roth. "Can I say something here. I welcome your homework and will expect a lot more in the few weeks we have available. But, we need to organize your research and discuss your findings item by item . . . "

Trends, Impacts, and Requisite Skills

With networking, citizens and clients will be more connected to the human service delivery system. Clients will be able to prepare themselves by browsing local, national, and international resource sites. Those with specialized problems will be able to examine the latest statistics and research on their problem. They will also be able to examine the resources available and familiarize themselves with appropriate interventions before deciding which intervention to choose. Many will try the less expensive and more convenient mutual support groups or self-help applications. Those choosing an on-line intervention requiring human interaction will be able to select their practitioner from anywhere in the world. Some see this as turning the treatment pyramid upside down because the first contact between the patient and the service delivery system is not with a specialist, but with the family and community (Ferguson, 1996).

Along with the increased information and freedom of service choice will come the advertising of services, questionable claims of success, and a "buyers beware" attitude from some providers. Clients will need skills in finding resources and evaluating what interventions are the most appropriate, cost-effective, and high quality.

Issues

Ownership of Information

In an information society, information is an owned resource. IT requires us to take a new look at record ownership; for example, clients can carry all their records on a small "smart" card. Different jurisdictions currently have very different rules about who owns the patient file. In some states, a client's record belongs to the client, while in other states, the record belongs to the practitioner or agency. In some states, official client information, such as symptoms, diagnoses, and treatment plans, is distinguished from practitioners' "personal" notes, such as associations and speculation. Clients have the right to see the official record, not the personal notes.

The provider as information owner is the most common practice at present. Clients surrender information to agencies in order to receive services. However, many issues remain. What rights do clients have to the information? Can clients who are in a state of distress be adequately advised of ownership and its implications? If they refuse to release ownership of information to the agency, can the agency refuse services? What limits does the agency have on the types of information it can collect? For example, must clients provide information not directly related to the services they requested? Some computerized social histories collect a variety of generic information thought "potentially" useful. Must the client provide all information requested? Can the agency give away client-related information or sell the information without the client's consent? If the information is sold, for example, for research purposes, must the client benefit from its sale? Does deidentifying the information change the rights each party has to the information? Does deidentification change the nature of transmitting client information outside the agency? How can clients understand what the release of information means when dealing with a multiagency consortium that agrees to "share" records? How long can the agency retain client information? How secure must this retention be? Must records be destroyed when they are not immediately necessary to help the client? Or, can client records be retained for research and trend analysis or "just in case" the client ever returns? If the information is used detrimentally at one point, is the agency or practitioner responsible? For example, being falsely labeled as a "cheat" or "deviant" when databases are merged may result in psychological stress. Is the practitioner or agency that originally collected the information liable for this psychological stress?

Client ownership also provokes many questions. If clients have ownership, what rights do the other parties have to the information? Can the clients pass on "use rights" to client advocates or to a malpractice lawyer? It may be necessary to divide the client records into parts, with each having different levels of ownership and use. Records may have some parts that can be deidentified and shared for research and trend analysis. Other parts could remain with the agency and be automatically destroyed when the intervention is concluded. Still other parts, such as personal notes of the practitioner, may not be officially part of a client record, although they may reside in the practitioner's personal files. Undoubtedly, this issue of ownership of client data is one that will be settled in the courts. Until then, guidelines are sorely lacking.

Privacy, Matching, Profiling, and Front-End Verification

Privacy concerns the right to keep information one considers personal concealed from others. The practices of matching, profiling, and front-end verification illustrate the importance of privacy and information ownership.

Matching is the electronic comparison of two or more sets of records using one or more common fields with the intent of finding records common or uncommon to more than one set. All Western countries are using, and often mandating, matching to an increasing degree to detect fraud, waste, and abuse. Privacy and confidentiality issues associated with matching concern inaccurate data, verification of hit matches, what is done with the records found during a match, and the absence of guidelines and oversight for handling problems such as prenotification of those involved. Most people are more supportive of matching to eliminate fraud if they think it will involve someone else. Of the public, 87 percent think that matching welfare recipient names to find fraud is justifiable, but only 68 percent think that matching income tax records with credit card records to find tax fraud is justifiable (U.S. Congress, Office of Technology Assessment, 1986).

Profiling is the electronic searching of one or more sets of records with the intent of finding indicators and characteristics thought to be associated with certain behavioral patterns. Examples are the profiling of airplane hijackers, drug traffickers, violent offenders, underreporting taxpayers, and child abusers. Profiling results in people being labeled and treated differently before they have done anything to warrant such actions. The major issues related to profiling include the accuracy of the data used to profile, the accuracy of the profile model, and what is done with the profile.

Front-end verification is a process of checking the accuracy and completeness of a record before the record is used. It is accomplished by electronically checking the record against similar information in one or more record sets. Front-end verification is different from matching in that it is done on an individual basis before services are received. Thus, it is used to prevent and deter rather than to detect and punish. Front-end verification is often used with applications for services, such as government benefits, unemployment benefits, credit, or loans. A major issue with front-end verification concerns the creation of a national identification system, as explained in the following quote:

> The use of front-end verification is creating a de facto national database covering nearly all Americans. The technological requisites for front-end verification lead to the establishment of individual databases for verification purposes and to the connection of these databases through on-line telecommunication linkages. This de facto national database is not a centralized database in the sense that all information is contained in one mainframe computer housed in one building. Instead, the present dominant approach is to create a "virtual" central databank by electronically (via direct on-line linkages or exchange of computer tapes) combining and comparing information from several separate, usually remote, record systems. If enough separate record systems are queried, the result can be the creation of a de facto electronic dossier on specific individuals. (U.S. Congress, Office of Technology Assessment, 1986, p. 68)

A more recent government report examined privacy on the Internet and found that approximately 85 percent of Web sites covertly collected personal information about the user, and 89 percent of children's sites surveyed collected personal information from children. Only 14 percent of sites collecting information provided notification, and only about 2 percent had a comprehensive privacy policy (Landesberg et al., 1998). Table 13.5 is a beginning attempt to formulate a set of principles and practices on security, privacy, and confidentiality. The United States can learn much from the Europeans, who have more thoughtful procedures on security, privacy, and confidentiality due to the adverse use of records during two world wars.

TABLE 13.5. Principles and Practices Regarding Security, Privacy, and Confidentiality

These principles outline an agency's responsibility for information collection, storage, retention, and use for voluntary clients. The overriding principle is that individuals should be able to control information about themselves. Even though one agrees with these principles, they are often difficult to put into practice. For example, in situations such as family therapy, multiple stakeholders exist and the security, privacy, and confidentiality of one may conflict with that of the others. Also difficult is "third party" information that is not verifiable by the agency.

Principles

- People should have easy access to an agency's information practices.

- People should be informed if identifiable information about them is to be forwarded outside an agency. They should be told to whom it will be transferred and what safeguards will be used to ensure the confidentiality of the information provided.

- People should know who potentially will own information about them before the information is collected. If they do not agree with the agency's ownership policies, they should still have service options available.

- People have a right to view information retained on them by agencies unless they or their guardians waive that right. The exception to this is information provided for which law guarantees anonymity, for example, in child abuse reports.

- Information should not be used by the agency in ways that those from whom it was collected would disapprove.

- People should know the length of time information about them will be retained and how it will be kept up to date.

- All information retained should be considered essential to the purpose for which the data were collected; that is, unnecessary data should not be collected.

- It should be clear from agency records what data are considered demonstrable or provable facts, direct observations, collectively agreed-upon judgments (for example, case conference conclusions), and opinions.

Practices Stemming from the Principles

- An agency should have written security, privacy, and confidentiality guidelines and procedures. These guidelines and procedures should be part of employee training and new employee orientation. They should be readily available to the public, for example, posted in the waiting room and on the Web site.

- One person in the agency should be responsible and have the resources necessary for ensuring the level of security, privacy, and confidentiality deemed appropriate by the agency and for ensuring that the agency is in compliance with all security, privacy, and confidentiality laws.

- Employees should know to whom, and in what circumstances, they can reveal agency data.

- All agency applications containing client data should be reevaluated yearly to ensure the current security procedures are adequate and followed.

- Verification techniques should exist to ensure information entered in any information system is accurate.

- Agencies should have a clear written process for clients and practitioners to question and appeal existing security, privacy, and confidentiality policies and procedures. Representatives of all parties concerned should be involved in any questioning or appeal.

- All client-identifiable information transferred via telecommunications must be transmitted securely, for example, encrypted before transfer.

- All information stored on an agency computer belongs to the agency unless otherwise stated, for example, all files and e-mail.

CONCLUSION

Although many of the past visions about IT and the human services have yet to be realized, dramatic changes have taken place in the past thirty years. It is becoming increasingly clear that we can replace the view of professional practice as primarily an art based on experience and intuition with one of practice as primarily a science based on processed information. However, we currently do not understand complex human service decision making well enough to develop supporting IT applications. So, before human services IT can expand beyond the management and routine practice levels, much research and prototyping are needed to rediscover and codify the information base of practice.

New concepts are needed; for example, no accepted term exists for describing information-based practice. Terms such as empirical practice, informed practice, and evidence-based practice are used, but the concepts are not well developed. New theories are needed; for example, one review of direct patient computer interviewing found the need for a new theory of stylistic presentation of information and user response. The researchers, who have a long history in working with automated interviewing, concluded:

> To design a computer interview, one must directly confront and understand the assumptions, content, and structure of the problem at hand. . . . The need to define all of these components concretely immediately reveals gaps and flaws in existing procedures. (Erdman, Klein, and Greist, 1985, p. 772)

The challenge to practitioners is to be educated IT consumers who can help design and use IT to solve client problems.

We have ended the era of stand-alone computers and entered the era of networked IT. The infrastructure of the information age is being built. Human service professionals must assume responsibility for the human service components of this infrastructure. These include developing applications for information and referral, interviewing, assessments, treatment, service monitoring, client tracking, service evaluation, client self-help, and education. Practitioners must not only address the use of IT within the human services but also monitor the impact of IT to prevent problems, such as privacy violations and dehumanizing systems. Many human services were born as a result of the miseries caused by the industrial revolution. We must monitor the information revolution so that the destructive forces of IT on our clients are minimized.

Historians say that the tallest buildings at our city centers during different time periods reflect that era's values. For example, churches dominated medieval city centers. Courthouses and state capitals dominated cities of the seventeenth and eighteenth centuries. Twentieth-century cities are dominated by tall glass banks and financial institutions. As we move into the information age, search engines and large information repositories are the largest structures being built in the center of cyberspace. We, in the human services, must erect structures that reflect our human values before the landscape is full. The information structures that exemplify how we should treat our global neighbors in need are waiting to be built.

REVIEW AND DISCUSSION QUESTIONS

1. Will machines ever be able to think?
2. For what purposes could you use a smart personal service robot?
3. Can the qualities that constitute friendship and intimacy be programmed into an IT application?
4. Can parts of "human nature" be replicated by an IT application? If so, which parts?
5. What does the following statement mean? The question of whether computers think is as relevant as the question of whether submarines swim.
6. To optimize the use of IT, must we eliminate humans from the system because they are the parts of the system that are unpredictable, unreliable, and liable to break down?
7. If human beings can be replaced by technology, should they be?

Glossary

access time: The time lapse from when a call for data is made until the data are delivered. Access time is frequently measured in milliseconds, or one-thousandth of a second.

algorithm: A well-defined procedure that leads to the solution of a problem.

alphanumeric: Composed of both numbers and alphabetic characters.

analog: Physical representation of data that bears an exact relationship to the data, for example, the etchings in the grooves of a phonograph record have a physical relationship to the stored sound. Contrast to digital.

application software: A computer program designed to solve a specific user/agency problem, for example, a payroll or client tracking system. Contrast to system software.

array: An arrangement of data into one or more dimensions. A two-dimensional array is a table with columns and rows.

artificial intelligence: A field of study concerned with developing computer systems with capabilities normally associated with human intelligence, for example, reasoning, learning, and self-improvement.

ASCII: Stands for American Standard Code for Information Interchange, which is a standard code for representing information to a computer.

assembly language: A programming language that uses symbols and abbreviations to represent the functions to be performed. Assembly language is a higher-level language than machine language and a lower-level language than general purpose languages such as COBOL, FORTRAN, and BASIC.

assistive technology: Any item, piece of equipment, or product system that is used to increase, maintain, or improve functional capabilities of individuals with disabilities.

asynchronous: A mode of data transmission that involves breaking the stream of data into single bytes so that each character or byte of data is sent sequentially, preceded by a start bit and followed by a stop bit. Asynchronous is also used to describe a form of interaction over a computer network whereby participants join the interaction at any time, such as a bulletin board system. Contrast to synchronous.

attribute: A property or characteristic of one or more entities, for example, color, weight, and gender can be attributes of the "person" entity.

authoring systems: Application software that allows users, such as educators and trainers, to construct modular sessions, such as lesson plans and tests.

bandwidth: Data transmission capacity during a specified time.

BASIC: Stands for Beginners' All-purpose Symbolic Instruction Code, which is a relatively easy-to-use, high-level language.

batch processing: A data processing mode in which similar transactions are held and then processed all at one time. Contrast with interactive processing.

baud rate: A term often used as a measure of character movement over a line, although it formally refers to the number of times per second the line signal can change states.

binary number system: A number system whereby two numerals, such as 0 and 1, are combined to represent all possible numbers.

bit: Short for binary digit, the smallest unit consisting of either a 1 or 0 for storing data in a computer, represented by two possible states, such as 0/1 or on/off.

bits per second (BPS): A measure of data transmission speed.

board: A thin, flat, plastic or fiberglass rectangle on which electronic components are soldered. Often called a computer card, a board is plugged into the bus structure of a computer. The main board is called the motherboard, and boards that plug into the motherboard are called daughter boards.

Boolean: Derived from the algebraic processes formulated by George Boole, for example, Boolean logic involving an operation that connects two states, as when one state is greater than or less than another state.

boot or bootstrap: Techniques, devices, or processes for loading the initial programs into a computer.

boundary: That which separates one system from another or a system from its environment.

BPS: Stands for Bits Per Second, which is a measure of data transmission speed.

branching: A programming technique whereby the program goes in one of several directions based on a comparison.

browser: A software application that allows users to view the World Wide Web.

browsing: The unplanned, casual search of the World Wide Web for anything of interest.

buffer: A computer component that accumulates data at one time or speed and releases it at another time or speed.

bugs: Errors in computer programs. The process of finding and correcting errors is called debugging.

bus: A pathway used to transmit signals, for example, a group of parallel wires on a computer board. Most computer components are connected through a bus structure.

byte: A group of bits that forms a storage location. Typically, a byte consists of 8 bits. One 8 1/2 x 11-inch double-spaced typed sheet of paper contains approximately 2,000 bytes (2K) of data (one K = 1,024 bytes).

CAI: See computer-aided or computer-assisted instruction.

case-based reasoning (CBR): The process of developing solutions to unsolved problems based on preexisting solutions of a similar nature.

cathode ray tube (CRT): A television-screen-like device used by a computer for displaying information.

central processing unit (CPU): The hardware components of a computer system that process data. The CPU, often called the brain of the computer, consists of an arithmetic/logic unit, a control unit, and high-speed memory.

character: Any alphabetic letter, number, or other symbol that, when used alone or in combination, has an agreed-upon meaning.

chat: Real-time text communication between users of a computer network.

client/server: A networking architecture whereby each device either runs applications (clients) or handles communications and resources between components (server). Contrast to peer-to-peer.

closed system: A system that does not interact with its environment. Contrast to open system.

coaxial cable: Cable consists of a center wire coated with insulation and surrounded by a grounded braided wire shield to minimize electrical and radio interference that is used to connect electronic devices.

COBOL: Stands for COmmon Business Oriented Language, a widely used, business-oriented, high-level programming language.

coding: The process of writing instructions for a computer.

compiled language: A type of computer language in which all program code is translated into machine code in one process and the compiled program is then executed. Contrast with interpreted language.

compiler: A computer program used to convert programs written in a high-level language into machine language for execution by the computer.

computer: A combination of electronic and mechanical devices that is capable of storing, retrieving, and performing arithmetic and logical operations on data according to programmed instructions.

computer-aided or computer-assisted instruction (CAI): The term used to describe the use of computing systems for education and training.

computer conference: Mechanisms that allow networked computer users to discuss topics using e-mail or other messaging systems. Other terms for computer conferences include newsgroups, listservs, lists, threaded discussion forums, or bulletin board systems (BBSs).

computing: The process of collecting, storing, manipulating, communicating, and using information in electronic form.

concerted suboptimization: An environment in which all subsystems interact according to an overall design (synergistically) to optimize the total system rather than optimizing the subsystems. An equivalent term in sports is teamwork.

confidentiality: A level of secrecy assumed or formally agreed upon by two parties with the expectation that shared information will be used consistent with the agreement.

conversational: Real-time interaction with the computer whereby the computer responds to user queries in the user's language and logic.

courseware: Application software used for instruction and training.

CRT: Stands for cathode ray tube, the basic display component of one type of computer display.

cursor: The movable highlighted or blinking symbol on a cathode ray tube (CRT) that shows the user where activity is taking place.

cybernetics: The study of feedback and control.

cyberspace: The nonphysical place where people meet and share resources using computer telecommunications.

data: Characters (letters, numbers, or symbols) that represent facts or events.

data administration: The group of tasks and processes associated with the management of data in an organization.

database: A collection of interrelated data, usually in the form of records and files, in which the data are stored and managed to minimize redundancy and to allow for easy manipulation and access. An agency database usually consists of fiscal, client, service, and staff files.

database management system (DBMS): Software that manages the collection, storage, manipulation, retrieval, integrity, and security of data in a database.

data dictionary: A database management module that contains a listing of information, such as the description, attributes, relationships, and users of the data items in a database.

data element: A label given one small unit or piece of information, for example, client date of birth. Synonymous with data item or field.

data entry: The process of preparing data in machine-readable form or entering data directly into a computer system.

data flow diagram: A tool for graphically illustrating the operations being performed on data, the procedures being followed, and the interconnection of the operations that are performed as data flow through a system.

data item: A label given one small unit or piece of information, for example, client's last name. Synonymous with data element or field.

data links: Communication lines or channels over which data are transmitted.

data processing: The automated activities in which programmed routines are used to store, manipulate, and retrieve data.

data warehouse: The collection of all the information in an agency and the systems to store, combine, and use that information.

DDP: See distributed data processing.

debug: The process of locating and correcting problems and inconsistencies in computer software so the desired outcomes from the computer can be achieved without error.

decision support system (DSS): An interactive computer-based system designed to assist users in making complex decisions. A DSS usually answers "what if"-type questions.

decision table: A structure for graphically presenting rules that specifies the conditions that must be tested and the actions that may be taken in a decision situation. A decision table is often called a logic table.

decision tree: A graphic presentation in which the "tree trunk" represents a decision problem and the branches represent alternative solution paths.

desktop publishing: Application software that provides users with the capabilities to typeset, lay-out, and print text, figures, and pictures at near print shop quality.

digital: The physical representation of data by a sequence of binary codes or bits. Contrast with analog.

disk operating system (DOS): See operating system.

display: An electronic component of a system that presents the information to the user.

distributed data processing: A computing environment in which the processing function is shared by two or more geographically separate computers connected by communications hardware and software.

documentation: Descriptive information, in written or electronic form, that explains the development, use, operation, and maintenance of a computer or application.

domain: A sphere or area of expertise, specialty, or practice, for example, medicine, psychiatry, child welfare.

dot matrix: A printing technology whereby letters and characters are formed using many small dots.

download: The moving of files from a remote computer to a local computer. Contrast with upload.

DSS: See decision support system.

dumb terminal: A terminal with no processing capabilities. Dumb terminals are often connected to mini- or mainframe computers.

duplex: A data transmission mode whereby data can be sent in both directions. In half duplex mode, data can be transmitted in only one direction at a time. In full duplex mode, data can be transmitted in both directions at the same time. Contrast with simplex.

emoticon: One or more ASCII characters used in electronic communications to express emotion, for example, : -) are ASCII characters that represent a sideways happy face to express humor or joy.

encryption: The process of coding or scrambling data so confidentiality can be controlled.

end user: The person or device that uses a computer system to solve a problem. Contrast with system developer or system manager. End user computing focuses computing power and responsibility at the end user level.

entity: An object or event about which information is stored in a database, for example, a person, a train, or a departure time.

entropy: A state of system decay, disorder, and uncertainty.

environment: The larger unit in which a system resides.

EPROM: Stands for Electrically Programmable Read Only Memory, which is memory embedded in computer chips that can be reprogrammed with special equipment.

ergonomics: The science of adapting technology to the comfort and health needs of users

expertise: Possession of high-level knowledge or experience in a specific domain, resulting in the ability to rapidly and consistently reach successful decisions to significant problems.

expert system: A computer software program that exhibits high performance in making decisions in complex domains, such as those relegated to human experts.

expert system shell: A set of expert system development tools that can be used to develop expert systems in any domain.

facsimile: An exact image or copy, often reproduced from one medium to another, such as printing on paper from electronic text in computer memory.

fiber optic cable: Cable comprised of many strands of hair-thin glass threads that allow electronic signals to be transmitted over light passing through the strands.

field: A label given to one small unit or piece of information, for example, client's last name. Synonymous with data element or data item.

file: A grouping of similarly constructed records treated as a unit, for example, a client file.

fire wall: A software or a software/hardware barrier between two networks on a computer.

firmware: Software that is inseparably combined with hardware, for example, software manufactured onto a ROM silicon chip.

flame e-mail: Hostile or insulting e-mail designed to arouse the emotions of the recipient to elicit an angry response.

floppy disk: A thin, flexible, plastic disk coated with ferrous oxide on which data can be magnetically stored.

flowchart: A diagram that uses standardized symbols to graphically express the sequence, logic, and interrelationship between the steps of a problem solution.

FORTRAN: A high-level programming language designed for scientific, mathematical, and engineering tasks.

freeware: Software for which the developers allow free distribution.

front-end verification: The process of checking the accuracy and completeness of a record before the record is used. One common front-end verification technique is electronically checking data against similar data in one or more databases.

FTP: Stands for File Transfer Protocol, which is a basic standard for uploading and downloading files.

geographic information systems (GIS): Information systems that work with geographic and spatial information and allow for spatial data analysis and mapping.

handshaking: A preliminary exchange of protocol information between computers that verifies that communication has been established and data transfer can proceed.

hard or rigid disk: A thin, rigid disk coated with ferrous oxide on which data can be stored.

hardware: The physical components of a computer system, such as the computer, printer, and storage devices. Contrast with software.

help desk: A technical support approach whereby support personnel and operations are placed in one office of an organization.

heuristics: Personal knowledge and inexact reasoning that enables a person to make educated guesses, to recognize promising approaches to problems, and to work with error-laden or incomplete information, for example, rules of thumb or judgments.

hexadecimal (hex): A numbering system in base 16 in which 16 different characters (1 through 9 and A through F) are used.

high-level language: A type of programming language that is similar to human language in structure and content and that requires very little knowledge of computer-specific codes on the part of the programmer, for example, Java or C. Contrast to low-level languages.

homeostasis: The steady or equilibrium state of a system.

home page: The initial page that users see when visiting an Internet site.

human services: Services that facilitate daily living by enabling individuals, families, and other primary groups to function, to cope, and to contribute.

hypermedia: An electronic publishing form that allows users to easily browse a document by jumping from one subject to another nonsequentially. Hypermedia publishing may include text (hypertext), data, graphics, pictures, video, and other media.

ill-structured decision: A decision that cannot be completely specified in advance.

inference: The process of deriving conclusions from facts and knowledge.

inference system: The component of an expert system that contains the reasoning, search, and control procedures that extract decisions from a knowledge base.

information: Data that have been aggregated or processed according to some model or rules to enhance their meaning, for example, the zip code number 76019-0129.

information system: A system of people, procedures, and equipment for collecting, manipulating, retrieving, and reporting data.

information technology (IT): The overarching term to describe technologies that process information, most often in electronic form.

input: Initial resources or start-up components that are acted on by a system.

input/process/output: The sequence of events that occurs within a system.

integer: Any positive or negative whole number or zero.

integrated software: Software applications that use similar commands and file structure, thus allowing the user to move back and forth between applications and functions, for example, a software package containing word processing, spreadsheet, and database applications.

interactive processing: A mode of communication with the computer whereby processing takes place as the transactions occur. The interaction with a computer is said to be interactive if each user's command elicits a response from the computer.

interface: The area of contact or overlap between systems.

Internet: A worldwide network of computer networks.

Internet service provider: An organization that provides computers with access to the Internet.

Internet site: A set of linked Internet pages that are typically developed and maintained by one individual or organization.

intranet: An organizational network that uses Internet tools and communication protocols.

joystick: An input device that uses a lever to control an electronic device. A joystick is frequently used in computer games.

keyboard: A component containing typewriter and/or calculator-style keys that is used for transmitting characters, letters, or numbers to a computer.

keypad: A calculator style device for transmitting numbers or other symbols.

knowledge: Descriptions and relationships derived from experts, literature, and research.

knowledge base: A large repository of structured knowledge.

knowledge-based systems: Computer programs that rely on the complex manipulation of large stores of task-specific knowledge. One type of knowledge-based system is an expert system.

knowledge engineering: The field of study concerned with the acquisition, representation, and manipulation of knowledge in computer systems.

LAN: See local area network.

language: A collection of symbols, characters, words, and their syntax for communicating with a computer, for example, BASIC or C.

lexicon: A list of vocabulary and rules for using the vocabulary. A lexicon is a tool used in software systems, such as in natural language processing.

light pen: An input device that is shaped like a small tubular flashlight and that either emits light to the CRT or senses light from the CRT.

LISP: A LISt Processing programming language suited for artificial intelligence applications.

listserv: A computer program that manages the distribution of e-mail to a list of subscribers.

local area network (LAN): Software and cabling that allows many computers in the same geographic area to be linked together to operate as a single integrated computing system.

low-level language: A computer language that is closely tied to the circuitry of the computer on which it runs. Contrast to high-level language.

machine language: Instructions for a computer in binary form that can be executed without translation by the electronic circuitry of the computer.

mainframe computer: A large computer, for example, one designed to support the information processing needs of a large organization, such as a statewide department.

management information system: An information system that primarily serves the needs of managers, typically those at the middle levels of an organization.

mass storage: An electronic medium for holding large amounts of information. The CPU cannot directly access data in mass storage without first loading the data into main memory.

matching: The electronic comparison of two or more sets of records using one or more common fields with the intent of finding records common or uncommon to more than one set.

medium: A means of information storage or transmission.

memory: The component of a computer system that magnetically or electronically stores data and information. Memory is often called storage; however, storage usually implies a longer retention than memory.

menu driven: A type of end user interface whereby the user responds to a list of options presented on the computer display.

microcomputer: A small computer, for example, one designed to support the information processing needs of a small agency of 1 to 25 employees.

microprocessor: The small semiconductor chip that is the core of the central processing unit.

microwave: An electromagnetic wave above 890 megahertz in the radio frequency spectrum on which data can be transmitted.

minicomputer: A medium-sized computer, for example, one designed to support the information processing needs of a medium-sized human service agency of approximately 25 to 200 staff.

MIS: See management information system.

model: A simplified replication of reality that aids understanding and/or prediction.

modem: A device for transmitting data across telephone lines.

motherboard: The main circuitry receptacle or frame in a computer. The motherboard may contain computer components and have receptacles for plugging in boards with additional components, such as a modem or sound card.

mouse: An input device in the shape of a small object with one or more buttons. When the mouse is moved on any surface, it moves a cursor on the computer display.

multiprocessing: A processing mode in which two or more processors in the same location are simultaneously executing instructions, as when several small computers are connected to a large mainframe.

multitasking: A processing mode in which the computer concurrently processes many different jobs in very small time slices.

nanosecond: One-billionth of a second.

natural language processing: A type of artificial intelligence application concerned with computerizing the capacity to comprehend human languages.

network: A collection of computers and peripherals that acts as one computer system.

Neural Network: A data analysis application, based on the workings of the human brain, that can be used to classify, model, estimate, and predict after learning patterns from many past examples.

node: One computer in a computer network.

number: A mathematical concept that denotes how many items or entities are in a group. Numbers can be manipulated mathematically.

numeral: A symbol or group of symbols that represents a quantity or number, for example, the Roman numeral III.

off-line: A processing environment in which no direct connection exists to provide input directly to the computer. Contrast to on-line.

on-line: A mode of communication with a computer whereby the user is in direct contact with the central processing unit and the computer responds rapidly to user commands. Contrast to off-line.

open system: Any system that interacts with its environment.

operating system: The integrated group of computer programs that supervise the operations of a computer, for example, the Windows operating system.

output: The elements leaving a process, or the act of expelling processed inputs.

parallel processing: A processing environment in which two or more processors share all other computing resources while simultaneously handling separate parts of the same problem.

parity: An error detection method used during data transmission. Parity refers to whether the total number of ON bits in 1 byte of transferred data results in an even or an odd number.

PASCAL: A high-level programming language designed to make it easy to write programs using structured programming techniques.

peer-to-peer: A network architecture whereby each node has equivalent capabilities and responsibilities. Contrast to client/server.

performance support systems (PSS): An IT application that improves performance by providing content-specific training when it is needed and in the format it is needed.

peripheral: Any hardware component separate from, yet tied to, the CPU of the computer, for example, keyboard, video displays, storage disks, or printers.

personal computer (PC): A computer designed for the data processing needs of one individual.

plotter: An output peripheral that enables the computer to control a pen moving over a piece of paper to draw graphs and pictures.

port: A connection for joining computer components together, for example, two computers connected by wires running from the port of one computer to the port of the other. A serial port allows data to be transmitted across a single wire one bit at a time. A parallel port allows multiple bits of information to be transferred simultaneously across multiple wires.

practitioner: In this text, a human service professional at the line level of an organization, for example, a psychiatrist, social worker, psychologist, rehabilitation worker, or counselor. Professional practitioners are more skilled and more highly paid than paraprofessionals and other line workers who receive expertise through on-the-job training, such as is typically the case with psychiatric attendants or food stamp eligibility workers.

printer: A device that forms characters and symbols on paper using ink or a related substance.

privacy: An individual's right to keep his or her possessions, including personal information, away from others.

process: The activity that converts input elements into output elements. The terms conversion, transformation, or throughput are often synonymous with process.

profiling: The electronic searching of one or more sets of records with the intent of finding specified pieces of information that can act as indicators thought to be associated with certain behavior patterns, for example, searching records for tax evaders.

program: A set of sequenced instructions that directs a computer to perform a series of tasks to solve a problem.

programmable decision: A decision for which detailed procedures can be established, for example, service eligibility determination. Contrast to a nonprogrammable decision, or decisions for which it is difficult to develop detailed procedures, for example, whether one should get married.

programmer: The person who translates a problem solution into instructions capable of being processed by a computer.

programming: The process of developing computer programs.

PROM: Stands for Programmable Read Only Memory, which is memory available on computer chips that has been programmed onto that chip. Once programmed, the information on a PROM chip cannot be changed.

protocol: A predetermined specification for the format and timing of messages between communicating devices.

pseudocode: The English-like statements that a programmer writes to explain how a program operates.

public domain software: Nonproprietary software that is available free. See also shareware.

query language: A high-level language that allows users to request information from a database using English-like commands.

RAM: See random access memory.

random access: A nonsequenced access method by which a device can directly find any location on the storage medium.

random access memory : Memory that allows the access device to go directly to the information requested without sequentially passing through the preceding information.

read-only memory: Memory resident on a computer chip that can only be read. A computer can only read the information programmed on the ROM device during manufacturing; it cannot write information to ROM memory.

real time: A processing environment in which the time between the user entering a command and the computer responding is short enough to affect subsequent use.

reasoning: One type of general underlying process for reaching conclusions to problems, for example, deductive, inductive, or probabilistic reasoning.

record: A set of related data items, for example, a client record.

register: A temporary, very high-speed information storage location inside the CPU.

ROM: See read-only memory.

routines: Previously validated series of instructions that are used by programmers.

RS-232: An Electronic Industrial Association standard interface for connecting computers with other computers and peripherals.

satisficing: Finding an acceptable alternative. Contrast with maximizing or examining all alternatives until the best solution is reached.

schema: A map of the overall logical structure of a database or problem solution.

security: The protection of hardware, software, and data by locks, doors, and other barriers such as passwords.

sequential access: An access method whereby a device must proceed sequentially from one location to another to get to the desired location. Contrast with random access.

shareware: Software freely distributed for examination for which users pay a fee only if the program is consistently used.

simplex: A data transmission mode whereby data can be sent in only one direction, such as from a computer to a printer. Contrast with duplex.

simulation: An experimental method that attempts to replicate a system or activity without building or operating the actual system or performing the activity.

software: Programs, procedures, and documentation, that is, the instructions that guide the computations and other operations of the computer. Contrast with hardware.

software package: A group of generalized programs that perform related functions, for example, a statistical software package.

spam: Unsolicited and unwanted electronic messages or junk e-mail, usually sent to a large number of recipients to advertise a product.

spreadsheet: A software package that allows users to manipulate and examine information in tabular format, that is, in columns and rows.

steering committee: A representative committee that guides the overall policy/planning, development, and implementation of a computing application.

storage: The component of a computer system that magnetically or electronically accepts, retains, and makes accessible data and information. See also memory.

streaming audio or video: A technology that allows audio or video files to play while they are downloading rather than after the audio or video file has completed downloading.

structured programming: A set of programming techniques for helping chain together the programming operations that solve a problem.

subroutines: Routines that are not stored as separate entities but are set apart in a computer program.

subsystem: A subset of a system. For example, a client tracking system and an accounting system are subsystems of a total agency information system.

The distinction between a system and subsystem depends on the level of observations.

supercomputer: A very large computer capable of rapidly processing large volumes of data for complex tasks, such as guiding rocket systems.

synchronous: A mode of data transmission that involves breaking the stream of data into similar sized groups of bytes. Synchronous is also used to describe a form of interaction over a computer network whereby participants are online in constant connection, as in a chat room. Contrast with asynchronous.

synergy: A state in which the total system output is greater than the sum of the outputs of all subsystems.

system: An assembly or set of related elements connected in an organized way and exhibiting certain properties, for example, goal directedness, hierarchy, and synergy.

system analysis: The process of analyzing a system to make recommendations on its improvement.

system software: Software that controls the internal operations of the computer and aids programming. Contrast with application programs.

TCP/IP: Stands for Transmission Control Protocol/Internet Protocol, which is the protocol used by all computers connected to the Internet.

technology: A set of prescribed actions that is grounded in scientific knowledge, practice, expertise, or ideology and that directs activities, decisions, and choices toward goal achievement.

telecommunications: Data transmission across telephone lines.

telehealth: The use of communications technologies to provide and support health care when the provider and patient are in different physical locations.

terminal: A device that allows the user to receive information from, and input information to, a computer. A hard copy terminal is similar to a typewriter. A video display terminal uses a keyboard along with a CRT.

throughput: The activity or action component of a system. Contrast to input and output.

time-sharing: The multiple use of a computing system whereby applications are divided, sequenced, and processed so rapidly and efficiently that users feel that they have the computer's total capabilities.

transaction: One data processing operation.

uniform resource locator (URL): The address that identifies a node on the Internet.

upload: The transfer of files from a local computer to a remote computer. Contrast to download.

user friendly: Software that is easy to use and tolerant of the user's interaction styles and mistakes.

utility program: A computer program that performs functions commonly used in computer programming, for example, alphabetic character sorting.

video display terminal (VDT): A computer terminal that contains a CRT for displaying data.

virtual: Something that exists in electronic form but not in the physical world, for example, the virtual world of a video game.

virtual memory: A combination of main memory and mass storage that allows users to assume they are working with a large amount of main memory.

virtual reality: A three-dimensional perception of reality accomplished by having each eye view separate computer screens using a helmet, goggles, or similar device.

viruses: Computer or communication programs designed to annoy recipients or damage their hardware and software.

volatility: The capacity of a storage medium to lose data when the electrical power is turned off. For example, RAM chips are volatile in that they lose all their memory when the electricity powering them is turned off.

well-structured decision: A decision that is completely specified in advance, such as deciding the amount of a payroll check. Contrast to ill-structured.

wide area network (WAN): A computer network that connects geographically separated nodes, e.g., a main office with a remote office.

windowing: A technique of dividing the computer display into areas called windows. Users can work in one window while monitoring the processes occurring in other windows.

word processing: The use of information technology to perform many of the standard functions of a typist, for example, collecting, storing, managing, editing, proofreading, formatting, and printing text.

World Wide Web (WWW or Web): A subset of Internet nodes that allows access using a standard graphical protocol.

References

Introduction

Forester, T. (1985). *The Information Technology Revolution.* Cambridge, MA: MIT Press, p. xiii.

Chapter 2: Basic Concepts and Historical Content

Boorstin, D.J. (1984). The lost arts of memory. *The Wilson Quarterly, 8*(2), 107.

Chapter 3: Professional Generic Applications and Assistive Technology

Armoni, A. (1998). Use of neural networks in medical diagnosis. *M.D. Computing, 15* (March/April), 100-101.

Bleckman, E., Rabin, C., and McEnroe, M. (1986). Family communication and problem solving with board games and computer games. In C. Shaefer and S. Reid (Eds.), *Game Play—Therapeutic Use of Childhood Games* (pp. 129-145). New York: John Wiley.

Bolen, R.M. (1997). Macromedia authorware. *Computers in Human Services, 14*(1), 77-84.

Bordnick, P.S. (1997). Methodologist's toolchest. *Computers in Human Services, 14*(1), 71-75.

Brodzinski, J.D., Crable, E.A., and Scherer, R.F. (1994). Using artificial intelligence to model juvenile recidivism patterns. *Computers in Human Services 10*(4), 1-18.

Burda, P.C., Starkey, T.W., Dominguez, F., and Vera, V. (1994). Computer-assisted cognitive rehabilitation of chronic psychiatric inpatients. *Computers in Human Behavior, 10*(3), 359-368.

Butterfield, B. (1998). Review of the Software Dragon Naturally Speaking Deluxe. *Computers in Human Services, 15*(1), 79-84.

Cahill, J.M. (1994). Health works: Interactive AIDS education videogames. *Computers in Human Services, 11*(1/2), 159-176.

Clarke, B. and Schoech, D.J. (1984). A computer-assisted therapeutic game for adolescents: Initial development and comments. In M. D. Schwartz (Ed.), *Using Computers in Clinical Practice: Psychotherapy and Mental Health Applications* (pp. 335-353). Binghamton, NY: The Haworth Press, Inc.

Cowan, L. (1994). OPTEXT adventure system-software development in practice—A case history. *Computers in Human Services, 11*(1/2), 101-108.

Cox, G.B. Erickson, D. Armstrong, H., and Harrison P. (1989). The AGENCY computer simulation model. *Computers in Human Services, 5*(3/4), 13-27.

Desrochers, M. (1996). Basic behavioral principles and their applications to people with developmental disabilities. *Computers in Human Services, 13*(1), 73-80.

Drisko, J.W. (1998). Using qualitative data analysis software. *Computers in Human Services, 15*(1), 1-19.

Engen, H.B., Finken, L.J., Luschei, N.S., and Kenny, D. (1994). Counseling simulations: an interactive videodisc approach. *Computers in Human Services, 11*(3/4), 283-298.

Falk, D.R., Shepard, M.F., Campbell, J.A., and Maypole, D.E. (1992). Current and potential applications of interactive videodiscs in social work education. *Journal of Teaching in Social Work, 6*(1), 117-136.

Flynn, J.P. (1985). MERGE: Computer simulations of social policy process. *Computers in Human Services, 1*(2), 33-52.

Flynn, J. (1987). Simulating policy processes through electronic mail. *Computers in Human Services, 2*(1/2), 13-26.

Gray, J.I. (1994). Problem solving in case management (PIC): A computer assisted instruction simulation. *Computers in Human Services, 11*(3/4), 269-282.

Gray, S.H. (1994). Poverty policy software and a violent crime database as training tools. *Computers in Human Services, 11*(3/4), 245-260.

Grebel, H. and Steyaert, J. (1993). *Social Informatics, Education on the Vocational Use of Information Technology in Schools of Social Work* (report to the Commission of the European Union). Eindhoven, Netherlands: Causa.

Hoefer, R. (1996). SimHealth. *Computers in Human Services, 13*(2), 87-90.

Hoefer, R.A., Hoefer, R., and Tobias, R.A. (1994). Geographic information systems and human services. *Journal of Community Practice, 1*(3), 113-128.

Janzen, F.V. and Lewis, R.E. (1990). Spreadsheet analysis in human services. *Computers in Human Services, 6*(1/2/3), 51-67.

Lambert, M.E. (1989). Using computer simulations in behavior therapy training. *Computers in Human Services, 5*(3/4), 1-12.

Lambert, M.E., Hedlund, J.L., and Vieweg, B.W. (1990). Computer simulations in mental health education: Current status. *Computers in Human Services, 7*(3/4), 211-229.

Lambert, M.E. and Vieweg, B.W. (1990). Computer enhanced education in the human services: An annotated bibliography. *Computers in Human Services, 7*(3/4), 355-402.

Luse, F.D. (1980). Use of computer simulation in social welfare management. *Administration in Social Work, 4*(3), 13-22.

MacFadden, R.J. (1991). Computer-assisted instruction in sexual abuse assessment: Does it work? *Computer Use in Social Services Network Newsletter, 11*(4), 12-15.

MacFadden, R. (1997). Keisha: A case simulation in failure to thrive. *Computers in Human Services, 14*(2), 51-56.

McLaughlin, F.S. and Pickhardt, R.S. (1979). *Quantitative Techniques for Management Decisions*. Boston, MA: Houghton Mifflin.

Oakley, C. (1994). SMACK: A computer driven game for at-risk teens. *Computers in Human Services, 11*(1/2), 97-99.

Olevitch, B.A. and Hagan, B.J. (1994). "How to get out and stay out: The story of Cathy": An interactive videodisc simulation for psychiatric wellness education. *Computers in Human Services, 11*(1/2), 177-188.

Patterson, D.A., Pullen, L., Evers, E., Champlin, D.L., and Ralson, R. (1997). An experimental evaluation of HyperCDTX: Multimedia substance abuse treatment education software. *Computers in Human Services, 14*(1), 21-38.

Poulin, J.E. and Walter, C.A. (1990). Interviewing skills and computer assisted instruction: BSW student perceptions. *Computers in Human Services, 7*(3/4), 179-197.

Quinn, P. (1996). HyperResearch. *Computers in Human Services, 13*(3), 91-95.

Rafferty, J. (1998). Changing to learn: Learning to change. *Computers in Human Services, 15*(2/3/4), 159-169.

Renz-Beaulaurier, R. (1997). The Mental Health Studios [CD-ROM]. *Computers in Human Services, 14*(1), 85-89.

Resnick, H. (1988). "Busted," A computerized therapeutic game, description, development and preliminary evaluation. In B. Gastonbury, W. LaMendola, and S. Toole (Eds.), *Information Technology and the Human Services* (pp. 103-116). Chichester, England: John Wiley and Sons.

Resnick, H. (1998). Paraphrase II: A listening skills training program for human service students. *Computers in Human Services, 15*(2/3/4), 89-96.

Resnick, H. and Sherer, M. (1994). Computerized games in the human services: A review. *Computers in Human Services, 11*(1/2), 17-28.

Ryan, E.B. (1994). Memory for Goblins: A computer game for assessing and training working memory skill. *Computers in Human Services, 11*(1/2), 213-217.

Satterwhite, R. and Schoech, D.J. (1995). Multimedia training for child protective services workers: Initial test results. *Computers in Human Services, 12*(1/2), 81-97.

Schoech, D. (1994). Multimedia toolbook. *Computers in Human Services, 10*(3), 65-71.

Schueren, B. (1986). Video games: An exploration of their potential as recreational activity programs in nursing homes. *Activities, Adaption and Aging, 8*(1), 49-58.

Seabury, B.A. (1993). Interactive video programs: Crisis counseling and organizational assessment. *Computers in Human Services, 9*(3/4), 301-310.

Steyaert, J. (1994). Soft computing for soft technologies: Artificial neural networks and fuzzy set theory for human services. *Computers in Human Services 10*(4), 55-67.

Stull, J.C. (1994). Convict: A computer simulation of the criminal justice system. *Computers in Human Services, 11*(3/4), 261-267.

Thomas, D. (1994). LIFE CHOICES—The program and its users. *Computers in Human Services, 11*(1/2), 189-202.

Thomas, D. (1998). Review of the software Age of Empires. *Computers in Human Services, 15*(1), 85-91.

Thompkins, P. and Southward, L.H. (1998). Geographic information systems (GIS): Implications for promoting social and economic justice. *Computers in Human Services, 15*(2/3/4), 209-226.

Vaarama, M. (1995). The Evergreen, software for planning services for the elderly. *Computers in Human Services, 12*(1/2), 169-178.

Chapter 4: Management Applications

Brown, L.A. (1996). *Designing and deeloping electronic Performance Support Systems.* Boston, MA: Digital Press.

Carr, C. (1992). Performance support systems—The next step? *Performance + Instruction. 31*(2), 23-26.

Grey, G.J. (1991). *Electronic Performance Support Systems.* Boston, MA: Weingarten.

Keen, P.G. and Morton, M.S. (1978). *Decision Support Systems: An Organizational Perspective.* Reading, MA: Addison Wesley.

Kulik, J.A. (1994). Meta-analytic studies of findings on computer-based instruction. In E.L. Baker and H.F. O'Neil Jr. (Eds.), *Technology Assessment in Education and Training* (pp. 9-33). Hillsdale, NJ: Lawrence Erlbaum.

Ladd, C. (1993). Should performance support be in your computer? *Training and Development, 47*(8), 23-26.

Leake, David B. (Ed.) (1996). *Case-Based Reasoning: Experiences, Lessons, and Future Directions.* Menlo Park, CA: AAAI Press/MIT Press.

MacNeil-Lehrer Report (1983). Artificial intelligence. Washington, DC: Public Broadcasting Service, April 22.

Miller, L.S. (1993). The optimum allocation of in-home supportive-type services in the multipurpose senior services program. *Computers in Human Services, 9*(1/2), 111-135.

O'Brien, J.A. (1995). *Introduction to Information Systems.* Chicago, IL: Richard D. Irwin.

Paul, L.G. (1996). PC docs. *PC Week, 13* (June 10), 39, 51.

Reynolds, A. and Araya, R. (1995). *Building Multimedia Performance Support Systems.* New York: McGraw-Hill.

Schoech, D. (1979). A microcomputer-based human service information system. *Administration in Social Work, 3*(4), 423-440.

Schoech, D. (1996). Performance support systems: Integrating information technology under practitioner control. *Computers in Human Services, 13*(3), 1-18.

Schoech, D. and Bolen, B. (1998). The worker safety advisor: A performance support system. *Computers in Human Services, 15*(2/3), 143-158.

Schoech, D., Cavalier, A., and Hoover, B. (1993). Using technology to change the human service delivery system. *Administration in Social Work, 17*(2), 31-52.

Schoech, D., Jennings, H., Schkade L.L., and Hooper-Russell, C. (1985). Expert systems: Artificial intelligence for professional decisions. *Computers in Human Services, 1*(1), 81-115.

Schoech, D. and Schkade, L.L. (1980). Computers helping caseworkers: Decision support systems. *Child Welfare, 59*(9), 566-575.

Schoech, D., Schkade, L.L., and Mayers, R.S. (1982). Strategies for information system development. *Administration in Social Work, 5*(3/4), 11-26.

Schuerman, J.R. and Vogel, L.H. (1986). Computer support of placement planning: The use of expert systems in child welfare. *Child Welfare, 65,* 531-543.

Stein, T. and Rzepnicki, T. (1983). *Decision Making at Child Welfare* (pp. 42-43). Washington, DC: Child Welfare League of America.

Texas Department of Protective and Regulatory Services (Ed.) (1997). *Worker Improvements to the Structured Decision and Outcome Model: The Child Welfare Decision Enhancement Project.* Austin, TX: Texas Department of Protective and Regulatory Services.

Wick, J. and Schoech, D. (1988). Computerizing protective services intake expertise. *Children and Youth Services Review, 10*(3), 233-252.

Chapter 5: Human Services IT Applications

Arbona, C. and Perrone, P.A. (1989). The use of the computer in counseling college students. *Computers in Human Services, 5*(3/4), 99-112.

Bezold, C. (1994). Mental health services in the 21st century: Challenges and vision. *Behavioral Healthcare Tomorrow, 3*(5), 86-88.

Binik, Y.M., Meana, M., and Sand, N. (1994). Interaction with a sex-expert system changes attitudes and may modify sexual behavior. *Computers in Human Behavior, 10*(3), 395-410.

Blonk, A.M., Van Den Bercken, J.H.L., and De Bruyn, E.E.J. (1996). Evaluation of DYSLEXPERT: A comparison of a knowledge-based system with experienced clinicians in the diagnosis of dyslexia. *Computers in Human Behavior, 12*(4), 567-586.

Boberg, E.W., Gustafson, D.H., Hawkins, R.P., Chan, C.-L., Bicker, E., Suzanne, P., and Berhe, H. (1995). Development, acceptance, and use patterns of a computer-based education and social support system for people living with AIDS/HIV infection. *Computers in Human Behavior, 11*(2), 289-311.

Colby, K.M. (1979). Computer simulation and artificial intelligence in psychiatry. In E.A. Serafinides (Ed.), *Methods of Biobehavioral Research* (pp. 145-156). New York: Grune and Stratton.

Daily, B.F. and Steiner, R.L. (1998). The influence of group decision support systems on contribution and commitment levels in multicultural and culturally homogeneous decision-making groups. *Computers in Human Behavior, 14*(1), 147-162.

Doheny-Farina, S. (1996). *The Wired Neighborhood.* New Haven, CT: Yale University Press.

Downing, J., Fasano, R., Friedland, P., McCullough, M., Mizahi, T., and Shapiro, J. (1991). *Computers for Social Change and Community Organizing.* Binghamton, NY: The Haworth Press, Inc.

Erdman, H.P., Greist, J.H., Klein, M.H., Jefferson, J.W., and Getto, C. (1981). The computer psychiatrist: How far have we come? Where are we heading? How far dare we go? *Behavior Research Methods and Instrumentation, 13*(4), 393-398.

Ferguson, T. (1996). Consumer health informatics: Turning the treatment pyramid upside down. *Behavioral Healthcare Tomorrow, 5*(February), 35-37.

Finn, J. (1996). Computer-based self-help groups: On-line recovery for addictions. *Computers in Human Services, 13*(1), 21-41.

Fortuna, D. (1996). Review of the software recDONOR. *Computers in Human Services, 13*(1), 81-87.

Gingerich, W.J. (1995). Expert systems. *Encyclopedia of Social Work* (Nineteenth Edition). Washington, DC: NASW, 917-925.

Glastonbury, B. (1985). *Computers in Social Work.* London: MacMillan Publishers, Ltd.

Gustafson, D., Wise, M., McTavish, F., Taylor, J.O., Wolberg, W., Stewart, J., Smalley, R.V., and Bosworth, K. (1993). Development and pilot evaluation of a computer-based support system for women with breast cancer. *Journal of Psychosocial Oncology, 11*(4), 96-93.

Harkonen, R.-S. (1995). Building the future: Communication camps—The real utopia. *Computers in Human Services, 12*(1/2), 133-140.

Hartje, J.C. (1993). Emerging trends in biofeedback. In B. Schlosser and K.L. Moreland (Eds.), *Taming Technology: Issues, Strategies and Resources for the Mental Health Practitioner* (pp. 73-75). Phoenix, AZ: American Psychological Association.

Hile, M.G. (1998). The history and function of the Target Cities management information systems: An introduction to the special issue. *Computers in Human Services, 14*(3/4), 1-7.

Hile, M.G. and Adkins, R.E. (1997). Do substance abuse and mental health clients prefer automated assessments? *Behavior Research Methods, Instruments and Computers, 29*(2), 146-150.

Hile, M.G. and Desrochers, M.N. (1994). Decision support in designing behavior treatments: The mental retardation expert. *Computers in Human Behavior, 10*(3), 325-332.

Lambert, M.E. (1994). Review of the software Therapist Helper. *Computers in Human Services, 10*(4), 83-89.

Lambert, M.E. (1998). Review of the software Overcoming Depression. *Computers in Human Services, 15*(1), 71-77.

Lambert, M.E., Hedlund, J.L., and Vieweg, B.W. (1990). Computer simulations in mental health education: Two illustrative projects. *Computers in Human Services, 7*(3/4), 231-245.

Malcolm, R., Sturgis, E.T., Anton, R.F., and Williams, L. (1989). Computer-assisted diagnosis of alcoholism. *Computers in Human Services, 5*(3/4), 163-170.

Margaliot, N. (1997). A model for the computerized allocation of personnel resources among local bureaus by a municipal department of social services. *Computers in Human Services, 14*(2), 1-16.

Marks, I.M., Shaw, S.C., and Parkin, J.R. (1998). Computer-aided treatments of mental health problems. *Clinical Psychology: Science and Practice, 5*(2), 151-170.

Mathison, K.S., Evans, F.J., Meyers, K., Rochford, J.M., and Wilson, G. (1984). An evaluation of computerized DSM-III diagnosis in a private psychiatric hospital. Paper presented at the fifty-first annual meeting of the National Association of Private Psychiatric Hospitals, Palm Springs, CA, January, p. 4.

Miller, L.S. (1993). The optimum allocation of in-home supportive-type services in the multipurpose senior services program. *Computers and Human Services, 9*(1/2), 111-135.

Modai, I., Saban, N.I., Stoler, M., Valevski, A., and Saban, N. (1995). Sensitivity profile of 41 psychiatric parameters determined by neural network in relation to 8-week outcome. *Computers in Human Behavior, 11*(2), 181-190.

Mundt, J.C., Kobak, K.A., Taylor, L.V., Mantle, J.M., Jefferson, J.W., Katzelnick, D.J., and Greist, J.H. (1998). Administration of the Hamilton Depression Rating Scale using interacative voice response technology. *M.D. Computing, 15* (January/February), 31-38.

Nartz, M. and Schoech, D. Use of the internet for community practice: A delphi study.

Nurius, P.S. and Hudson, W.W. (1993). *Human Services, Practice, Evaluation and Computers.* Pacific Grove, CA: Brooks/Cole.

Oyserman, D. and Benbenishty, R. (1997). Developing and implementing the integrated information system for foster care and adoption. *Computers in Human Services, 14*(1), 1-20.

Renz-Beaulaurier, R. (1997). The Mental Health Studio. *Computers in Human Services, 14*(1), 85-89.

Rheingold, H. (1993). *The Virtual Community.* Reading, MA: Addison-Wesley.

Rohrbaugh, J. and Johnson, R. (1998). Welfare reform flies in New York. *Government Technology, 11*(June), 58.

Sander, F.M. (1996). Couples group therapy conducted via computer-mediated communication: A preliminary case study. *Computers in Human Behavior, 12*(2), 301-312.

Schneider, S.J., Schwartz, M.D., and Fast, J. (1995). Computerized, telephone-based health promotion. II. Stress management program. *Computers in Human Behavior, 11*(2), 205-214.

Schneider, S.J. and Tooley, J. (1995). Self-help computer conferencing. *Computers and Biomedical Research, 19*(3), 274-281.

Schoech, D. and Bolen, B. (1998). The Worker Safety Advisor: A performance support system. *Computers in Human Services, 15*(2/3), 143-158.

Schoech, D.J., Cavalier, A.R., and Hoover, B. (1993). Using technology to change the human services delivery system. *Administration in Social Work, 17*(2), 31-52.

Schoech, D., Jensen, C., Fulks, J., and Smith, K. (1998). Developing and using a community databank. *Computers in Human Services, 15*(1), 35-53.

Schwab, J.A. and Wilson, S.S. (1989). The continuum of care system: Decision support for practitioners. *Computers in Human Services, 4*(1/2), 123-140.

Schwab, J.A., Bruce, M.E., and McRoy, R.G. (1985). A statistical model of child placement decisions. *Social Work Research and Abstracts, 21*(2), 28-34.

Selmi, P.M., Klein, M.H., Greist, J.H., Johnson, J.H., and Harris, W.G. (1982). An investigation of computer-assisted cognitive-behavior therapy in the treatment of depression. *Behavior Research Methods and Instrumentation, 14*(2), 181-185.

Selmi, P.M., Klein, M.H., Greist, J.H., Sorrell, S.P., and Erdman, H.P. (1990). Computer-administered cognitive-behavioral therapy for depression. *American Journal of Psychiatry, 147*(1), 51-56.

Shaw, S.C. and Marks, I.M. (1996). "Fear Fighter," behavioural self-help for agoraphobia on computer multimedia—A new system. *European Psychiatry, II*, 271s.

Simmons, W.W. (1979). The Concensor: A new tool for decision-makers. *The Futurist, 13*(2), 91-95.

Taber, C.S. and Timpone, R. (1994). The Policy Arguer: The architecture of an expert system. *Social Science Computer Review, 12*(1), 1-24.

Wakefield, R.A. (Ed.) (1985). Home computers and family empowerment. *Marriage and Family Review, 8*(1/2), 83-101.

Weinberg, N. (1996). Compassion by computer: Contrasting the supportiveness of computer-mediated and face-to-face interactions. *Computers in Human Services, 13*(2), 51-63.

Chapter 6: The Process of Developing IT Applications

Dorsey, L.T., Goodrum, D.A., and Schwen, T.M. (1993). Just-in-time knowledge performance support: A test of concept. *Educational Technology, 23*(11), 21-29.

Hile, M. (Ed.) (1998). The history and function of the target cities management information systems. Special issue. *Computers in Human Services, 14*(3/4).

Hile, M.G., Callier, J.M., Schmoock, J., Adkins, R.E., and Cho, D. (1998). St. Louis target city information system. *Computers in Human Services, 14*(3/4), 119-137.

Krepco, M.A., Marks, B.J., Garnett, D.U., Snell, L., and Olson, L. (1998). Dallas target cities safety network management information system. *Computers in Human Services, 14*(3/4), 29-49.

Moyer, D. (1997). Journey to the brave new world of data automation technology—Are we ready? *Computers in Human Services, 14*(2), 17-34.

Neilson, R. (1985). The role of the federal government in social service systems development. *Computers in Human Services, 1*(2), 53-63.

Newkham, J. (1982). Lessons that have been reinforced in implementing a computerized MIS. *Computer Use in Social Services Network, 2*(2), 3.

Perrone, G. (1997). *Structured Analysis with Case Tools.* Englewood Cliffs, NJ: Prentice Hall.

Schoech, D., Schkade, L.L., and Mayers, R.S. (1982). Strategies for information system development. *Administration in Social Work, 5*(3/4), 25-26.

Topper, A., Ouellette, D., and Jorgensen, P. (1993). *Structured Methods: Merging Models, Techniques, and Cases.* New York: McGraw-Hill.

Yang, C. and Pascale, C. (1993). Effects of computer system performance and job support on stress among office workers. *Advances in Human Factors/Ergonomics, 19,* 931-936.

Yourdon, E. (1991). *Modern Structured Analysis.* Englewood Cliffs, NJ: Prentice Hall

Yourdon, E. and Argila, C.A. (Ed.) (1996). *Case Studies in Object-Oriented Analysis and Design.* Englewood Cliffs, NJ: Prentice Hall.

Zefran, J. (1984). Analysis of the information needs of a private practice. In M. Schwartz (Ed.), *Using Computers in Clinical Practice* (pp. 19-39). Binghamton, NY: The Haworth Press, Inc.

Chapter 7: Applying Systems and Decision-Making Theories

Berlin, S.B. and Marsh, J.C. (1993). *Informing Practice Decisions.* New York: Macmillan.

Boulding, K.E. (1956). General systems theory—The skeleton of science. *Management Science, 2,* 197-208.

Cohen, M.E. and Auslander, G.K. (1996). Utilization of aggregate information in social work: Deductive and inductive strategies. *Computers in Human Services, 13*(2), 17-31.

Dewey, J. (1910). *How We Think.* New York: D.C. Heath and Co.

Etzioni, A. (1968). *The Active Society.* New York: The Free Press.

Hile, M.G. (1998). The history and function of the Target Cities management information systems: An introduction to the special issue. *Computers in Human Services, 14*(3/4), 1-7.

Keen, P.G. and Morton, M.S. (1978). *Decision Support Systems: An Organizational Perspective.* Reading, MA: Addison Wesley.

Kelley, K. (1997). New rules for the new economy: Twelve dependable principles for thriving in a turbulent world. *Wired* (September), 186-197.

Kettlehut, M.C. and Schkade, L.L. (1991). Programmers, analysts and human service workers: Cognitive styles and task implications for system design. *Computers in Human Services, 8*(2), 57-79.

Lewin, K. (1947). Group decision and social change. In T.M. Newcomb and E.L. Hartley (Eds.), *Readings in Social Psychology* (pp. 330-344). New York: Holt.

Robey, D. and Taggart, W. (1982). Human information processing in information and decision support systems. *MIS Quarterly, 6*(2), 61-73.

Rubinstein, M.F. (1975). *Patterns of Problem Solving.* Englewood Cliffs, NJ: Prentice Hall.

Schein, E.H. (1961). *Brainwashing.* Cambridge, MA: Center for International Studies, M.I.T.

Schkade, L.L. and Potvin, A.R. (1981). Cognitive style, EEG waveforms and brain levels. *Human Systems Management, 2,* 329-331.

Schoech, D. and Schkade, L.L. (1981). Human service workers as the primary information system user. In R.R. Schmitt and J.H. Smolin (Eds.), *Urban, Regional and Environmental Information: Needs, Sources, Systems, and Uses—Papers from the Annual Conference of the Urban and Regional Information Systems Association* (pp. 71-81). Washington, DC, Urban and Regional Information Systems Association (URISA).

Simon, H.A. (1977). *The New Science of Management Decision* (Revised Edition). Englewood Cliffs, NJ: Prentice Hall.

Simon, H.A. (1997). *Administrative Behavior: A Study of Decision-Making Processes in Administrative Organizations* (Fourth Edition). New York: Free Press.

Springer, S.P. and Deutsch, G. (1981). *Left Brain, Right Brain.* San Francisco, CA: W.H. Freeman.

Van Gigch, J.P. (1978). *Applied General Systems Theory* (Second Edition). New York: Harper & Row.

Witkins, H.A. (1971). *Manual: Embedded Figures Test, Children's Embedded Figures Test, Group Embedded Figures Test.* Palo Alto, CA: Consulting Psychologists Press.

Zeleny, M. (1982). *Multiple Criteria Decision Making.* New York: McGraw-Hill.

Chapter 8: Assessing Human Service Information Needs

Arthur Young and Company (1983). *Position Classification Study.* Austin, TX: Texas Department of Human Resources.

Berlin, S.B. and Marsh, J. (Eds.) (1993). *Informing Practice Decisions,* Englewood Cliffs, NJ: Prentice Hall.

de Groot, L., Gripton, J., and Licker, P. (1986). *The Digital Social Worker: Microcomputers in Clinical Social Work Practice Final Project Report* (Project No. 4558-1-32). Canada: National Welfare Grants Directorate, Health and Welfare.

Emmert, N. and Schoech, D. (1991). Effectiveness of a computer-based placement decision support system. *Residential Treatment for Children and Youth, 9*(1), 61-73.

Fortune, A.E. (1981). Communication processes in social work practice. *Social Service Review, 50*(1), 93-128.

Franklin, J. and Thrasher, J. (1976). *An Introduction to Program Evaluation.* New York: Wiley.

Hile, M.G. (1989). Two automated systems for behavioral assessment of clients with mental retardation or developmental disabilities. *Computers in Human Services, 5*(3/4), 183-191.

Newcombe, T. (1997). Prodigal system: California's SAWS. *Government Technology, 10*(13) (December), 126-130.

Schoech, D. and Schkade, L.L. (1981). Human service workers as the primary information system user. In R.R. Schmitt and H.J. Smolin, *Urban, Regional, and Environmental Information: Needs, Sources, Systems, and Uses—Papers from the Annual Conference of the Urban and Regional Information Systems Association (URISA)* (pp. 71-81). Washington, DC: URISA.

Schwab, A.J., Bruce, M.E., and McRoy, R.G. (1985). A statistical model of child placement decisions. *Social Work Research and Abstracts, 21*(2), 28-34.

Stein, T.J. and Rzepnicki, T.L. (1983). *Decision Making at Child Welfare Intake.* New York: Child Welfare League of America.

Texas Department of Protective and Regulatory Services (Ed.) (1997). *Worker Improvements to the Structured Decision and Outcome Model: The Child Welfare Decision Enhancement Project.* Austin, TX: Texas Department of Protective and Regulatory Services.

Chapter 9: Hardware and Software Influences on IT Development

Dangel, R.F. and Polster, R.A. (1984). *Winning! Specialist Handbook* (Second Edition). Arlington, TX: American Children's Foundation.

Chapter 10: Database Management Influences on IT Development

California computer system bites the dust (1997). *Wired News,* November 21: <http://www.wired.com/news/politics/story/8715.html>.

Dutka, A.F. and Hanson, H.H. (1989). *Fundamentals of Data Normalization.* Reading, MA: Addison Wesley.

Ikujiro, N. and Hirotaka, T. (1995). *The Knowledge-Creating Company.* New York: Oxford University Press.

Chapter 11: Networking, Telecommunications, and Internet Influences on IT Development

Butterfield, B. and Schoech, D. (1997). The Internet: Assessing the world of information. In R. Edwards (Ed.), *Encyclopedia of Social Work* (Supplement), (pp. 151-168), Washington, DC: National Association of Social Workers.

Grant, G.B. and Gorbman, L.M. (1998). *The Social Worker's Internet Handbook.* Harrisburg, PA: White Hat Communications.

Menon, G.M. (1998). Gender encounters in a virtual community: Identity formation and acceptance. *Computers in Human Services, 15*(1), 55-69.

Rheingold, H. (1993). *The Virtual Community: Homesteading on the Electronic Frontier.* Reading, MA: Addison Wesley.

Tanenbaum, A.S. (1996). *Computer Networks.* Englewood Cliffs, NJ: Prentice Hall.

Chapter 12: Managing, Supporting, and Evaluating IT Applications

Batchilder, M. (1997). Leveraging technology boosts incomes and productivity. *The NonProfit Times, 11*(13) (September), 26-27.

Bellerby, L.J. and Goslin, L.N. (1982). Managing for success: Assessing the balanced MIS environment. *Administration in Social Work, 5*(3/4), 69-81.

DeLone, W.H. and McLean, E.R. (1992). Information systems success: The quest for the dependent variable. *Information Systems Research, 3*(1), 60-95.

Garrity, E. (1998). *Information Systems Success Measurement.* Hershey, PA: Idea Group Publishing.

Gibson, C.F. and Nolan, R.L. (1974). Managing the four stages of EDP growth. *Harvard Business Review, 52*(1), 80.

Hile, M. (Ed.) (1998). The history and function of the Target Cities management information systems. *Computers in Human Services, 14*(3/4), 1-7.

Huff, D. (1993). *How to Lie with Statistics.* New York: W.W. Norton and Company.

Kanungo, S. (1998). An empirical study of organizational culture and network-based computer use. *Computers in Human Behavior, 14*(1), 79-91.

Kidd, R. (1995). Oklahoma Dept. of Human Services does it right. *Government Technology, 8*(August), 50-51.

Moyer, D. (1997). Journey to the brave new world of data automation technology—Are we ready? *Computers in Human Services, 14*(2), 17-34.

Nolan, R.L. (1979). Managing the crises in data processing. *Harvard Business Review, 57*(2), 115-126.

Saunders, C.S. and Jones, J.W. (1992). Measuring performance of the information systems function. *Journal of Management Information Systems, 8*(4), 63-82.

Savaya, R. and Waysman, M. (1996). Factors implicated in the integration of clinical information systems into human services agencies: A concept map. *New Technology in the Human Services, 9*(2), 15-22.

Sharon, N. (1996). The help desk: Its design, function and effectiveness. *Computers in Human Services, 13*(2), 1-15.

Sircar, S., Schoech, D, and Schkade, L.L. (1982). Approaches for evaluating information systems. *Information and Referral, 4*(1), 50-65.

Chapter 13: Trends, Issues, and the Future

Bowers, C.A. (1998). The paradox of technology: What's gained and lost. *Thought and Action, 14*(1), 49-57.

Erdman, H.P. and Foster, S.W. (1988). Ethical issues in the use of computer-based assessment. *Computers in Human Services, 3*(1/2), 71-78.

Erdman, H.P., Klein, M.H., and Greist, J.H. (1985). Direct patient computer interviewing. *Journal of Consulting and Clinical Psychology, 53*(6), 760-773.

Ferguson, T. (1996). Consumer health informatics: Turning the treatment pyramid upside down. *Behavioral Healthcare Tomorrow, 5*(February), 35-37.

Glastonbury, B. (1985). *Computers in Social Work.* London: Macmillan.

Grebel, H. and Steyaert, J. (1993). *Social Informatics, Education on the Vocational Use of Information Technology in Schools of Social Work* (report to the Commission of the European Union). Eindhoven, Netherlands: Causa.

Hammer, A.L. and Hile, M.G. (1985). Factors in clinicians' resistance to automation in mental health. *Computers in Human Services, 1*(3), 1-25.

Hudson, W.W., Nurius, P.S., and Reisman, S. (1988). Computerized assessment instruments: Their promise and problems. *Computers in Human Services, 3*(1/2), 51-70.

Lamson, R.J. (1995). Virtual therapy: The treatment of phobias in cyberspace. *Behavioral Healthcare Tomorrow, 4*(1), 51-53.

Landesberg, M.K., Levin, T.M., Curtin, C.G., and Lev, O. (1998). *Privacy Online: A Report to Congress.* Washington, DC: Federal Trade Commission.

Long, M. (1985). Turncoat of the computer revolution: An interview with Joseph Weizenbaum. *New Age*(December), 47-51, 76-78.

Mundt, J.C., Kobak, K.A., Taylor, L.V.H., Mantle, J.M., Jefferson, J.W., Katzelnick, D.J., and Greist, J.H. (1998). Administration of the Hamilton Depression Rating Scale using interactive voice response technology. *M.D. Computing, 15*(1), 31-39.

Pervan, G. (1997). Information systems management: An Australasian view of key issues—1996. *Australian Journal of Information Systems, 5*(1) (September).

U.S. Congress, Office of Technology Assessment (1986). *Federal Government Information Technology: Electronic Record Systems and Individual Privacy.* Washington, DC: U.S. Government Printing Office, June.

Author Index

Subject Index

Page numbers followed by the letter "f" indicate figures; those followed by the letter "t" indicate tables.

HAWORTH Social Administration
Simon Slavin, EdD, ACSW
Senior Editor

HUMAN SERVICES TECHNOLOGY: UNDERSTANDING, DESIGNING, AND IMPLEMENTING COMPUTER APPLICATIONS IN THE SOCIAL SERVICES by Dick Schoech. "A comprehensive, clearly written text for students and human service professionals who need to understand the impact and use of information technology in human service practice." *Jerry Finn, PhD, Associate Professor, Department of Social Work, University of New Hampshire*

LOBBYING FOR SOCIAL CHANGE, SECOND EDITION by Willard C. Richan. "Outlines the basic steps grassroots activists must take to exert pressure on politicians and bring about change in public policy.... Provides step-by-step advice on setting an agenda, understanding policymakers, and arguing one's case. " *Chronicle of Philanthropy*

PERFORMANCE EVALUATION IN THE HUMAN SERVICES by Wayne Matheson, Cornelius Van Dyk, and Kenneth Millar. "A most welcomed breakthrough in rethinking a necessary, and yet too often misunderstood and misapplied, opportunity to enhance the delivery of human services." *Administration in Social Work*

COMMUNITY ORGANIZATION AND SOCIAL ADMINISTRATION: ADVANCES, TRENDS, AND EMERGING PRINCIPLES by Terry Mizrahi and John D. Morrison. "Administrators and organizers will find in this work a blend of research and practical significance in the critical area of societal organization for today and tomorrow." *Journal of the American Association of Psychiatric Administrators*

SOCIAL WORK ETHICS ON THE LINE by Charles S. Levy. "A useful synopsis for experienced practitioners to refresh and refocus their attention. . . useful to students and teachers in facilitating discussion. . . a good resource for agency executives who want to initiate in-service training on ethical decision making." *Social Work* (Journal of the National Association of Social Workers)

RESEARCH UTILIZATION IN THE SOCIAL SERVICES: INNOVATIONS FOR PRACTICE AND ADMINISTRATION edited by Anthony J. Grasso and Irwin Epstein. "Should be required reading for social work students as well as practitioners and researchers interested in informed and accountable practice." *Social Work* (Journal of the National Association of Social Workers)

BEYOND ALTRUISM: SOCIAL WELFARE POLICY IN AMERICAN SOCIETY by Willard C. Richan. "Provides a helpful framework for organizing the multiplicity of roles and tasks social workers undertake.... Richan has written an interesting and readable textbook in social policy." *Social Thought*

SOCIAL ADMINISTRATION: THE MANAGEMENT OF THE SOCIAL SERVICES, SECOND EDITION, Volumes 1 and 2 edited by Simon Slavin. "Remarkably comprehensive. Volume 1 presents both theory and case materials to give the student of social administration a textured understanding of the social agency and its dilemmas. Volume 2 walks the student through the very practical problems and challenges of budgeting personnel policy and computer usage. Both volumes are highly recommended to students and practitioners alike." *Larry Hirschhorn, PhD, Management & Behavioral Center, The Wharton School, University of Pennsylvania*

For Product Safety Concerns and Information please contact our EU representative GPSR@taylorandfrancis.com Taylor & Francis Verlag GmbH, Kaufingerstraße 24, 80331 München, Germany

T - #0012 - 090625 - C0 - 229/152/25 [27] - CB - 9780789001085 - Gloss Lamination